Major Aspects of American Government

McGRAW-HILL SERIES IN POLITICAL SCIENCE

Joseph P. Harris, *Consulting Editor*

Adrian · Governing Urban America: Structure, Politics, and Administration
Adrian · State and Local Governments
Bone · American Politics and the Party System
Chase · The United Nations in Action
Christenson and McWilliams · Voice of the People: Readings in Public Opinion and Propaganda
Ebenstein · Political Thought in Perspective
Ferguson and McHenry · American Federal Government
Ferguson and McHenry · American System of Government
Ferguson and McHenry · Elements of American Government
Field · Governments in Modern Society
Frank · Cases on the Constitution
Gosnell, Lancaster, and Rankin · Fundamentals of American Government: National, State, and Local
Gosnell, Lancaster, and Rankin · Fundamentals of American National Government
Gross · The Legislative Struggle
Haas and Whiting · Dynamics of International Relations
Hartmann · Basic Documents of International Relations
Holloway · State and Local Government in the United States
Mangone · A Short History of International Organization
McClosky and Turner · The Soviet Dictatorship
Millett · Government and Public Administration
Millett · Management in the Public Service
Neumann · European and Comparative Government
Pierson and Gil · Governments of Latin America
Powell and Parker · Major Aspects of American Government
Pritchett · The American Constitution
Pritchett · American Constitutional Issues
Riemer · Problems of American Government
Roche and Stedman · The Dynamics of Democratic Government
Rodee, Anderson, and Christol · Introduction to Political Science
Svarlien · An Introduction to the Law of Nations
Turner · Politics in the United States: Readings in Political Parties and Pressure Groups
Turner and Vieg · The Government and Politics of California
Vandenbosch and Hogan · Toward World Order
Waldo · Ideas and Issues in Public Administration: A Book of Readings
Wilson · The American Political Mind
Wilson · Police Administration

NORMAN J. POWELL and DANIEL P. PARKER
Department of Political Science
Baruch School, The City College
City University of New York

Major Aspects of American Government

McGRAW-HILL BOOK COMPANY, INC.
New York San Francisco Toronto London

MAJOR ASPECTS OF AMERICAN GOVERNMENT

 Library of Congress Catalog Card Number 62-19250

PREFACE

A DECENT DEFERENCE to the opinions of readers requires a preliminary note by the editors on the book they have put together, and it is toward that end that these introductory remarks are set forth under the following captions: A. Organization; B. Selection of the Readings; C. Editors' Comments; D. Coverage; E. Acknowledgments.

A. Organization. American government is one unit. It is no aggregate of operations, such as political analysis; no mere sum total of the spelling out of American values; of documents, like the Constitution; of splinters called Congress, the Presidency, and the Judiciary; of processes such as politics; of ideas like freedom; of concepts, relations, organizations, and institutions, such as public opinion, pressure groups, and propaganda; of operations, such as foreign policy; of people and policies combining to perform public administration.

Nevertheless, we cannot talk about everything at once, and so we have grouped the subject matter into eleven topics, and talked about the eleven one at a time, working out the sequence in accordance with the apparent logical and psychological utility of the arrangement. Thus, it seemed evident that the material concerned with political analysis should be placed first; such material is a useful preliminary to the examination of all the other topics.

Comparable rationale prompted the positioning of "Public Administration." Included as a topic because of the distinctiveness and significance of the subject matter both as a field of study and work, "Public Administration" was placed last to give readers maximum preliminary political science material for making choices about their major intellectual and occupational interests.

The fact is, of course, that the subject matter of the book can be organized in many ways; professors, students, and other readers remain free to use any other arrangement they may prefer.

B. Selection of the Readings. The readings are taken from public and other sources including varied kinds of periodicals, classic writings, speeches, hearings, reports, polls, congressional debates and judicial opinions, presidential press conferences and television-script selections, speeches and articles from magazines published in Britain, the Soviet Union, and Communist China. The objective has been to make available materials that deal with important subjects in an informative and interesting fashion.

Choosing the materials has been an extraordinary amalgam of pleasure and pain. It has been thrilling to seek and to find challenging and perceptive and vivid writing on major aspects of American government. Equally, it has been a corrosive experience to carve out beautiful materials tentatively included and to edit down eminently creative writing. For example, an earlier draft of this book paired the 1960 campaign speeches of John F. Kennedy and Richard M. Nixon at the Alfred E. Smith Memorial Dinner. The final manuscript omits the Nixon speech, limiting itself simply to the fascinating one by Kennedy. It was a searing experience to delete the Nixon speech, as it was lacerating to eliminate other items, such as insightful testimony on the proposed Department of Urban Affairs or the Senate debate in 1958 on the Kennedy-Ives Bill, starring Kennedy and Goldwater and featuring the National Association of Manufacturers.

Comparably, the editors flinched as they decided to include one or another item while they excised segments from the commentary of their articulate and astute authors.

Ernest Hemingway once remarked that the quality of a manuscript can be judged by the quality of the writing discarded. Readers cannot peer into editorial wastebaskets; the editors can but hope that readers will share the pleasures of the final draft of this book.

C. Editors' Comments. Editors' comments introduce each of the chapters and each of the articles or other readings within a chapter. Depending on the apparent requirements of the section and the individual reading, the comments vary in purpose. Sometimes the comments are designed to explain main ideas in the chapter or in a given reading, sometimes to stimulate the reader's interest in the materials, sometimes to supplement the materials.

For example, guided by experience, the editors emphasize the quality and fame of *The Federalist* papers. In the absence of such cuing commentary, some modern readers of political science are apt to respond to *The Federalist* in somewhat the fashion they would react to Sanskrit or at the least to peculiarly and unnecessarily difficult writings.

Another illustration is the editorial comment introducing the article from the Soviet magazine *International Affairs*. Our experience has been that even apparently well-informed people have thought the article's reasoning to be substantially valid. Therefore, it has seemed fruitful to include a comment identifying the central fallacy of the magazine article.

An instance of another kind of editorial comment is the introduction to the chapter on public administration. Intended to supplement and illuminate the readings in this chapter, the introductory material identifies salient ideas and ways of thinking about the subject.

D. Coverage. Only occasionally is there an effort to include materials covering "both sides" of an issue. Our reasoning is this: (1) Citing two sides of a question is misleading in present-day America. Current issues have many aspects rather than two sides. Talk of two sides is simplistic. (2) The readings have been selected on the assumption that in a real situation the citizen is exposed to a particular unit of material at a given time and place. Realistically, therefore, the student should learn how to dissect such material and how to analyze the data and views that he encounters. Therein, incidentally, lies the justification of the inclusion of the unconventional reading represented by the first chapter, "Political Analysis."

E. Acknowledgments. It is a pleasure, finally, to record three acknowledgments. One is the considerable obligation to the Alumni Association of the Bernard M. Baruch School of Business and Public Administration of the City College of New York. At a vital point, the alumni extended a loan to us that aided in carrying this book forward. Our second great debt is to Dean Emanuel S. Saxe, Assistant Dean Samuel F. Thomas, Prof. Thomas G. Karis, Riordan Roett, Henry W. Morton, and David E. Powell—for stimulating conversation, helpful advice, useful criticisms, pungent commentary, eviscerating analysis, and active encouragement. Our third enormous debt is to the successive waves of students we have had over the years. College students are precious spirits; we are grateful for their company, past and present and, we hope, future.

NORMAN J. POWELL
DANIEL P. PARKER

CONTENTS

CHAPTER 1

POLITICAL ANALYSIS

HIGH AMONG the objectives of any program for teaching American government is the aim of helping the student to think analytically and creatively about public affairs. Few of us can say with Pablo Picasso, "Je ne cherche pas; je trouve." Particularly in politics, assuming understandings and information to be the citizen's interest, the notion "I do not seek; I find" is false. Good thinking in public affairs is achieved only by adopting a questioning and curious attitude, by setting out to weigh and examine. Long ago the British philosopher Jeremy Bentham observed that political truths "flourish not in the same soil as sentiment. They grow among thorns; and they are not to be plucked, like daisies, by infants as they run." Accordingly, the following material describes ways in which competent political analysis can be facilitated.

Cautions in Thinking

[Norman J. Powell, "Cautions in Thinking about American Government," chapter from the manuscript of a book in preparation.]

This chapter makes the assumption first that there exist useful ways of thinking about public affairs, that these can be identified, that there is profit in thinking about ways of thinking about public affairs. No implication exists that methods of analysis are peculiar to politics; actually, as in any complex subject matter, the individual can but use every point of his IQ. We suggest simply that political materials are useful sources for describing caveats and pitfalls that the citizen can helpfully examine.

Long ago Edmund Burke said that "No lines can be laid down for civil or political wisdom," adding, "They are a matter incapable of exact definition. But though no man can draw a stroke between the confines of day and night, yet light and darkness are upon the whole tolerably distinguishable." There is no formula for thinking well about American government that has the exactitude or relative clarity and readiness of application of a recipe for cooking baked Alaska.

What can be devised are general guides—"rules" seems too rigid and pretentious a term—that can be serviceable to the citizen who tries to be intellectually competent. There, in fact, is the preliminary necessity: that the citizen, the student, the reader, the listener work at the job of thinking; that he adopt a probing attitude and a searching mind-set; that he deliberately make the effort to stretch his intellectual capacity to its political limits.

The ten propositions below are first approximations, not a how-to-think-about-public-affairs formulary. They are couched in what-to-do form, not to supply a ready-made key to governmental issues, but to present the material realistically in a fashion applicable to the analysis and evaluation of political thinking wherever encountered.

1. *Figure out the meaning of the statement under consideration; then examine and evaluate the evidence cited to support the statement.*

The questions to ask of any political communication are these: What does the statement say? What data can be offered in substantiation? How persuasive are the data?

The leading requirement is concerned with the nature of the conclusion being urged upon us by any writer or speaker. Before you can assess, accept, or reject any political point, you need to know what it is.

Not infrequently you resolve a question when you find out what it means. An illustration is the assertion of a speaker at a public hearing on the budget for school construction in one municipality. At one point, the chairman of the hearing noted that the budget would really reflect the priorities of the community inasmuch as far more money was being requested than was available. Thereupon, the speaker rose to say, "I am not at all concerned with priorities, as we feel that all the schools should be constructed immediately," and then went on to tell about the city's educational needs. Look closely at the statement, and you see that the speaker said this: to decide whether and when schools should be built, you need only to determine that the schools are useful. Such an assertion is a flight from reality. Two elements are omitted from the statement: the community's ability to pay for its public services and the relative necessity for additional schools as against, say, hospitals or police protection.

Comfortable words in politics require especially close inspection because they massage already firmly held concepts whose relevance is undeniable—to issues other than the one being examined. "The logical standard," said a onetime President of the United States, "by which to make valid comparisons of opposing party doctrines is the degree in which it conforms to American ideals, promotes real progress, is faithful to concepts expounded in the founding documents and stimulates national greatness." Every good American believes in American ideals, in progress, in the worth of the Declaration and the Constitution, in the greatness of the United States. This listing strokes our neurons gently and lulls the thought process as it tells us in essence that good party doctrine furthers the United States. The American's belief in Americanism must be separated out from a quite different idea: that political parties differ in their Americanism. Taking the former Chief Executive's statement seriously about the way to compare political parties would require the citizen to decide whether Democrats or Republicans are more American. Few less rewarding or more pointless political activities could be devised.

An example of the utility of searching first for meanings in a statement comes from an un-American source. Talking about a Marxist party congress on one occasion, Lenin said, "we shall ideologically oppose those decisions of the Congress which we regard as being in error. But at the same time, we declare before the entire Party that we are against every schism. We stand for subordination to the decisions of the Congress." The citizen's responsibility is to tarry when he reads such a complex statement to see what the author has said. Lenin here has said something that is impossible: he will reject the decisions he considers wrong and, simultaneously, he will accept those decisions, whatever they may be.

Whatever the meaning of a political proposition, its evaluation necessitates an analytic process that tends to be as uncomfortable as it is difficult. Much fun has been made of the inclination of people to behave as though good thinking unnecessarily complicates their existence. There is the cartoon showing a group in a courtroom while a lawyer is examining a man in the witness box. A woman in the jury is leaning over to say to her neighbor, "I don't listen to the evidence. I like to make up my own mind." A companion piece is the often-quoted cartoon showing the man saying, "I don't listen to both sides of an argument; I just find it confusing." Commenting on "realistic appraisals of the limits of action in foreign policy," one observer notes: "Whereas such appraisals are nearly always complicated, tentative, easily distorted, and uncertain, the recipes and formulas of demagogues and utopians are bold and militant, emotional and, for desperate souls, almost always satisfying." After all, political argument, like all social communication, has many roles. The rational citizen is a unit who is partly a nonintellectual man interpreting political data in a manner that helps to fulfill his personality needs; his difficulties in dealing with political evidence are not only intellectual.

Perhaps the most important single cue for the citizen-as-public-affairs-analyst is that he self-consciously search for and dissect data to check their relevance and probative value. The argument bathed in political language may not even have been dipped in political proof.

Illustrative is the radio interview of a mayoralty candidate in a great city at the time one of the other municipalities in the same state had embarked on a spend-as-little-as-possible relief program. Concern about increasing welfare expenditures had been translated into a heated political issue, much of the discussion centering on the idea of a rigorously administered public welfare program. Some critics had tarred the program as uncivilized, others had maintained that the plan was essential to protect the community from undesirable people. Conversation between the candidate and the interviewer went somewhat as follows:

INTERVIEWER: What do you think of the New Welfare Program?

CANDIDATE: I am, as you know, the State Comptroller, and part of my job is to audit the bills and finances of the city that has produced this new welfare plan, so that it would be most unethical of me to comment on its details. But I don't want to seem to anybody to be dodging the question. So I'll be glad to give you a direct answer anyway.

INTERVIEWER: Excellent, please do so.

CANDIDATE: There are two crucial things I want to say. And these are on the essence of the matter, and that is the important issue of relief itself. One is that I am entirely in favor of giving adequate assistance to anybody in this country and in this state who needs relief; nobody ought to go hungry in this great state of ours. There is a second thing to be said too, and that is I am against chiseling on relief and we ought to be sure that anybody who is chiseling and cheating should be removed from the relief rolls and kept off. Let's have what we make sure is a program of help to needy people, and one which at the same time is efficiently run.

The candidate's response is on the theme of the New Welfare Program, and to the cursory eye or ear—especially if the speech is given with great apparent earnestness—may seem to answer the question. The talk is about relief, cheating, needy people, efficiency, and is certainly concerned with public welfare. What is more, the candidate announced that he was answering the question. Actually, of course, he did not answer the interviewer's question at all. His statement was responsive to two questions not asked: (a) Should needy people, such as those who are hungry, be given help? (b) Should a public welfare program be administered honestly and efficiently? The candidate's answer is no more than an affirmation of what everybody believes; it is a response to what is not an issue.

The gap between data and conclusion may rival the distance between data and relevance. Again the citizen needs to keep his eye on the distinction between evidence and interpretation. Political syllogisms are a case in point: A favors (or opposes) X, B favors (or opposes) X, therefore A and B are ideologically intertwined (or antagonistic). Let the Soviet leader verbally attack the President of the United States and let an American politician do so as well; it does not follow that the American politician and the Soviet leader are ideological cronies. If Communists support public housing and Senator Robert A. Taft also did so, the inference that Senator Taft was a Communist or a Communist dupe is nonsense. Antipathy to communism and an interest in decent housing for Americans are wholly compatible. Anticommunism may be a good political motive and a bad social taskmaster. In any event, the man who is on the same planet as the Soviet Union may or may not be a Communist; additional evidence is needed.

What extends to all political thinking is the citizen's obligation at the outset of any inquiry to work hard at the thinking process and, along the way, to look for meanings and proof before adopting a judgment.

2. *Look at least twice at the political question under consideration to make sure it is the one that is actually at issue. The nature of the question is a critical determinant of the answers and the further questions that are put.*

Any complex area of significant governmental concern can be approached in a thousand ways, and each way sets the terms of reference for the analysis that follows. The alumnus shows more insight than his social science professor in the story of the old graduate who came upon his professor of long ago in the act of writing out the questions for his next examination. Observing that the questions were the same as those he had had to answer twenty-five years previously, he commented on this to the professor. The pedagogue replied, "You might at least have learned this much during your four years here, that it is not the questions that change, but the answers."

Half a truth in this instance is worse than none. For the question is a guide to the information and the arguments that we ought to look for; it sets the frame of the answer. With the wrong or obsolescent or obsolete questions we are sure to find the wrong answers. Questions must change as circumstances and needs change, as we become more aware of our emerging social characteristics and requirements.

An illustration is the man who inveighs against big government, saying, "I am against any increase in the size or scope of government. Whatever it is that is proposed for anything new or expanded in governmental activity or power, I am opposed to it."

For instance, anyone arguing for an increased military effort is also arguing for enlarged Federal activities; nobody argues for a bigger army or navy or air force by creating or adding to the size of private armies. The implicit question in our friend's antigovernment declaration is: Shall we oppose or favor an increase in government? A revised and more useful form of the question might be: What combination of public and private enterprise will carry forward the general welfare in application to specific areas, like television, steel manufacture, banking, housing, defense, tax collection, or highway construction?

The superiority of the suggested rewrite lies in its awareness that American society is dynamic, that the country's difficulties mount in number and complexity, that business, labor, and agriculture also get bigger, that American government must also expand or it cannot govern, that the question is not whether government shall reach out, but where and how government will grow or not in company with increases in the power of other segments and forces in the United States. The essential defect of the original draft demanding simply that government stay at its present size is that it is an implicit plea for reaction, a distraction from useful analysis of a current problem to a wistful effort to accomplish the impossible by returning to the way things used to be.

To put one of the major questions confronting the United States as Big Government versus Freedom is quite as misleading as to talk of Communism versus Capitalism. Communism is both a political and an economic system, but capitalism is only one form among many that are possible within democracy. In somewhat comparable fashion, big government may (or may not) further freedom; the baldly stated options suggest what is not true: that expanding government is incompatible with liberty.

The field of arms control–disarmament provides another example of the importance of style in framing political questions. Two forms of a significant question are: (a) Is disarmament possible? (b) Is arms control possible? Each statement of the question at issue leads to the presentation of different data, different conclusions, and different approaches to international affairs. Define the basic problem as "disarmament" and you then talk of such matters as historical failures to achieve disarmament, the cataclysmic consequences to any country if the other breaks an agreement, and the accompanying built-in pressures not to risk the total vulnerability of disarmament, and you end with such interpretations as "Red or Dead" alternatives. Define the issue as "arms control" and you see that "the loom of history" offers somewhat relevant positive accomplishments, and in any case the scope of the arms-reduction problem is narrowed so as to stimulate efforts to work out practicable agreements.

To ask one question rather than another, even on the same general subject matter, is to begin the consideration of different issues whose outcomes are foreshadowed in the way the question is put. Full appreciation of what is involved in every case of political inquiry demands that the individual possess enough information about the issue to know the direction in which he is aiming the question. A little knowledge may be a useful thing in guiding a question fruitfully. At the minimum, a protection for the individual is to know beforehand that he always runs the hazards of question-tipping and answer-weighting in politics.

The point is exemplified in the famous tenth number of *The Federalist.* In this paper, James Madison seeks to demonstrate that a great virtue of the proposed Constitution is the excellence with which the Constitution deals with the problem of factions, the problem on which civilizations throughout history have foundered. By this time, the sophisticated reader will anticipate that the analysis cannot continue creatively unless there is a definition of the term "factions." Evidently, its meaning will be crucial in the exposition, and the individual may reasonably be suspicious of the talents or scruples of any writer who does not define critical, complex terms such as "faction."

Madison does define what he is talking about:

> By a faction, I understand a number of citizens, whether amounting to a majority or a minority of the whole, who are united and actuated by some common impulse of passion, or of interest, adverse to the rights of other citizens, or to the permanent and aggregate interests of the community.

At least one aspect of the definition is clear and relevant here. Even majorities may be factions, and they must be controlled by an effective Constitution. The definition tells us firmly that Madison implicitly trusted neither the rich nor the poor, neither the well-born nor the ill-born. The current verbal obeisance to majorities is not Madisonian.

In the remainder of this *Federalist* paper Madison brilliantly analyzes the kinds of controls over both majorities and minorities which are apposite and are set forth in the Constitution. Along the way, Madison has given us an illustration of the manner in which the definition of a central term has been used to point and advance the analysis toward a predetermined objective—not necessarily obvious to the casual or unwary reader or listener. Think of how different Madison's argument and conclusions would have been if "factions" had been limited simply to minorities.

Not all political definitions and questions are subtle and elusive ways of prompting desired answers. Sometimes the bias or set may be altogether plain. For example, when William Henry Harrison ran for the Presidency in 1840, his supporters made much of Harrison's simplicity as exemplified by his preference for hard cider, rather than expensive wines. The comment of William Cullen Bryant, the Democratic editor and well-remembered poet, was an effort to focus attention on what was important: "The question is not whether Harrison drinks hard cider. . . . The question is what he and his party will do if they obtain power."

Twentieth-century analogues are everywhere. "Keep Cool with Coolidge" is an imprecise cue about the important questions in a presidential election campaign. Rhymes or trick plays with candidates' names or physical characteristics assume that politics is a branch of show business and suggest that an attractive real or metaphorical grin is the basic political answer to any question.

Extreme weighting tends to produce questions that are essentially rhetorical, not so much asking a question as using a rising inflection while affirming a thesis. An example comes from a newspaper editorial reproduced in the *Congressional Record* at the time President John F. Kennedy first proposed the creation of a Federal Department of Urban Affairs:

> What the cities need far more urgently than Federal "concern" for their failings is a hard look by their own administrators and citizens at what Federal housing programs already are doing to them. What is happening as the result of paper plans imposed upon them from Washington whether relevant to local problems and conditions or not? What has been the effect of municipal rubber-stamping of Federal standards and specifications, imposed under the threat of withdrawal of Federal funds? What has been the effect on cities of swallowing projects which in the absence of local control had been better not begun at all?

The editorial's questions strike at selected aspects of city politics and administration and presume answers to preliminary unasked questions summed up in ideas like "imposed" and "rubber-stamping." The concluding point here is simple. Questions shape answers. You must reexamine implicit or explicit questions to be sure they are the ones that will facilitate the search for valid political conclusions.

3. *Test a political assertion by turning the thesis on its head, by searching for interpretations other than the one given.*

"A little learning," said Alexander Pope, "is a dangerous thing." The art commentator, Bernard Berenson, remarked paradoxically, "Too much learning is a dangerous thing, as much as having too little." George Bernard Shaw remarked truly that youth is so wonderful a thing that it is a shame to waste it on young people; paradoxically, one may add that maturity is a wonderful thing, and it is a shame to waste it on old people. Lord Acton's phrase has become hackneyed: "Power tends to corrupt and absolute power corrupts absolutely." At the same time, the Acton phrase may be stood on its head with equal truth: The absence of power tends to corrupt and the total absence of power corrupts absolutely. Or another variation is plausible: Power tends to promote responsibility; absolute power is not an issue in the United States. For the fact of the matter is that virtually any sweeping generalization with much truth in it is likely also to have much falsehood in it. Useful indeed is the citizen's habit of turning around and around in his head the complex declaration he sees and hears to see what happens to the sense of a thesis when it is inverted or stretched out to meet a complement.

A seventeenth-century British pamphleteer states that a "man who will be master of argument, must do like a skilful General, who sendeth scouts on all sides, to see whether there may not be an enemy. So he looks around to see what objections can be made, and not go in a straight line, which is the ready way to lead him into a mistake."

This is a proposition with application to a variety of political cases. For example, a senator says that another "prominent man" was shocked at President Dwight Eisenhower's invitation to Premier Khrushchev to visit the United States in 1959. A later speaker then remarks that it is reasonable to believe the senator's statement to be true, because the prominent man has never denied the report that he made the statement. The listener's rational scouts will readily develop alternative explanations why the absence of a denial is fallible evidence that the alleged statement was made; e.g., perhaps the prominent man wished to give the charge no further publicity and nourishment, or maybe he wished not to get into a fracas with the senator.

Another example of the use in looking for various interpretations is comment about motivations influencing public figures. Thus, Chief Justice John Marshall, the man who did so much to create the Constitution we know, has been the subject of a good deal of investigation and effort to explain his great nation-making decisions. In that vein, one writer suggests a key to Marshall's "unyielding economic conservatism," and perhaps his dynamic drive as well:

> . . . the fact that, in the common phrase, he was a self-made man who came up the hard way. Like so many who fight their way to the top against original odds, he had scant sympathy for those less able or less fortunate or less determined whom he left behind and beneath; successful, respected, well-to-do by dint of his own efforts, he identified himself completely with the class to which he had climbed.

The assumption, of course, is that the man who has climbed to success has little sympathy for the people who have not risen, but identifies himself with successful people. The reader then has the obligation to turn the idea around in the attempt to inquire into its validity, and to ask the question: How often, if at all, do self-made men retain their feeling for common men; how often, if at all, do men who were born in highly fortunate circumstances behave in one way or another in relation to the needs and the problems of ordinary people?

What becomes plain is that we have no evidence of the frequency with which self-made men or non-self-made men abjure the unsuccessful many; so that what we can say of the suggested explanation of Marshall's behavior is that the explanation either does or does not explain the situation competently. The reader can but think of instances in his experience, of the aristocratically born Franklin D. Roosevelt and the commonly born Abraham Lincoln, who argued and politicked on behalf of ordinary people, or of other examples, necessarily imprecise, of one or another hypothesis of what makes a public figure run.

Certainly the politically sophisticated citizen will search deliberately for interpretations which are not necessarily identical with those attached to a governmental event. One more example ought to be cited. "The shadow of the Pentagon hangs over the United States," said one commentator, who continued:

> The signs can be seen in the Federal Government. The Government is acquiring a military face. The Pentagon is spending most of the Federal income, and military men are taking over many civilian duties. By 1957, some 7,500 officers were on duty at non-military posts at home and abroad. Two hundred generals and admirals were among them. A general—not a civilian—even in charge of the Immigration and Naturalization Service, which lets fascists in and deports anti-fascists.

Disentangling the slanted material from the rest of the statement, we find the basic data are clear enough. Great sums of Federal money are going for Federal purposes; military personnel are staffing a great number of posts traditionally thought of as civilian in nature. Out of these data stem the conclusion that "the Government is acquiring a military face" and the implication that a militarist is replacing a previously civilian emphasis.

Neither the conclusion nor the implication is inescapable. The basic data can certainly be reinterpreted: considerable amounts of public money are being appropriated to keep America nonmilitarist; sizable military expenditures are an indispensable part of America's effort to remain free; extending the use of military men (but keeping them under civilian control) is an accompaniment of the new kinds of technical and professional tasks facing the United States in its search to maintain its democracy. To be noted, of course, is that there are vast amounts of other data not cited either in the original or revised explanation supporting the idea that the face of the United States is, as it was, civilian.

The moral is plain: set out deliberately to pull and push all political conclusions so as to find out whether reinterpretations may be superior to the one proffered by a writer or speaker.

4. *Determine whether figures of speech and proverbs are used to say something interestingly, not to prove anything.*

A metaphor, a parable, and a cliché are inferior substitutes for rational analysis and data in politics; at best they suggest hypotheses for exploration; at worst, they halt or mislead thought. The saying we have heard ten thousand times tends to guide us toward interpretations not necessarily supported by the weight of the data. For example, a highly vulnerable cue to truth is contained in the notion that there is a golden mean, that a middle ground between conflicting assertions is most likely to be the most nearly true ground. One historian likens the man who seeks a middle course between antagonistic statements to the "little chap who, asked for the square of the number two, when one neighbor whispered 'four' and the other 'eight,' thought he had hit the mark in answering 'six.'"

Further exemplification of the way in which ancient sayings can mislead is the partial truth, "Where there is smoke, there is fire." Actually, there can be smoke without fire just as there can be fire without smoke and in either case the application to politics is nil. The citizen who takes a mass of political accusation and noise as indicating clearly that the object of the accusation is guilty of *something* may, of course, be right; but he may be wrong, the political innuendo and mud being merely the work of a man interested—intentionally or not—in deceiving the citizenry into thinking that there must be *some* basis for the uproar. Suppose that a public figure is attacked as a Communist dupe and an incompetent and alleged to be involved with a man who was a friend of somebody else who lived in the same apartment house as another person who was a sex deviate. These are attention-arresting charges and, made with literary gusto and dramatic flair by, let us say, a senator, could well produce reams of publicity without a bit of substantiation. Even if the central figure were utterly pure, the difficulties confronting the United States *could* explain great public interest in the whole affair.

"A good maxim," notes one writer, "like any other tool, requires judicious handling." Take the illustration of Abraham Lincoln's declaration that a nation cannot endure "half slave and half free." A fair question is: "Why not?" The remark has a neat literary swing. "Slave" and "free" are interestingly opposed, and the arithmetic division by two is presumably a figure of speech to make the point that freedom is inevitable. Implied is the thought that as in pregnancy, there can be no touch of liberty, that "all or none" is the sweeping assumption whereby to test the presence or absence of freedom. Yet it is surely conceivable that in a particular nation there could be large numbers of unfree people and numbers of free people. In a specific country, say the Soviet Union, the governing oligarchy may maintain unfreedom through a skillfully brewed mixture of force, propaganda, political organization, and confusing ideology. In politics, an eloquent statement and a valid conclusion are distinguishable.

Political witticisms and aphorisms furnish another example of political unthought by literary reference. Here are a few timeworn instances:

When a diplomat says yes, he means maybe; when he says maybe, he means no; when he says no, he is no diplomat.
The only battle that counts is the last battle.

Now a series of definitions:

Idealism: If you have two cows, you milk them both, use all the milk you need, and have enough left for your neighbors.
Socialism: If you have two cows, you keep one and give the other to the man next door.
Communism: If you have two cows, you give both to the government; then the government gives you back a little milk.
Imperialism: If you have two cows, you steal somebody's bull.
Capitalism: If you have two cows, you sell one and buy a bull.
New Dealism: If you have two cows, the government shoots one; you milk the other, then dump half the milk down the sink.
Nazism: If you have two cows, the government shoots you and takes the cows.
Realism: If you have two cows, they're both dry.

Running through these literary effusions are two characteristics: they are wrong, and they conform to stereotypes that push and shove in our heads. Thus, it may safely be presumed that when some diplomats say yes, they mean certainly; that when they say maybe, they are inviting further discussion; that when they say no, they mean no. As Harold Nicolson, the brilliant foreign-affairs analyst, has observed, one of the most important assets of the modern diplomat is that he be known as clear and honest.

Even in classical military warfare, it was probably wrong to say that only the last battle counted. In modern warfare the saying is faulty indeed; by the time the last battle is fought, it may be that the nation has been so exhausted and devastated that the outcome of the battle is inconsequential. Certainly, as Richard Neustadt points out, "in political warfare, the outcome for a President depends as much or more on the *first* battle. These are battles that decide his public image and create a pattern for his Washington reputation."

That the definitions of the isms cited above were framed by a believer in capitalism should be immediately clear. The Communist would presumably define capitalism as: "You never do have two cows; the banker has all the cows and the landlord puts water into the milk you get." These are quips, not evidence; they are ways of saying something that people already believe; they sound persuasive to people who have accepted the message before hearing the data. "A proverb," said Voltaire, "is not a reason." Similarly, a good story or an interesting phrase is not sound documentation and whimsey is not valid argumentation.

5. *Assess political evidence primarily to see whether it is representative, rather than whether it is merely true.*

Much of political perversion consists less of telling lies than of telling part of the truth; equally, it is never possible to tell the truth, the whole truth, nothing but the truth in politics. Whatever may be said by anyone embodies selection and arrangement, involves organization and emphasis, highlighting and omission. In politics, particularly because of the complexities and extent of its subject matter, truth may be false, or at least deceptive; falsehood may be true, or at least not fabrication.

The listener must be wary of what is unsaid; the reader must be careful about what is between the lines. In all cases, a sensible question is: Is the "proof" an adequate sample of the significant data relevant to the issue under consideration?

Statistical materials are rich in examples of misrepresentation through partial truth telling. A historian gives a Soviet instance:

> Malenkov, for example, told the Nineteenth Party Congress (1952) that the total number of cattle on Soviet farms had been raised by 1948 to the level of 1940. A 1957 Soviet publication corroborated this statement but also gave additional data which completely altered the picture. In choosing 1940 for the comparative figure, Malenkov inflated the apparent recovery. The number of cattle in 1940 was appreciably less than in 1938, 1939, or even 1941. Moreover the number of cattle on Soviet farms in 1948 was almost

17 million less than it had been in 1928, and 8 million less than the figure for the farms of Imperial Russia in 1916. This puts a very different face on the matter, especially when the figures are seen in relation to the population increases between 1916 or 1928 and 1948.

None of these figures was invented, but they are fictional anyway. In this case, the base years picked for comparison were designed to dupe the people listening. By design or not, political arithmetic can be deceptive by appropriate manipulation of every step in the computations, extending from the definition of the terms used to the choice of the method of statistical calculation.

To protect himself against the illicit use of numerical materials, the citizen may seek easy, unwarranted comfort in dismissing all statistics as species of lies. Yet it would seem less than sensible to wave away a whole class of potentially valuable information because some of the data can be twisted. The citizen would find it more useful to ask silent questions of the statistical data with the expectation that honest, competent tabulations tell the reader both what the statistics are and, very importantly, how they were derived.

The ways in which political statistics can be approached are exemplified in a commentary by Chester Bowles. Often deplored as a sure road to the poorhouse, the mounting public debt can be viewed as a correlative of America's growth:

> There is no doubt that the total American debt—public and private—has increased in the past years. Since 1945 local and state debt has risen 400 per cent and private debt 300 per cent.
>
> But in this same period our federal debt has increased only 5 per cent. In 1945 the figure stood at $279 billion. This corresponded roughly to $2,000 for every man, woman and child in the country, adjusted to 1958 prices.
>
> In the fall of 1959 the nation's debt stood at $285 billion. This came to a little over $1,600 for each person in the country—or $400 per person less in 1958 prices than it was in 1945.
>
> Yet this is but a part of the story. Everybody knows that a private debt of $10,000 is less of a burden to a man earning $15,000 than to one earning $5,000. So it is with our national debt.
>
> Since 1945 our gross national product has more than doubled. Thus we are far better able to carry the national debt these days than we were then.

Unadorned, the raw figures may well sound near-cataclysmic to the future of American government: after all, in 1945 the Federal debt came to $2,000 for every person in the country, and by 1959 the debt had soared further by another 6 billion dollars. Standing alone, however, the figures are incomplete; they do not represent adequately the impact of the debt. With the addition of the Bowles computations, the meaning of the statistical pattern changes appreciably to indicate that the American national debt is not necessarily a path to perdition.

Not only numerical information requires close examination to make sure that it is descriptive and representative of the universe from which it has been selected. To qualitative data, too, the question may be put: whether whatever evidence has been cited is typical of the category from which it is drawn.

Several examples will illustrate the necessity for testing qualitative specifics to see whether they are representative samples from whatever governmental universe is being explored. On one occasion, during a 1954 discussion in the Security Council of the United Nations, the Soviet delegate quoted from an article allegedly written by the American delegate in 1930:

> When the northern man with his taste for doing and acting comes in contact with the tropical man with his taste for submission and endurance, the tropical man always submits. It should be accepted as a fact and programs for change should be based on this premise as a point of departure.

The American delegate promptly repudiated the doctrine in the article as "highly offensive"; the observer interested in forming an opinion about the American's attitudes toward "tropical man" would have to ask whether this single citation from a 1930 article is a cue suggestive of the delegate's attitudes and behavior long afterward when the delegate was a quarter-century older, working in a different role in a different world.

The intellectual problem for the citizen is to avoid the pitfall of incomplete data so pictured that a total situation is erroneously described. The charge is made, let us say, that a Federal agency concerned with foreign aid has supplied striped pants for Greek undertakers and bathtubs for Egyptian camel drivers. The full data were that shoes had been supplied for the Greek army, and sanitary facilities had been provided to Egypt so as to stamp out a form of hookworm. In a partial sense it could be said that clothes had been supplied to Greece, and bathtubs to Egypt. The charges have somewhere around a fortieth-cousin relationship to truth. To make a determination about the validity of the criticism of the foreign-aid program, the reader needs to separate the picturesque language of the unfriendly commentary from the proof and ask whether the evidence presented is descriptive of what the Federal agency actually did; more generally, whether any evidence necessarily selected from a great mass of materials typifies the array of specific items and arguments and figures that could have been presented.

6. *Use authoritative sources on political matters the way a sensible man uses a lamppost—for illumination rather than support.*

"My principal merit, if I may claim any in public affairs," said Benjamin Franklin on one occasion, "is that of having been always ready and willing to receive and follow good advice." We may applaud the Franklin idea: it is generally good sense to use other people's experience and wisdom. The alternative is for the citizen to seek to become omniscient and painfully to make his own mistakes as he takes the highroad to learn everything himself. At the same time, there is nowhere an easy-to-find-and-use key to an ultimate authority that may be consulted on any sensitive and complicated mundane matter. In politics particularly the citizen who would find it comfortable to rely on the expert encounters difficulties along the whole rational way.

The man who looks for the support of experts searches for a nonexistent standard of valid political thinking. For experts may be wrong, and the individual who places utter reliance on political authority remains vulnerable to error. What is more, one of the most notable characteristics of the experts is the frequency with which they disagree with one another, and individuals continue in any event to have the problem of deciding which experts to accept. Rounding out the impediments to letting authorities do the thinking for ordinary people in politics is the fact that often enough there is no source of unquestionable authority in politics.

The susceptibility of the expert to error has been exemplified throughout all American—and not only American—history. The near unanimity of the authorities in 1941 in believing that the Soviet Union would collapse in a few weeks under the Nazi onslaught, the near unanimity of the experts in 1948 in believing that Thomas Dewey would win over Harry Truman in the presidential election, the contempt of the French Academy of Sciences in rejecting the ideas of Pasteur, the action of ten thousand authorities on ten thousand occasions, bear testimony to the extent to which experts can be merely mistaken or devastatingly wrong.

When the experts agree, they can all be wrong anyway; when they disagree at least some must be wrong. Which are to be accepted in part or as a whole, which rejected, is not a determination that can effectively be made simply by reference to the authorities' conclusions. For instance, in one leading work the writer said: "Strange as it may sound today, the statesmen of 1787 intended to make the process of constitutional amendment an easy one." In contrast, the author of a second important volume on American government declared: "The amending of the federal Constitution was clearly intended to be a difficult procedure." A triad of possible differences of judgment is neatly completed by the statement from a long-time classic book on American government: "Desiring that the new fundamental law should neither be virtually impossible to amend, as the Articles had been, nor yet capable of too swift and easy change, the framers devised somewhat difficult, but not prohibitive, amending procedures. . . ."

More useful than asking these authorities for their answers to whatever questions we may have in mind is to ask for the proof on which they base their judgments. Such inquiry would remind us first of the difficulties in figuring out the intentions and motives of the Constitution makers—or any other protagonists in a major governmental drama. Then we could see that the basic data include the small number of formal amendments and the great number of changes effected through nonformal means. To the citizen the significant information is, after all, the data about the extent and kind of constitutional modifications that have been made, information that the ordinary man obtains by finding out especially what is the evidentiary basis of the experts' conclusions.

Information about the background and qualifications of the expert in politics is of no great use to the layman. There would seem to be little point to the question of when the expert in politics is an expert. First, the citizen has no equipment for deciding the relative worth of different qualification patterns. He has no reliable way of calibrating, let us say, a Ph.D. from Yale

University, as against a second man's five years of service in a state Legislature, or a third man's reading and reflecting that produced a series of magazine articles. Every political scientist, in fact, knows other political scientists with extensive formal qualifications in teaching, writing, or government experience who, nevertheless, have odd, unjustified opinions about significant aspects of public affairs. Thus, to take an obvious illustration, Lenin and Marx are not similarly evaluated as authorities by everyone.

Second, the value of the expert to the man interested in acquiring considered opinions lies in the expert's communication of data and insights. With such materials provided by the expert, the citizen can more readily think out his own conclusions on a substantial, informational foundation.

Suppose you are interested in finding out the meaning of the word "democracy." You will find one definition in an unabridged dictionary, a second in the *Encyclopedia of the Social Sciences*, and a train of others in other sources. No automatic criterion reveals which of these interpretations can most reasonably be taken as authoritative. Nobody is an authority on the meaning of the term; there are only varying views with differing substantiation for the diverse opinions. Unhappily or not, there is no substitute for the necessity that you plow through the job of puzzling out for yourself the significance of the term. Equally, although there is nowhere in politics a safe reservoir of secure answers to great political questions, all is not drearily hopeless for the man willing to try to think. There are lots of authoritative sources, expert materials, and stimulating ideas available to the interested individual to help him form his own discriminating judgments about public affairs.

7. *Make use of political semantics as an exercise in finding and assessing political evidence, rather than as a process of ignoring or lamenting other people's verbal sins.*

Words do not dangle in mid-air devoid of connection with an environment, a ground, a context. On the contrary, words are always tied to a person, a thing, an idea, an event—a something, whatever it may be. In one of the Disraeli novels, a cynical statesman says that "with words we govern men." What validity is held by the aphorism hinges on the relations between the substance of the words and the mainsprings of human thought and action. The powerful words in the United States are words we have all seen and heard many times: political-looking terms like democracy and Constitution; nonpolitical-looking terms like mother, family, love; names like Washington, Franklin Roosevelt, Stalin, Khrushchev. Every one of these words is a reference to something real in our experience, our education in and out of school, the values we hold dear or reject vehemently. Words are symbols and stand for entities entangled with sentiments and behavior.

Naturally, the political leader, seeking to influence his audience, encases his message in language calculated to evoke a desired reaction. "Democracy" in the United States is a positive symbol; so are good housing, good medical care, individualism, and varied other objects of American favor. Any incumbent public official or aspirant to office, whatever the nature of the proposals or ideas he urges, will label what he says as a contribution to good care of the American's health or the maintenance of his sturdy self-reliance.

When Earl Browder campaigned for the American Presidency in 1936, his slogan was, "Communism is twentieth-century Americanism." This coherence between an individual's language and the value system of the people he wants to reach is hardly a unique phenomenon or peculiar to the United States. It was in the eighteenth century in Britain that a member of Parliament took occasion to warn lovers of liberty that they must not be misled by the specious title of a bill. "I dare say," he observed, "if the High Priest of the Spanish Inquisition was to come among us to introduce his system of inquisition here, he would call it an act for the better support and protection of religion."

Similarly, the man who wants to destroy civil liberties in the United States would form an organization with some such title as "Society for the Protection and Advancement of Civil Liberties." To be added, of course, is that the individual who seeks to maintain and extend civil liberties would likewise use such a name for his organization. "Good" words are not the special province of the politician practicing semantic sleight of hand, just as they are not reserved for the politician who operates with his verbal sleeves rolled up to show that he is engaging in no ideological skulduggery.

In approaching the problems of political semantics, the citizen can distinguish three types of attitudes. The words used in political discourse may be thought of as unfortunate, emotional obstacles to clear thinking, or as the overwhelmingly important essence of the matter under examination, or as normal ways of communications requiring close inspection to sift out data from conclusions.

Language in politics may mislead or confuse the observer by design, but not necessarily so. "No one," said Henry Adams, "means all that he says, and yet very few say all they mean, for words are slippery and thought is viscous." Take the fact that considerable verbal skill is required to say anything abstract and complex, add that the political orator may have a great emotional attachment to what he is saying, multiply the combination by the audience's probable indifference to political communication and most people's lack of background information, sprinkle the result with the consequent necessity that a speaker talk loudly and dramatically, omitting hard-to-follow and dull material to keep his uninterested, uninformed audience: the product is a political language pattern that is likely at best to be inexact.

The point of possibly unintentional semantic obfuscation is further illustrated by a quotation from Justice Holmes: "A word is not a crystal, transparent and unchanged; it is the skin of a living thought and may vary greatly in color and content according to the circumstances and the time in which it is used." Words like "bomb," "war," and "peace," allusions to the major concerns of our time, exemplify the Holmes thought. Throughout human history the word "war" has described relatively small numbers of military people using instruments of violence as savage as they could contrive, but limited anyway in scope and intensity. It offends intellectual and emotional sensibilities to use the same word "war" to refer to the devastation of nuclear warfare or the horrors of bacteriological or chemical or other kinds of extermination that modern technology develops. In fine, the use of old attitude- and meaning-encrusted words shrinks our understandings of public affairs.

Whether political deception, self-inflicted or not, is deliberate in specific instances involves data ordinarily not at hand; in any event, it can be argued that the semanticist's intentions are far less significant than his behavior. It is what is done that counts, and what is done need not be hinged to the words used. Thus, the German military strategist Clausewitz once remarked, "A conqueror is always a lover of peace." Copying this comment in his diary, Lenin added, "Ah! Ah! Witty!" The Nazi organizations which collected 60,000 aged and insane people from the German public-assistance institutions and then gassed them in "clinics" were called not the "Organizations for Murdering Helpless People" but the "Charitable Foundation for the Transportation of the Sick" and the "Charitable Foundation for Institutional Care."

The task for the politically creative individual is to peel off the conclusions from a given statement, get at the factual core (if any), and then decide what conclusion is warranted by the facts.

Plenty of examples exist in politics of the utility of what may be called operational definitions, of the value in Justice Holmes's advice: "We must think things, not words." Thus, at the time Congress was considering the "Jensen Amendment," aimed at reducing Federal payrolls, one observer declared that the measure would better be described as "kicking out the bureaucrats," an aim "with which only a few political sophisticates might take issue." The sensible citizen would take neither the neutral nor the biased-looking descriptions as the basis for a conclusion: for him to have a judgment, he needs to see what the amendment actually does, how its provisions work.

One speaker at a Communist meeting proposed that "workers," a term with limited appeal in the United States, be dropped in favor of "the people." The audience denounced the idea as a "fascist formulation"; "we must not encourage such myths," said one spokesman. Whatever the term used in the discourse, the thinking person would inquire closely into the nature of the data presented about whom—and remember the tendency of interested people to use language they consider effective rather than precise.

When the British once withdrew their support from one Yugoslav group to back another, the Government issued a directive: the forces formerly described as "patriots" were now to be called "terrorist gangs," the people previously called "red bandits" were now to be designated "freedom fighters." When a reviewer in a British professional journal of international affairs commented on a new book, he protested: "The emergence of former British colonies as autonomous nations is represented as a loss to the British Empire instead of a gain to the Commonwealth." In Nazi Germany, when Joseph Goebbels took charge of the propaganda program, he named himself Minister for Public Enlightenment. The American who hears talk of "coexistence" thinks in terms of "live and let live." But it may be in concrete circumstances that someone else means by "coexistence" war by less bloody means or some other unexpected interpretation.

A commonplace in politics is the use of such terms as liberal, conservative, left, right, reactionary, radical, left extremism, right extremism. Witty references underscoring one aspect of a complex totality are popular: "A liberal is a radical with a family" or "A right extremist is a man with one of the best minds of the twelfth century." Nothing should be clearer than the worn-out character of such verbiage in present-day America (or elsewhere for that matter). Is it right or left in the United States to urge a pay-as-you-go governmental policy emphasizing enormous taxes and public budgets that take into account the impact of all expenditures on the economy? Is it left or right deviationist, or neither, in the Soviet Union to seek greater production of consumer goods? Even if you could determine whether something is liberal or conservative or in any other category, you have progressed not at all in the search for valid political conclusions.

What remains always is the necessity to ascertain and evaluate evidence in the light of whatever the criterion may be. A term like "extremism" is a summary—and useless—reference. It is the content summarized under the label that is significant in cuing a decision about the value or threat of an organization. Of course, the organization will name itself something like the Foundation to Advance American Welfare, and different commentators will attach to it varying epithets, all requiring further examination. Does the organization wish to impeach the Chief Justice of the Supreme Court? On what basis? Is this basis persuasive? Are there other judgmental bases that are relevant besides that presented by the organization itself? What do other apparently knowledgeable sources of information say? Questions like these the citizen should seriously ask (and find answers to), instead of restricting himself to a label, common and accepted or not.

Either the citizen breaks down a summary term to analyze its meaningful components or he has no adequate ground for political thought. And not every potentially deceptive term has the obvious political coloration of emotion-stained words. What seem like ordinary words can be verbal traps, especially where the reference is to some remote entity. The word "Africa" is an example, as may be seen from the commentary of one observer:

> Africa is not a unit in any sense: neither geographical, climatic, racial, cultural, linguistic nor historical. There are only Africas, vaguely defined by the points of the compass: North, South, East and West, alike only in their immensity and their emptiness.
>
> Even within these Africas each huge enough to be a subcontinent in itself, there is no uniformity of terrain, of language, of custom, of civilization.
>
> Algeria is as different from the Congo as Canada is from Brazil—and, incidentally, the distance from Algiers to Elisabethville is about as great as that from the St. Lawrence to the Amazon. For over five thousand miles this enormous continent stretches from the Straits of Gibraltar to Port Elizabeth.

The man who thinks of American relations to an Africa that is primitive or hot or homogeneous in any other major characteristic is wrong, and he can be right only if he inquires into the particular political, cultural, or other constituents he discusses.

To the individual who aspires to hold firmly rooted political opinions, any language in politics is an invitation to further study and analysis of the things under the words.

8. *Find and seek to control the nonintellectual components and ramifications of your political opinions and behavior.*

Every man has preconceptions and frustrations and unwarranted biases; the obligation of the citizen is to try to shrink their impact in warping a productive view and analysis of the evidence. No man can be altogether objective in removing his prejudices from the consideration of a problem, but every man can recognize his vulnerabilities and set out deliberately to build safeguards against them.

There is a Velázquez painting, *The Maids in Waiting*, which illustrates the interrelation between the citizen and the issue he confronts. In the painting, the artist is before a large canvas. The King and Queen are reflected in a small mirror at the back. The Infanta Margarita and her attendants are in the foreground. Thus "the painting is not only a celebration of the court of Philip IV, but also of Velázquez's own place there, an analysis of the problem of the relationship between the artist, the subject and the spectator, and between 'illusion' and 'reality.' "

In each man's head is a picture of the world around him and a conceptualization of the forces which make things what they are; all of us work hard to keep the world in coherent relation with our values and our wishes, our needs and our aspirations. The wit takes one aspect of this relation when he says, "The demand for fair play is as usual merely the hypocritical exterior of a demand for substantial favoritism." Less brutally, another observer widens the scope of this proposition and introduces a qualification, "The fact is that our societies, our governments, and we as individuals are constantly under the sway of a legendary world against which the real world can hardly prevail."

The political world is no system of complex arithmetic, of quantified weights and measures and balances fixed without relation to people's feelings. Exemplifying another aspect of the connection between the political and the personal world is the statement of George Orwell, author of the famous political novel *1984*: the book "wouldn't have been so gloomy if I hadn't been so ill."

When President McKinley spent the night in prayer for divine guidance, he wound up by deciding to annex the Philippines. Following the bombardment of Veracruz in 1914, President Wilson assured the world that "the United States had gone to Mexico to serve mankind." One could suspect that the predispositions of each man had facilitated enormously the process of resolving the pressures acting on him by coming to a conclusion that proved comfortable to live with.

Justice Holmes once declared, "I always think of a remark of Brooks Adams that the philosophers were hired by the comfortable class to prove everything is all right. . . . When I say that a thing is true, I mean that I cannot help believing it. . . . I therefore define the truth as the system of my limitations, and leave absolute truth for those who are better equipped."

The philosophers are not alone in searching for evidence that everything they like is all right; other people too search for data and interpretations that help to make things acceptable. Thus, if a man has been frustrated by a life of failure, he can find it useful to explain the absence of successes by the activities of the Communists, the Fascists, the Rich Men, Wall Street, Propagandists, Extremists, Jews, Catholics, the Interests, or, more simply, They and Them. The man who has just lost his job can assist himself to maintain his integrity and convince himself that he remains a fine fellow; he needs only to lay the loss of his work to the machinations of the grimy fellow with a beard who undoubtedly gets together with other grimy men with beards to plot the discomfort of our hero.

All this sounds, of course, like somebody else, but the citizen will reach a little nearer to seeing things as they are if he will perceive that he is a first cousin to the other fellow just described. Few things, for example, are more natural than to expect the foreigner to be a fool or a villain or otherwise objectionable, and even a student may fall into the error of assuming his own superiority. (Undoubtedly, it is possible that the student *is* superior; the point is that the assertion should be proved. One thinks of the man who goes to the psychoanalyst because of an inferiority complex, and then is crushed when the analyst assures him that he has no complex at all; he really is inferior.)

The readiness of the citizenry to see politics as a tool for nourishing their psyche is no secret from the political campaigner. "Political campaigns," says one historian, "are designedly made into emotional orgies which endeavor to distract attention from the real issues involved, and they actually paralyze what slight powers of cerebration man can normally muster." Let the issue be, say, whether electrical power is to be produced and distributed by a public agency or by a privately owned organization. The campaigner knows that most of us lack interest and concern about technical matters, that we are prejudiced in favor of people who started from humble surroundings, that we prefer entertaining comments to discussions of difficult, abstruse issues. The result is that the aspirant for public office is likely to remind us that he has nine children (and, if the constituency is Lithuanian, that one daughter is married to a man of Lithuanian extraction), to exhibit his attractive wife on all occasions, to let people know he was a poor boy. These days, no campaigner will use a log cabin as his symbol, but he might make his headquarters in Indiana even if he has spent his life on Wall Street. All these are ways of halting thought, of diminishing the probability that we will examine the arguments laid before us: the anti-intellectualism of the political campaign becomes a reflection of the fact that so many of us vent our unhappiness as we can, and when the opportunity arises, by appropriate projection upon our political leaders.

It is because political analysis for some of us is an exercise in finding bases for justifying ourselves to ourselves that we tend to avoid data that conflict with our interest and, if we cannot avoid the data, to interpret them in accordance with some attractive fiction in our minds. So people are more likely to talk politics with people who share their views, more likely to read the newspapers that say what they would like to have said, listen to the radio and television shows that mirror the notions they already have, "see" and "hear" in coherence with judgments held before looking and listening. And the term "people" includes the student, the reader, the writer, and everybody else. The sole variable is the extent to which we are conscious of the phenomenon and knowingly devise ways of constraining our prejudices. The rich man's son who joins the Communist Party in order to set the world aright is presumably not responding to evidentiary data but to messages from his own psyche; in these circumstances, the best-intentioned information campaign of the American politician is hardly apt to be maximally successful in educating him.

In the phrase of one historian, the caution for the citizen to bear in mind is that he must watch his emotional commitments "as an athlete watches his diet." Awareness of undue emotional considerations is first; then comes the effort to exclude such irrational factors. The attempt will never be wholly achieved, but partial achievement would appear possible and worth the try, the likelihood of success varying substantially with the individual's freedom from severe emotional distress and great desperations. The beginnings of political understanding lie in self-understanding.

9. *Approach all political materials warily, but recognize that data produced by an open society are more reliable than those issued by totalitarian governments. As one instance, American data are more reliable than Soviet data.*

We do not suggest that American political data are without great defects, or that the data have special virtues because of the special virtues of Americans. We do suggest the invalidity of the occasional undergraduates' and others' equal disdain for all sources of information, rejecting all as emanating from individuals and organizations eager to justify and aggrandize themselves, intent on influencing enemies, converting neutrals, and making friends. Not chauvinism, but a demonstrable basis underlies our proposition.

Two kinds of data are relevant: ideological and governmental. We take each in turn and concentrate on the Soviet Union as the archetype of the totalitarian state.

Communism takes every aspect of the community to be a way of carrying forward the Communist idea. Bourgeois morality is taken to be a propaganda device whereby the ruling class holds and wields its power and has nothing to do with guiding the behavior of the Communist. "Statistics," said Lenin on one occasion, "is an instrument of the class struggle." Stuart A. Rice, then president of the International Statistical Institute, quoted a 1950 Moscow "conference on methodology" at which the chief of the Soviet Central Statistical Administration "identified the main obstacle to the development of statistical science as the formal mathematics school of thought which considers statistics to be a universal science for the study of nature and society based ultimately on the mathematical law of large numbers and not on Marxist-Leninist theory." At this conference, Rice said, statistics was pronounced a social science whose tasks and theoretical foundations are formulated in the works of Marx, Lenin, and Stalin and was used purely to aid in building a Communist society. Rice concluded: "These theses suggest the existence of an unbridgeable gulf between Soviet conceptions and those which have guided the development of modern science since the heliocentric theory of Copernicus, founded on empirical observation, triumphed over medieval dogma."

A decade later, Nikita Khrushchev told a Soviet Writers' Congress: "Writers are a type of artillery. They clear the way for our forward movement and help our party in the Communist education of the workers. . . . You must brainwash people with your works." When L. F. Ilyichev spoke in December, 1960, on "The Twenty-Second Party Congress and the Tasks of Ideological Work," he declared, "The tasks of the Soviet press are clear: to fight, with all its strength, talent, ability and Party zeal, and jointly with the people, for the implementation of the program of communist construction. . . . The Soviet press always has been and will be the spokesman for the ideas of our party and the herald of the people's thoughts and vital interests."

In contrast is the frequently stated emphasis in the United States on reporting data as they are, instead of attempting to "educate" people in some fashion. American practice falls short of the proclaimed ideals of the statistician, the newspaper, the scholar, or other reporting source in this country. Nevertheless, the Soviet-press ideal virtually guarantees that Soviet-announced data are those that are useful for the government to define and issue; American data, on the contrary, are not constrained to further governmental objectives and may, in fact, operate in a reverse direction to embarrass governmental interests.

Moreover, there is in our government a structural and procedural basis for believing that American data are more likely than Soviet data to be trustworthy. It lies in the characteristics of the American government and society: our openness, the stimuli and the encouragements to factual accuracy, and comprehensiveness given through separate and independent checks on all major species of data, the balances in informational competition.

If the governmental figures or other data are issued by a Republican administration, Democrats will inspect the material carefully and sometimes provide rival data. If the data are Federal, then state and local agencies may furnish their own versions. If the statistics are from an executive agency, the Congress gets ample opportunity to say its say. If the Department of Agriculture reports anything, farmers' organizations may publish a competitive interpretation, and a consumer group may report that the public agency and the agricultural organizations are both wrong and announce yet a different array of data. One newspaper says this, a second declares that, and a television program still something else.

On one occasion some years ago, the Bureau of Labor Statistics released cost-of-living data. Union groups, whose wage agreements were tied to cost-of-living changes, promptly challenged the figures, industrial groups challenged the unions' challenge, and into the fray leaped various other groups with varying views; the upshot was a well-examined numerical index with known characteristics.

Out of the totality of conflicting and cross-checking claims and counterclaims in the United States, the interested citizen has extensive opportunity to become aware of the nature and attributes of important information about public affairs. On the other hand, the American citizen finds in the Soviet Union no informational sources independent of the Soviet government. Where there are no checks on official data, the validity of the data becomes questionable or, at the least, uncertain. All information, American or not, official or not, requires cautious evaluation, but American data have been subjected to extensive and intensive commentary and analysis, whereas the Soviet materials have undergone no comparable public examination and verification.

10. *Wind up your political thinking with some sort of consciously adopted conclusion, and include as possibilities a confession of ignorance and a resolution of inaction.*

It is a false notion that any man who is sensible enough to be an American is correlatively justified in holding and acting on an opinion stretching to any aspect of public affairs. It is equally false that any American's political judgments are as good as anybody else's. More than sincerity and good intentions and American birth are necessary coin for defensible opinions.

Assume, for example, the great issue confronting the United States in 1962, when the Soviet Union resumed thermonuclear testing: Ought the United States to resume testing? Assume also that the criterion for the answer lies in another question: Will the resumption of testing advance the welfare of the American people? Assume that the overriding American interests are to achieve peace combined with security, and a core issue becomes: Is testing needed to protect American military retaliatory capacity against a possible surprise attack from the Soviets? To this question nobody but people in possession of detailed, technical, and secret information could have a reply in which more than zero confidence could be placed. Almost anybody with an IQ, say of 120 or more, could take part merrily in the game of to-and-fro arguments on atmospheric nuclear testing. On one side were such contentions as: alienation of "world opinion"; poisoning the atmosphere and producing genetic injuries; worsening of U.S.-Soviet relations; increased momentum given to arms race and further testing after the testing followed by enormous additional military expenditures. On the go-ahead-and-test side were arguments that summed up to the necessity to safeguard the American democracy.

The outcome of stacking such arguments in two or more piles cannot fruitfully be one whereby the ordinary individual, educated and intelligent or not, makes a decision and then cries out loudly that anyone who disagrees is an approximation to a traitor or perhaps a fool. Ordinary people just do not have the information and skills for a creative choice; in a democratic society, they cannot and do not make highly specialized governmental decisions. There are occasions when even the generally knowledgeable citizen sensibly acknowledges his ignorance, is hopeful, and does nothing.

Readiness to have judgments on all public issues is no more pointless than to have opinions on none but those for which all the facts are in. All the facts are never in, and in politics always there are more data and varying interpretations in relation to suggested questions and proposed solutions. Characteristically, many social scientists end a monograph with the comment that more research is necessary for a firm conclusion. In the political world around us perfect data or altogether-convincing answers are not everywhere to be found. The typical choice for the citizen is not between the Scylla of the utterly nonrational and the Charybdis of the completely rational. Instead, the selection is among options of intermediate merit, the ultimate preference perhaps being fairly stated as one which is apparently the "least worst" of the lot available, whether the subject be Congressional redistricting, financing a school bond issue, or supporting a United Nations action in an African nation.

The citizen's necessity to avoid hasty and ill-considered conclusions is not met with the error of what one political scientist has called "the indecision which is born of intellectual integrity." The sensible man takes his political judgments as tentative, avoiding the position of the fanatic: "the man who does what God would do if God had all the facts." Dean Rusk once talked of a negotiator who was "supremely confident as only a closed mind can be." There are personality advantages, psychological comfort, and emotional ease in "knowing" neatly formulated answers. Yet, as in democracy, where things are always shifting and things often look politically untidy, so in the open mind there is continuing change in deciding on appropriate questions and answers—reflecting the real world of politics in a free society.

"Man," said Justice Holmes, "is born to act. To act is to affirm the worth of an end, and to persist in affirming the worth of an end is to make an ideal." Abjure talking and reading and listening about politics and doing *something* political, and you finish as political nothingness. The good citizen makes a point of gathering what data he can get, forms a judgment when he can, and then does what he can—all with knowledge of the possibility that he is wrong, that his dissident neighbor is not necessarily an objectionable creature and may, in fact, be right in whole or in part. We learn to think, to discuss, and to do politics in part by political thinking, discussing, and doing. There is civic wisdom in the injunction that it is better to light one candle than to curse the darkness.

CHAPTER 2

THE AMERICAN VALUE SYSTEM

AMERICAN GOVERNMENT is a product of the total culture of the United States—of its assumptions and aspirations, its practices and ideals, its economics and technology, its social organization and personal attitudes, its physical environment. These are interconnected complex bundles of sentiments, habits, institutions, and forces which make American government different from and similar to governmental systems to be found elsewhere in the world.

It is because a nation's politics are inextricably interwoven with the remainder of its forms and bonds and manifestations that Woodrow Wilson remarked that "after years of study, he had only one final conviction of government, and that was that the same sort of government was not suitable for all nations."

Only if the student takes cognizance of the assumptions and setting in which the American political system is imbedded, can he understand the operations and meanings of governmental activities and grasp significant ideas about public affairs. It is easy, and it is wrong, for the American to presume that all decent people believe and act like Americans; it is equally easy and wrong to suppose that anything political exists in and of itself.

An example is the report of the American survey team in the Far East who studied a fishing village and made a variety of recommendations designed to double the output of the village. The American recommendations were tried out by the village, found effective indeed, and so the villagers proceeded to cut in half the amount of time they had previously given to fishing activities.

Another illustration is the action of the students and the mothers who picket the United Nations headquarters with signs proclaiming that the demonstrators WANT A WORLD IN PEACE NOT PIECES. The notion that tactics which are apposite for internal American domestic politics are quite as appropriate for the world around us is mistaken; the Soviet or other foreign leadership is unlikely to quail before the American mother who leads the child bearing the poster, PLEASE LET ME GROW UP TO BE A MOMMY.

Political life is but one aspect of life, and American political life is but one phase of the life that all of us lead. The values implicit in the concern of a mother for her child have political manifestations in the United States, just as the American stress on material success has political correlatives different from those associated with a foreigner's ideal realized in behavior that coheres with *his* values.

Illustrating the connection between mother-child and politician-constituency relations, whether in the United States or elsewhere, is the hypothesis that values learned by children persist into maturity and find political expression. For example, where youngsters are taught to be dependent by their parents, they may exhibit as adults political dependency evidenced in greater readiness to embrace totalitarian government.

The two readings that follow are designed to give the student a point of departure for thinking about American government with awareness of non-American and nongovernmental considerations.

Changes in American Values

This is a review article on Max Lerner's best-selling book, *America as a Civilization: Life and Thought in the United States Today* (Simon and Schuster, Inc., New York, 1957). At the time Lerner's book was published, one critic said the book was "significant" and perhaps even more: "Some 200 years ago Denis Diderot compiled an encyclopedia—and started the French Revolution." Not every critic was equally laudatory; another commentator objected to Lerner's "middle-of-the-road stance that leaves him not only free of bias but bereft of viewpoint," and concluded that "the middle of the road is a good place to be hit by the traffic of history, but a poor place to gauge its destination."

The author of the article is Clyde Kluckhohn, who was professor of anthropology and chairman of the Department of Anthropology at Harvard University. Kluckhohn wrote a number of books and other publications including, in collaboration with others, *How the Soviet System Works.*

[Clyde Kluckhohn, "Shifts in American Values," *World Politics,* vol. 11, pp. 252–261, 1959.]

Lerner ably reviews a succession of European observations upon the United States, from the "wonder and excitement" in de Tocqueville and Mrs. Trollope's horror at American vulgarity down to Sartre's description of jazz as a cultural expression and his contemptuous comparison of American conformity to the respectful prostitute. He soundly considers the image which drew millions of immigrants to "the land of opportunity" and the changes in image correlated with the dwindling of this stream to a trickle. Throughout the book there are wise observations on the situational differences which make for distortion of our images of the rest of the world and vice versa. For example, he points out that the economic experience of most Americans since 1945 makes it next to impossible for them to identify with the problems of the underdeveloped economies in Asia and Africa.

In a section in the final chapter he recapitulates "The World's Image of America." Most of these furrows have been well plowed by others: the fear of American power in the light of our political immaturity; the

"Athens complex" of European intellectuals; surviving racist discriminations; "American materialism"; the feedback from Communist propaganda; the nationalistic overtones of some of our acts and utterances ("the American century"). Lerner does make strongly two points that are less worn with discussion:

(1) "In this civil war raging in the mind of European and Asian man there is a danger of underestimating the pull that America still exerts on both. What attracts them is less the image of American power than of the American personality and social structure. Even many of the Russians —whatever their propagandists may teach them about American 'imperialism' and 'war-mongering'—are drawn toward the American personality. The case histories of Russian defectors into Germany and Austria, and of Hungarian refugees fleeing to the United States, show a residual sympathy for American society which two generations of Communist dogma have not been able to efface" (p. 928).

(2) "The Asian, newly liberated from colonialism or struggling to be liberated, finds in America a Devil symbol which serves to channel both his resentments and his newly felt sense of triumph. When Europeans take America apart, they are taking apart something they have come to regard as close to themselves. . . . In the case of Asia there is the sense neither of a shared past nor of a common destiny. . . . America is viewed as the outsider, the giant who typifies what is held hostile in the Western way of life. . . . The Americans, who have only recently begun to face toward Asia, have made their appeal mainly as a society of freedom and abundance, of food and sanitation. They have not understood the deep Asian resentments which are further embittered by the image of America as a storehouse crammed with commodities. They have missed the fact that for the peoples of the Far East the American living standards seem incredible because they are incommensurable in terms of Asian experience. They fail to offer these people a compassable earthly vision, just as they fail to offer in spiritual terms a vision that will sustain the Oriental hunger for renunciation" (p. 932).

These things seem to me well and powerfully said. Yet I should like to have seen a more extensive development of some of the themes in the body of the book. I think the negative pole of the ambivalence in the world image of the United States rests not only upon envy of our wealth and power but also upon resentment at our sheer success—in certain realms. I was in India at the time the first Sputniks were announced. Rather to my surprise, warmth of feeling toward this country perceptibly rose. The sources of this shift were undoubtedly complex. For one thing, these events heightened Indian fear of the Colossus to the north. But Indians also made explicit sentiments which can be crudely abstracted as follows: "For once you people are not leading the world in technology. You are humanly fallible like the rest of us. We feel closer to you."

While I agree fully with Lerner that one can underestimate the attraction that the image of the United States still has for the peoples of the world and that this rests in part on certain human qualities that representative Americans have, I believe Lerner deals altogether too perfunctorily with changes in the image of America between the pre-Civil War period and the mid-twentieth century. As G. T. Robinson has pointed out with passionate eloquence, the United States of the early nineteenth century did not appear to foreigners just as a land of economic opportunity and political freedom. It was likewise looked to as the country where the most daring and most promising social experiments were taking place, where a splendid way of life—to be shared in not by a selected few but by all citizens—was not only dreamed of but in process of creation. Today the image is quite different. Abroad, Americans seem to be determined to preserve certain values which are precious to them and aspired to by others. They seem capable of courage and of certain kinds of generosity (as Lerner documents). But the freedoms Americans talk about now strike Asians and Africans as old freedoms, restricted freedoms, negative freedoms. The success story (for ourselves) remains palpable. The excitement of ideas for others is largely gone. A fresh vision of a brave new world for Americans and for all mankind is lacking. Only some achieved goods are to be conserved and —with some qualifications—diffused to other peoples. And, of course, Asians and Africans are increasingly sensitive to Bernard Shaw's paraphrase of the Golden Rule: "Don't do unto others as you would have them do unto you; their tastes may be different."

There is much to be said along these lines, and Lerner in fact says a good deal of it himself. For example, I think he is fundamentally correct in remarking: "One may see in these polar impulses the proof that American life is deeply split. One may prefer to see them as contradictory parts of a bewildering puzzle. Or one may see them as signs of an effort, on a grander scale than ever in history, to resolve the conflicting impulses that are to be found in every civilization but each of which occurs here with a strength and tenacity scarcely witnessed elsewhere" (p. 73). But what Lerner fails to accent is the consequence for the picture other countries have of us of the circumstance that in recent times the United States has not adequately communicated to the world the fact that it is indeed still engaged in a basically idealistic attempt to resolve on a titantic scale the huge contradictions that always and everywhere imperil the good life in a mass society.

This stricture, whether just or not, is only a facet of the sole major criticism I would make of this book, viewed in terms of its own organization and purpose. Max Lerner, largely tacitly, assumes a greater stability of the core American values than I think justified by the evidence. There is no doubt about the tremendous continuities in the American value system. All scholars are substantially agreed on this point. Nor is it at all the case that Lerner is blind to change in general. He painstakingly chronicles almost every sort of concrete phenomenon: alterations in sexual mores; the new status of the second sex (which he calls, fittingly enough, "The Ordeal of the American Woman"); heightened values placed upon recreational and aesthetic activities; etc. He titles one section: "Morals in Revolution."

And yet, if I read him correctly, he postulates implicitly only evolution and not revolution as regards the ten or a dozen central moral premises of American civilization. He sees some increasing breakdown of the operative codes, some growth of hypocrisy as regards morals, where I see widespread questioning and overt rejection of principles that were dominant and considered as axiomatic (at least in the key middle classes) from the founding of the Republic until about 1920—and considerably after that in the older generation. . . .

. . . let me sketch, as a counterfoil to Lerner's treatment, my view that during approximately the past generation the first fundamental shift in American values in our history has occurred. There would be little disagreement between Lerner and me as to the facts, though I had access to some extremely pertinent unpublished research reports. On the whole, however, my account is compatible with Lerner's so far as the data go, and indeed isolated items of generalization and inference are identical. There is nevertheless sizable divergence in emphasis and in interpretation. Looking to the future, I believe that the most essential thing to say about life and thought in the United States today is that some value premises have already changed radically and others are in rapid process of change. This reader did not draw such a conclusion from careful study of Lerner's text. . . .

Numerous investigations conducted within the past five years suggest that the value premises of Americans who were in their twenties about a generation ago differ in some striking features from those of the same age-grade in 1950 and later. Many of these studies deal with college students in the two periods. But others make content analyses of advertisements in the *Ladies' Home Journal,* published utterances of the business elite, value themes in the most popular songs and best-selling novels. Stouffer's *Communism, Conformity, and Civil Liberties,* based upon highly sophisticated polling techniques, revealed important generational differences in values. What impresses me is the extent to which the results of researches independently conducted with varying methods upon varying samples and media converge in their main outlines. I shall comment only upon those findings which appear to me to have been neglected—at least in their abstract dimensions—by Lerner.

The most pervasive value shift is what W. H. Whyte, Jr., has called "the decline of the Protestant Ethic." Connected with and influenced by this fundamental shift are a number of others. The degree to which these shifts may plausibly be traced to a weakening of the Puritan Ethic varies considerably. Perhaps a more logical interpretation would be that all changes, including that in the core ethical conception, are the products of still deeper processes which have not yet been satisfactorily analyzed or named. At any rate, I am sure that all of the shifts are interconnected and mutually reinforcing and that the decline of the Protestant Ethic is ubiquitous and a convenient point of central reference.

Looking forward optimistically, planning and working toward the future —this hallmark of the Puritan Ethic has surely waned. At any rate, the distant future has been drawn into the very near future. One has children, several of them, now while one can, because who knows where the husband will be after the savings have been accumulated that will "provide properly" for them? If there is a bit of capital, it is used as a down payment on a house, "for the house will mean a great deal to us and the children now and you can't tell if inflation will wipe out our savings anyway or if all college education will be provided by the government when the children are ready for it."

One might call this new value orientation "hedonistic and present-time." I do not, however, employ "hedonism" in its pejorative sense, for it strikes me that there is considerably less hedonism of this sort than there was in the decade after World War I. I mean, rather, the value which Puritanism never placed upon recreation (except as a means to the end of more effective work), pleasure, leisure, and aesthetic and expressive activities. Americans enjoy themselves more and with less guilt than ever before.

Moreover, there has been a remarkable diversification and broadening of the base of leisure-time activities within the population. Between 1940 and 1950 ticket sales for the legitimate theater and the opera went up 85 per cent as against only 42 per cent for motion pictures. Attendance at concerts of serious music jumped 88 per cent; more dollars were spent for them in 1951 than for baseball. By 1951 there were 659 "symphonic groups" in the United States, and the number of towns and cities having regular concert series had doubled since 1940. Sales of paintings, attendance at art museums, and the number of art museums have increased at an almost fantastic rate. The sales of art supplies were ten times as great in 1949 as in 1939. Gardening, photography, participation in sports, foreign travel—all gained fabulously. In part—but only in part—these changes were a reflection of economic prosperity. Americans have long been comfort-loving, and they continue to be, but their activities, aesthetic and expressive, have expanded greatly beyond mere "comfort." To mention only one further example: there is the "boom in American history."

Barzun has linked the spread of aesthetic interests to the new value emphasis upon the immediate social group. The Puritan Ethic centered upon individual "conscience": i.e., "internal" standards. There is abundant evidence that external or "social" pressures receive much more stress today. This is what Ralph Barton Perry has termed "collective individualism": marked sensitivity to the approval of others, an often compulsive need to be liked, an unquestioning acceptance of the standards of the group with which one primarily identifies. This is Riesman's "other-directed," "radar-oriented" type of character; Fromm's "personality of the market place."

The vulgar label is "conformity," but this is a label which masks too many unexamined questions. In particular, little attention has been given to the psychological aspect. What kind of conformity is it? My evidence indicates that, however much behavioral compliance there may be, there is far from complete "internal" acceptance of any one conventional point of view on everything or any general notion that the deviation of others from that viewpoint is "wrong" or "bad." Indeed, I would argue that the American has matured somewhat since de Tocqueville wrote of him: "Not only does he mistrust his strength, but he even doubts of his right; and he is very near acknowledging that he is in the wrong, when the greater number of his countrymen assert that he is so. The majority do not need to force him; they convince him."

Is contemporary American "conformity" really a conformity of anxiety or automatism? Or is it a fairly deliberate conformity of choice which follows upon the weakening of the Puritan Ethic, with its demands for exhibitionistic achievement, unbridled "individualism," and competition? An outward conformity of behavior or an inward conformity of thought and feeling? We must remember that much of the indignation over the conformity of the young comes from the intellectuals who in the 1920's and 1930's made nonconformity a cardinal virtue and whose ego stature is diminished if their children flaunt this value.

I think it certainly possible that today's kind of conformity may actually be a step toward more genuine individuality in the United States. I sense that in the younger generation conformity is less of a personal and psychological problem, less tinged with anxiety and guilt. If one accepts outwardly the conventions of the face-to-face group, one may have greater psychic energy to develop and fulfill one's private potentialities as a unique person.

Conformity may also be a reaction to exhaustion brought about by the speed and number of changes in American life and that of the world. At all events, I am convinced that much of the contemporary conformity springs from deliberate and somewhat reflective choice based upon realization of the uncertainty of things and upon recognition of the implacable necessities of gigantic organizations. Surely one can see around one that "inconspicuous consumption" now rivals "conspicuous consumption," that many now wish "to keep down with the Joneses." What use to strive endlessly for achievement, to compete blatantly with one's neighbors and with one's rivals in the occupational sphere? Is it not, rather, more sensible to enjoy what one can while one can, to keep the surface of things harmonious? Why elect to live and work in the ulcer belt?

However much conformity may have increased, no one can argue that attention to the psyche of the individual has dropped out of the picture. On the contrary, concern with "mental health," with the proper psychological atmosphere at home and in the school, and with psychotherapy has risen to proportions that some have, understandably, regarded as obsessive. This rise has been associated with the domestication of psychoanalysis on the American scene and the immense increase in psychological self-consciousness.

While conformity in some sense is probably a heightened value for the younger generation, the data indicate that this goes along with a greater tolerance for diversity in others and indeed a prizing of diversity as a value in itself. Several recent studies show that American college students rank higher in these values than do various European, Asian, and African student populations. I believe that heterogeneity is itself becoming one of the organizing principles of American culture. This tendency has, I suspect, two origins.

One goes back to the impact of the bewildering rapidity of change and is reflected in an implicit premise of much American life: you never can tell what strange oddment of information will be interesting or indeed useful in an unforeseen context. Americans therefore are devoted to crossword puzzles, to newspaper columns of the "Believe It or Not" type, to TV programs of the "$64,000 Question" variety. Americans perhaps are following a way of thinking suited to a world in which generalizations are hard to apply.

The other origin lies, I think, in increased experience with cultural diversity and a diminished certainty about the infallible superiority of "the American way of life" in every last idea and detail. One of the massive facts of the last twenty years is the vast jump in the number of Americans who have actually seen other cultures. Twenty million (Lerner) have served in the armed forces, and a high proportion of these have been abroad. It would be naive to assume that a majority of them have been much affected one way or the other, and we all know from personal observation that sometimes the effects are negative. Nevertheless, some are enlightened, and the consequences of this in the body politic gradually cumulate. It is difficult in the military setting to have other than somewhat artificial and superficial experiences—though a surprising number of individuals manage to do so. Americans traveling in foreign countries since 1945 for pleasure and as civilian representatives of government or business have better opportunities, and the American masses are far less isolated from firsthand or one-remove contact with "foreign ways"—other than those of immigrants, who were traditionally looked down upon and were, in any case, for the most part not drawn from the "higher" levels of their cultures. Finally, there is the circumstance that all fairly well-informed Americans, even if themselves untraveled, are aware—however grudgingly—that the realities of international politics will not permit the writing-off of other values and customs as simply "ignorant" or "stupid."

These influences—and others of a more personal and psychological nature—have brought about, even in those who choose themselves to conform to the patterns of their American peer group, a diminution of the single-mindedness of devotion to "the American way," and that positive attachment to diversity as a value which the investigations of Charles Morris, Gordon Allport, and others have revealed.

Among those who have rejected the Puritan Ethic in whole or in part or who are, at most, apathetic toward its tenets, there is frequently an extremely active search for explicit values that educated men and women who accept mass organizations as the normal centers of their lives can live in and live by. This is evidenced by the "return to religion," by the staggering number of articles on ethics and values in literary and middle-brow journals, by the fact that business groups (e.g., the Advertising Council and the Corning Glass Works) have staged expensive round tables on this subject. The trend is intensified by the concern of thoughtful citizens with the widespread belief abroad that American values are either negative or status quo ones (preservation of the eighteenth-century values of the founding fathers).

The "return to religion" is certainly a phase of the renewed search for explicit values. However, except for the fundamentalist and emotional sects, I doubt that this ordinarily represents a daily seeking for divine guidance in one's daily life or taking the pleasing of a personal God as one's primary goal. Rather, I think, the "return to religion" a manifestation of two more fundamental value shifts: (a) increasing stress upon affiliation with stable groups; (b) increasing recognition of the need for explicit and shared values. And I would emphasize more than Lerner that one of the outstanding differences between the climate today and that of a generation ago is the striving for new values that are positive and explicit.

To sum up, let me catalogue more generally and explicitly than does Lerner some of the fresh values that are visibly emerging among Americans:

(1) Strictly personal values are receding in importance—so far as the accepted code is concerned—at the expense of more publicly standardized "group values," whether those of an organization, a community, a social class, a profession, a minority, or an interest group.

(2) But there has been a concomitant rise in the "psychological values" related to mental health, the education and training of children, and the like.

(3) The value placed upon "future success" has receded in favor of "respectable and stable security" seen in a shorter time range.

(4) Aesthetic values have risen notably in the hierarchy.

(5) The value of institutionalized religion is greater, but primarily in terms of changes 1 and 3 above (need for group affiliation and stability) rather than in terms of intensified personal religious life.

(6) "Heterogeneity" is becoming one of the organizing principles of the dominant American value system.

(7) There is an increased overt concern for abstract standards; there is greater prizing of explicit values.

Crossing the Culture Bars

In tandem with politics, technology has created a world in which the informed American citizen needs not only to understand himself but also to have some equipment with which to follow intelligently what he reads and hears about emerging and alien nations. There is grace in the reference to the United States as the oldest of the new nations; there is likewise gross error in the phrase. For in the variety of cultures spread across the world, there are values and assumptions far afield from those we have met so often.

Not only the obviousness of language differences obstruct communication and respect and acceptance between Americans and others. There are differences reflecting spiritual and behavioral distinctions among all peoples, Americans included. Talk of "developing countries" becomes a misleading way of gathering dissimilar entities under a single caption. Political thought is simplified, but it is also steered wrongly. South Vietnam and Ghana and Brazil and Turkey are not usefully put under the same analytic umbrella in political thinking, as the article below suggests.

Although the article seems to discuss the training of American technicians for overseas assignments, what it says is pertinent to the effort of the modern American seeking to understand a world he never made and only parts of which he has seen and experienced in person.

John D. Montgomery, the author, is director of the Center for Development Research and Training, African Studies Program, at Boston University. His publications include *Forced to Be Free, Cases in Vietnamese Administration,* and *The Politics of Foreign Aid.*

[John D. Montgomery, "Crossing the Culture Bars: An Approach to the Training of American Technicians for Overseas Assignments," *World Politics,* vol. 13, pp. 544–560, 1961.]

American failures in technical assistance involve two types of erroneous cultural assumptions: those induced by blindness to our own national cultural idiosyncrasies, and those induced by the uncritical transfer of assumptions from one set of personal experiences in technical assistance to another setting. The first might be characterized as the notion that all people are like us; the second, by the hypothesis that all other people are alike because, or at least insofar as, they are not like us. For purposes of this discussion I shall refer to them respectively as "national" and "transfer" cultural errors.

Cultural rigidities on our part—the "national" errors—are an exact parallel to the doubts, apathies, and suspicions that we so often observe as peculiarities in the receiving cultures. In fact, the limitations on our own self-perception have made others seem even more peculiar than they really are.

These self-limiting cultural factors I sometimes call the "beanbag syndrome" because of an experience that my wife and I shared in Saigon. The American Women's Association there, over 250 strong, engaged in a number of charitable activities on their own initiative. They were especially attentive to orphanages and hospitals. One of their benevolences was an elaborate project for the hand artisans among the American wives: to make some 300 cloth dolls vaguely resembling cats, filled with beans. (The culture-sensitive American women did not want to offend the Vietnamese by using rice, a much cheaper commodity but one in somewhat short supply as food.) These were presented to orphanages for use as Christmas gifts, with the understanding that any surplus could be sold in a self-help fund-raising scheme. Tours of inspection during the ensuing weeks revealed that while none of the beanbags had entered the Saigon marketplace, neither had any reached the hands of the Vietnamese orphans. Upon inquiry it developed that the dolls, each the product of several hours of painstaking work, had been slit open and the beans removed, cooked, and eaten, while the decorated cloth was either discarded or used to make rather small and odd-looking handbags. The project was not, in short, an economic success: the generous club-women had been looking at Vietnamese orphans, but seeing American children.

The three main features of this miniature self-help operation present an object lesson about American foreign aid. First, it was undertaken from the purest of motives, and with no hope of personal gain. Second, an undoubted benefit resulted (if a meal of beans can be thus defined). Third, the inefficiency of the relationship between intentions and results suggests that the effort involved might have been better applied in some other fashion.

Examples of the "beanbag syndrome" in technical assistance are provided by countless stories of misused or underused tools: the laundress in Indochina who was given an ironing board so she would no longer squat on the floor to do her ironing, and who after repeated urgings by her mistress to "use it" was discovered squatting on it precariously as she performed her task; or the sawing off of the long-handled hoes given to Egyptian farmers to replace the faz, the traditional short-handled wooden implements used in the backbreaking posture familiar to travelers in the Near East; or the discarding of unfamiliar food from the CARE packages in Bolivia so that the cans at least could be used in cooking. Scores of such examples have been reported as evidence of a failure in transmission. They have been used in the popular literature to discredit the entire foreign aid process. They are illustrations of the "beanbag" effect in its simplest, most obvious form. They are typical of many gifts offered by the United States in the form in which they have been useful to us.

The "beanbag syndrome," long observed in the physical aspects of technical assistance, can also be identified in the tools of the mind that are involved whenever institutions are to be transplanted. Without indulging in an exhaustive examination of the American culture as a source of ideas and techniques, it is obvious that the pragmatic tenor of our institutional behavior is not a cultural universal; that the idea of "economic man" means something different in the African bush than in the American college classroom; that the virtues of cleanliness are not everywhere self-evident; that the concept of advancement by individual merit is an affront to certain orders of society; that the ticking clock as a symbol of efficiency has not measured the timeless golden days of most village headmen within commuting distance of the equator. All of these culturally induced attitudes are characteristic of Western society, especially in its American variant.

It is true, of course, that study of non-Western societies where these attitudes are not prevalent may succeed in alerting technicians to some of the dangers of ethnocentricity. But these are not always revealed in studies of foreign cultures by themselves: no one would study a non-Western culture in terms of the notion that it assigns "uncleanliness" or "inefficiency" a place in its hierarchy of values. It is not enough to study the peculiarities of non-Western peoples if we are to identify the difficulties likely to arise in the transmission of technical knowledge and attitudes to them. Some attention must also be devoted to American ways of doing things that collide with those of non-Western cultures. . . .

Still another useful approach, not yet attempted systematically, would be to start by considering ourselves as a coherent, unitary culture, at least as we approach the rest of the world through our technical assistance programs, and then isolate and identify those of our characteristics that have seemed strange and repellent to those we have tried to influence. By the study of enough examples drawn from experience in technical assistance, it may be possible to identify, minimize, and perhaps avoid repeating some of our standard national errors.

One of the principal assumptions in American technical assistance is our cultural exaltation of the written word. Centuries of Roman and Anglo-Saxon adjudication of contracts and written agreements have left their mark, until the written word is now considered altogether more binding as an obligation than other agreements. Like the Muslims, we are "people of the book." We do not like to think of agreements as capable of fluctuating with changes in the conditions that gave rise to them. Our Constitution is legalistically considered changeless except by written amendment; and when its words are given new meanings, someone always objects. Even so, the uncertainty can be eventually resolved, again in writing; and the Supreme Court simply uses more written words to define the new (or "rediscovered") meanings of old ones. After each decision, the "social contract" is once more fixed, until it is challenged anew.

In many societies, however, the written word is a last resort in expressing or identifying agreement, and contract obligations shift with changing needs. President Ngo Dinh Diem of Vietnam, one of the few Asian leaders who has been counted a "reliable" friend of the United States, has been characterized by aid officials as wholly unconcerned with our written bilateral agreements. Vietnamese guarantees of contributions from the national budget to various programs have not always been scrupulously kept; agreements to undertake governmental reorganization to administer projects supported by American funds have also been loosely interpreted; and as a result Americans have felt cheated. These derelictions appear reprehensible to American technicians and diplomats, but they are perfectly normal to Vietnamese officials. The latter explain that Vietnamese are more concerned with accomplishing the end result of a project than with undertaking all the obligations assumed as a condition to an agreement. Yet the Vietnamese society is a relatively sophisticated one. It has, if anything, a surplus of lawyers, and it enjoys a rigid—not to say, static—bureaucratic system. On the administrative level, in contrast to the diplomatic, the orders transmitted from the central government are fulfilled with terrifying literalness. To minor officials in Vietnam, written words are coats of mail. This again shocks the American bureaucrat, because at the working levels he is accustomed to finding enough flexibility to permit discretionary changes in policy in the field, to be followed, if necessary, by subsequent justifications. Thus one might say that in Vietnamese governmental circles the written word conveys rigid orders, but not rigid obligations, while traditions in the United States are nearly the reverse.

In some cultures, however, the written word serves neither purpose. The assumptions of literacy and the usefulness of contracts and written agreements break down still further in non-literate societies which have only recently adapted themselves to the Western alphabet. Speaking of the continent of Africa, Margery Perham asserted that "Until the very recent penetration by Europe the greater part of the continent was without the wheel, the plough and the transport animal; almost without stone houses or clothes except for skins; without writing and so without history." Yet the traditions of such a society may be well established. It has its agreements, arrived at by careful group negotiation; and they will be remembered by its elder citizens in terms of the general atmosphere of negotiation and purpose as understood at the time. That is one reason why the slow processes of reaching agreement are so important in some non-Western societies. A consensus reached by careful soundings may be of much greater importance to this group than a cold written contract, enforcement of which would be all but impossible. The procedure enjoined upon the technician under such circumstances may well be a patient, step-by-step series of negotiations at which communal understanding is reached for each point under consideration. The detailed written agreement may even have to be abandoned altogether, or at least delayed until implementation has begun. In general, dependence upon signed contracts, which appears to be the pattern enjoined by ICA for technical assistance operations, sometimes makes the Americans seem rigid, impersonal, irrational, and unresponsive to the actual conditions of the society. The Marouf, a spontaneous, unplanned gesture of friendship in some Arabic countries, is almost never possible in foreign aid.

A closely related assumption of the American culture is reliance upon fixed standards of measurement and the expectation that reports and statistical data can become a basis for evaluating progress or success. It is obvious that such standards do not exist in most underdeveloped societies, where lengths and weights are calculated in terms of human sizes and shapes, and even distance may be measured in terms of the number of cheroots or pipefuls of tobacco smoked while walking at a normal pace between two points. There are still millions of people unaccustomed to a cash economy or to measuring farm output. Reports of national income, farm productivity, and even population cannot be more reliable than the accuracy of the intricate measurements that are reported in the farms and villages of the country concerned. . . .

Another assumption related to the Western preoccupation with the written word is the unexpressed view adopted uncritically in underdeveloped countries that the only valid learning is book-learning, that the only education is formal schooling, and that education provides the road to advancement in a backward society. This has given rise to a preference for degrees and certificates in evaluating individual technicians, civil servants, and their counterparts, although these may bear little relation to the needs or habits of a developing society. The United States, which often seems peopled with degree-bearing citizens, has led the way in easing some of the needlessly strenuous academic disciplines bequeathed to the underdeveloped countries by the colonial powers; but the implication of this relaxation has not yet been accepted in practice by our own diplomats and technicians or by European-trained Africans and Asians, who are still impressed by degrees. They still tend to believe that the way to develop a leader is to send him to school. It is American universities, on the whole, that have had to try to find substitutes for academic courses and degrees that will at once satisfy the bias toward book-learning and fulfill the needs of the underdeveloped countries. In this effort they have already earned the scorn of European scholars, and at the same time failed to come to grips with another cultural obstacle: the fact that in many underdeveloped societies, knowledge, especially from book-learning, is not necessarily power. Many highly educated men from underdeveloped societies, chosen for leadership through education in a "fair" competition with other candidates, will continue to encounter disappointment and frustration as they discover that leadership may demand other qualities often unrelated to book-learning, technical skills, and even a Westernized conscience.

Still another fundamental assumption in American life that is carried into most technical assistance activities is the tradition of relying upon individual incentives to increase productivity, whether on the farm or in the government office. This approach assumes that changes in ways of doing things can be induced by offering increased earnings or improved efficiency. But although economic motives are widespread in the underdeveloped world, they are not necessarily related to individual betterment. This is particularly true in subsistence economies or societies in which strong family ties would deprive an individual of the benefits of increased earning power. In Africa it has been noted that certain tribes possess extensive kinship systems that offer the basic means of social security. Members of these societies cannot always be induced to accept more efficient ways of farming by holding out the advantages of increased income to individuals. The old ways are easier; and most increases in an individual's income would only be absorbed by the indigent members of the kinship group. Resettlement efforts have been known to fail to achieve their economic objective because the large farms that were originally established as part of the development scheme were surreptitiously broken up into smaller uneconomic holdings and divided among the kinship group. Nor have the members of the family always been willing to band together to gain the benefits of large-scale operations, such patterns of co-operative activity being foreign to much of Africa. The result is that the large-scale practices that would have provided the economic foundation of the resettlement could not be followed by either individuals or families. What is "economic" to Westerners may not be so at all to others.

Certain attitudes toward the role of government have also permeated American technical assistance operations. Not many Americans are conscious of the fact that they look upon their government as a service institution, but this is the basis of nearly all of their complaints about government. Certain institutional procedures such as Congressional review, patronage appointments and removals, and the requirements of public morality all tend to make the civil servant conscious of his role in rendering public service. Bureaucrats must be courteous if not actually responsive to public desires. In many parts of the world, however, this is not the case: civil servants in Asia are often direct heirs of the Mandarin tradition, in which public service is largely irrelevant to public office. In other parts of the world, civil servants as a class are the lineal descendants of men performing public functions as personal servants to the king or chief. Service to the people, and the designing of government operations to accommodate the convenience of the public, are products of some of the most sophisticated traditions of democratic history. Many aid projects that have depended for their success upon the dedication of the civil servant to fulfilling his responsibilities in the public interest have failed because the individuals involved in the system possessed an entirely different—and, from their point of view, equally legitimate—conception of their role. Thus a servicio in Guatemala abandoned a program for training agricultural extension workers in order to engage in research for the purpose of improving the strains of plantation crops; public health trainees in Ethiopia returned from a course in the United States to take care of their own extended families and ignored other groups; and when an American technician found a warehouse filled with drugs which a Vietnamese official had failed to distribute, that worthy said, "You Americans are too sentimental. People will die anyhow." All of these examples represent points of view entirely appropriate (or at least acceptable) in the societies in question, based on different cultural causes, and alike only in repudiating the concept of the government as an organ of service to its citizens.

Americans are commonly accused of pretending to omniscience in technical matters. It is true that many of them tend to think of American history as providing verifiable facts and even universal truths of economic and technical development; but such pretenses are usually greatly softened by experiences in another culture. A technician who has learned that his knowledge cannot be simply translated into a foreign tongue may also have learned how to transmit it in an immediate situation. The discovery that techniques have a cultural dimension may help eliminate one set of errors, only to introduce another; for a successful adaptation to one culture may lead a technician to a new set of assumptions about his omniscience. He may now fancy that he possesses the key to "the non-Western culture."

The assumptions that individual technicians develop out of their own successful experiences are compounded by a practical administrative need: that of simultaneously operating scores of foreign aid programs on a global basis. Sixty-five different countries now receive various forms of American aid, and the necessity of accommodating so many requirements makes it necessary to standardize operations in South Asian, Near Eastern, African, and Latin American cultures. Thus the individual technician's tendency to treat one like another (the fallacy of universalizing from one success) is compounded by the administrative necessity for treating all alike.

These factors have led to a second set of cultural errors, which I have called "transfer" errors because they represent a variety of individual experiences and technical assumptions carried from one assignment to another. They lead to errors of transmission which represent rigidities on the part of American technicians that are even more confusing to outsiders than those arising from ethnocentric blindness. The assumptions are not American; they are foreign to both the donor and the host culture. They arise from insufficiently examined experiences in other cultures.

It is difficult to generalize about these transfer cultural errors, although I suspect that the phenomenon itself is recognizable enough. In some respects post-Geneva Viĕtnam was like postwar Greece, especially as seen by an American foreign aid technician. Both were torn by civil disorder, both still threatened by Communists and the failure of democratic institutions, and both industrially underdeveloped. Indeed, cultural and social resemblances could be enumerated until a plausible case could be made that Vietnam and Greece were for practical purposes culturally identical. Improbable as this seems, members of the American aid mission actually made such assumptions about Vietnamese commercial potentialities based on these superficial resemblances. The consequences were to prove puzzling and frustrating to both sides. Similarly, technicians who moved from Korea to Taiwan—to choose a somewhat more likely cultural confusion—have been distressed at the nature and extent of cultural and institutional differences. The techniques used in introducing community development to the Philippines were not crowned by equal success in Iran.

Transfer errors are essentially individual and perhaps non-recurrent phenomena, and are therefore somewhat more difficult to approach through a broadside group-training process than national errors, which presumably represent common problems for all participants. But even transfer errors could be grouped according to general patterns. A number of them have arisen out of regional or racial confusions based on the assumption that Asians, Africans, Middle East Arabs, or other foreign people are culturally alike. Others have been produced by historical assumptions, such as those derived from the rather superficial resemblances among different countries emerging from the British or French colonial experiences in India and Malaya or in Indochina and Africa. A third set of transfer errors might be traced to confusions arising out of political similarities among "oriental despotisms," "neutralist countries," or "tribal" and "patron" party systems that may hide more than they reveal. Still others might arise out of differences in administrative and political relationships between the American and host government's technicians, leading to misunderstanding of motives and procedures. . . .

This discussion may have conveyed an impression of cultural bluntness on the part of American technicians that is both unfair and misleading. The fact is that Americans are not at all indifferent to the sensitivities and opinions of others. Americans are in some ways distressingly unsure of themselves. They are anxious to be liked and respected. When the British wrote best-sellers about their achievements as cultural innovators, they used Rudyard Kipling's Victorian "empire builders" as a prototype; while the Americans have typically accepted books like *The Ugly American* as providing recognizable, if equally unrealistic, depictions of their neo-Victorian efforts overseas. Neither the French, Belgians, nor Russians have worked abroad with so little public sympathy at home for their problems and achievements, or so great an uncertainty about the appropriateness of their being there at all. Few Americans would presume to live in the bush as the British have and attempt to bring the natives into submissiveness by sheer self-confidence. Our tradition has not permitted us to assume the burden of actually governing any backward peoples for very long, largely because the Declaration of Independence really did state something approaching our complex political-value system. Our political self-restraint has inhibited us from building empires of long standing, and in recent years we have dared offer advice only because of the distinction we make between "political" and "technical." Even this self-restraint has not fully protected us, however, for while our society distinguishes between "politics" and "techniques," many underdeveloped cultures do not. We have begun to learn that the advice we offer in the belief that it is politically sterile sometimes sounds to the listener like an invasion of national sovereignty. Such misunderstandings have been so frequent that American technicians now welcome training that facilitates crossing these culture bars and avoids generating unnecessary antagonisms while trying to offer assistance. . . .

National and transfer cultural errors have not yet been directly confronted in the training programs offered to technical assistants. Yet like Plato's state, cultural factors are writ larger than individual characteristics. They are more easily seen because they are multiplied endlessly in the experience of thousands of individuals. Moreover, members of a single culture can discuss their group peculiarities with much less sensitiveness than they can their personal limitations (though this is not usually true as between members of different cultures). Recognition of one's cultural peculiarities does not suggest offensive judgments of "right" or "wrong" or of "acceptability" or "rejection." Cultural factors are also more susceptible to protracted group training than individual characteristics. They can be treated as an organic, inseparable element in the process of technical assistance, and thus can be introduced in discussions of many phases of overseas operations rather than occupying a single lecture or two. Finally, from the operational viewpoint, specific cultural patterns can sometimes be changed once they are recognized. Thus, for example, some written contracts have been waived in the implementing of projects in West Africa; academic requirements for admission to universities have been relaxed in offering study and observation grants, replacing the traditional forms of book-learning as the legitimate avenue to leadership; and civic action and self-help community programs unlike anything in the United States are being developed with American aid in places where the national civil servants themselves may be disinterested in devising modes of rendering service to the public. . . .

New approaches can then open the way to a more imaginative adjustment of American techniques to non-Western cultures, and perhaps contribute to a better understanding of the processes of rendering foreign aid.

CHAPTER 3

RATIONALE OF THE CONSTITUTION

A BRITISH PRIME MINISTER once called the American Constitution "the most wonderful work ever struck off at a given time by the brain and purpose of man." An American abolitionist was quite as extreme in his description, but aimed his language in the opposite direction, labeling the Constitution as "a covenant with death and an agreement with hell." These days, the Constitution is rather more likely to be held in reverence equaling that accorded to motherhood. In any case, the American Constitution of the latter part of the twentieth century is a document whose words are no more a definition of American political and governmental practice than is, as Henry Steele Commager says, the Thirty-Nine Articles a description of the Episcopal Church or the charter of the Standard Oil Company a statement of the business and other activities of the Standard Oil Company.

The American Constitution is only in part the document which is at the back of an introductory textbook in American government; essentially, the Constitution of the United States is also the interpretations of the Supreme Court, the behavior of the Congress and the President, and the words and acts of the other major institutions—political and nonpolitical and parapolitical. The sum total is no mere organization of words; it is also a system of values in operation. When the student looks at the American Constitution—or at any other constitution—he should know that constitutions are not made of words but are, in the ultimate, spiritual expressions. So far as words can convey essential spirit and basic rationale, the three essays reproduced below are explanations of major aspects of the American Constitution. The essays are three of the eighty-five letters of which *The Federalist* consists. Originally written to several New York newspapers to persuade the electorate to support what was then the proposed Constitution, each letter was signed "Publius," a pseudonym for James Madison, Alexander Hamilton, and John Jay.

Thomas Jefferson said *The Federalist* was "the best commentary on the principles of government which has ever been written." Carl Van Doren called it "the masterpiece of all thinking and writing about federal government"; Woodrow Wilson said that "These papers were henceforth to be the chief manual of all students and historians of the constitution. And their style, with its unfailing lucidity, its cogency without artificial emphasis, its unmistakable distinction and elevation of tone, matched their matter. This was the masterpiece of letters in the sober kind bred by revolution." Francis W. Coker remarked that "no other work has been so frequently cited in discussions on doubtful points of constitutional interpretation." Edward Bourne talked of it as one of "the political classics of the world"; Charles Beard referred to it as a "noble piece of writing that has been given immortality." When Edward R. Murrow delivered a Lincoln's Day speech in 1962, he noted that a small United States Information Agency library in Africa had had repeated requests for *The Federalist.*

The tenth essay is the most famous paper in the collection; numbers 47 and 51 are also highly valued as a brilliant elucidation of basic aspects of the American Constitution. Written by James Madison, all are penetrating commentaries on politics not limited to the situations and problems of any time or place.

Peel off layers of politics, economics, and social analysis in *The Federalist* papers and you will see that the Constitution is the embodiment of a theory of human nature, as well as an essay in governance by free men. Thus, number 51 declares that no man is an angel, and experience has taught mankind that responsible government necessitates precautions auxiliary to a dependence on the people. Whether the man is twentieth-century or colonial American, a New Totalitarian or an Old Constitutionalist, he is less than the angels.

The American governmental system assumes that constitutional goverance is not to be achieved by giving unrestrained power to the rich, or to the poor, or to the wellborn or to the lowly but, instead, by a complex configuration of political arrangements that are hinged to psychological assumptions. A freewheeling generalization is implicit in *The Federalist* papers: simple governments are irresponsible governments.

The Federalist No. 10: Factions

Among the numerous advantages promised by a well-constructed Union, none deserves to be more accurately developed than its tendency to break and control the violence of faction. The friend of popular governments never finds himself so much alarmed for their character and fate, as when he contemplates their propensity to this dangerous vice. He will not fail, therefore, to set a due value on any plan which, without violating the principles to which he is attached, provides a proper cure for it. The instability, injustice, and confusion introduced into the public councils, have, in truth, been the mortal diseases under which popular governments have everywhere perished; as they continue to be the favorite and fruitful topics from which the adversaries to liberty derive their most specious declamations. The valuable improvements made by the American constitutions on the popular models, both ancient and modern, cannot certainly be too much admired; but it would be an unwarrantable partiality, to contend that they have as effectually obviated the danger on this side, as was wished and expected. Complaints are everywhere heard from our most considerate and virtuous citizens, equally the friends of public and private faith, and of public and personal liberty, that our governments are too unstable, that the public good is disregarded in the conflicts of rival parties, and that measures are too often decided, not according to the rules of justice and the rights of the minor party, but by the superior force of an interested and overbearing majority. However anxiously we may wish that these complaints had no foundation, the evidence of known facts will not permit us to deny that they are in some degree true. It will be found, indeed, on a candid review of our situation, that some of the distresses under which we labor have been erroneously charged on the operation of our governments; but it will be found, at the same time, that other causes will not alone account for many of our heaviest misfortunes; and, particularly, for that prevailing and increasing distrust of public engagements, and alarm for private rights, which are echoed from one end of the continent to the other. These must be chiefly, if not wholly, effects of the unsteadiness and injustice with which a factious spirit has tainted our public administrations.

By a faction, I understand a number of citizens, whether amounting to a majority or a minority of the whole, who are united and actuated by some common impulse of passion, or of interest, adverse to the rights of other citizens, or to the permanent and aggregate interests of the community.

There are two methods of curing the mischiefs of faction: the one, by removing its causes; the other, by controlling its effects.

There are again two methods of removing the causes of faction: the one, by destroying the liberty which is essential to its existence; the other, by giving to every citizen the same opinions, the same passions, and the same interests.

It could never be more truly said than of the first remedy, that it was worse than the disease. Liberty is to faction what air is to fire, an aliment without which it instantly expires. But it could not be less folly to abolish liberty, which is essential to political life, because it nourishes faction, than it would be to wish the annihilation of air, which is essential to animal life, because it imparts to fire its destructive agency.

The second expedient is as impracticable as the first would be unwise. As long as the reason of man continues fallible, and he is at liberty to exercise it, different opinions will be formed. As long as the connection subsists between his reason and his self-love, his opinions and his passions will have a reciprocal influence on each other; and the former will be objects to which the latter will attach themselves. The diversity in the faculties of men, from which the rights of property originate, is not less an insuperable obstacle to a uniformity of interests. The protection of these faculties is the first object of government. From the protection of different and unequal faculties of acquiring property, the possession of differing degrees and kinds of property immediately results; and from the influence of these on the sentiments and views of the respective proprietors, ensues a division of the society into different interests and parties.

The latent causes of faction are thus sown in the nature of man; and we see them everywhere brought into different degrees of activity, according to the different circumstances of civil society. A zeal for different opinions concerning religion, concerning government, and many other points, as well of speculation as of practice; an attachment to different leaders ambitiously contending for pre-eminence and power; or to persons of other descriptions whose fortunes have been interesting to the human passions, have, in turn, divided mankind into parties, inflamed them with mutual animosity, and rendered them much more disposed to vex and oppress each other than to co-operate for their common good. So strong is this propensity of mankind to fall into mutual animosities, that where no substantial occasion presents itself, the most frivolous and fanciful distinctions have been sufficient to kindle their unfriendly passions and excite their most violent conflicts. But the most common and durable source of factions has been the various and unequal distribution of property. Those who hold and those who are without property have ever formed distinct interests in society. Those who are creditors, and those who are debtors, fall under a like discrimination. A landed interest, a manufacturing interest, a mercantile interest, a moneyed interest, with many lesser interests, grow up of necessity in civilized nations, and divide them into different classes, actuated by different sentiments and views. The regulation of these various and interfering interests forms the principal task of modern legislation, and involves the spirit of party and faction in the necessary and ordinary operations of the government.

No man is allowed to be a judge in his own cause, because his interest would certainly bias his judgment, and, not improbably, corrupt his integrity. With equal, nay with greater reason, a body of men are unfit to be both judges and parties at the same time; yet what are many of the most important acts of legislation, but so many judicial determinations, not indeed concerning the rights of single persons, but concerning the rights of large bodies of citizens? And what are the different classes of legislators but advocates and parties to the causes which they determine? Is a law proposed concerning private debts? It is a question to which the creditors are parties on one side and the debtors on the other. Justice ought to hold the balance between them. Yet the parties are, and must be, themselves the judges; and the most numerous party, or, in other words, the most powerful faction must be expected to prevail. Shall domestic manufactures be encouraged, and in what degree, by restrictions on foreign manufactures? are questions which would be differently decided by the landed and the manufacturing classes, and probably by neither with a sole regard to justice and the public good. The apportionment of taxes on the various descriptions of property is an act which seems to require the most exact impartiality; yet there is, perhaps, no legislative act in which greater opportunity and temptation are given to a predominant party to trample on the rules of justice. Every shilling with which they overburden the inferior number, is a shilling saved to their own pockets.

It is in vain to say that enlightened statesmen will be able to adjust these clashing interests, and render them all subservient to the public good. Enlightened statesmen will not always be at the helm. Nor, in many cases, can such an adjustment be made at all without taking into view indirect and remote considerations, which will rarely prevail over the immediate interest which one party may find in disregarding the rights of another or the good of the whole.

The inference to which we are brought is, that the CAUSES of faction cannot be removed, and that relief is only to be sought in the means of controlling its EFFECTS.

If a faction consists of less than a majority, relief is supplied by the republican principle, which enables the majority to defeat its sinister views by regular vote. It may clog the administration, it may convulse the society; but it will be unable to execute and mask its violence under the forms of the Constitution. When a majority is included in a faction, the form of popular government, on the other hand, enables it to sacrifice to its ruling passion or interest both the public good and the rights of other citizens. To secure the public good and private rights against the danger of such a faction, and at the same time to preserve the spirit and the form of popular government, is then the great object to which our inquiries are directed. Let me add that it is the great desideratum by which this form of government can be rescued from the opprobrium under which it has so long labored, and be recommended to the esteem and adoption of mankind.

By what means is this object attainable? Evidently by one of two only. Either the existence of the same passion or interest in a majority at the same time must be prevented, or the majority, having such coexistent passion or interest, must be rendered, by their number and local situation, unable to concert and carry into effect schemes of oppression. If the impulse and the opportunity be suffered to coincide, we well know that neither moral nor religious motives can be relied on as an adequate control. They are not found to be such on the injustice and violence of individuals, and lose their efficacy in proportion to the number combined together, that is, in proportion as their efficacy becomes needful.

From this view of the subject it may be concluded that a pure democracy, by which I mean a society consisting of a small number of citizens, who assemble and administer the government in person, can admit of no cure for the mischiefs of faction. A common passion or interest will, in almost every case, be felt by a majority of the whole; a communication and concert result from the form of government itself; and there is nothing to check the inducements to sacrifice the weaker party or an obnoxious individual. Hence it is that such democracies have ever been spectacles of turbulence and contention; have ever been found incompatible with personal security or the rights of property; and have in general been as short in their lives as they have been violent in their deaths. Theoretic politicians, who have patronized this species of government, have erroneously supposed that by reducing mankind to a perfect equality in their political rights, they would, at the same time, be perfectly equalized and assimilated in their possessions, their opinions, and their passions.

A republic, by which I mean a government in which the scheme of representation takes place, opens a different prospect, and promises the cure for which we are seeking. Let us examine the points in which it varies from pure democracy, and we shall comprehend both the nature of the cure and the efficacy which it must derive from the Union.

The two great points of difference between a democracy and a republic are: first, the delegation of the government, in the latter, to a small number of citizens elected by the rest; secondly, the greater number of citizens, and greater sphere of country, over which the latter may be extended.

The effect of the first difference is, on the one hand, to refine and enlarge the public views, by passing them through the medium of a chosen body of citizens, whose wisdom may best discern the true interest of their country, and whose patriotism and love of justice will be least likely to sacrifice it to temporary or partial considerations. Under such a regulation, it may well happen that the public voice, pronounced by the representatives of the people, will be more consonant to the public good than if pronounced by the people themselves, convened for the purpose. On the other hand, the effect may be inverted. Men of factious tempers, of local prejudices, or of sinister designs, may, by intrigue, by corruption, or by other means, first obtain the suffrages, and then betray the interests, of the people. The question resulting is, whether small or extensive republics are more favorable to the election of proper guardians of the public weal; and it is clearly decided in favor of the latter by two obvious considerations:

In the first place, it is to be remarked that, however small the republic may be, the representatives must be raised to a certain number, in order to guard against the cabals of a few; and that, however large it may be, they must be limited to a certain number, in order to guard against the confusion of a multitude. Hence, the number of representatives in the two cases not being in proportion to that of the two constituents, and being proportionally greater in the small republic, it follows that, if the proportion of fit characters be not less in the large than in the small republic, the former will present a greater option, and consequently a greater probability of a fit choice.

In the next place, as each representative will be chosen by a greater number of citizens in the large than in the small republic, it will be more difficult for unworthy candidates to practice with success the vicious arts by which elections are too often carried; and the suffrages of the people being more free, will be more likely to centre in men who possess the most attractive merit and the most diffusive and established characters.

It must be confessed that in this, as in most other cases, there is a mean, on both sides of which inconveniences will be found to lie. By enlarging too much the number of electors, you render the representatives too little acquainted with all their local circumstances and lesser interests; as by reducing it too much, you render him unduly attached to these, and too little fit to comprehend and pursue great and national objects. The federal Constitution forms a happy combination in this respect; the great and aggregate interests being referred to the national, the local and particular to the State legislatures.

The other point of difference is, the greater number of citizens and extent of territory which may be brought within the compass of republican than of democratic government; and it is this circumstance principally which renders factious combinations less to be dreaded in the former than in the latter. The smaller the society, the fewer probably will be the distinct parties and interests composing it; the fewer the distinct parties and interests, the more frequently will a majority be found of the same party; and the smaller the number of individuals composing a majority, and the smaller the compass within which they are placed, the more easily will they concert and execute their plans of oppression. Extend the sphere, and you take in a greater variety of parties and interests; you make it less probable that a majority of the whole will have a common motive to invade the rights of other citizens; or if such a common motive exists, it will be more difficult for all who feel it to discover their own strength, and to act in unison with each other. Besides other impediments, it may be remarked that, where there is a consciousness of unjust or dishonorable purposes, communication is always checked by distrust in proportion to the number whose concurrence is necessary.

Hence it clearly appears, that the same advantage which a republic has over a democracy, in controlling the effects of faction, is enjoyed by a large over a small republic,—is enjoyed by the Union over the States composing it. Does the advantage consist in the substitution of representatives whose enlightened views and virtuous sentiments render them superior to local prejudices and schemes of injustice? It will not be denied that the representation of the Union will be most likely to possess these requisite endowments. Does it consist in the greater security afforded by a greater variety of parties, against the event of any one party being able to outnumber and oppress the rest? In an equal degree does the increased variety of parties comprised within the Union, increase this security? Does it, in fine, consist in the greater obstacles opposed to the concert and accomplishment of the secret wishes of an unjust and interested majority? Here, again, the extent of the Union gives it the most palpable advantage.

The influence of factious leaders may kindle a flame within their particular States, but will be unable to spread a general conflagration through the other States. A religious sect may degenerate into a political faction in a part of the Confederacy; but the variety of sects dispersed over the entire face of it must secure the national councils against any danger from that source. A rage for paper money, for an abolition of debts, for an equal division of property, or for any other improper or wicked project, will be less apt to pervade the whole body of the Union than a particular member of it; in the same proportion as such a malady is more likely to taint a particular county or district, than an entire State.

In the extent and proper structure of the Union, therefore, we behold a republican remedy for the diseases most incident to republican government. And according to the degree of pleasure and pride we feel in being republicans, ought to be our zeal in cherishing the spirit and supporting the character of Federalists.

PUBLIUS.

The Federalist No. 47: Power Distributed

Having reviewed the general form of the proposed government and the general mass of power allotted to it, I proceed to examine the particular structure of this government, and the distribution of this mass of power among its constituent parts.

One of the principal objections inculcated by the more respectable adversaries to the Constitution, is its supposed violation of the political maxim, that the legislative, executive, and judiciary departments ought to be separate and distinct. In the structure of the federal government, no regard, it is said, seems to have been paid to this essential precaution in favor of liberty. The several departments of power are distributed and blended in such a manner as at once to destroy all symmetry and beauty of form, and to expose some of the essential parts of the edifice to the danger of being crushed by the disproportionate weight of other parts.

No political truth is certainly of greater intrinsic value, or is stamped with the authority of more enlightened patrons of liberty, than that on which the objection is founded. The accumulation of all powers, legislative, executive, and judiciary, in the same hands, whether of one, a few, or many, and whether hereditary, self-appointed, or elective, may justly be pronounced the very definition of tyranny. Were the federal Constitution, therefore, really chargeable with the accumulation of power, or with a mixture of powers, having a dangerous tendency to such an accumulation, no further arguments would be necessary to inspire a universal reprobation of the system. I persuade myself, however, that it will be made apparent to every one, that the charge cannot be supported, and that the maxim on which it relies has been totally misconceived and misapplied. In order to form correct ideas on this important subject, it will be proper to investigate the sense in which the preservation of liberty requires that the three great departments of power should be separate and distinct.

The oracle who is always consulted and cited on this subject is the celebrated Montesquieu. If he be not the author of this invaluable precept in the science of politics, he has the merit at least of displaying and recommending it most effectually to the attention of mankind. Let us endeavor, in the first place, to ascertain his meaning on this point.

The British Constitution was to Montesquieu what Homer has been to the didactic writers on epic poetry. As the latter have considered the work of the immortal bard as the perfect model from which the principles and rules of the epic art were to be drawn, and by which all similar works were to be judged, so this great political critic appears to have viewed the Constitution of England as the standard, or to use his own expression, as the mirror of political liberty; and to have delivered, in the form of elementary truths, the several characteristic principles of that particular system. That we may be sure, then, not to mistake his meaning in this case, let us recur to the source from which the maxim was drawn.

On the slightest view of the British Constitution, we must perceive that the legislative, executive, and judiciary departments are by no means totally separate and distinct from each other. The executive magistrate forms an integral part of the legislative authority. He alone has the prerogative of making treaties with foreign sovereigns, which, when made, have, under certain limitations, the force of legislative acts. All the members of the judiciary department are appointed by him, can be removed by him on the address of the two Houses of Parliament, and form, when he pleases to consult them, one of his constitutional councils. One branch of the legislative department forms also a great constitutional council to the executive chief, as, on another hand, it is the sole depository of judicial power in cases of impeachment, and is invested with the supreme appellate jurisdiction in all other cases. The judges, again, are so far connected with the legislative department as often to attend and participate in its deliberations, though not admitted to a legislative vote.

From these facts, by which Montesquieu was guided, it may clearly be inferred that, in saying "There can be no liberty where the legislative and executive powers are united in the same person, or body of magistrates," or, "if the power of judging be not separated from the legislative and executive powers," he did not mean that these departments ought to have no PARTIAL AGENCY in, or no CONTROL over, the acts of each other. His meaning, as his own words import, and still more conclusively as illustrated by the example in his eye, can amount to no more than this, that where the WHOLE power of one department is exercised by the same hands which possess the WHOLE power of another department, the fundamental principles of a free constitution are subverted. This would have been the case in the constitution examined by him, if the king, who is the sole executive magistrate, had possessed also the complete legislative power, or the supreme administration of justice; or if the entire legislative body had possessed the supreme judiciary, or the supreme executive authority. This, however, is not among the vices of that constitution. The magistrate in whom the whole executive power resides cannot of himself make a law, though he can put a negative on every law; nor administer justice in person, though he has the appointment of those who do administer it. The judges can exercise no executive prerogative, though they are shoots from the executive stock; nor any legislative function, though they may be advised with by the legislative councils. The entire legislature can perform no judiciary act, though by the joint act of two of its branches the judges may be removed from their offices, and though one of its branches is possessed of the judicial power in the last resort. The entire legislature, again, can exercise no executive prerogative, though one of its branches constitutes the supreme executive magistracy, and another, on the impeachment of a third, can try and condemn all the subordinate officers in the executive department.

The reasons on which Montesquieu grounds his maxim are a further demonstration of his meaning. "When the legislative and executive powers are united in the same person or body," says he, "there can be no liberty, because apprehensions may arise lest THE SAME monarch or senate should ENACT tyrannical laws to EXECUTE them in a tyrannical manner." Again: "Were the power of judging joined with the legislative, the life and liberty of the subject would be exposed to arbitrary control, for THE JUDGE would then be THE LEGISLATOR. Were it joined to the executive power, THE JUDGE might behave with all the violence of AN OPPRESSOR." Some of these reasons are more fully explained in other passages; but briefly stated as they are here, they sufficiently establish the meaning which we have put on this celebrated maxim of this celebrated author.

If we look into the constitutions of the several States, we find that, notwithstanding the emphatical and, in some instances, the unqualified terms in which this axiom has been laid down, there is not a single instance in which the several departments of power have been kept absolutely separate and distinct. New Hampshire, whose constitution was the last formed, seems to have been fully aware of the impossibility and inexpediency of avoiding any mixture whatever of these departments, and has qualified the doctrine by declaring "that the legislative, executive, and judiciary powers ought to be kept as separate from, and independent of, each other as THE NATURE OF A FREE GOVERNMENT WILL ADMIT: OR AS IS CONSISTENT WITH THAT CHAIN OF CONNECTION THAT BINDS THE WHOLE FABRIC OF THE CONSTITUTION IN ONE INDISSOLUBLE BOND OF UNITY AND AMITY." Her constitution accordingly mixes these departments in several respects. The Senate, which is a branch of the legislative department, is also a judicial tribunal for the trial of impeachments. The President, who is the head of the executive department, is the presiding member also of the Senate; and, besides an equal vote in all cases, has a casting vote in case of a tie. The executive head is himself eventually elective every year by the legislative department, and his council is every year chosen by and from the members of the same department. Several of the officers of state are also appointed by the legislature. And the members of the judiciary department are appointed by the executive department.

The constitution of Massachusetts has observed a sufficient though less pointed caution, in expressing this fundamental article of liberty. It declares "that the legislative department shall never exercise the executive and judicial powers, or either of them; the executive shall never exercise the legislative and judicial powers, or either of them; the judicial shall never exercise the legislative and executive powers, or either of them." This declaration corresponds precisely with the doctrine of Montesquieu, as it has been explained, and is not in a single point violated by the plan of the convention. It goes no farther than to prohibit any one of the entire departments from exercising the powers of another department. In the very Constitution to which it is prefixed, a partial mixture of powers has been admitted. The executive magistrate has a qualified negative on the legislative body, and the Senate, which is a part of the legislature, is a court of impeachment for members both of the executive and judiciary departments. The members of the judiciary department, again, are appointable by the executive department, and removable by the same authority on the address of the two legislative branches. Lastly, a number of the officers of government are annually appointed by the legislative department. As the appointment to offices, particularly executive offices, is in its nature an executive function, the compilers of the Constitution have, in this last point at least, violated the rule established by themselves.

I pass over the constitutions of Rhode Island and Connecticut, because they were formed prior to the Revolution, and even before the principle under examination had become an object of political attention.

The constitution of New York contains no declaration on this subject; but appears very clearly to have been framed with an eye to the danger of improperly blending the different departments. It gives, nevertheless, to the executive magistrate, a partial control over the legislative department; and, what is more, gives a like control to the judiciary department; and even blends the executive and judiciary departments in the exercise of this control. In its council of appointment members of the legislative are associated with the executive authority, in the appointment of officers, both executive and judiciary. And its court for the trial of impeachments and correction of errors is to consist of one branch of the legislature and the principal members of the judiciary department.

The constitution of New Jersey has blended the different powers of government more than any of the preceding. The governor, who is the executive magistrate, is appointed by the legislature; is chancellor and ordinary, or surrogate of the State; is a member of the Supreme Court of Appeals, and president, with a casting vote, of one of the legislative branches. The same legislative branch acts again as executive council of the governor, and with him constitutes the Court of Appeals. The members of the judiciary department are appointed by the legislative department, and removable by one branch of it, on the impeachment of the other.

According to the constitution of Pennsylvania, the president, who is the head of the executive department, is annually elected by a vote in which the legislative department predominates. In conjunction with an executive council, he appoints the members of the judiciary department, and forms a court of impeachment for trial of all officers, judiciary as well as executive. The judges of the Supreme Court and justices of the peace seem also to be removable by the legislature; and the executive power of pardoning in certain cases, to be referred to the same department. The members of the executive council are made EX-OFFICIO justices of peace throughout the State.

In Delaware, the chief executive magistrate is annually elected by the legislative department. The speakers of the two legislative branches are vice-presidents in the executive department. The executive chief, with six others, appointed, three by each of the legislative branches, constitutes the Supreme Court of Appeals; he is joined with the legislative department in the appointment of the other judges. Throughout the States, it appears that the members of the legislature may at the same time be justices of the peace; in this State, the members of one branch of it are EX-OFFICIO justices of the peace; as are also the members of the executive council. The principal officers of the executive department are appointed by the legislative; and one branch of the latter forms a court of impeachments. All officers may be removed on address of the legislature.

Maryland has adopted the maxim in the most unqualified terms; declaring that the legislative, executive, and judicial powers of government ought to be forever separate and distinct from each other. Her constitution, notwithstanding, makes the executive magistrate appointable by the legislative department; and the members of the judiciary by the executive department.

The language of Virginia is still more pointed on this subject. Her constitution declares, "that the legislative, executive, and judiciary departments shall be separate and distinct; so that neither exercise the powers properly belonging to the other; nor shall any person exercise the powers of more than one of them at the same time, except that the justices of county courts shall be eligible to either House of Assembly." Yet we find not only this express exception, with respect to the members of the inferior courts, but that the chief magistrate, with his executive council, are appointable by the legislature; that two members of the latter are triennially displaced at the pleasure of the legislature; and that all the principal offices, both executive and judiciary, are filled by the same department. The executive prerogative of pardon, also, is in one case vested in the legislative department.

The constitution of North Carolina, which declares "that the legislative, executive, and supreme judicial powers of government ought to be forever separate and distinct from each other," refers, at the same time, to the legislative department, the appointment not only of the executive chief but all the principal officers within both that and the judiciary department.

In South Carolina, the constitution makes the executive magistracy eligible by the legislative department. It gives to the latter, also, the appointment of the members of the judiciary department, including even justices of the peace and sheriffs; and the appointment of officers in the executive department, down to captains in the army and navy of the State.

In the constitution of Georgia, where it is declared "that the legislative, executive, and judiciary departments shall be separate and distinct, so that neither exercise the powers properly belonging to the other," we find that the executive department is to be filled by appointments of the legislature; and the executive prerogative of pardon to be finally exercised by the same authority. Even justices of the peace are to be appointed by the legislature.

In citing these cases, in which the legislative, executive, and judiciary departments have not been kept totally separate and distinct, I wish not to be regarded as an advocate for the particular organizations of the several State governments. I am fully aware that among the many excellent principles which they exemplify, they carry strong marks of the haste, and still stronger of the inexperience, under which they were framed. It is but too obvious that in some instances the fundamental principle under consideration has been violated by too great a mixture, and even an actual consolidation, of the different powers; and that in no instance has a competent provision been made for maintaining in practice the separation delineated on paper. What I have wished to evince is, that the charge brought against the proposed Constitution, of violating the sacred maxim of free government, is warranted neither by the real meaning annexed to that maxim by its author, nor by the sense in which it has hitherto been understood in America. This interesting subject will be resumed in the ensuing paper.

PUBLIUS.

The Federalist No. 51: Ambition Counteracts Ambition

To WHAT expedient, then, shall we finally resort, for maintaining in practice the necessary partition of power among the several departments, as laid down in the Constitution? The only answer that can be given is, that as all these exterior provisions are found to be inadequate, the defect must be supplied, by so contriving the interior structure of the government as that its several constituent parts may, by their mutual relations, be the means of keeping each other in their proper places. Without presuming to undertake a full development of this important idea, I will hazard a few general observations, which may perhaps place it in a clearer light, and enable us to form a more correct judgment of the principles and structure of the government planned by the convention.

In order to lay a due foundation for that separate and distinct exercise of the different powers of government, which to a certain extent is admitted on all hands to be essential to the preservation of liberty, it is evident that each department should have a will of its own; and consequently should be so constituted that the members of each should have as little agency as possible in the appointment of the members of the others. Were this principle rigorously adhered to, it would require that all the appointments for the supreme executive, legislative, and judiciary magistracies should be drawn from the same fountain of authority, the people, through channels having no communication whatever with one another. Perhaps such a plan of constructing the several departments would be less difficult in practice than it may in contemplation appear. Some difficulties, however, and some additional expense would attend the execution of it. Some deviations, therefore, from the principle must be admitted. In the constitution of the judiciary department in particular, it might be inexpedient to insist rigorously on the principle: first, because peculiar qualifications being essential in the members, the primary consideration ought to be to select that mode of choice which best secures these qualifications; secondly, because the permanent tenure by which the appointments are held in that department, must soon destroy all sense of dependence on the authority conferring them.

It is equally evident, that the members of each department should be as little dependent as possible on those of the others, for the emoluments annexed to their offices. Were the executive magistrate, or the judges, not independent of the legislature in this particular, their independence in every other would be merely nominal.

But the great security against a gradual concentration of the several powers in the same department consists in giving to those who administer each department the necessary constitutional means and personal motives to resist encroachments of the others. The provision for defense must in this, as in all other cases, be made commensurate to the danger of attack. Ambition must be made to counteract ambition. The interest of the man must be connected with the constitutional rights of the place. It may be a reflection on human nature, that such devices should be necessary to control the abuses of government. But what is government itself, but the greatest of all reflections on human nature? If men were angels, no government would be necessary. If angels were to govern men, neither external nor internal controls on government would be necessary. In framing a government which is to be administered by men over men, the great difficulty lies in this: you must first enable the government to control the governed; and in the next place oblige it to control itself. A dependence on the people is, no doubt, the primary control on the government; but experience has taught mankind the necessity of auxiliary precautions.

This policy of supplying, by opposite and rival interests, the defect of better motives, might be traced through the whole system of human affairs, private as well as public. We see it particularly displayed in all the subordinate distributions of power, where the constant aim is to divide and arrange the several offices in such a manner as that each may be a check on the other—that the private interest of every individual may be a sentinel over the public rights. These inventions of prudence cannot be less requisite in the distribution of the supreme powers of the State.

But it is not possible to give to each department an equal power of self-defense. In republican government, the legislative authority necessarily predominates. The remedy for this inconvenience is to divide the legislature into different branches; and to render them by different modes of election and different principles of action, as little connected with each other as the nature of their common functions and their common dependence on the society will admit. It may even be necessary to guard against dangerous encroachments by still further precautions. As the weight of the legislative authority requires that it should be thus divided, the weakness of the executive may require, on the other hand, that it should be fortified. An absolute negative on the legislature appears, at first view, to be the natural defense with which the executive magistrate should be armed. But perhaps it would be neither altogether safe nor alone sufficient. On ordinary occasions it might not be exerted with the requisite firmness, and on extraordinary occasions it might be perfidiously abused. May not this defect of an absolute negative be supplied by some qualified connection between this weaker department and the weaker branch of the stronger department, by which the latter may be led to support the constitutional rights of the former, without being too much detached from the rights of its own department?

If the principles on which these observations are founded be just, as I persuade myself they are, and they be applied as a criterion to the several State constitutions, and to the federal Constitution, it will be found that if the latter does not perfectly correspond with them, the former are infinitely less able to bear such a test.

There are, moreover, two considerations particularly applicable to the federal system of America, which place that system in a very interesting point of view.

First. In a single republic, all the power surrendered by the people is submitted to the administration of a single government; and the usurpations are guarded against by a division of the government into distinct and separate departments. In the compound republic of America, the power surrendered by the people is first divided between two distinct governments, and then the portion allotted to each subdivided among distinct and separate departments. Hence a double security arises to the rights of the people. The different governments will control each other, at the same time that each will be controlled by itself.

Second. It is of great importance in a republic not only to guard the society against the oppression of its rulers, but to guard one part of the society against the injustice of the other part. Different interests necessarily exist in different classes of citizens. If a majority be united by a common interest, the rights of the minority will be insecure. There are but two methods of providing against this evil: the one by creating a will in the community independent of the majority—that is, of the society itself; the other, by comprehending in the society so many separate descriptions of citizens as will render an unjust combination of a majority of the whole very improbable, if not impracticable. The first method prevails in all governments possessing an hereditary or self-appointed authority. This, at best, is but a precarious security; because a power independent of the society may as well espouse the unjust views of the major, as the rightful interests of the minor party, and may possibly be turned against both parties. The second method will be exemplified in the federal republic of the United States. Whilst all authority in it will be derived from and dependent on the society, the society itself will be broken into so many parts, interests, and classes of citizens, that the rights of individuals, or of the minority, will be in little danger from interested combinations of the majority. In a free government the security for civil rights must be the same as that for religious rights. It consists in the one case in the multiplicity of interests, and in the other in the multiplicity of sects. The degree of security in both cases will depend on the extent of country and number of people comprehended under the same government. This view of the subject must particularly recommend a proper federal system to all the sincere and considerate friends of republican government, since it shows that in exact proportion as the territory of the Union may be formed into more circumscribed Confederacies, or States, oppressive combinations of a majority will be facilitated: the best security, under the republican forms, for the rights of every class of citizens, will be diminished; and consequently the stability and independence of some member of the government, the only other security, must be proportionately increased. Justice is the end of government. It is the end of civil society. It ever has been and ever will be pursued until it be obtained, or until liberty be lost in the pursuit. In a society under the forms of which the stronger faction can readily unite and oppress the weaker, anarchy may as truly be said to reign as in a state of nature, where the weaker individual is not secured against the violence of the stronger; and as, in the latter state, even the stronger individuals are prompted, by the uncertainty of their condition, to submit to a government which may protect the weak as well as themselves; so in the former state, will the more powerful factions or parties be gradually induced, by a like motive, to wish for a government which will protect all parties, the weaker as well as the more powerful. It can be little doubted that if the State of

Rhode Island was separated from the Confederacy and left to itself, the insecurity of rights under the popular form of government within such narrow limits would be displayed by such reiterated oppressions of factious majorities that some power altogether independent of the people would soon be called for by the voice of the very factions whose misrule had proved the necessity of it. In the extended republic of the United States, and among the great variety of interests, parties, and sects which it embraces, a coalition of a majority of the whole society could seldom take place on any other principles than those of justice and the general good; whilst there being thus less danger to a minor from the will of a major party, there must be less pretext, also, to provide for the security of the former, by introducing into the government a will not dependent on the latter, or, in other words, a will independent of the society itself. It is no less certain than it is important, notwithstanding the contrary opinions which have been entertained, that the larger the society, provided it lie within a practical sphere, the more duly capable it will be of self-government. And happily for the REPUBLICAN CAUSE, the practicable sphere may be carried to a very great extent, by a judicious modification and mixture of the FEDERAL PRINCIPLE. PUBLIUS.

CHAPTER 4
CONGRESS IN ACTION AND INTERACTION

When the student thinks of other legislative forms in comparison with the American Congress, he should remember the long roots of the American national legislative body. Before the Congress came into being, there had been a long, long line of gestation and development. Predating the Congress were the colonial legislatures, in turn transplantations, adaptations, and modifications in the new civilization of the legislative and other experiences of a mother country whose Parliament was already an ancient body with ancient prerogatives and concepts. It was in the thirteenth century that the principle was established that no statute enacted by Parliament could be abrogated, except by Parliament; in the thirteenth century also came the acceptance of the proposition that no taxes were to be levied without the consent of Parliament.

In the latter sixteenth century Sir Thomas Smith stated that the Parliament of England "representeth and hath the power of the whole realme both the head and the bodie. For everie Englishman is entended to be there present, either by person or by procuration and attornies, of whatever preheminence, state, dignitie, or qualities soever he be, from the Prince (be he King or Queen) to the lowest person of England, and the consent of Parliament is taken to be everie man's consent." "Representative government in evolution," Charles Beard noted, is "one aspect of the movement of civilization." There were centuries of hard experience and strong custom and firm attitudes on which the Congress was built; it was not the product of great minds who plucked the congressional essence out of thin ideals and airy objectives.

The Congress is no simplistic governmental organ. In modern times, one writer whose field of expertise is the American Congress, has written of the Senate that it "is so complex an organization that it can remain largely incomprehensible to some who have spent the better part of a lifetime in and around it." Characterizing Congress are various, complex procedures; numerous foci of power and activity; extensive avenues of approach and retreat in promoting, frustrating, circumventing, crippling, enfeebling, invigorating, improving, destroying, or performing ten thousand other operations on would-be or has-been or will-be legislative ideas and acts; the result is much like a Jackson Pollock painting and looks like a conglomeration with neither beginning nor end—nor, in fact, a middle.

Fortunately, the intelligent political consumer will find the task of understanding Congress rather more manageable than that of identifying meanings in abstract-expressionist paintings. The citizen needs to let his fancy roam, within the limits of his analytic abilities. An example is the question: Who writes the laws enacted by Congress? Before giving the obvious answer, the congressmen, the student may well put another question: What characteristics are needed by the individual who writes proposed laws? The answer is not difficult to work out: much information about the issue under consideration; considerable interest; more or less ready access to the congressman; a substantial amount of time and extensive facilities to devote to the problems inherent in framing legislative ideas. Now the issue has shifted to figuring out what kind of person or group has the attributes just enumerated: expertise, status, interest, time, facilities. Two kinds of people possess these prerequisites: governmental bureaucrats and interest-group leaders.

That somewhere about 90 per cent of legislation in America originates in or around public agencies or pressure groups becomes an intelligible statistic. In line with these figures are such data as the fact that the Pendleton Act, establishing the merit system in Federal civil service, was substantially the work of the National Civil Service Reform Association, or the point that the Social Security Act of 1935, introduced by Senator Robert F. Wagner, was prepared in the United States Department of Labor.

An associated phenomenon takes place: Legislation tends to take on the characteristic deemed desirable by pressure groups and bureaucracies. For instance, the contribution of professional social workers to the preparation of the 1935 Social Security Act was in part an effort to enact into law the values and standards of the social work profession.

Anything that has national importance finds its way into the congressional dialogue (as well as vast wastelands of lesser significance). The nature of that dialogue is subjected to pressures so insistent and varied, confronted with problems so technical and urgent, faced with indicated solutions that are so complicated and systematic, that there is a solid base for the question put by one analyst: "Can Congress survive?" Another leading commentator remarks that in a real sense Congress is "a procedural abstraction," for it is not recognized and does not act as a single unit. Less kindly, a famous British authority has described Congress as "a debating society adhering to an executive."

The common American assumption is that Congress is the nation's policy-making agency, its representative organ, and its sounding board. Another view is far more accurate: that Congress can be described as an agency which makes broad selections between competing policies submitted for its inspection; that gerrymandering in the House and the weighting of areas rather than people in the Senate make the Congress only very approximately representative and, in any case, not more representative of the American population than the President; that much of the congressional task is to act as a counterweight to the Presidency and much of its activity consists of helping to make public affairs more vivid and dramatic than would be the case without the charismatic people who serve so often as legislators.

Congress Debates Its Rules: a Case Study in Legislative Packing and Unpacking

The subject of the debate appears to be the question of whether the size of the House Committee on Rules should be increased from twelve to fifteen, and a good part of the discussion centers around the arguments against having a small group of committee members act as a bottleneck hindering consideration of proposed legislation.

Actually, the question at issue was this: Who is to control the legislative bottleneck? For it is clear that the House of Representatives, a body with hundreds of members, needs a committee to serve as a traffic cop or bottleneck or whatever metaphorical equivalent is educed for an agency that will figure out what bills ought to come to the floor of the House for debate, the amount of time to be taken for their consideration, and the conditions to be set for enabling the legislative debate to be carried forward. On control of the bottleneck by Representative Smith and his allies as against control by supporters of the President and of the Speaker would hinge resolution of part of the issue of what was to be the character of the legislation the Congress would enact.

A good part of the debate has been excised here because of space limitations. The student may, however, be able to see that congressmen often talk right past each other in their effort to reach not their colleagues but their constituents back home; how the congressman documents his support of or opposition to the change in the rules by asserting in either case his opposition to the Soviet Union, his support of the United States of America, his belief in good traditions and sound customs, his preference for freedom and for representative government, his eagerness to avoid quarrels, his interest in legislation that will promote the public welfare, his desire for democratic legislative procedures, his antipathy to subversive activities. The resolution under consideration was attacked as an effort to pack the Rules Committee; the resolution could equally have been defended as an attempt to unpack the Rules Committee. For the student—or for anybody else—it is not always easy to figure out the definition of a particular public-affairs problem or the nature and strength of the argumentation surrounding the problem, but of one thing the reader or the auditor may be sure: the American congressman or other political leader will entwine his commentary around enthusiasm for the symbols that are dear to you and to me.

After the debate, the Committee on Rules was increased to fifteen. Voting for the increase were 195 Democrats and 22 Republicans; against the resolution were 64 Democrats and 148 Republicans.

The *Congressional Quarterly* reported lobbying was extensive during the dispute on the committee, including groups like the National Association of Manufacturers, American Farm Bureau Federation, Chamber of Commerce of the United States, the American Medical Association, the National Association of Real Estate Boards, and the National Lumber Manufacturers Association. These organizations have been opposed to an increased Federal role in such programs as health care for the aged, expanded urban-renewal legislation, and minimum-wage legislation.

Ranged in favor of the committee change apparently were such groups as the AFL-CIO, the National Education Association, Americans for Democratic Action, American Municipal Association, U.S. Conference of Mayors, and National Farmers Union, all organizations that have campaigned vigorously for expanded governmental action in socioeconomic areas.

It is noteworthy that after the Committee on Rules was expanded, neither congressional catastrophe nor legislative Elysium followed and, in fact, one of the two Democrats added to the committee voted against presidential recommendations on significant social legislation shortly after the committee was altered. The struggle of diverse interests and changing personalities and evolving leadership continues; Congressional procedural arrangements remain the focus of unending efforts to maintain or change the status quo amid charges and countercharges of committee packing, unpacking, and repacking.

[Debate on the Rules of the House of Representatives of the United States Congress, *Congressional Record,* Jan. 31, 1961, pp. 1502–1519.]

MR. TRIMBLE. Mr. Speaker, I call up House Resolution 127 and ask for its immediate consideration.

The Clerk read as follows:

Resolved, That during the Eighty-seventh Congress the Committee on Rules shall be composed of fifteen members.

MR. TRIMBLE. Mr. Speaker, as is customary, I yield 30 minutes to the gentleman from Ohio [Mr. Brown] and at this time I yield myself such time as I may consume.

Mr. Speaker, this is one assignment that I did not seek.

I have deep affection for all parties involved in this controversy, and I have deep respect for the rules of the House.

I am a Democrat. I have always fought my political battles in the battle-scarred uniform of the Democratic Party, and I shall continue to do that. However, I have firm belief in the position that with the majority rests the responsibility. If the Republican Party were in the majority here today and had the Speaker and they were seeking some means of assuring the leadership leeway to conform to their full responsibilities, as the majority I would vote with them on a similar resolution.

We are a two-party system. My prayer is that never in this great land of ours will we become so confused and mixed up with different parties that we will become the victim of the lack of authority to function as a majority that exists in some of the states of Europe and of Asia. I believe in a two-party system. Of course, as a Democrat, I naturally want the Democrats always to be leading, at least one jump ahead.

Another thing, we in this Hall of the House of Representatives and all the people of the United States are brothers and sisters. We are partners in this great enterprise called America, and the necessity of affirming our leadership abounds. We are the beneficiaries of a Republic dedicated to us by the trials, sacrifice, blood, and tears from Plymouth Rock, Jamestown, Lexington, Bunker Hill, Valley Forge, clear on through to Pork Chop Hill and Heartbreak Ridge in Korea.

Yes, it is my country. It is your country. It is our country. And it is challenged today as it has never been challenged before by a shrewd, wily, calculating, relentless foe. As we sit here in this Chamber today the Russian Bear has its claws in the front door of our yard, and in the backyard there is a Red dragon as long as the back porch. So the challenge is ours.

. . . I hope as we vote upon this resolution that when it ends, whichever way it goes, we can return to our work without malice, without bitterness, without selfishness, proud of the heritage that is ours of a great Republic dedicated to the proposition that freedom is ever dearer than life itself.

. . . Mr. Speaker, I yield 4 minutes to the gentleman from Texas [Mr. Kilday] for the purposes of debate.

(MR. KILDAY asked and was given permission to revise and extend his remarks.)

MR. KILDAY. Mr. Speaker, I know of no one who wanted this conflict to come to the floor of the House. I know of no one who could have prevented it from coming here. There is a situation existing which no one can deny. We have reached a stalemate in our Committee on Rules, a stalemate produced because of tie votes of 6 to 6. What is the basic cause of our difficulty? Reflect for only a second. The basic cause is self-evident—it is very simple, and that is that the Committee on Rules is composed of an even number of Members and, therefore, is prone to tie votes. Our Founding Fathers realizing the danger of tie votes in a deliberative body, and as the Senate must always be composed of an even number, two from each State, provided a mechanism in the other body for breaking a tie vote and permitted the Vice President, not a Member of that body, to vote in order to break a tie. But, no mechanism was provided in the House of Representatives. Why? Because the House is presided over by a Member of this body; and, in addition, because it was always contemplated that the House would consist of an odd number or an uneven number of Members. In providing for the first Congresses until after the taking of the first census, each State in the Union was assigned a finite number of Members to sit in those Congresses before the first census could be taken. Each State was assigned a finite number and it added up to 65—an uneven number. Congresses very close in time to the Constitution fixed the membership of the House at an uneven number.

. . . If you think there is something sacrosanct about the number 12 on the Committee on Rules, there is no reason for that feeling. It was created as a standing committee of the House in 1880. Prior to that time, it existed as a select committee. When the Committee on Rules was created in 1880 it consisted of five Members. That continued until 1910 when the number was increased to 11 members and in 1917 to 12 members and in 1935 to 14 members and in 1945 and since that time, it has consisted of 12 members. So that the numbers on the Committee on Rules have been changed, and have been changed a number of times since that committee has been in existence.

The rules of the House provide the number to be on a committee, but they do not provide the manner in which those numbers shall be distributed between the majority and the minority. What happens? At the beginning of each Congress, the Speaker of the House and the minority leader agree upon the ratio to be assigned to these committees, and it has invariably conformed to the ratio of representation of the two parties in the House of Representatives, as nearly as it has been possible to do so.

That is not true as to the Committee on Rules, under the custom and the unbroken tradition of the House. The majority party, by custom and tradition, always has a 2-to-1 majority on the Committee on Rules. Under the strength of 12, there have been 8 Democrats and 4 Republicans when the Democrats have controlled the House, and 8 Republicans and 4 Democrats when the Republicans have controlled the House. Why? For the simple and all important reason that the Committee on Rules is an arm of the leadership of the majority party. The majority party has the right to bring to the floor of the House the legislative proposals of the committees. Once a proposal is on the floor, each member is a free agent to consider, to decide, and to vote as he sees fit.

. . . MR. BROWN. Mr. Speaker, I yield myself 8 minutes.

Mr. Speaker, naturally I have not been too happy in recent weeks over the misinformation, misrepresentation, falsehoods and slander which have been directed against the committee of which I have had the honor to serve for 18 years. There has been much said that is absolutely untrue and not according to the facts. Therefore, I think, Mr. Speaker, that this is the time and place to look at the record.

This resolution was designed and introduced for one purpose and one purpose only, to pack the Rules Committee so as to give either one individual, or a limited few, the power to completely control all of its decisions and actions.

It is exactly similar to the 1937 attempt of Franklin Delano Roosevelt to pack the Supreme Court so as to obtain the favorable decisions he desired.

Never before has an attempt been made to pack any House committee to control its legislative decisions, although the membership of other committees has been changed at times for different but proper purposes.

If the Rules Committee is packed it will be possible for those in control to withhold from or send to the floor for action any and all legislation. More sinister and dangerous is the fact it will be possible for the committee to report any closed or gag rule desired, so as to prevent Members from offering amendments to a bill, or otherwise work their will thereon. Rules could also be reported to waive points of order, so any given bill could carry provisions otherwise contrary to House rules, and even to statutory law.

If the Rules Committee can be packed to obtain political decisions, other committees of the House can likewise be packed. The Ways and Means Committee could be packed to get from it the Forand type of Federal aid bill previously rejected by the committee, or the kind of tax laws some may desire. The same situation could apply to all other legislative committees.

. . . There is no reason to believe that the Rules Committee, as now constituted, will or can prevent any important legislation from receiving consideration by the House, for the House of Representatives can always work its will on legislative matters.

Wednesday of each week is designated as Calendar Wednesday, at which time the chairman of any House legislative committee can call up a bill for immediate consideration without obtaining a rule to make such action in order.

By a simple majority of the membership signing a discharge petition any bill can be called up for prompt consideration by the full House.

Any measure can also be called up under suspension of the rules procedure and acted upon promptly, providing the Speaker approves.

Bills and resolutions from the Committees on Ways and Means, Appropriations, and House Administration, are usually brought to the floor for action without a rule.

In my nearly a quarter of a century of service here I have never known of a single instance, when the House leadership desired a bill to be brought to a House vote, that such measure was not voted upon.

So actually it is only power which is being sought by this resolution—power to prevent any individual Member, as well as any minority, from a vote or free expression on legislative bills. This is power no little group, no Speaker, no President should seek. This is power no little group, no Speaker, no President, should have.

The majority leadership already have the means and the powers to bring any legislation before the House for consideration. Such have long been exercised.

. . . Mr. Speaker, I yield 2 minutes to the gentleman from Missouri [Mr. Curtis].

MR. CURTIS of Missouri. Mr. Speaker, I take this time to restate a position.

I doubt very much if anything said here is going to change many views on the subject. Essentially, I feel that this is an instance where two wrongs do not make a right.

. . . I remember in the 83rd Congress when we won by a majority of 6 at which time we packed the Rules Committee, if one wants to use that term, 2 to 1, or 8 to 4, the Ways and Means Committee 15 to 10, the Appropriations Committee 30 to 20. The principle is a sound principle, and I think in this instance we make a mistake as the Republican Party to oppose this basic proposal.

Finally, may I say that I hope as the result, if this is to prevail, that a third wrong does not come into the fore, and it might. History indicates it might. I hope if this comes about there will not be these gag rules coming out of the Rules Committee waiving points of order, actually forbidding the Members of the House to work their will on certain legislation.

. . . MR. TRIMBLE. Mr. Speaker, I yield 8 minutes to the gentleman from Virginia [Mr. Smith].

(MR. SMITH of Virginia asked and was given permission to revise and extend his remarks and to include extraneous matter.)

MR. SMITH of Virginia. Mr. Speaker, let me say at the beginning I am very sorry that I am not given what I consider a fair amount of time in which to discuss this matter. I will have to be brief and quick and I will not be able to yield to anyone.

In the first place, a lot of people around here these days talk about this being a matter of a quarrel between the Speaker and myself. I have served with the Speaker of this House for 30 years. I have no quarrel with the Speaker. He has a right to his convictions, I claim the right to mine.

. . . When I make this pledge to the Speaker and to the Members of this House, it is a pledge I made when I first became chairman of the Rules Committee. That is, I will cooperate with the Democratic leadership of the House of Representatives just as long and just as far as my conscience will permit me to go. Some of these gentlemen who are laughing maybe do not understand what a conscience is. They are entitled to that code, and I think I am entitled to mine.

. . . I was surprised to see the Committee on Armed Services engage in this assault on the Rules Committee, because I challenge anybody on that committee to mention any measure that they ever asked for since I have been a member of the Rules Committee that has been held up for a minute. The members of that committee know this is true. There are very few bills that have been held up by the Committee on Rules as compared to the legislative committees of the House. Do you know that there were some 15,000 bills introduced in this House in the last Congress, and do you know that 90 percent of them died in committee and were never reported; in other words, the legislative committees refused or neglected to report 90 percent of the bills and the Committee on Rules less than 10 percent of the bills that came before them.

Now, there is what I want to say to you, and I want to make it a matter of record. There has been a lot of talk about who is interested in this thing. I do not know whose fight this is on the Committee on Rules. I have heard it was the President's. He never said anything to me about it; never made any request of me. Why, this morning the newspapers said it was Khrushchev. Now, I never heard from Khrushchev and I have not heard from Castro, but I have heard from some other people.

. . . Now, I add one other thing to this. There has been some talk about my going out and milking cows once or twice. Well, I will make this statement, that so far as I am concerned there will not be any delay, any undue delay on any call that the leadership makes to hold hearings in the Committee on Rules, if these proposals are accepted. If the resolution is adopted I make no commitments.

. . . Under leave to extend my remarks, I include a copy of a letter sent to all Members of the House last Saturday:

January 28, 1961

Hon. Carl Vinson,
Hon. Francis E. Walter,
House of Representatives,
Washington 25, D.C.

Dear Carl and Francis:

You called on me yesterday afternoon to discuss a solution to the controversy of packing the Committee on Rules of the House. You left me to discuss further a proposal which we three thought might be mutually satisfactory. I have heard nothing further from you and assume that all efforts to settle have been rejected. I, therefore, want it clearly understood what we, who oppose the packing scheme, have offered to do.

We have offered to interpose no obstacles in the Committee on Rules to the five major bills that the President has publicly announced as his program for this session.

We have offered to support a change in the rules to deprive the Committee on Rules of jurisdiction to prevent bills from going to conference.

We have brought out of the Committee on Rules a resolution which the leadership can pass in the House next Tuesday if they have the votes, or adopt the wiser course of waiting until the Committee on Rules in the opinion of the leadership, acts in a manner contrary to the wishes of the House, at which time the leadership can bring it up, and pass it, and stack the committee, any time the House wishes in the next 2 years.

Those of us who oppose this packing scheme have offered every honorable solution for the sake of harmony.

Sincerely yours,
HOWARD W. SMITH

THE SPEAKER. The time of the gentleman from Virginia [Mr. Smith] has expired.

MR. BROWN of Ohio. Mr. Speaker, I yield 4 minutes to the gentleman from Illinois [Mr. Arends].

MR. ARENDS. Mr. Speaker, let us ask ourselves one simple, basic question. What is the real purpose of this pending resolution to amend the rules of the House to provide for an increase in the size of the Rules Committee?

Admittedly, this committee has tremendous power. Its primary function is to review legislation reported to the House and to determine how and when it shall be considered on the floor. The membership of this committee has, for the most part, consisted of senior Members of the House with a broad knowledge of governmental matters and legislative procedures. Traditionally, the ratio has been 8 to 4 majority controlled.

Every committee of the House, as we all know, is vested with great power. Each can determine what bills before it shall be considered, rejected, or reported, and in what forms.

But this committee power, of the Rules Committee or any other committee, is not a power without limit. The rules of the House provide ways and means by which the majority can work its will, and often has, in the consideration of any measure.

The pending resolution does not change the functions of the Rules Committee. It does not in any way take away its powers, which it has and should have for the orderly consideration of legislation.

I ask again what is the purpose of this resolution? It is obvious. The obvious purpose of this resolution is to "pack" the committee. It is proposed here to convert a screening committee, a senior deliberative committee, into a "rubber stamp" committee for whatever our new President may propose and subject to the dictates of our Speaker.

. . . MR. BROWN of Ohio. Mr. Speaker, I yield 4 minutes to the gentleman from New York [Mr. Miller].

MR. MILLER of New York. Mr. Speaker, the President of the United States said in this chamber on yesterday, and I quote:

> Our Constitution wisely assigns both joint and separate roles to each branch of the Government, and a President and a Congress who hold each other in mutual respect will not permit nor attempt any trespass.

So, regardless of some newspaper comments to the contrary, this is solely a matter for us to determine—the organization and size of our own Rules Committee.

. . . MR. TRIMBLE. Mr. Speaker, I yield 3 minutes to the gentleman from Pennsylvania [Mr. Walter].

MR. WALTER. Mr. Speaker, I rise in support of the resolution to enlarge the Rules Committee of the House.

It is just about 24 hours ago when we heard in this House, the sobering but stirring message of the President of the United States. As of the minute he spoke, the eyes of the world, particularly the hostile eyes that watch us from behind the Iron Curtain, focused on us in the House of Representatives.

Every move we make is going to be watched by our friends and enemies alike. Every mistake we make is going to be magnified by hostile propaganda so as to make even our friends believe that the Nation and its representatives do not stand back of the President of the United States.

The great young man who addressed us yesterday laid down foundations for action. He courageously undertook commitments. However, the fulfillment of his commitments on which the survival of this Nation and, indeed, the survival of freedom depends, is our job.

. . . MR. BROWN of Ohio. Mr. Speaker, I yield 4 minutes and 50 seconds to the gentleman from Minnesota [Mr. Judd].

MR. JUDD. Mr. Speaker, this proposal to pack the Rules Committee in order to make it a rubber stamp for anyone in the Congress or outside it, is one of the easiest to vote against that I have faced in 18 years.

. . . We are grown men and women. Every one of us here knows that frequently Members go to the Rules Committee members and say, "Please hold up that legislation. I do not think it is good, but if it does come out, there is so much pressure in my district that I will have to vote for it."

Are the Members of Congress to be Representatives? Or are we to be reduced to mere delegates of the largest or most powerful groups at home? Are we to be just like the flag on a cash register, registering whatever button is pushed by somebody else? If they push the 10-cent button, the 10-cent flag goes up, without any thought or judgment on our part? If they push the "aye" button, the "aye" flag goes up? Our country is a Republic. It was not expected by the founders that the people themselves could make direct decisions on the complicated issues that come along. It was expected that the people in a given district would select one of their number in whose character, ability, and judgment they had confidence, and send him to Congress to give his full time to studying issues and making decisions in the interest of the Nation.

My title is not Representative of Minnesota. It is U.S. Representative—from the State of Minnesota. I have only one mandate here, and that mandate is to help govern this country the best I can as one member of the board of directors of the United States of America, the greatest organization the world has ever known.

. . . Should this House be intimidated into abandoning sound committee procedures developed and tested through more than 170 years—and giving the stablest and best government the world has known?

Just what are the good ends that justify such bad means?

Furthermore a packed Rules Committee can be expected to bring out bills under gag rules, making it impossible for Members to propose, debate, and act on amendments. Is that democratic? Is that proper protection of the rights of the minority?

If the proposal before us were one to modify or take away some of the powers of the Rules Committee, that would be a different issue. But this resolution does not alter in the slightest the autocratic powers it is claimed the Rules Committee has. It merely packs the Committee so it will be a rubber stamp in the hands of the Speaker, without appearing to be so. I cannot believe that is being candid, democratic or wise—whoever the Speaker may be.

. . . MR. BROWN. Mr. Speaker, I yield the balance of my time to distinguished minority leader, the gentleman from Indiana [Mr. Halleck].

THE SPEAKER. The gentleman from Indiana is recognized for 7 minutes.

MR. HALLECK. Mr. Speaker, I want to say at the outset that I am opposed to this legislation. I hope to state some legitimate reasons for that opposition.

I am against it because it is unwise, unjustified, untimely, unnecessary and, therefore, unsupportable. I am not suffering under any illusion here about changing the votes of some of my friends on the right, or possibly even on my side. There have been pressures exerted in this controversy that perhaps would far exceed any argumentative effort on my part. We have even had Mr. Khrushchev dragged into the controversy. I would just like to say that if the President really is concerned about his ability, as reported from unknown sources at the White House, to deal with Mr. Khrushchev if this resolution is not adopted, I would like to have word direct from down there.

I have had an avalanche of mail, most of it handwritten, from people opposed to this resolution. And why are they opposed to it? They are concerned about rash and reckless platform promises repeated in the campaign, some of it added to by some of the task force reports.

As I read that mail from the people of this country, right-thinking people by the millions, I am convinced they are afraid that this effort signals a collapse of the opposition to such unwise measures. They are afraid the floodgates will be let down and we will be overwhelmed with bad legislation.

. . . I ask you to vote against this resolution.

MR. TRIMBLE. Mr. Speaker, I yield the balance of the time on this side to the gentleman from Texas [Mr. Rayburn].

MR. RAYBURN. Mr. Speaker, whether you vote with me today or not, I want to say that I appreciate your uniform kindness and courtesy that has been displayed toward me. This issue, in my mind, is a simple one.

We have elected to the Presidency a new leader. He is going to have a program that he thinks will be in the interest of and for the benefit of the American people.

I think he demonstrated on yesterday that we are neither in good shape domestically nor in the foreign field. He wants to do something about that to improve our situation in the United States of America and in the world. . . . Now, I have a letter here that if I were easily insulted, it would do rather so to me. The gentleman from Virginia [Mr. Smith], chairman of the great Committee on Rules, sent out a letter, and in that letter he used the words "stack" and "pack" four times. The gentleman from Virginia, nor any other Member of this House, can accuse me of ever packing any committee for or against anything. It is a reflection on the majority leader. It is a reflection on our great committee on committees on the Democratic side of the House. And, talk about packing. Away back in 1933 we had a tremendous contest in this House. One side won. They put up a man for membership on the Committee on Rules; our side put up their man, and we at that time packed the Committee on Rules with the gentleman from Virginia [Mr. Smith].

MR. MC CORMACK. Mr. Speaker, will the gentleman yield?

MR. RAYBURN. I yield to the gentleman from Massachusetts.

MR. MC CORMACK. I might say that I was a member of the committee on committees, and my friend, the gentleman from Virginia, is the only Democratic Member in my 33 years that was elected by the committee on committees to the Committee on Rules when he was not recommended by the then Speaker and the majority leader. He was the choice of those of us who were defeated. Might I also say that this is a procedural matter; entirely a procedural matter. The former Speaker of this House, the gentleman from Massachusetts [Mr. Martin], is paired in favor of it. He recognizes the justice of it. Might I also say to my Republican friends, the other night on television my good friend, the gentleman from Virginia [Mr. Smith] said he was very happy to have the Republicans on his side. This is only a fair proposition and one that should be adopted.

MR. RAYBURN. I thank the gentleman from Massachusetts [Mr. McCormack] for his splendid contribution.

And then in 1939, the gentleman from Mississippi [Mr. Colmer] came to me and said he very much desired to go on the Committee on Rules. I told him I thought it was a mistake for him to go on the Committee on Rules, for various reasons. But he insisted and then we packed the committee with Mr. Colmer.

But a strange thing is in this House today. The Democrats have eight members on the Committee on Rules who have served there, some of them a long time, six of them—and I do not think they are long-haired radicals, either, who want to destroy the country—six of the eight are supporting this resolution today to add three Members to the Committee on Rules. To me that is very significant. The gentleman from Virginia [Mr. Smith] says that he is not going to report anything that violates his conscience and then winds up his talk on the floor by saying you have nothing to fear from the action of the Committee on Rules.

Let us move this program. Let us be sure that we can move it. And the only way that we can be sure that this program will move when great committees report bills, the only way it can move, in my opinion, my beloved colleagues, is to adopt this resolution. . . .

. . . MR. JOHANSEN. Mr. Speaker, there is a single issue before the House today. It is the issue of power—power to push the program of the new administration through the House with a minimum of effective resistance and with a maximum of speed and conformity to the wishes of the executive branch.

. . . Some days ago the arch-liberal columnist, Doris Fleeson, commented that the then President-elect has "all but promised to use—his Presidential powers—to the utmost." Miss Fleeson added the amazing observation, without any indication of regret, that "recent history suggests that—the Presidential powers—are subject to very little practical interference by the courts or Congress."

What is here proposed today is to reduce still further this already "very little practical interference" by Congress.

I oppose such action as I will continue to oppose those items in the President's program which I believe contrary to the best interests of our Nation.

I might add that after listening to the President's recitation on yesterday of the very numerous and, in many instances in my judgment very unwise, proposals, which he contemplates sending to Congress, it becomes more imperative than ever that we preserve such checks and restraints on pressure tactics exercised both by the executive branch and by powerful minority groups as we now possess.

Let no one be mistaken about it. If this resolution passes, it will be only the beginning of the pressure tactics.

MR. YATES. Mr. Speaker, the resolution which the House votes on today presents such an elementary proposition for democratizing the procedure of the House that one wonders how it is possible for any Member to oppose it.

. . . By this resolution the responsibility for passing upon legislation will be transferred to the body where it rightfully belongs, namely in the membership of the House. If a major legislative committee of the House after serious consideration has passed a bill, certainly it deserves to be heard by the membership of the House—not necessarily passed, Mr. Speaker—but a chance to be heard.

Mr. Speaker, public opinion throughout the country supports the resolution. The *Chicago Sun-Times* in its very perceptive editorial of January 29, 1961, entitled "Let the House Vote," points out that although it supported Republican candidates for President, U.S. Senator, and a number of Republican candidates for the U.S. House of Representatives, it believes that the

Republican leadership of the House is doing the wrong thing in opposing this resolution.

. . . Mr. Speaker, under leave to extend my remarks in the *Record,* I attach the editorial of the *Chicago Sun-Times,* dated January 29, 1961, entitled "Let the House Vote":

> This newspaper supported the Republican candidates for President and U.S. Senator from Illinois as well as a number of Republican candidates for the U.S. House of Representatives. We believe, nevertheless, that the Republican leadership in the House is doing the wrong thing in opposing Speaker RAYBURN's proposal to break the hold that six Congressmen have over all legislation. The 20 or so Republicans who are expected to be with RAYBURN on the vote Tuesday are showing commendable nonpartisanship on a matter of principle.
>
> . . . There are only two ways the committee can be circumvented. Legislation can be brought to the floor by a petition signed by half (219) of the House Members. This is a long and tedious process and many Representatives, wishing to dodge taking any stand on controversial matters, won't sign up. Any legislation can be brought up on Wednesdays if it can be squeezed in, but any bill so called up must be disposed of that day. Highly controversial legislation should not be railroaded through in 1 day, even if the votes are there to do it.

MR. BLATNIK. Mr. Speaker, I rise in support of the resolution increasing the size of the Rules Committee to 15 members. No more important issue or decision has faced this House in several decades or will face this House this year or for many years to come. On this vote hinges not the power or prestige of individuals or groups comprising this body, but rather the answer to the question of whether the majority will shall rule in this House in considering legislation which will determine the future course of national and world events in these critical times insofar as this House is able to shape them.

. . . The Rules Committee never was intended to be a super, all-seeing, all-knowing independent overseer of the House of Representatives. It is not for the Rules Committee to decide what the House shall consider, but rather the order and the conditions in which it shall consider the legislative proposals favorably reported to the House by the various legislative committees. While the committee may be the traffic coordinator of the House, assuring the orderly procedure of this body, it is not and was never intended to be the arresting officer, judge and jury of legislation. That is the function and duty of the legislative committees. It is for the Rules Committee to simply establish orderly rules of procedure under which these proposals can be considered.

. . . Mr. Speaker, in the Subcommittee on Rivers and Harbors, of which I am chairman, we consider hundreds of individual navigation projects affecting the well-being of many communities and areas throughout the country. We consider the projects that come before us carefully and approve those with adequate cost benefit ratios. No question of party loyalty is raised, no political considerations are made. These projects are considered solely on their merits. I raise this point, Mr. Speaker, to emphasize that this is all I ask of the Rules Committee. To permit us, the Members of the House, the right to consider on their merits the various legislative proposals hammered out of legislative committees after what is often days and even weeks of hard work and lengthy consideration. Is this too much to expect? Obviously, to the present membership of the Rules Committee it is. They have forsaken the fundamental basic tenet of our Republic—the will of the majority shall prevail. They have flaunted principles and precepts which we hold dear. They have ignored the needs of the Nation and taken unto themselves powers never delegated to them. Such a situation cannot be tolerated any longer. The membership of the Rules Committee must be increased so as to convert it into an instrument of responsible party leadership.

Mr. Speaker, I extend to you the heartfelt best wishes and thanks of all of us concerned with the problem confronting us this afternoon. Your leadership has been an inspiration to us all. History will record your valiant efforts. I urge the adoption of the resolution.

MR. ALGER. Mr. Speaker, my opposition to the enlargement of the Rules Committee is the clear and present danger that I see of disruption of the democratic legislative procedure.

I concede the right of the leadership to recommend the addition of members to the committee, and the correctness of a 2-to-1 majority so that the majority party can control the programing of legislation. That is their responsibility and duty. But I do oppose and protest the intent at this time of liberalizing the committee to become expressly a rubberstamp of the administration's program. The procedures of the House are now adequate to consider and adopt any legislation desired by the House.

. . . MR. LINDSAY. Mr. Speaker, I support the resolution to enlarge the Committee on Rules. My reasons can be briefly and simply stated.

First, the Committee on Rules should be the agent, not the master of the House. Second, I value and will fight for my right to debate and to vote for or against measures on the floor of the House. The country has a right to expect the same. . . .

. . . MR. SCHWENGEL. Mr. Speaker, I recognize this question of membership on the Rules Committee as an extremely important one.

It is vital to the independent work of this Congress.

At issue, it seems to me, are two questions: one of precedent and the other whether or not the administration's program and the program of the loyal opposition will both have a full and fair consideration before this House.

Mr. Speaker, the party of my choice presents a moderate but adequate program for America. In the last campaign, Mr. Nixon received 49.7 percent of the vote cast for President while running on the Republican platform compared to 49.8 percent received by the winner running on the platform adopted in Los Angeles. Then there are hundreds of thousands of people, as we know, who did not vote for either candidate.

These figures indicate, Mr. Speaker, that the loyal opposition has a mandate, too. It is a mandate to use every honorable means to assure ourselves and the country that our program, as reflected in the platform adopted in Chicago by the Republican Party, be given a chance for a full and fair hearing in this House and an opportunity to be voted on by its Members.

. . . MR. SCHERER. Mr. Speaker, the packing of the Rules Committee has some extremely serious implications which may not be apparent at first blush.

The public has been bombarded with the propaganda that the present Rules Committee bottles up so-called progressive, leftwing legislation. So it is proposed that we pack the Rules Committee with leftwingers to break the bottleneck and open the spending floodgates. Has anyone stopped to think what this new, leftwing Rules Committee will do with some so-called conservative, constructive legislation?

There is an omnibus bill now pending before the Congress which contains 17 provisions to tighten the internal security laws of this nation, to correct some of the asinine decisions of the Supreme Court which have wrecked our security program. When this bill reaches this new stacked Rules Committee, it will not have a Chinaman's chance of getting to the floor. It will make the present Rules Committee under the chairmanship of Judge SMITH smell like a rose by comparison.

There is another more serious evil in this committee-packing business. Once you set the precedent and people realize it can be done, what's going to happen to some other committees?

All of us are aware of the movement afoot to abolish the House Committee on Un-American Activities. Since the American people at the crossroads are behind this committee, there is no chance of getting rid of it, but you can destroy its effectiveness by packing it with a few Roosevelts and Cellers. Let these liberals get their foot in the door by packing this Rules Committee and then just watch them move against the Committee on Un-American Activities and possibly two or three others that they do not like.

It is dangerous business. We are playing with fire.

MR. POFF. Mr. Speaker, the new year opened with the word "purge" in the air. Even those who planned the deed used the word. But the word struck the public ear with a note which grated against the moral sensitivity of the people. The tone sounded somehow of purification, pasteurization, cleaning of the unclean. Synonyms came to mind—exile, banishment. The people rebelled against the concept of elimination of opposition by physical expulsion. A new concept was proposed which some artist of semantics first called numerical adjustment. And which some realist later called packing.

. . . MR. ADDONIZIO. Mr. Speaker, the U.S. House of Representatives is probably the most democratic legislative body in the world. It is revered as a temple of responsive government, a symbol of our freedoms. I know that every one of us is proud and honored to be a Member.

But like all human creations, the structure of this House is marred by some flaws. One of the most serious of these, it seems to me, is displayed in every session of Congress by the operation of the Committee on Rules. Surely it is an incredible situation when, in a body supposedly devoted to responsible and equitable majority rule, 6 men have the power to decide in which direction 437 shall move. Surely it is even more incredible that these men, who are not even the duly elected leaders of their respective parties, hold such dictatorial power as to prevent the consideration by this House of important and often vital legislation.

. . . Mr. Speaker, our committees are generally composed of experienced and knowledgeable men and women from both parties and from all sections of the country. Many of them are experts in their fields. They often devote months to the study of specific legislation in those fields. The bills they report are usually, and justifiably, treated with respect by this House.

Yet how often have we been witness to the spectacle of measures so conceived throttled by the capricious will of half the Committee on Rules? How often have committee chairmen been ordered to modify in line with the biases of the Rules Committee, measures their committees have reported, on penalty of having the bills completely withheld from floor consideration? We are all familiar with numerous incidents of this kind. They make a mockery of democratic procedure.

. . . MR. CONTE. Mr. Speaker—Through trial and error our predecessors from the 1st Congress through the 86th have developed a wondrously effective system to enable 437 men to deal with the more than 10,000 legislative measures which are introduced in the House of Representatives during almost every session of Congress. It makes good sense for a body of 437 men to charge a committee of 31 men to report to the body its recommendations on all proposed legislation dealing with Banking and Currency. The Members ordinarily seek election to the committees with jurisdiction of a field in which they are most qualified and most interested. And in this body more than a few of the Members are nationally and internationally recognized experts in the fields of the committees and subcommittees on which they serve. After the committee has heard the testimony of those who favor and those who oppose the legislation, after the committee has weighed the merits of the legislation and reported its recommendation to the full body, then the Members of the full body have the evidence they need to be able to discuss the issues intelligently on the floor and decide whether enactment of the legislation would be in the best interest of the Nation and the people who elected them.

. . . MR. HALPERN. Mr. Speaker, I support this resolution. I do so because I believe enlarging the membership of the House Rules Committee is a reasonable and moderate solution to a serious problem.

. . . Each Congressman—Democrat and Republican alike—has a responsibility to act in the public interest. Getting legislation, controversial or otherwise, to the floor of the House is in the public interest and the resolution before us is a reasonable proposal to expedite legislation.

. . . MR. TRIMBLE. Mr. Speaker, I move the previous question.

The previous question was ordered.

THE SPEAKER. The question is on the resolution.

MR. BROWN of Ohio. Mr. Speaker, on that I ask for the yeas and nays.

The yeas and nays were ordered.

The question was taken; and there were—yeas 217, nays 212, answered "present" 1, not voting 4.

Seniority and the Legislative Process

Seniority is not mentioned in the rules of either the Senate or the House of Representatives, and what has been called "the seniority rule" is a congressional usage and no more. The political scientist's stress on seniority as a significant barrier (or aid) to the legislative process arises from the crucial nature of the congressional committee and the power of its chairman. Tending in effect to be a miniature House or Senate, the committee in turn tends to become what the chairman makes of it.

In assessing the argumentation about seniority, the student should remember that a touch of political ingenuity may save an immensity of governmental trouble. At least some of the difficulties in the seniority system may be met through approaches other than the abolition of the system itself. Thus, former Congressman Stewart Udall has cited the rules and procedures of the House Committee on Interior and Insular Affairs as an example of the fashion in which the arbitrary power of a chairman can be reduced: in that committee, the rules provide that bills are automatically referred to standing subcommittees whose jurisdiction is clearly defined, and subcommittee chairmen are chosen on the basis of seniority. Illustrated here, incidentally, is the paradoxical effort to limit the effects of the seniority system in part by choosing subcommittee chairmen through seniority, so as to lessen the rewards and punishments available to committee chairmen.

The author of the following article, Congressman Emanuel Celler of New York, is chairman of the House Committee on the Judiciary. Congressman Celler's appraisal of the seniority rule was published at about the same time as the research of a political scientist who found, after a quantitative investigation, that his "analysis does not make as clear a case against seniority as many of the critics of the system seem to claim. Chairmen are older on the average than their colleagues, and yet with luck a number of younger men are singled out for chairmanships. The districts which produce chairmen are not as stagnant as is often suggested, and the degree of party unity and presidential support among chairmen is not as low as many believe. The picture, however, is far from the ideal held by the proponents of majority rule."

A familiar political truth emerges from consideration of the evidence in and around this article: the machinery for the internal operation of the Congress is apt to be remote from the interest and concern of the citizen, close to the concern and potential for power of the congressman, and as susceptible to change as congressmen can tolerate under the circumstance that their survival hinges on getting along with diverse individuals and assorted groups.

[Representative Emanuel Celler, "The Seniority Rule in Congress," *Western Political Quarterly,* vol. 14, part 1, pp. 160-167, March, 1961.]

It is a rare session of Congress that does not produce its share of proposals to abolish that perennial red herring—the so-called "seniority rule." This long-standing congressional tradition, under which the House and the Senate organize their working committees, has become as popular a target as sin itself. It is intermittently bombarded by Democrats and by Republicans, by liberals and by conservatives, depending largely upon whose ox is being gored.

I do not entirely understand why this should be so. True, it is sometimes expedient to explain the defeat of a locally popular measure in terms of the tyranny of a committee chairman. Also, able and energetic young men and women who come to Congress and find the best seats occupied will understandably chafe at the tardiness with which their talents are recognized and rewarded by assignments to coveted posts. Thus, a distinguished United States Senator, after two years of service, called the seniority rule a "strait-jacket," described it as "rigid, inflexible, and unyielding," and urged its discontinuance as "the sole determinant of Congressional sovereignty and influence" in committee chairmanships and assignments. An example of the intermittent assaults upon congressional seniority is the joint resolution, H.J. Res. 253, of the 86th Congress, which would have rendered senators and representatives who have served twelve years ineligible for re-election for a two-year period.

But the tendency to attack the seniority principle has not been confined to members of Congress, nor, indeed, to politicians. Students of political science regularly excoriate the rule for theoretical imperfections which no method of selection designed by human beings could conceivably eliminate. Even members of the working press—practical men and women who know their way around Capitol Hill—fall in with this approach. The seniority bugaboo is always good for a couple of sticks on a dull Monday, or for a feature in the Sunday Supplement, predicting what the Hill "leadership" will or will not "permit," with the clear implication that the congressional power is too narrowly held and dictatorially exercised.

From the tone of some of its critics, one would suppose that the seniority principle is firmly entrenched and sanctified by law, and that little short of a constitutional amendment could dislodge it. Properly speaking, however, it is not a rule at all, but is rather a custom or convention. Although operative in both the Senate and the House for many years, it is embodied in no formal rule of either chamber. And, far from being sacrosanct, seniority has been overridden by both parties, when circumstances appear to require. Instances of this include the ouster of Stephen A. Douglas from the chairmanship of the Senate Committee on Territories in 1859, and the removal of Charles Sumner from the chairmanship of the Committee on Foreign Relations in 1871. It was a Democratic caucus that ousted Douglas, a Republican caucus that removed Sumner. Moreover, the rigor of the seniority rule has been modified in the current practice of Senate Democrats to allow no senator a second committee choice until each freshman shall have received at least one major committee assignment.

Recurrent criticisms also create the impression that the seniority criterion has wrested control of legislation from the members of Congress and concentrated it in the hands of autocratic committee chairmen, for the gratification of their personal whims. Yet despite these repeated assertions, no steps are even taken to change the basic operation of the system. Like the weather, much is said, but nothing done about it.

Just what role does seniority actually play in the operation of Congress, and why, if it is as unsatisfactory as its critics assert, has it not long been abandoned?

My thirty-eight years of continuous service in the House of Representatives, spent first in acquiring the experience and understanding of legislative work which are implicit in "seniority," and more recently in the exercise of the responsibilities that go with a committee chairmanship, have given me a better than average opportunity to observe the working of the system. I believe that the seniority principle, though far from perfect, performs an indispensable function in the organization of the Congress, and that the alternatives that have been offered as a cure for its deficiencies would aggravate, rather than relieve them. . . .

As concerns the method of designating chairmen of standing committees, foreign countries today fall into two principal categories. The parliamentary organization and practice of the seventeen countries that compose the British Commonwealth are modeled on that of the Mother of Parliaments—the English House of Commons, where the practice appears to be for the Speaker to appoint the chairmen of standing committees.

Elsewhere among the fifty-seven parliaments that are members of the Interparliamentary Union, the general practice is for the chairmen of committees to be elected by the committees themselves. A curious departure is found in the Bundestag where chairmen of committees are allotted proportionally among the parties. The number of chairmen of committees allotted to a parliamentary party corresponds to the number of members of the different parliamentary parties. Chairmen of different committees are nominated by parliamentary parties on the basis of agreement between the parties. The chairman is then formally elected in committee. Up to the present, the chairmen proposed by the parliamentary parties have always been elected.

Appraisal of the American system against this background must take into account the realities of the legislative process. Neither house of Congress could conceivably give detailed attention to all the facets of its legislative program in regular session. Preliminary consideration of legislative proposals is therefore delegated to standing committees, which, with the aid of specialized subcommittees, study the bills, conduct investigations, hear and attempt to reconcile divergent needs and views, and finally report a measure to the full body. Thereafter the committee members perform their individual responsibilities in the ensuing debate. In addition, each committee has the task of keeping itself informed as to the effectiveness with which existing laws within its jurisdiction are being enforced.

What is more, legislation destined for ultimate enactment frequently fails of passage in the Congress in which it is initially introduced. Indeed, it is not unusual for legislative history of a measure to extend over more than two biennia. In such cases, although new bills must be introduced in each new Congress, the committee has a virtually continuing responsibility for managing, or processing, the legislative issue.

Against this background, the rationale of the seniority principle becomes evident. Over the years, manifestly, the effectiveness of a committee will bear a direct relationship to the stability of its personnel. If the legislative committees were to be reshuffled after each election—beyond what is necessitated by the retirement of members and the arrival of new ones—all issues pending unresolved in the House, and to a lesser degree those pending in the Senate would require consideration de novo. The time and effort necessarily expended by committee members in familiarizing themselves with the nature of the committee's work, the intricacies of its problems, and the identity and character of interested parties would indeed be lost. What has been said of the members applies with peculiar force to the committee's chairman. Upon the chairman rests the administrative responsibility for the committee's program and for the functioning of the subcommittees. He supervises the professional staff. Continued availability of the chairman's accumulated expertness, experience, and prestige is a central factor in a committee's effectiveness. Interruption of his tenure, other than is necessitated when the control of the Chamber passes from one political party to the other, would needlessly impair the efficiency of the committee's operations.

Fundamentally, the seniority system avoids the waste implicit in instability of committee composition and management. It invokes the presumption that, other things being equal, the man or woman with the greatest experience in a particular job is best fitted to participate and to lead in its performance. To quote Luce, in his work on legislative procedure, "Whatever the activity, we all know that experience counts for more than anything else, and promotion by seniority is nothing but the recognition of this." Since a senior congressman is more experienced than his junior, and since all congressmen aspire to posts of influence, choice of committee assignments may safely be left to seniority. Within a committee, similarly, since effectiveness is presumptively related to length of uninterrupted service, the seniority ladder properly defines the succession to the chairmanship.

The seniority criterion for selecting committee chairmen has the added virtue of being objective. It automatically eliminates the intrigues, deals, and compromises that characterize election campaigns. By the same token, committees are able to get down to work immediately, without having first to bind the wounds of disappointed aspirants to leadership.

To counter these salient advantages, opponents of the system offer two principal criticisms. The first is addressed to its alleged effect upon the functioning of the committees. Here it is contended that the capacity to achieve re-election has no necessary relation to the qualities ideally embodied in a chairman; that under a seniority rule the potential contribution of an exceptionally able young legislator is sacrificed to the entrenchment of an aging incumbent whose energies may be waning; and that the relative inviolability of the custom operates to immunize chairmen against retribution, no matter how arbitrary and dictatorial their conduct of office.

Each of these claims has surface plausibility—and each has been overstated. Although seniority, alone, does not guarantee superior ability, success in effectively serving the state or district remains an indispensable attribute of the perennially successful candidate for election. The most backward electorate will not indefinitely return a congressman who wholly fails to serve its needs. Such a man is retired, if not in an election, then in a primary contest. By and large, the so-called "safe" state or district is one that has been getting the kind of representation it wants. And inevitably, the affirmative qualities that keep a man in office do contribute to his effectiveness as a committee chairman.

Each of us must some day lay down his burdens, but nature has not uniformly decreed when this must be. Some men remain vigorous and effective in their eighties; others may fail at fifty. As stated by Gross in *The Legislative Struggle,*

> The seniority system has often been mistakenly attacked on the ground that it puts too much power in the hands of old men. This argument misses the real implications of the seniority system. Age alone does not cause diminution of mental vigor, alertness, and leadership ability. Nor does it mean that a man becomes more conservative. Some of the outstanding liberals in Congress have been old men who have fought valiantly despite the other handicaps of age. . . .

Public servants with long tenure should be able to retire with a measure of security, and recent amendments of the retirement system make this increasingly possible for members of Congress. But most men know when they have had enough, and I fear that by imposing compulsory retirement of committee chairmen upon the attainment of any particular age we would as often lose as gain in terms of the vigor and capacity of the successor. With respect, also, to the criticism that able young legislators with special skills must today go too long without appropriate outlet for their talents, it is noteworthy that increasing use of subcommittees, as well as select committees, are enabling greater utilization of such members in chairmanships.

By far the most serious of this group of criticisms is that which implies arbitrary, one-man rule of committees. It is true that the prerogative of calling meetings and the control of agendas gives some chairmen wide powers, sometimes amounting to the practical equivalent of a veto. But it would be a mistake to attribute this to the seniority system. Seniority does no more than designate the chairman; it does not write the committee's rules of procedure, nor does it prescribe despotism in the conduct of the committee's affairs. Recent years have seen an increasing incidence of well-developed rules of procedure for the governance of committee business. It is always possible for the members of a committee to outvote its chairman. That this happens from time to time is wholesome. That it does not happen more often is as reasonably attributable to the respect and confidence with which the members regard their chairman as to any sinister implication of dictatorship. I believe that the charge of dictatorship is often an attempt to saddle the chairman with sole responsibility for the committee majority's unwillingness to act.

As Luce puts it: "Somebody must lead. If it is not the strong, it will be the weak. If it is not the experienced, it will be the inexperienced. Otherwise chaos." Under any method of selection, the chairman will remain the committee's most powerful member. The cure for despotism, where it may still exist, is not to deprive the committee of the services of its most seasoned member, but to insist on democratic procedures. In this way, the committee itself can guarantee that the chairman will act as a guide and leader, responsive to the will of the majority, and not as a dictator.

The other major objection that has been leveled at the seniority system is that it concentrates the power implicit in chairmanships in congressmen from so-called one-party states and districts, at the expense of areas whose political complexion is mixed. It is further asserted that the prestige and influence of a high-seniority congressman becomes a political asset in warding off assaults upon his tenure, thus further entrenching him in office. Here, again, some truth and some exaggeration are encountered.

In a Democratic Congress, like the present one, the argument is usually illustrated by pointing to the preponderance of southerners, traditionally more conservative than northern and western Democrats, at the helms of the committees. It is true that of 36 standing committees in the House and the Senate, 21 are headed by men from the South. On the other hand, many important chairmanships are in the hands of northerners and westerners. Indeed, the dean at this writing among Senate Democrats, in his eighties, is the exceptionally able Senator Carl Hayden, chairman of the Committee on Appropriations, who speaks for Arizona. So, too, the states of Nevada, Washington, New Mexico, and Missouri, none of them classed as southern, are represented among Senate committee chairmanships.

In the House, likewise, the important Committees on Appropriations, Banking and Currency, Education and Labor, Foreign Affairs, Government Operations, Interior and Insular Affairs, Judiciary, Public Works, and Un-American Activities, are chaired by men from non-southern states, including New York, Illinois, Pennsylvania, Missouri, Kentucky, and Colorado. And four of the six House committee chairmen having the greatest length of uninterrupted service are from non-southern states. Numerous northerners are also chairmen of powerful subcommittees.

Withal, it cannot be denied that the seniority system produces some disproportion in the distribution of committee chairmanships. Whether this justifies abandonment of the rule raises the question whether the one-party districts can properly be penalized, simply for being able to make up their minds, by being deprived of the fruits that normally accrue from the acquisition of experience and expertness by their representatives. Such considerations tend to become academic, however, unless some satisfactory substitute for the existing rule can be found.

It is my conviction that the reason why the seniority principle has not long been abandoned lies not only in its demonstrable advantages but also in the difficulties that beset alternative proposals. I know of no substitute for the present system whose disadvantages would not outweigh its benefits. Proposals to require chairmen to step down at a specified age, or after a specified period of service, and to rotate chairmanships among committee members having a specified period of service would destroy continuity without necessarily producing more capable leadership. Proposals to elect chairmen in party caucuses would additionally give rise to campaigning with its attendant evils—again without any real assurance of the election of the best fitted candidate. Resort to secret ballot would slightly, but not wholly obviate this objection. The practice of foreign parliaments in which chairmen are predominantly elected by committee members may be appropriate in situations in which the members are themselves selected by lot. Such a system, however, makes knowledge or interest on the part of the committee members improbable. In systems like our own in which a premium has always been placed on continuity, election by committee members would be subject to all the infirmities of election by caucus. Appointment by the Speaker would generate inordinate pressures upon him from within and without Congress and would inordinately enlarge his power over legislation. I doubt whether the present Speaker would want such power. None of these alternatives would go to the real heart of the problem—the evolution of committee procedures that will guarantee democratic functioning.

I suspect that we shall continue to follow the custom of respecting seniority in the selection of congressional committee chairmen, not because it is perfect, but because it is better than any other method that has yet been proposed. And we could do much worse, for, to paraphrase Speaker Rayburn, the rules of both Houses of Congress are such that a determined majority can always work its will.

White House and Congress

Presidential Aide Lawrence O'Brien's picture is on the cover page of the issue of *Time* from which the item below is taken. Shown behind O'Brien is an outline of a stick that looks like a governmental-building pillar from which there dangles an appetizing-looking carrot. The carrot-and-stick theme of the picture represents a well-known combination of techniques for getting people to do something: guile and force, persuasion and coercion. Precisely this point is the one conveyed in the title of James M. Burns's biography of Franklin D. Roosevelt, *Roosevelt: The Lion and the Fox.*

Concerned with material that lies close to the heart of the American governmental system, the article may be viewed from varied perspectives, including: the weight in the checks-and-balances system of a man few people have heard of working in communications machinery which has, nevertheless, focused attention on him; the intensity of the executive effort and the necessity for extraformal instruments to soften the congressional-presidential clash and achieving legislative-program objectives; the characteristics of a liaison man, why he was selected for the job, what makes him effective; the impact of national magazine coverage on the future behavior of the politicians mentioned (and those not mentioned); the image and the reality of congressional–White House relationships; the relations of technique and purpose in achieving legislative programs.

["White House & Congress: Power, Patronage and Persuasion," *Time*, Sept. 1, 1961, pp. 10–15.]

THE ADMINISTRATION

The Man on the Hill

In his walnut-paneled White House office, Lawrence Francis O'Brien held a hurried conference with his aides. He had been warned by Vice President Lyndon Johnson that an important Southern Senator was wavering on an Administration bill. "See what you can do with him," O'Brien told a staffer. Then, as the meeting broke up, O'Brien turned to his telephone and called another Senator to thank him for a favorable vote the previous week. "I didn't want you to think we didn't notice and appreciate what you did," said O'Brien in a low Yankee twang. "The President mentioned it at the leadership meeting this morning."

During that same morning, O'Brien heard warnings, gave orders and expressed gratitude in a dozen other telephone calls; he talked to Congressmen, lobbyists, Democratic National Chairman John Bailey and Secretary of State Dean Rusk. Between calls, he raced downstairs three times for quick conferences with President Kennedy. Then he was off to Capitol Hill for a meeting with Lyndon Johnson and Senate Majority Leader Mike Mansfield in the Vice President's office. After lunching on the run, O'Brien talked to a dozen Congressmen, examined the fever charts of a dozen pending bills. Returning to the White House in midafternoon, he held another staff conference, saw the President again, greeted North Carolina's visiting Democratic Governor Terry Sanford, finally shrugged into his jacket and left for the Mayflower Hotel, where a Democratic National Committee cocktail party for Congressmen was in full swing.

All in all, that day last week was a relatively relaxed one in the life of Larry O'Brien, 44, whose job as President Kennedy's Special Assistant for Congressional Relations makes him one of the most important of all New Frontiersmen—with responsibility for seeing to it that the Kennedy Administration's programs become public law.

A Problem of Climate. To the casual observer, that responsibility might seem simple. After all, Democrat Jack Kennedy took office from Republican Dwight Eisenhower with lopsidedly Democratic majorities in both the U.S. Senate and the House of Representatives. But Kennedy won his way to the White House by such a perilous plurality (118,000 votes out of a national total of 68 million) that he could in no sense be considered to have a mandate that might compel Congressmen to go along with him. Indeed, many winning Democratic Representatives and Senators who led Kennedy on the ticket within their own constituencies, could reasonably decide that they knew better than the young President about what was good for the people.

In such a political climate, the job of convincing or, if necessary, pushing the Congress into following the Administration has become one of the toughest and most sensitive in Washington. It requires keen understanding of the equations of politics. The President's man on Capitol Hill must know instinctively which Congressmen will respond to deference or flattery, which ones require threats or pressures from home, which ones will leap at the hint of presidential support in the next campaign. O'Brien possesses such understanding in good measure. And he is an expert in the political uses of power, patronage and persuasion.

Check It with Larry. In his operations on Capitol Hill, O'Brien's greatest asset is the all-out backing of the President himself. In the first days of the New Frontier, Jack Kennedy made it obvious to Congressmen that Liaison Man O'Brien was armed with all the authority he might need. Senators and Representatives calling Kennedy with political proposals invariably were asked: "Have you checked that with Larry O'Brien?" They soon got the idea.

O'Brien knows precisely how far the President will go in making legislative concessions to Congress. More than once, when approached by Democratic congressional leaders with suggestions for compromises that might speed Administration programs through the Senate or House, O'Brien has accepted on the spot, without having to refer to the President.

As a man who prefers the carrot to the stick in his operations, O'Brien uses the power of the presidency sparingly. Time and again, congressional leaders have urged him to recommend that President Kennedy intervene directly in legislative matters. Time and again, O'Brien has refused, acting only in crucial cases when a presidential telephone call or White House talk with a key Congressman is most timely and can be most effective.

The Friendly Lobbies. Other top Administration officials follow the President's lead in helping O'Brien move New Frontier programs through Congress—and it is indeed a crusty legislator who is not flattered by a friendly telephone call, made at O'Brien's suggestion, from a member of the Kennedy Cabinet.

O'Brien has also made effective use of the pressures that can be brought to bear on Congressmen by the liberal lobbies that abound in Washington—notably that of the A.F.L.-C.I.O., under its own able legislative man, Andy Biemiller. When Administration legislative interests coincide with those of a particular lobbying group, O'Brien makes certain that one of his staffmen compares notes and coordinates efforts with the lobbyists. Intelligence is exchanged, a list is made of Congressmen whose votes might be swayed, and high-tempo lobbying techniques, ranging from direct-mail campaigns to carefully arranged visits from constituents, are turned on the solons.

The Use of Patronage. Just before O'Brien took over as President Kennedy's liaison representative to Congress, he conferred with Republican Dwight Eisenhower's man on the Hill, Bryce Harlow. From Harlow, O'Brien received a piece of sage advice: not to get too overtly involved with patronage problems. Said Harlow: "With patronage, you will have to turn down ten men for every one you say yes to. You make people unhappy instead of happy."

O'Brien has followed that advice—up to a point. Officially, patronage is left to Democratic National Committee Chairman John Bailey, who works in consultation with O'Brien Staffman Dick Donahue. But O'Brien knows well that patronage is still a potent political instrument; he makes recommendations to Bailey on major appointments, and his suggestions receive top-priority consideration. Thus, when the 14 members of the Italian-American congressional bloc threatened to vote against the Administration's feed-grain bill just to demonstrate their power, O'Brien quickly found out what was on their minds: no man of Italian descent had been appointed to a major Administration post. O'Brien promised to look into the matter for them, the bloc voted right, and a few weeks later the White House was pleased to announce the appointment of Salvatore Bontempo as head of the State Department's consular service. For good measure, Michel Cieplinski was named as Bontempo's assistant, mollifying an eleven-member Polish-American group in the House.

All Congressmen now know that, although John Bailey is the nominal dangler of political plums, O'Brien is really the man to see when they have a patronage problem.

Worlds Apart. For all the political power tools that he can command, Larry O'Brien's greatest strength lies in his personal relationships with the members of Congress. He can talk their language. Like them, he is a political pro. He has the pro's disdain for windmill-tilting amateurs. "The eggheads," he says, "want the candidate to win on his own terms, to defy the party and interest groups. The egghead thinks it's worthwhile to be defeated. I think it's worthwhile to be elected." This same pragmatic professionalism sets O'Brien apart from many of the other men who surround President Kennedy. "I don't know what I'm doing in this crowd," O'Brien once mused. "I didn't go to Harvard, and I'm not athletic. I don't even play touch football.". . .

After the war, Larry O'Brien returned to Springfield to manage the O'Brien Realty Co.—which had grown to include a gas station and a parking lot in addition to the restaurant—and to get back into politics. In Best Man Foster Furcolo, Organizer O'Brien had a ready candidate. Having come up through the wards, Furcolo was ready for the big time, and O'Brien was eager to handle his campaign for Congress. With his usual attention to detail, he gridded the Second Massachusetts District into 60 units, recruited a corps of "secretaries," and kept a swarm of volunteers busy mailing campaign letters to their friends.

During that first Furcolo campaign, O'Brien devised many of the campaign techniques that later became standard operating procedure for John Kennedy's state and national efforts. But 1946 was a Republican year, and Furcolo was defeated by a scant 3,295 votes. As soon as the returns were in, O'Brien went methodically to work on the 1948 campaign. And in the second Furcolo race, O'Brien brought in a winner, with a 15,000 plurality. In gratitude, Foster Furcolo asked O'Brien to come to Washington as his administrative assistant. Two years later, the two friends came to a mysterious and bitter parting of the ways (neither man will reveal the reason), and Larry O'Brien came back to Springfield vowing that he had quit politics forever.

Tea and Telephones. It was one of the briefest retirements in political history. Within six months O'Brien was hard at work, organizing Massachusetts for John Kennedy, then a third-term Congressman and an unannounced aspirant to the Senate. Kennedy had known O'Brien casually for five years, had spotted him as a campaign organizer of rare talent. Within a year, O'Brien had recruited 350 secretaries, 18,000 volunteer Kennedy workers. By the time Kennedy formally announced his Senate candidacy, O'Brien was all ready with a purring state-wide political machine. The O'Brien brain was a supermarket of political innovations: the campaign tea parties, with Kennedy's mother and sisters pouring (and an omnipresent guestbook to provide O'Brien with the names and addresses of potential campaign workers); the expanding "O'Brien Manual," a handbook of organizational instructions written in language that any amateur could understand; the O'Brien Home Telephone Technique, rounding up women volunteers who would each call all the people listed on a single page in the telephone book, ask for support and offer transportation to the polls. Explains O'Brien: "The key to this is the full utilization of womanpower. Normally, women are wasted in a campaign. They have children. They can't come to headquarters."

To the Kennedy team, O'Brien was and is more than a skillful political organizer. He has the experience and understanding to serve as a bridge between the Democratic Old Guard and the New Frontier. The bright, eager young men around Jack Kennedy have always baffled and often offended the Skeffingtons of Massachusetts; but Larry O'Brien can talk to politicians in their own language and win them over. "He was the essential transition man for us with the Old Guard," says Bobby Kennedy. At the same time, O'Brien was an invaluable professor of political science for the likes of Bobby, Kenny O'Donnell, Dick Donahue and other young members of the Kennedy group who were rank political amateurs in Kennedy's successful 1952 senatorial campaign. They have since become a closeknit, highly professional team that is known in Administration circles as "the Irish Mafia."

Big Thoughts. As a first-term Senator, Jack Kennedy had a legislative record that was nothing to brag about. But his political appeal was such that in 1956, when Democratic Presidential Nominee Adlai Stevenson threw the vice presidential nomination up for grabs at the party's Chicago convention, Kennedy made a wildly disorganized eleventh-hour attempt for the prize. He lost to Estes Kefauver, but by so narrow a margin that it set the Kennedyites to thinking really Big Thoughts. Recalls Larry O'Brien (who had not even attended the convention): "After that convention, we began to realize that Kennedy could go all the way."

With Larry O'Brien and his organization working as though their own lives were at stake, Kennedy won re-election to the Senate in 1958 by close to 900,000 votes, the biggest plurality in Massachusetts history. Kennedy's reputation as a prime vote getter—presumably on a national scale—was correspondingly enhanced. And so, in late February 1959, Jack Kennedy called a special presidential strategy session at his father's Palm Beach home. Present were Brothers Bobby and Teddy Kennedy, Brothers-in-Law Sarge Shriver and Steve Smith, Adviser Ted Sorensen—and Larry O'Brien. In the first formal planning for a Kennedy effort to reach the White House, O'Brien was assigned the job of establishing Kennedy organizations throughout the U.S.

Courthouse v. White House. Carrying out that assignment, O'Brien crossed the nation nine times, traveling 100,000 miles, talking deep into every night, stoking himself with three packs of Pall Malls, a Niagara of black coffee each day. He set up the local organizations, staffed mostly by enthusiastic amateurs in the states where Kennedy had to win presidential primaries to have any real hope for the Democratic nomination. O'Brien could also talk turkey with such patronage-minded politicians as a local West Virginia leader who told him bluntly: "I'm not interested in the White House. I'm interested in the courthouse."

The primaries won, O'Brien was in Los Angeles setting up Kennedy headquarters a full month before the Democrats met to choose their candidate for President. In Los Angeles, O'Brien's elaborate telephone and walkie-talkie system of instant, 24-hour communication with the convention floor and each state delegation headquarters was a marvel of modern political efficiency. After the convention, O'Brien applied all his tried and true organizational techniques to Kennedy's winning campaign against Republican Richard Nixon. "It was dog work," he recalls, "but it was worthwhile: it worked." Jack Kennedy's own postelection appraisal of O'Brien: "The best election man in the business."

Immediately after Election Day, O'Brien drew an arduous assignment: checking the qualifications, background, weak points and strong suits of nearly 10,000 prospective officials in the new Administration. One afternoon in Palm Beach, going over the lists of names with O'Brien, Kennedy casually notified him of his new job: "By the way, I think this role of congressional liaison is for you." As a graduate of both houses, Kennedy gave O'Brien a warning against the pitfalls of intimacy. "In politics," the President-elect told him, "you don't have friends. You have allies."

The Unfigurables. In his campaigning travels, Larry O'Brien had come to know many Congressmen—but he had never dealt with them in their legislative capacity. Now it was time for just such dealing. First O'Brien huddled with a select group of Capitol Hill veterans, sought to make a knowledgeable estimate of the political shape of the 87th Congress. It was decided that the Senate, with a minimum amount of attention, would back most of the Kennedy program. But the House of Representatives was a different matter. The presession analysis showed that there were about 180 certain House votes for most New Frontier Programs, about 180 votes that were almost equally sure to go against the Administration. That left between 75 and 80 votes that were more or less unfigurable.

Next, O'Brien met early in February in his Mayflower Hotel suite with three of the canniest young Democratic members of the House: Missouri's Richard Bolling, New Jersey's Frank Thompson and Alabama's Carl Elliott.

Bolling had already gone over the list of New Frontier legislative proposals, estimated as things stood that only one—the housing bill—was a sure shot for House passage. The conferees ran through the entire roster of 437 Representatives—name by name, back-home problem by back-home problem, interest by interest and prejudice by prejudice. "We decided," recalls one of the men who sat in on the Mayflower session, "that we had two target areas, the Eastern industrial Republicans and the moderate-to-conservative Southerners. We figured there were 40 Southerners we couldn't touch—but we've modified that since, because we have touched some of them."

As his staff contact man with Southern Representatives, O'Brien wisely selected Henry Hall Wilson Jr., 39, a North Carolinian who had done yeoman service for Candidate Kennedy in Wilson's native state during the 1960 campaign. Wilson knew little about legislative dealing with members of Congress. "But we figured he could learn," says Dick Donahue. "The most important thing was to get our own man, so that if he had any ties he had 'em to Larry instead of to a bunch of people he's known and become obliged to on the Hill."

The Absolute Key. In their studies of the House balances of power, O'Brien and his congressional advisers decided that there was a key man: Georgia's Carl Vinson, chairman of the Armed Services Committee and one of the two or three most influential Southerners in the House. They decided that it was vital to lure Vinson away from the conservative camp; he could, among other things, bring at least a score of Southern votes along with him. Says Bolling: "Vinson was absolutely the key to the whole session." O'Brien concentrated his own efforts on Vinson. The old gentleman won O'Brien's genuine admiration—and O'Brien won his. As it has happened since that time, Carl Vinson and his house followers have voted down the line for the New Frontier's programs.

The first major Administration legislative item to come up for floor vote in Congress found O'Brien with his organizational fences not yet in place. It was the feed-grains bill, which found rural and urban Congressmen bitterly divided. About the only appeal that O'Brien and his staffers could make to Democratic Congressmen was not to let the President down on his first bill—"Let's win this one for Jack, Jackie and little Caroline." The bill passed the House by seven votes—and since then O'Brien has been able to move more sophisticated weapons into action on behalf of the Administration program.

His bulky (5 ft. 11½ in., 187 lbs.) frame and his reddish, whisk-broom thatch are a familiar sight in the Capitol's corridors. In turn, Larry has made it his business to meet nearly all the inhabitants of Capitol Hill at a marathon succession of cocktail parties and at leisurely Sunday brunches on the O'Brien's Georgetown terrace, with Wife Elva presiding at meals that include O'Brien potatoes. But O'Brien has remembered the Kennedy warning: although he is liked by nearly everyone, Republican as well as Democrat, on the Hill, he has made use of only one close friend: Representative Eddie Boland, the Congressman from O'Brien's own district. (It was Boland who was the earliest to spot Jack Kennedy's presidential potential. In 1946 he told O'Brien: "Kennedy's a real comer. He can go all the way.") On the Hill, Boland's office has become an anteroom to O'Brien's headquarters, and other Congressmen have come to regard the Springfield Democrat as the resident of Capitol Hill who has the most direct line to O'Brien.

The Tough Way. In the heat of battle, when persuasion fails, O'Brien is perfectly willing to play it the tough way. When Louisiana's penny-pinching Representative Otto Passman decided to block a $600 million request for Latin American aid money in his House appropriations subcommittee, O'Brien's operatives went quietly behind his back, lined up enough votes to pass the bill over the chairman's objection; Passman eventually voted for the appropriation himself, rather than have it known he could not control his committee. Again, during the aid-to-education debate, Chicago's Representative Roman Pucinski threatened to kill the public school measure by tagging onto it a parochial school amendment. O'Brien appealed to Chicago Boss Dick Daley, who immediately telephoned Pucinski: "Who sent you there, me or the bishop?" he growled. "And who's going to keep you there, me or the bishop?" Pucinski has since remembered who sent him there. . . .

He does know that there is a time to compromise. Says he: "As realists, we want to get as much of our program through as we can. If you feel that you are getting as much as you can, all right. If you don't get as much as you can you've failed." On that basis, no one can say that Larry O'Brien has failed.

CHAPTER 5

THE PRESIDENCY AS POWER AND MYTH

MANY GOVERNMENTS have officials with the label "President," and every now and then a visit from a foreign dignitary to the White House will be followed by a release embodying some verbal handshaking between "the two Presidents." In point of fact the visiting President, from wherever he may be, may be a totalitarian ruler or he may possess lesser power; in no case will he be a firm analogue to the American President. For the American Presidency is a unique institution; every President comes to office already equipped with all the powers that all his predecessors have held and used—if he can manage to retain and maintain those powers.

Harry Truman once described the Presidency as the place "where the buck stopped." Any commentator on the Truman concept of the Presidency is in somewhat the position of the second lieutenant who took as his subject for a speech to a group "The Military Mistakes of Napoleon Bonaparte." But the analyst may observe, nevertheless, that the presidential figure of speech is inexact. One may wonder whether there is a buck, or whether, instead, there is an unending series of actions, counteractions, challenges, accusations, claims of credit for good intentions and high accomplishments, charges of blame for evil motives and inept performance, cries of havoc, and sounds of accomplishment.

If there is an unemployment, a housing, a defense, or other problem, the President can blame the Congress for not having adopted intact presidential proposals, the Congress can blame the President or some government department or bureau for not having carried out adequately the excellent program it had forwarded. The pressure group can complain that too little or too much of this or that has been done or undone. The courts are also available as objects of denunciation or praise, as are previous Presidents and previous congressmen and political party leaders.

Accordingly, the Presidency is not the terminus of political action in the United States; it is an area within a continuous spiral. What the President proposes stems from another source and is in any event not adopted for all time; the President can pass the buck to Congress, who can pass the buck to an executive agency, who can pass it to an interest group or another instrumentality, who can pass it along or change it or bury it, sometimes in a burning spotlight of public attention, sometimes in other more obscure ways.

The readings below are concerned with major aspects of the presidential campaign, the election machinery, definition and exercise of the presidential power, and "improvements" in the Presidency.

Presidential Campaign Speech: the Art of Persuasion

Shortly before the 1960 presidential election John F. Kennedy spoke at the sixteenth annual Alfred E. Smith dinner, delivering an address that is a work of superb political art. Theodore H. White says that Kennedy had originally been reluctant to accept the invitation to this Catholic event on the ground that his Catholicism would be unnecessarily accentuated. White also remarks that Kennedy must have decided to speak with a light touch, as is indicated by the nature of the speech and the fact that for a couple of days before the dinner Kennedy's aides had been circulating through the press asking, "Do you know any jokes?"

The speech exemplifies some of the principal attributes of presidential campaign tactics: the attempt to gain everybody's favor and the absence of analysis of substantive issues. To the citizen the value of the campaign speech lies in the opportunity to observe the candidate as a man and a personality, rather than as a talking ideology.

[*Freedom of Communications, Final Report of the Senate Committee on Commerce, Prepared by Its Subcommittee of the Subcommittee on Communications: The Speeches, Remarks, Press Conferences, and Statements of Senator John F. Kennedy, August 1 through November 7, 1960,* S. Rep. No. 994, pt. 1, 87th Cong., 1st Sess. (1961), pp. 666–669.]

I am glad to be here at this notable dinner once again and I'm glad that Mr. Nixon is here also.

Now that Cardinal Spellman has demonstrated the proper spirit I assume that shortly I will be invited to a Quaker dinner honoring Herbert Hoover.

Cardinal Spellman is the only man so widely respected in American politics that he could bring together amicably at the same banquet table for the first time in this campaign two political leaders who are increasingly apprehensive about the November election, who have long eyed each other suspiciously and who have disagreed so strongly both publicly and privately —Vice President Nixon and Governor Rockefeller.

Mr. Nixon, like the rest of us, has had his troubles in this campaign. At one point even the *Wall Street Journal* was criticizing his tactics. That's like the *Osservatore Romano* criticizing the Pope. But I think the worst news for the Republicans this week was that Casey Stengel had been fired. It just shows that perhaps experience doesn't count.

On this matter of experience, I had announced earlier this year that if successful, I would not consider campaign contributions as a substitute for experience in appointing ambassadors. Ever since I made that statement, I haven't received one single cent from my father.

One of the inspiring notes that was struck in the last debate was struck by the Vice President in his very moving statement warning the children of the nation and the candidates against the use of profanity by Presidents and ex-Presidents when they're on the stump.

And I know after fourteen years in the Congress with the Vice President that he was very sincere in his views about the use of profanity.

But I am told that a prominent Republican said to him yesterday in Jacksonville, Fla., "Mr. Vice President, that was a damned fine speech." And the Vice President said: "I appreciate the compliment, but not the language." And the Republican went on: "Yes, sir, I liked it so much that I contributed $1,000 to your campaign." And Mr. Nixon replied: "The hell you say."

However, I would not want to give the impression that I am taking former President Truman's use of language lightly. I have sent him the following wire:

> "Dear Mr. President: I have noted with interest your suggestion as to where those who vote for my opponent should go. While I understand and sympathize with your deep motivation, I think it is important that our side try to refrain from raising the religious issue."

One of the subjects that interests candidates and those who write about candidates is whether 1960 will be another 1928. I have had some interest in that question myself. And looking at the speeches of Governor Smith in the 1928 campaign, I am struck by the continuity of the themes.

The 1928 and the 1960 campaigns with all of the obvious differences have much in common. In 1928 as in 1960 the Yankees won the pennant; the Postmaster General was promising efficient mail delivery at last; farm purchasing power was down some 20 per cent in 1928, compared to eight years earlier, just as it is today; 3,000,000 people had left the farms in that period, just as they have in the last eight years.

The stock market was unstable, and two-thirds of all corporate profits went to one-fourth of 1 per cent of the corporations.

In September, 1928, the Republican candidate for the Presidency declared: "Real wages have improved more during the past seven and one-half years than in any similar period in the history of our country."

He spoke of the country's unparalleled progress. He stressed American comfort, hope and confidence for the future are immeasurably higher than they were seven and a half years ago.

The Democratic candidate in 1928 questioned how stable our prosperity was. He pointed to the pockets of distress. He warned of a farm depression. He criticized Administration farm vetoes. He stressed, and I quote him, "the necessity for the restoration of cordial relations with Latin America." And he called for more effective action against disarmament.

The Democratic nominee in 1928 spoke thirty years ago tonight about building a stronger America, strengthening not only our economy but our sense of moral purpose and our public duty.

In all of these and other ways 1960 and 1928 may be sisters under the skin. Some say that this will also be true when the ballots are counted, that the religious convictions of the candidates will influence the outcome more than their convictions on the issues.

But this is where I believe that 1928 and 1960 are very different.

Regardless of the outcome and regardless of these similarities, I do not believe the American voter in 1960 is the same as the American voter of 1928, for we live in a different world. There are a billion more people crowding our globe and every American can hear the rumble of a distant drum.

The next President will have a budget twenty-five times as large as that of the candidates in Al Smith's time.

And he will face problems unprecedented in that time or at any time in our long history—automation and unemployment, farm surpluses and food shortages; a high cost of living in the midst of an economic slump; new nations, new leaders—the world is different across the street and on the other side of the moon.

The white race is in the minority, the free enterprise system is in the minority and the majority are looking at us harder and longer than they ever looked before.

The people who live in the tenements of Africa and Asia and Latin America want to fight their way out of the slums. The Lower East Side of the world is looking for help, and unlike 1928, the Lower East Side of the World has a voice and a vote.

The world is large, John Boyle O'Reilly wrote: "The world is large when weary leagues two loving hearts divide, but the world is small when your enemy is loose on the other side."

In 1960 as never before our enemy is loose on the other side. In 1928, the voters, perhaps, could be excused for not seeing the storm coming—the depression, the Japanese conquest of Manchuria, Hitler's rise and all the rest.

But in 1960, the citizens of this country face the great question of whether freedom will not only endure but whether it will also prevail.

Thus, 1960 and 1928 are very different.

It will be with this view of America that we shall accept the fortunes of Nov. 8, 1960, be they favorable or unfavorable—good or bad. The American people in 1960 see the storm coming. They see the perils ahead. 1960 is not 1928.

I am confident that whatever their verdict, Republican or Democratic, myself or Mr. Nixon, that their judgment will be based not on any extraneous issue but on the real issues of our time, on what is best for our country, on the hard facts that face us, on the convictions of the candidates, and their parties, and on their ability to interpret them.

When this happens then the bitter memory of 1928 will begin to fade and all that will remain will be the figure of Al Smith, large against the horizon, true, courageous and honest, who in the words of the Cardinal, "served his country well. And having served his country well, nobly served his God."

Accepting an Election Defeat (or Victory): the American Way

Richard M. Nixon delivered these gracious comments on the occasion early in 1961 of the joint session of the House and Senate held for the purpose of counting the electoral votes cast in the 1960 presidential election. As presiding officer of the Senate, Nixon had the responsibility of announcing the outcome of the vote, and thus exemplifying one of the central characteristics of the American democracy: the good grace with which the loser accepts the election results instead of setting out immediately to remedy through violence the judgment of the electorate.

At the same time, in the United States the winner tolerates the continued efforts of losing candidates and groups to organize, to propagandize, and to campaign again.

Here is illustrated no small glory of the American governmental system: the civilized way in which presidential changes are sought and made, indeed, one of the main ways in which a free society stays free.

[Remarks by the Vice President of the United States, *Congressional Record,* Jan. 6, 1961, p. 284.]

. . . THE VICE PRESIDENT. Mr. Speaker, since this is an unprecedented situation I would like to ask permission to impose upon the time of the Members of this Congress to make a statement which in itself is somewhat unprecedented.

I promise to be brief. I shall be guided by the 1-minute rule of the House rather than the unlimited time rule that prevails in the Senate.

This is the first time in 100 years that a candidate for the Presidency announced the result of an election in which he was defeated and announced the victory of his opponent. I do not think we could have a more striking and eloquent example of the stability of our constitutional system and of the proud tradition of the American people of developing, respecting, and honoring institutions of self-government.

In our campaigns, no matter how hard fought they may be, no matter how close the election may turn out to be, those who lose accept the verdict, and support those who win. And I would like to add that, having served now in Government for 14 years, a period which began in the House just 14 years ago, almost to the day, which continued with 2 years in the Senate and 8 years as Vice President, as I complete that 14-year period it is indeed a very great honor to me to extend to my colleagues in the House and Senate on both sides of the aisle who have been elected; to extend to John F. Kennedy and Lyndon Johnson, who have been elected President and Vice President of the United States, my heartfelt best wishes, as all of you work in a cause that is bigger than any man's ambition, greater than any party. It is the cause of freedom, of justice, and peace for all mankind.

It is in that spirit that I now declare that John F. Kennedy has been elected President of the United States, and Lyndon B. Johnson Vice President of the United States.

Political Science Professors Look at the Electoral College

Senator Estes Kefauver, committee chairman, mailed a questionnaire to political scientists who were heads of departments of political science or government in American universities and colleges. The purpose of the questionnaire was to poll the political scientists for their opinions of various plans which have been proposed for "reform" of the electoral college.

Among other points that emerge from the replies, two are prominent. One is the considerable agreement among political scientists that some sort of change should be made in the current method of electing the President set forth in the Constitution. Agreement by nine out of ten Americans on any complex issue is surprising; agreement by nine out of ten political scientists on the inadequacy of a present constitutional arrangement is extraordinary indeed. If one of the greatest capacities of the expert is his ability to differ with his fellows, it is the political expert who is especially competent at finding diagnoses and therapies alternative to those of his colleagues.

A second point that comes out of the tabulation is the wide disagreement among the political scientists as to the constitutional change in the method of electing the President that should be adopted. Particular interest is attached to the finding that the political scientists are evenly distributed between favoring and opposing a proportional division system by which each state's electoral votes would be divided according to percentages of the popular vote; this proposed fair-looking system has found vocal support among congressmen and people generally in the community.

[*Nomination and Election of President and Vice President and Qualifications for Voting, Hearings before the Subcommittee on Constitutional Amendments of the Senate Committee on the Judiciary,* 87th Cong., 1st Sess., pt. 3 (1961), pp. 692–694.]

ANSWERS TO POLITICAL SCIENTISTS' QUESTIONNAIRE

Question No. 1. Do you favor any amendment to the Constitution which would change our present method of electing the President?

	Number	Percentage of total
Yes	230	90.6
No	24	9.4

Question No. 2. Do you feel the office of elector should be abolished?

	Number	Percentage of total
Yes	182	71.7
No	62	24.4
Unanswered . .	10	3.9

Question No. 3. Do you favor retaining the present electoral voting strengths of the States?

	Number	Percentage of total
Yes	154	60.7
No	85	33.4
Unanswered . .	15	5.9

Question No. 4. Do you favor election of the President by national direct popular vote?

	Number	Percentage of total
Yes	87	34.2
No	160	63.0
Unanswered . .	7	2.8

Question No. 5. Do you favor a proportional division system by which each State's electoral votes would be divided according to percentages of the popular vote?

	Number	Percentage of total
Yes	119	46.9
No	124	48.8
Unanswered . .	11	4.3

Question No. 6. Do you favor a proportional division system which would divide only the electoral votes of States in which the minority candidate receives some minimum percentage of the popular vote?

	Number	Percentage of total
Yes	47	18.5
No	188	74.0
Unanswered . .	19	7.5

Question No. 7. Do you favor the district system under which two presidential electors would be selected at large and the balance in single-elector districts in each State?

	Number	Percentage of total
Yes	41	16.2
No	199	78.3
Unanswered . .	14	5.5

Question No. 8. Do you favor some plan other than those mentioned?

	Number	Percentage of total
Yes	5	2.0
No	187	74.3
Unanswered . .	60	23.7

Question No. 9. Do you favor any change in the present method of election of the President in the House of Representatives when no candidate receives a majority?

	Number	Percentage of total
Yes	142	55.9
No	96	37.8
Unanswered . .	16	6.3

Question No. 10. If so, do you favor election by a majority of the House and Senate in joint assembly with each member having one vote?

	Number	Percentage of total
Yes	130	51.2
No	69	27.2
Unanswered . .	55	21.6

Assessing an Election System

Whether or not the student accepts Prof. David B. Truman's conclusions in the letter below, he should find highly instructive this example of systematic and analytic thinking about election systems, a subject whose obscurity is matched by its importance. An effective system of elections has the notable characteristic of producing responsible leadership, but rounding out the essentials of optimum national election arrangements are other attributes: simplicity, speed, intelligibility, coherence with the selection of congressmen.

Of especial interest is the point that the all-or-none system of distributing electoral-college votes in presidential elections is a method for giving to urban areas considerable weight which helps to balance the substantial weight given to rural areas in the Congress. Correlated with this numerical advantage given to the highly industrialized states with large populations is the fact that such states tend to have concentrations of minority groups, so that in effect the procedure of giving all the electoral votes to the candidate with the greatest number of popular votes in any states is a way of giving great political importance to minority groups, such as Catholics, Negroes, and Jews.

Behind ideas of balance and equity and accuracy and speed in political arithmetic lie the problems in the Executive and in Congress of support for and opposition to the great social and other programs of our time.

[*Nomination and Election of President and Vice President and Qualifications for Voting, Hearings before the Subcommittee on Constitutional Amendments of the Senate Committee on the Judiciary*, 87th Cong., 1st Sess., pt. 3 (1961), pp. 673–676.]

. . . Columbia University in the City of New York,
New York, N.Y., July 7, 1961

Senator Estes Kefauver,
Chairman, Subcommittee on Constitutional Amendments, Committee on the Judiciary, U.S. Senate, Washington, D.C.

Dear Senator Kefauver: I am very glad to respond to the request of Mr. James C. Kirby that I convey to you in writing my comments on various of the Senate joint resolutions concerning Federal elections that are currently before your subcommittee. I regret that I was unable to accept his invitation to testify in person.

With your permission I shall confine my observations to the 12 resolutions dealing with the nomination and election of the President and Vice President. . . .

In assessing these proposals I start from four general assumptions that I should like to regard as principles. First, an election system, especially one designed for the choice of a Chief Executive, should be as simple as possible. A simple scheme has the double virtue of being readily comprehensible to the electorate, an intangible but significant value, and of offering a minimum number of points for dispute, for litigation, or for improper manipulation. Second, an appropriate system should provide for making the choice of a President as quickly as possible and for making it with as little residual doubt as possible concerning the legality of the winner's title. I need not tell you that in the life of any political system occasions for a change of government are critical. Perhaps especially under a system of popular elections, operating in conditions of acute and chronic international tension, it is often more important that a decision concerning the constitution of the legitimate government be made quickly and with finality than that it conform precisely to some standard of equity. Third, in an arrangement of popular elections it is imperative that the system foster and protect stable and responsible leadership in the party structure. For an electorate to choose wisely, its decision should be able to take account not merely of the qualifications of two individuals but as well of the sets of persons with whom they will principally have to work if they are elected. Where the latter are subject to constant change, the evidence demonstrates beyond much doubt that responsibility is undermined. Fourth, a system for choosing the President cannot properly be assessed apart from that for selecting the Members of the Congress, and any system that is defensible must provide for an appropriate balance within the system as a whole, so that no major interest in the country, especially none which is peculiarly exposed to problems of critical dimension, should be without effective voice.

In connection with this last assumption it is appropriate to say that no one can with complete confidence predict the full range of consequences that may result from the operation of any untried system. Since, as I would argue, the limitations of the present arrangements are known and are far from intolerable, the burden of proof lies with the sponsors of change to demonstrate that their proposals would not predictably produce disadvantages of greater magnitude. . . .

The Myth of Presidential Power

The substance of a discussion on the *Third Programme,* a series intended for what some Americans would call "eggheads," this article is taken from *The Listener,* a British periodical which regularly prints the texts of talks given over the British Broadcasting Corporation. Norman Hunt, the author, is a lecturer in politics at Oxford University. It is of interest that Hunt's effort to explore the presidential power becomes principally an examination of executive-legislative relationships.

Accustomed to thinking of the President as the most powerful politician in the world, the American may be taken aback at the apparent contradiction in Hunt's conclusion that the President "simply will not have the power a British Prime Minister can command."

In any case, the American reader is apt to think of monumental differences between the British and American contexts which have helped produce the quite intelligible differences between the Presidency and the Prime Ministry in action: the relative homogeneity of the British as compared with the comparative heterogeneity of the American people in terms of ethnic origin, race, religion; the relatively small size of Britain in contrast to the continental sprawl of the United States, the unitary system in Britain as against American federalism, the historical development of the British political party arrangements which gave the British a disciplined party system so different from the freewheeling nature of American parties; differences in economics; social attitudes which have carried with them British-American distinctions in viewing and operating the top executive in the two countries.

The import of these differences is not necessarily that the Americans and the British ought to exchange their concepts of optimum executive-power arrangements; much more useful for the student is an understanding of why the Presidency is what it is, and whether modifications would be useful or possible.

[Norman Hunt, "The Myth of Presidential Power," *The Listener,* Jan. 26, 1961, pp. 163–165.]

For a country that worships progress the United States possesses a Constitution which in some fundamental respects is downright archaic—especially where it affects the Presidency. For the eighteenth-century Constitution makes it impossible for a twentieth-century President to live up to his responsibilities. Quite simply, the Founding Fathers gave the President too many duties and too little power.

Today the President's duties are so onerous and varied that they are far beyond the capacity of a single individual. In the modern United States no President, however gifted and hard-working, can be at once titular and ceremonial head of the State, leader of his political party, chief diplomat personally in charge of foreign policy, chief initiator of new domestic policy, Commander-in-Chief of the Armed Forces, and, finally, boss of the vast administrative machine to which he personally makes hundreds of appointments.

When the Constitution was drafted in 1787 it was possible for one man to combine all these roles. Those were spacious and leisurely days; governments were best which governed least; the country consisted merely of thirteen States clustered on the eastern seaboard of the North American continent and separated by 3,000 miles of difficult water from the nearest major foreign power. Since then the world has become dangerously smaller, the United States vastly larger, and the problems of government infinitely more complex. All these changes have made the job of the President much bigger and much more demanding than the Founding Fathers ever imagined. In recent years the President's duties, but not his powers, have been extended considerably. For example, recent legislation requires the President to recommend to Congress whatever action seems necessary to maintain full employment; and he has also been given the ultimate responsibility of being conciliator in labour disputes.

Partly because the Founding Fathers did not realize how big a job the President would eventually have to do, the Constitution is ridiculously sparing in the powers it gives him. A twentieth-century President is also the victim of Montesquieu's blindness and George III's folly. Montesquieu wrongly thought that individual liberty in eighteenth-century England was the product of a strict separation of powers between King, Lords, Commons, and Courts. This became hallowed political dogma which the authors of the United States Constitution uncritically accepted when they drew it up. George III's personal attempt to subvert their liberties seemed only to reinforce Montesquieu's ideas. So they rigidly excluded the President and his advisers from Congress so that each would always be a check on the other.

The Constitution gives the President only three powers which he can use at all independently of Congress. First, he can pardon criminals—but that is hardly important politically. Secondly, he can veto bills passed by Congress; but that is negative rather than positive because the President cannot use the veto to force Congress to act in a particular way. He cannot veto a part of a bill only—so he frequently has to accept an unwanted and even harmful clause in a bill as the price of having any legislation on that subject at all. And ultimately, of course, Congress can override a President's veto if it can muster a two-thirds majority against him.

The third power which the President can wield at all independently of Congress is the so-called "executive power." This is fairly nebulous, and, strictly speaking, does not give the President much more than the duty of seeing—in the words of the Constitution—"that the laws be faithfully executed." Here, it is true, there is some scope of political manoeuvre, for the President can sometimes decide how fully and how strictly a law is to be implemented. The Sherman Anti-Trust Act is a good example of this. There have been times when American Presidents have enforced it vigorously and gone in for trust-busting in a big way—as Theodore Roosevelt did. At other times, Presidents have virtually ignored the Act—as happened in the nineteen-twenties. More recently, President Eisenhower simply decided not to spend the extra money Congress thought ought to be devoted to the air force. But the scope for Presidential initiative here is limited. Theodore Roosevelt could prosecute the trusts only because Congress had given the necessary authority; and the Anti-Trust Act could hardly have been neglected if Congress had otherwise determined.

So the President's independent powers amount to little. In fact, they are still more restricted than I have so far suggested. Even within his own executive branch of government, where the President is at least the nominal boss, there are important limitations. All his main appointments have to be approved by the Senate, and this approval is by no means automatic. Then the President has to cope with the Independent Regulatory Commissions. These bodies, set up by Congress to regulate such things as inter-State commerce, tariffs and communications, are beyond Presidential control. The President can appoint the commissioners, but he cannot dismiss them, nor can he give them instructions. It is rather as if in England the Board of Trade and the Ministry of Transport were independent of the Cabinet and the Prime Minister.

Powers Shared with Congress

The President does have more important powers than I have so far mentioned—power to formulate general policy, for example, and financial powers —but these are in a real sense shared powers—they are shared with Congress; and they are shared in such a way that the last word is usually with Congress and not with the President. In the final analysis, therefore, the power of the President of the United States depends on his ability to get his way with Congress.

The problem here is not merely whether the President's party has a majority in both the Senate and the House of Representatives—or even how big those majorities may be. For the fact is that no Congress, whatever its political complexion, likes to rubber-stamp Presidential proposals. Congress considers it is doing its job only if it behaves independently of the President —and this means thwarting him as much as possible. This natural tension between President and Congress is heightened by their representing different and often opposing forces. Congress is composed of men who are, and who think of themselves as, the representatives in Washington of the local interest of their district or State—interests which are now of a continental diversity; the President, in contrast, is the embodiment of the national interest. Then again, Congress over-represents rural areas, while urban votes are the decisive factor in electing the President.

That hallowed but ridiculous principle, the separation of powers, gives full play to these natural antagonisms. In England, where we have the good sense not to exclude members of the government from Parliament, an M.P. usually supports his Prime Minister's proposals because that is a recognized way of eventually getting a place in the Cabinet; in any event, if he votes against his government, it may fall. For a Member of Congress, thanks to the separation of powers, the situation is totally different. Since he is excluded from the government, support for it will not bring him promotion. Nor will it bring him headlines in the national and local newspapers. A Congressman gets the biggest headlines when he opposes the President. Since there is no possibility that such opposition can bring the government down before the end of its fixed four-year term, there is little wonder that Congress can indulge its natural inclinations to behave as independently of the President as possible.

Traditionally, the President and Congress find it easier to co-operate with each other during the first few months after the election, the so-called "honeymoon period." Then, if the President's party has a majority in Congress, the relationship is amicable, if not exactly loving. But President Truman made the best comment on this when he said: "If that's the honeymoon, then God help marriage."

What power, then, has the President to overcome the constitutionally inborn waywardness of his Congressional partner? The short answer is—none at all. Though the President and Congress are, in all that really matters, indissolubly joined together for better or worse, there is no promise that Congress will love, honour, or obey—and, worse still, there is no constitutional means of enforcing such obedience. All that the President can do is to try to use influence.

The President's View of His Job

Here a good deal will depend on the President's own view of his job. Presidents like Theodore Roosevelt, Woodrow Wilson, and Franklin Roosevelt believed that they should provide strong and decisive leadership. As Theodore Roosevelt put it: "My belief was that it was not only his [the President's] right but his duty to do anything that the needs of the nation demanded unless such action was forbidden by the Constitution or by the Laws." President Wilson endorsed this when he wrote: "The President is at liberty both in law and conscience to be as big a man as he can. His capacity will set the limit." The high-water mark in this sort of attitude was reached when Franklin Roosevelt once said: "In the event that the Congress should fail to act, and act adequately, I shall assume the responsibility and I will act."

Not unnaturally, Presidents with these views have been much more influential than men like President Taft and President Coolidge. Taft's belief was, as he put it: "The President can exercise no power which cannot be fairly and reasonably traced to some specific grant of power, or justly implied and included within such express grant as proper and necessary." And Coolidge's line was even weaker: "I have never felt," he wrote on one occasion, "that it was my duty to attempt to coerce senators or representatives or to make reprisals. The people sent them to Washington. I felt I had discharged my duty when I had done the best I could with them." President Eisenhower has, for the most part, behaved more like a Taft or a Coolidge than a Roosevelt.

But even Franklin Roosevelt, for all his bold beliefs in Presidential initiative, found there were times when he could accomplish little—though sometimes, of course, he seemed to be a virtual dictator. Nothing illustrates the fundamental inadequacy of Presidential power better than these fluctuations.

Fluctuations in Roosevelt's Influence

Roosevelt's influence was at its maximum between 1933 and 1936 and again from 1940 to his death, primarily because the country was in a state of crisis. In 1933 the crisis was economic: banks were toppling; there were over 12,000,000 unemployed. Congress, not knowing what to do, virtually abdicated its functions and did what the President recommended—especially during the famous first "hundred days." The crisis of the second world war gave Roosevelt similar authority. And by virtue of being Commander-in-Chief, Roosevelt was able personally to control the economy in ways which would certainly not have been accepted in peace time. Yet in the years between these two periods of national crisis—that is, from 1936 to 1940—Roosevelt's influence was considerably reduced, and there was nothing he could do about it. He sought to dominate Congress as completely as he succeeded in doing during the two crisis periods; he used the same tactics and methods—but they no longer had the same effect. For in the last analysis, Roosevelt's political armoury for the battle with Congress consisted only of the arts of personal persuasion. And when there is no national crisis these are not enough.

Of the aids to such personal persuasion patronage was, perhaps, the most important then, as it is now. The thousands of jobs which a new President has to fill are a powerful means of influencing Congressmen who have so many and such deserving constituents. Franklin Roosevelt showed a nice appreciation of this when, on taking over the Presidency in 1933, he announced that the distribution of patronage would be delayed until Congress had passed the necessary emergency measures. But generally, once the jobs have been distributed, the President's influence begins to decline. Gratitude is not the most powerful of human emotions, especially in the breasts of American Congressmen. And now that a President is restricted by the Constitution to two terms of office only, patronage is even more of a wasting asset than it used to be.

Apart from this wasting asset what other means can a President use to get his way with Congress? He can appeal to public opinion—as Franklin Roosevelt did in his famous radio fireside chats; here Roosevelt in his first term mobilized such public support for his proposals that Congressmen found it expedient to do as he wanted. But a President cannot do this too frequently; and whatever impact he makes depends greatly on his personality. Then there is the regular press conference, which is another means of seeking to mobilize public opinion behind the President. Mr. Kennedy's decision that some of his press conferences will be televised live will certainly increase their impact on the public. But even this will hardly guarantee that Mr. Kennedy will get his way with Congress.

All Presidents, therefore, devote much time to man-management—the men in question being Congressmen. President Coolidge used an institution known as the "White House breakfast"—and the newspapers made a great deal of the President meeting political leaders over sausages and griddle cakes. But they were not a great success politically—or even socially, for that matter. Nor do President Eisenhower's breakfasts seem to have been more effective. Perhaps breakfast is the wrong time to appeal to a man's better nature anyway. Other more successful methods have ranged from the strategic timing of Presidential messages to Congress, and the delivery of these messages in person, to regular interviews with the more important Senators and Representatives. But whatever the techniques, they are a totally inadequate basis for Presidential power. There is no guarantee that they will be successful; they place inordinate demands on the President's time; and they make a President devote too much of his thinking to tactics instead of to policies. President Truman summarized it all admirably when he said: "I sit here all day trying to persuade people to do the things they ought to have sense enough to do without my persuading them. . . . That's all the powers of the President amount to."

How will all this affect President Kennedy? Clearly the Constitution does not give him anything like enough independent authority to ensure that he will be as powerful a President as he would obviously like to be. But he will inherit from the Eisenhower regime two enormously valuable legacies—a greatly strengthened Cabinet and the National Security Council. The American Cabinet has never been as powerful an instrument as its British counterpart. Even so, it is an extraordinary fact that only under Eisenhower was it equipped with a secretariat—a job Lloyd George belatedly did for the British Cabinet as long ago as 1916. Eisenhower has also similarly strengthened and developed the National Security Council which, since its formation in 1947, has become a sort of super-Cabinet. These common-sense innovations have had two obvious and important consequences. Before taking vital decisions the President can now be reasonably certain that he has before him, in the Cabinet and the National Security Council, all the relevant information and points of view. Secondly, when he has approved the decisions arrived at in these two bodies, it is now much more likely that the decisions will be followed by the appropriate co-ordinated action in the departments and agencies concerned.

These Eisenhower legacies will not, of course, give Mr. Kennedy any new constitutional powers, but they will enable him to wield the existing powers more effectively, particularly in the sphere of foreign affairs. For here Congress is not the heavy millstone round the President's neck that it is in home affairs, though it could play havoc with a foreign policy which needed a lot of dollars; and the Senate can always refuse to ratify a treaty—as it did with the Treaty of Versailles. But the Eisenhower legacies will not help Mr. Kennedy with the Independent Regulatory Commissions or ensure that he will get his way with Congress in home affairs. At one time Mr. Kennedy no doubt had in mind trying to emulate Franklin Roosevelt's first hundred days when Roosevelt bombarded Congress with a whole series of radical measures which were meekly accepted. But today, Mr. Kennedy has not the great popular majority behind him that Roosevelt had; and so far there is no national crisis to make Congress stampede in the direction Mr. Kennedy wants. There is the further handicap, too, that within Congress the all-powerful committee chairmanships are for the most part held by Southern Democrats strongly opposed to the sort of liberal legislation Mr. Kennedy seems to have in mind; although here the influence of Vice-President Lyndon Johnson will no doubt help. Yet this provides a final illustration of the limitations on Presidential power. The fact has to be faced that Mr. Kennedy simply will not have the power a British Prime Minister can command.

Senator John F. Kennedy Discusses the Presidency

Well before his nomination and election to the Presidency, Senator Kennedy described his conception of the nature of the nation's highest office. Any student who sees the President of the United States as a disembodied omnipresence and omniscience should have his preconceptions thoroughly jolted by this speech.

[Address by John F. Kennedy, *Congressional Record,* Jan. 18, 1960, pp. A353–354.]

. . . Text of Senator Kennedy's Speech

The modern presidential campaign covers every issue in and out of the platform from cranberries to creation. But the public is rarely alerted to a candidate's views about the central issue on which all the rest turn. That central issue—and the point of my comments this noon—is not the farm problem or defense or India. It is the presidency itself.

Of course a candidate's views on specific policies are important, but Theodore Roosevelt and William Howard Taft shared policy views with entirely different results in the White House. Of course it is important to elect a good man with good intentions, but Woodrow Wilson and Warren G. Harding were both good men of good intentions; so were Lincoln and Buchanan; but there is a Lincoln Room in the White House and no Buchanan Room.

The history of this Nation—its brightest and its bleakest pages—has been written largely in terms of the different views our Presidents have had of the Presidency itself. This history ought to tell us that the American people in 1960 have an imperative right to know what any man bidding for the Presidency thinks about the place he is bidding for, whether he is aware of and willing to use the powerful resources of that office; whether his model will be Taft or Roosevelt, Wilson or Harding.

Not since the days of Woodrow Wilson has any candidate spoken on the presidency itself before the votes have been irrevocably cast. Let us hope that the 1960 campaign, in addition to discussing the familiar issues where our positions too often blur, will also talk about the presidency itself, as an instrument for dealing with those issues, as an office with varying roles, powers, and limitations.

Criticizes Eisenhower

During the past 8 years, we have seen one concept of the Presidency at work. Our needs and hopes have been eloquently stated—but the initiative and follow-through have too often been left to others. And too often his own objectives have been lost by the President's failure to override objections from within his own party, in the Congress or even in his Cabinet.

The American people in 1952 and 1956 may have preferred this detached, limited concept of the Presidency after 20 years of fast-moving, creative Presidential rule. Perhaps historians will regard this as necessarily one of those frequent periods of consolidation, a time to draw breath, to recoup our national energy. To quote the state of the Union message: "No Congress . . . on surveying the state of the Nation, has met with a more pleasing prospect than that which appears at the present time."

Unfortunately this is not Mr. Eisenhower's last message to the Congress, but Calvin Coolidge's. He followed to the White House Mr. Harding, whose sponsor declared very frankly that the times did not demand a first-rate President. If true, the times and the man met.

But the question is what do the times—and the people—demand for the next 4 years in the White House?

Rules Out Casual Bystander

They demand a vigorous proponent of the national interest—not a passive broker for conflicting private interests. They demand a man capable of acting as the commander in chief of the Grand Alliance, not merely a bookkeeper who feels that his work is done when the numbers on the balance sheet come out even. They demand that he be the head of a responsible party, not rise so far above politics as to be invisible—a man who will formulate and fight for legislative policies, not be a casual bystander to the legislative process.

Today a restricted concept of the Presidency is not enough. For beneath today's surface gloss of peace and prosperity are increasingly dangerous, unsolved, long-postponed problems—problems that will inevitably explode to the surface during the next 4 years of the next administration—the growing missile gap, the rise of Communist China, the despair of the underdeveloped nations, the explosive situations in Berlin and in the Formosa Straits, the deterioration of NATO, the lack of an arms control agreement, and all the domestic problems of our farms, cities, and schools.

This administration has not faced up to these and other problems. Much has been said—but I am reminded of the old Chinese proverb: "There is a great deal of noise on the stairs but nobody comes into the room."

The President's state of the Union message reminded me of the exhortation from "King Lear" that goes: "I will do such things—what they are I know not . . . but they shall be the wonders of the earth."

In the decade that lies ahead—in the challenging revolutionary sixties—the American Presidency will demand more than ringing manifestoes issued from the rear of the battle. It will demand that the President place himself in the very thick of the fight, that he care passionately about the fate of the people he leads, that he be willing to serve them at the risk of incurring their momentary displeasure.

As Chief Executive

Whatever the political affiliation of our next President, whatever his views may be on all the issues and problems that rush in upon us, he must above all be the Chief Executive in every sense of the word. He must be prepared to exercise the fullest powers of his office—all that are specified and some that are not. He must master complex problems as well as receive one-page memorandums. He must originate action as well as study groups. He must reopen the channels of communication between the world of thought and the seat of power.

Ulysses Grant considered the President "a purely administrative officer." If he administered the Government departments efficiently, delegated his functions smoothly, and performed his ceremonies of state with decorum and grace, no more was to be expected of him. But that is not the place the Presidency was meant to have in American life. The President is alone, at the top—the loneliest job there is, as Harry Truman has said.

If there is destructive dissension among the services, he alone can step in and straighten it out—instead of waiting for unanimity. If administrative agencies are not carrying out their mandate—if a brushfire threatens some part of the globe—he alone can act, without waiting for the Congress. If his farm program fails, he alone deserves the blame, not his Secretary of Agriculture.

"The President is at liberty, both in law and conscience, to be as big a man as he can." So wrote Prof. Woodrow Wilson. But President Woodrow Wilson discovered that to be a big man in the White House inevitably brings cries of dictatorship.

So did Lincoln and Jackson and the two Roosevelts. And so may the next occupant of that office, if he is the man the times demand. But how much better it would be, in the turbulent sixties, to have a Roosevelt or a Wilson than to have another James Buchanan, cringing in the White House, afraid to move.

Nor can we afford a Chief Executive who is praised primarily for what he did not do, the disasters he prevented, the bills he vetoed—a President wishing his subordinates would produce more missiles or build more schools. We will need instead what the Constitution envisioned: a Chief Executive who is the vital center of action in our whole scheme of Government.

As Legislative Leader

This includes the legislative process as well. The President cannot afford—for the sake of the office as well as the Nation—to be another Warren G. Harding, described by one backer as a man who "would, when elected, sign whatever bill the Senate sent him—and not send bills for the Senate to pass." Rather he must know when to lead the Congress, when to consult it and when he should act alone.

Having served 14 years in the legislative branch, I would not look with favor upon its domination by the Executive. Under our government of "power as the rival of power," to use Hamilton's phrase, Congress must not surrender its responsibilities. But neither should it dominate. However large its share in the formulation of domestic programs, it is the President alone who must make the major decisions of our foreign policy.

That is what the Constitution wisely commands. And, even domestically, the President must initiate policies and devise laws to meet the needs of the Nation. And he must be prepared to use all the resources of his office to insure the enactment of that legislation—even when conflict is the result.

By the end of his term Theodore Roosevelt was not popular in the Congress—particularly when he criticized an amendment to the Treasury appropriation which forbade the use of Secret Service men to investigate Congressmen.

And the feeling was mutual, Roosevelt saying: "I do not much admire the Senate, because it is such a helpless body when efficient work is to be done."

Quotes Wilson on Senate

And Woodrow Wilson was even more bitter after his frustrating quarrels. Asked if he might run for the Senate in 1920, he replied: "Outside of the United States, the Senate does not amount to a damn. And inside the United States the Senate is mostly despised. They haven't had a thought down there in 50 years."

But, however bitter their farewells, the facts of the matter are that Roosevelt and Wilson did get things done—not only through their Executive powers but through the Congress as well. Calvin Coolidge, on the other hand, departed from Washington with cheers of Congress still ringing in his ears. But when his World Court bill was under fire on Capitol Hill he sent no messages, gave no encouragement to the bill's leaders, and paid little or no attention to the whole proceeding—and the cause of world justice was set back.

To be sure, Coolidge had held the usual White House breakfasts with congressional leaders—but they were aimed, as he himself said, at "good fellowship," not a discussion of "public business." And at his press conferences, according to press historians, where he preferred to talk about the local flower show and its exhibits, reporters who finally extracted from him a single sentence—"I'm against that bill"—would rush to file tongue-in-cheek dispatches, proclaiming that: "President Coolidge, in a fighting mood, today served notice on Congress that he intended to combat, with all the resources at his command, the pending bill. . . ."

But in the coming years we will need a real fighting mood in the White House—a man who will not retreat in the face of pressure from his congressional leaders—who will not let down those supporting his views on the floor. Divided Government over the past 6 years has only been further confused by this lack of legislative leadership. To restore it next year will help restore purpose to both the Presidency and the Congress.

As Party Leader

The facts of the matter are that legislative leadership is not possible without party leadership, in the most political sense—and Mr. Eisenhower prefers to stay above politics (although a weekly news magazine last fall reported the startling news, and I quote, that "President Eisenhower is emerging as a major political figure"). When asked, early in his first term, how he liked the "game of politics," he replied with a frown that his questioner was using a derogatory phrase. "Being President," he said, "is a great experience . . . but the word 'politics' . . . I have no great liking for that."

But no President, it seems to me, can escape politics. He has not only been chosen by the Nation—he has been chosen by his party. And if he insists that he is "President of all the people" and should, therefore, offend none of them—if he blurs the issues and differences between the parties—if he neglects the party machinery and avoids his party's leadership—then he has not only weakened the political party as an instrument of the democratic process—he has dealt a blow to the democratic process itself.

I prefer the example of Abe Lincoln, who loved politics with the passion of a born practitioner. For example, he waited up all night in 1863 to get the crucial returns on the Ohio governorship. When the Unionist candidate was elected, Lincoln wired: "Glory to God in the highest. Ohio has saved the Nation."

As a Moral Leader

But the White House is not only the center of political leadership. It must be the center of moral leadership—a "bully pulpit," as Theodore Roosevelt described it. For only the President represents the national interest. And upon him alone converge all the needs and aspirations of all parts of the country, all departments of the Government, all nations of the world.

It is not enough merely to represent prevailing sentiment—to follow McKinley's practice, as described by Joe Cannon, of "keeping his ear so close to the ground he got it full of grasshoppers." We will need in the sixties a President who is willing and able to summon his national constituency to its finest hour—to alert the people to our dangers and our opportunities—to demand of them the sacrifices that will be necessary. Despite the increasing evidence of a lost national purpose and a soft national will, F.D.R.'s words in his first inaugural still ring true: "In every dark hour of our national life, a leadership of frankness and vigor has met with that understanding and support of the people themselves which is essential to victory."

Roosevelt fulfilled the role of moral leadership. So did Wilson and Lincoln, Truman and Jackson and Teddy Roosevelt. They led the people as well as the Government—they fought for great ideals as well as bills. And the time has come to demand that kind of leadership again.

And so, as this vital campaign begins, let us discuss the issues the next President will face—but let us also discuss the powers and tools with which we must face them.

For we must endow that office with extraordinary strength and vision. We must act in the image of Abraham Lincoln summoning his wartime Cabinet o a meeting on the Emancipation Proclamation. That Cabinet had been arefully chosen to please and reflect many elements in the country. But "I ave gathered you together," Lincoln said, "to hear what I have written own. I do not wish your advice about the main matter—that I have determined for myself."

And later, when he went to sign after several hours of exhausting handhaking that had left his arm weak, he said to those present: "If my name oes down in history, it will be for this act. My whole soul is in it. If my and trembles when I sign this proclamation, all who examine the document ereafter will say: 'He hesitated.'"

But Lincoln's hand did not tremble. He did not hesitate. He did not equivcate. For he was the President of the United States.

It is in this spirit that we must go forth in the coming months and years.

Top Politicians Talk about Presidential Campaigns

The excerpts below are from hearings held before a Senate subcommittee concerned with proposed amendments to or improvements in Federal election laws. The first statement is by John M. Bailey, chairman of the Democratic National Committee both through the 1960 presidential campaign and subsequent to the election of President John F. Kennedy; the second is by Senator Thruston B. Morton of Kentucky, who served as chairman of the Republican National Committee through the Nixon-Kennedy campaign. Discussing such matters as the financing of political campaigns, the relations of television to presidential campaigning and fund raising, increasing participation and turnout in elections, and attitudes toward a national presidential primary, Bailey and Morton complement each other, making interlocking points.

The topics considered here plow close to the center of America's political heart. Money, voting qualifications, nominating processes—these are aspects of American politics that go a long way toward determining what kind of person with what kind of interest can run for public office and win.

Two ramifications of these topics may usefully be identified, and both concern money in politics. First, money is a necessary but insufficient condition to the winning of national elections; after all, people vote as they do for a hundred reasons not intimately connected with the byproducts of a well-financed political campaign; for example, the economic status of the voter, his education, his religion, his residence in a rural or urban area, the political preferences of his friends, his family, the influence of other members of his face-to-face and informal groupings. Yet, it should be added, the potential weight of finances in primary elections is undoubtedly great because the factors that operate in primaries are not these differentiating Democrats from Republicans as in general elections. Studies of the role of finances in elections have investigated general rather than primary elections in which, ordinarily, Democrats oppose Democrats and Republicans compete with Republicans.

There is a second aspect that should be underscored: the issue of money in politics is not the same as the problem of corruption in politics. The cynic who curls his political lip on the assumption that the costs of democracy are the illicit spoils of the inside few who feed at the political finance trough is mistaken.

Nobody has corruption statistics with which to document quantitatively the assertion that American politics is or is not pure in comparison either with other countries or with our own past. But there would seem to be a good case for the conclusion that the politician in a democratic society is likely to behave more nearly in accord with high ethical standards than is the totalitarian leader. The reason is simply stated: only in a democratic society is there full public inspection of the politician's past and present, only in a democracy is there the continuing check of the interest group, the mass media of communications, the competing political party; the point is not that the democratic politician is equipped with especially pure genes, but that he behaves more responsibly than his totalitarian analogue because he has fewer places and ways to hide.

[*Proposed Amendments to and Improvements in the Federal Election Laws, Hearings before the Subcommittee on Privileges and Elections of the Senate Committee on Rules and Administration,* 87th Cong., 1st Sess., pt. 3 (1961), pp. 190–196.]

MR. BAILEY. . . . Political campaigns at every level, whether or not we agree with some of the ways in which they are conducted, are a valuable means of public education. They cause many people to think about Government problems and issues who do not pay much attention to these subjects between campaigns. And it goes without saying that when our country broadened the suffrage, what we had in mind was a popular vote by an informed electorate.

The cost of conducting campaigns has become astronomical with the development and expansion of new media of communication, particularly radio and television, coupled with the rapid growth of our population.

I think that one of the fields in which we should be most interested and in which you gentlemen should be most interested is the cost of communications media today, and I might say, in passing, that one of the interesting features of the cost of those media—and this I know from my own experience as a town chairman and a State chairman—is the fact that for some reason or other radio and TV networks look upon political advertising as seasonal.

That attitude has caused increases in the rates during political campaigns. It is hard enough to raise money, but when you advertise in the radio and TV media they increase their rates with the result that not only have you the original costs but this increased cost, too.

And I think another interesting thing about campaign expenditures is that the only people you do not owe money to after a campaign is over are the news media, the radio and the television people, because they are paid cash on the barrel.

These, I believe, are the reasons why we are now reexamining the traditional methods of raising campaign funds and asking ourselves whether new legislation may not be necessary.

I would like to comment briefly on several proposals.

One proposal, made in several varieties, calls for the allocation of Federal funds to the political parties for presidential campaigns. I support such an allocation of Federal funds. I think the parties should account for the manner in which these funds are expended, but I do not think the Federal funds should be earmarked for any special purpose.

I wrote that last night but since then I have thought it over and I believe, Senators, that we would be better off to have a drawing account if the Federal Government is going to appropriate $1, $2, or $3 million, so that we would then have the right to draw against that fund by presenting bills to some accounting office.

I think there would be a better public feeling if we were allowed so much to spend but were not given the actual money. We would file a bill itemizing so much television time and so much newspaper advertising, for example, and then be reimbursed or paid directly by the Federal Government.

I think the people would feel better that way if the Government gave us a grant of a million, 2 million, or 3 million, or whatever should be decided upon. . . .

Any allocation of Federal funds should be handled in such a way that it would not create a monopoly for the present two major parties and make it difficult or impossible for a new party, supported in its views by a sizable portion of the electorate, to obtain its fair share of Federal funds.

Another proposal calls for either tax deductions or tax credits for political contributions. Since the effort here is to broaden the base of financial participation, I suggest that a tax deduction will not be too helpful, since most taxpayers use the table form or the standard deduction.

I favor a tax credit, to be applied at three levels, for contributions to a national party, a State party, and to Federal candidates. I would suggest that a $5 contribution at each of these levels, or a total of $15 should be deducted directly from the amount owed the Federal Government for income tax.

In other words you have not only a national campaign but campaigns for congressional candidates and State party campaigns. If you allowed a tax credit on those three levels, $5 for national candidates, $5 for congressional candidates, and $5 for the State party, I think you would be getting at the real objective that you are trying to reach.

If the people were allowed a tax credit I think that they would be more willing to make a contribution.

As I said, I would suggest that a $5 contribution at each of those levels, or a total of $15, should be deducted directly from the amount owed the Federal Government for income tax.

We have worked hard and long at the Democratic National Committee to encourage small contributions and to broaden the base of financial support.

We have some support on this idea, but we find that while it looks fine on paper, it does not work out. We now have a $10 membership drive. We sent out 750,000 letters on that drive.

I think we received, at last counting, about 18,000 replies, and our "Dollars for Democrats" is another program which has been good on the basis of getting a lot of people to participate in political activity, but the number of dollars that we receive would in no way run a campaign.

This is one of the problems you find. Many of these ideas follow the Ruml plan, which was to get $5 from everybody, but some of these ideas do not work out and we are lucky to get back our costs.

Every time you start one of those plans you wonder if you will get back as much as it cost you without even adding the man-hours and the expense of headquarters and everything else that go into the program.

We are going to make a drive on our sustaining membership plan, because I think that we can accomplish something but, as I say, out of 750,000 letters—and there is another problem of obtaining good mailing lists. It's very competitive. . . .

Another proposal calls for removing the meaningless and openly evaded ceiling of $3 million on expenditures by the national committees. I urge that a reasonable ceiling be adopted, and at the same time, that we seek some workable way to prohibit unlimited or excessive spending.

You all know, and you have heard it discussed, that the Republican National Committee and the Democratic National Committee are limited to $3 million so they form the Nixon Committee or the Kennedy-Johnson Committee which can then each spend $3 million more. You can form the A committee, the B committee, the C committee, and you can spend as much money as you can collect.

I am not sure—but I think or I understand the limitation goes back to 1939 or 1940 when this present ceiling was set.

SENATOR CANNON. I think it was 1939.

MR. BAILEY. The Hatch Act. Is that not when the Hatch Act was passed?

Of course, expenses have gone up since then. With travel by airplane, with the candidates reaching far and wide, travel expenses are tremendous. Many people may think that candidates should not have to appear everywhere in person, but I do not think there is any substitute for letting the people see the man—the candidate.

You may see him on television and you may hear him on radio, but there is nothing that so stimulates the people's interest as seeing him as he is.

A proposal has been made to shorten the duration of presidential campaigns by legislation. A short campaign would benefit the Democratic Party in the next election, but I believe that the duration of campaigns should be determined by the problems of each party and the interests of the public.

Of course, we have no desire for partisan advantage. The party in power would have a great advantage if the campaign were shortened. I think the Democratic Party had their convention in August in 1956, and my staff tell me that the problems of getting ready are terrific.

This theory of a shorter campaign is fine, but unless you have a cut and dried convention, unless you know who the candidate is going to be, then all the candidates who are in contention must have markups. They have to get everything all set to go.

If you had a presidential convention in September then you would have only September, October, to November and there are brochures, buttons, party platforms, and all kinds of literature and materials to prepare. This is mechanical work which requires time and thought.

The party in power could be working on it for a year and be all ready to go. But what about the party out of power? Who would solve that problem? The candidate would also have that problem.

In Connecticut we used to hold our convention in September and we found that we had to move it back. We now have by law our State nominating conventions between the 1st of June and 15th of July.

As far as actual campaigning goes, I think that no campaign starts, so far as the public is concerned, until after Labor Day. Many times you feel that it doesn't start until after the world series is over and then you have the problem of reaching the great mass of people.

In connection with problems of political fund raising, I would like to suggest that the Congress consider the allocation of Federal funds to cover expenses incurred by an incoming administration between the dates of the election and the inauguration.

Federal funds could be used to cover certain expenses. These expenses will not fall again on the Democratic Party for some time, but we found after President Kennedy was elected that there was a period from November to January in which the Democratic Party had to spend nearly $350,000 while the President was preparing to take over the Government. . . .

I have one final suggestion to offer in connection with encouraging participation—both as contributors and as voters—in presidential campaigns, and this is a little bit aside from the question of campaign expenses.

I would hope that the States will find ways to make it possible for the millions who are now disenfranchised during presidential elections because of unduly restrictive residence requirements and outdated absentee voters laws to cast their votes in the presidential election of 1964. Given a chance to vote, I believe that many of these people would contribute to their parties and their enfranchisement would certainly make the election outcome more truly representative of the will of the people.

I think that we would be encouraged if the States would allow people to vote for the presidential candidate even if they were not eligible to vote for the State or local candidates in presidential years. Many people who move from one State to another, due to the voting requirements, lose their right to vote in the next State so there is no place where they can vote for President.

We offered a constitutional amendment in Connecticut providing for those people to vote for presidential candidates in presidential years who were qualified voters in some other State but had not qualified under our State law.

SENATOR CANNON. One of the proposals that has been under discussion here is that of extending the election period from 1 day to 2 days.

Do you think this might solve part of the problem of greater participation on the part of the voters?

MR. BAILEY. No; I do not think so. I really do not.

I think if you extend it to 2 days, there will be too many problems. What are you going to do with the ballot boxes especially in those towns or States where they vote by paper ballot?

Who is going to watch them all night? And, are you going to lock up the voting machines? Who is going to hold the keys to them?

I think that this is not a problem of voter participation. It is more a problem of educating the people to want to vote.

In certain States you get a great percentage of those who are eligible to vote. In discussing the failure of citizens to vote, and again I must refer to local experience, in Connecticut 89 to 92 percent of the people eligible to vote did vote. You could not do better than that if you held elections for 3 days, but the problem in back of that is, Who are eligible to vote? Whether you call it registration or whatever you call it in the strictness of the voting. Also, there is no uniform voting law.

And there is something else. I come from a State, an old State. We are still bound by our 1818 constitution on the qualifications of voters. They must go to the town hall where they must be sworn in before a majority of the board of elections and they must be physically present there.

Now, in California it is easier. In supermarkets deputy registrars register the voters and we then have more people eligible. We still have, in Connecticut, literacy tests requiring a reading of part of the constitution in English. This makes it very difficult for some of the Puerto Ricans and others who come into our State. I often think that the percentage figure is "pulled out of the air." I often think that there are only so many people voting out of those eligible to vote, and I do not think we use the right words. It is not those "eligible to vote." It is those who could be voters if they were qualified or if they were registered.

I think we get a much greater proportion of those voting who are eligible to vote.

SENATOR CANNON. Would you advocate a Federal law in this respect for uniformity?

MR. BAILEY. I do not think you can get one any more. I think that is a matter for the States. I think, again, that it is a matter of education.

It is still up to the States to set the qualifications of voters.

SENATOR CANNON. It is sort of an endless job.

As you point out, some of the States have such outmoded systems at the present time that it is a question of how you are going to get the States to change, to take action in that particular field. It poses a very real problem.

In referring to expenditures, you say that you would favor adoption of a more reasonable ceiling insofar as the present $3 million expenditure by a national committee is concerned.

What do you consider a "reasonable ceiling"?

MR. BAILEY. Well, to be realistic, what did we spend last time? We spent in the neighborhood of $10 million.

What the Republicans spent, I do not know. And whether or not there ›uld be a lower ceiling than that or whether that could be a realistic ceil-ng is difficult to determine.

How much is really spent on elections today? I think the *New York 'imes* in October said there would be perhaps $100 million spent in the .ection. This is money that is spent by a national committee. It is spent just n a national level. But when you go down to the town committees and the ındidates running for the legislature and for the State senate and for Con-ress and to the State committees, and the independent committees in the tates, you keep adding it up and especially in a two-party State where the ›mpetition is keen with advertising every night in the newspapers and with ›ot announcements which are very expensive—I would say that figure given y the *New York Times* is realistic but that it is not what I believe should e the ceiling.

I think that if there is going to be a proper accounting, the ceiling is just number that you pick out. As I say, we spent, from what I understand om your colleague, Senator Jackson, who was the chairman during the ımpaign, and whatever I say, is hearsay, because I was doing other things -that it was in the neighborhood of $10 million.

SENATOR CANNON. You also indicated that we should seek some workable 'ay to prohibit unlimited or excessive spending and, of course, if that is one then, perhaps, the need for the limit is—

MR. BAILEY. Is reduced.

SENATOR CANNON. Reduced.

MR. BAILEY. Well, I said that. On your question of the Federal grant, sup-ose you did provide not a grant but a fund to draw upon for television, ıdio, and the rest, and you said that the national committee might spend much and the United States would pay that debt, what would be the re-ılt?

We would have to keep within that limit and this is one of the big prob-ms.

We never have the money the Republicans have. It boils down to the ıct that spot announcements continue to go on. They are expensive and the campaign draws to a close it is decided, "Well, if we spend just a little ıore money on television and get it into the homes just as often as we ın—the campaign looks awfully close and since we have spent all of this ıoney we would rather spend a little more and win than lose."

SENATOR CANNON. Do you have any specific recommendation to make for workable method to prohibit this unlimited or excessive spending?

MR. BAILEY. When you say "excessive" I think it is well described that way, ı overabundance of television, radio, and newspaper advertising.

Whether or not you could limit the amount to be spent for those media education is something I do not know. I think it is a matter to be dis-ıssed and thought about.

I think the important thing that we ought to keep in mind is the Federal ›ntribution could well be given on the grounds of educational benefits to ıe people and only for expenditures in those fields.

And I think it is vitally important to the American people that they be fully informed of the issues; that they be fully informed as to what the candidates stand for.

I think it is just as important for the Federal Government to spend money for this as it is for anything else that you can imagine because while we who are in public life like to believe that everybody reads all these things in the newspapers, we know that isn't true. It takes constant repetition before the people finally begin to realize what the candidates are talking about and what the issues are.

> [*Proposed Amendments to and Improvements in the Federal Election Laws, Hearings before the Subcommittee on Privileges and Elections of the Senate Committee on Rules and Administration,* 87th Cong., 1st Sess., pt. 2 (1961), pp. 123–130.]

. . . SENATOR CANNON. Senator Morton, I wish to welcome you here this afternoon as a witness before the subcommittee to give your views on any of the legislative matters presently before the subcommittee. Your experiences as a U.S. Senator and, until recently, as chairman of the Republican National Committee have provided you with broad knowledge of the U.S. elective system and of many inadequacies or defects which are in need of correction. If you have a written statement to accompany your oral remarks we shall be happy to receive it for inclusion in the printed hearings. . . .

SENATOR MORTON. In general, I would say that during the frustrations o the campaign, especially the financing of the campaign, we all groped fo a broader base for, and a more effective way of, obtaining contributions.

Of course, we all give some thought to why should not the Federa Government pay for a portion of this since it is required of us to put ou candidates before the public, using the various expensive electronic medi of today, television and radio, in addition to advertisements in newspaper and periodicals.

After the heat of the election is over, even though the debts are sti with us, we begin to have second thoughts as to whether or not ther should be any Federal grant or any tax benefit to a contributor to a politic cause.

I think in this whole area we must move slowly. I think that, certainl some of the bills which you have before you go pretty far into congressiona gubernatorial, and other elections.

I think that if anything is done it should be confined to the election (the President and the Vice President. And let's feel our way. I was som what intrigued with a plan which would provide so much per vote, let say 5 cents per vote, to be paid after the election to a political party organiz tion which ran its candidate in 40 or more States and got more than percent of the national vote.

Also it would be the responsibility of the party, who was the recipien to show that the money had actually been spent for substantive, informati programs, television and radio, and not just for spot announcements. Ev that, I think, perhaps is undesirable.

One of these bills—our colleague Senator Mansfield's bill, I believe it is—makes a grant of Federal funds and requires the parties to have their conventions after September 1.

I certainly concur in what Senator Mansfield is trying to achieve in shorter campaigns. I think we can learn a lesson from the British as to the length of campaigns. They do it in about 30 days. Geographically, there is a great difference between England and the United States.

In England they run in their own district under a parliamentary system. So I do not think we could go to that extreme, but I do think that the long drawn-out campaign is not only costly but terribly tiring to the participants.

And I also think it becomes tiring to some of the citizens of our country before it is over.

I point out that the parties, themselves, can shorten the campaign by holding their conventions at a later date. And I think that there will always be between the two major parties a degree of cooperation in the matter of setting their convention dates. It has become traditional that the party that is out of power has its convention first. That is natural, because they have a greater job of organization to do in setting up their campaign.

They do not have the departments of government as a source of research and the Cabinet members and the heads of agencies as a source of aid in the campaign. But I think that that can be worked out voluntarily without legislation.

I think that the question of financial contributions can be worked out. The situation is improving even though the costs have gone up immeasurably. This was the most expensive campaign in the history of our country, as we all know. But in many States, in our own party, and I know it is true in the Democratic Party, they have broadened the base of contribution.

They have developed a plan similar to the plan that is employed by the community chest and the united givers appeals and put it on a year-round basis, regardless of whether it is an election year or not, or, a year-in and year-out basis, I should say.

I think that if we want to broaden contributions, as we all do, I am sure, that one way to do it most effectively would be to permit a contribution in certain modest limits, not to exceed, certainly, $100, and to be treated as a deductible item for tax purposes just as the contribution to a charitable organization or a church is treated today.

I think that this might stimulate a broader base of giving.

I am not in favor of the proposals that have been brought forward to just forgive taxes, let's say, up to $20 for a political contribution. If we are going to do that we might as well go ahead and just let the Federal Government appropriate that much money, because it is the same thing.

I think there ought to be some sacrifice to making a political contribution just as there is some sacrifice to making a contribution toward any worthy charitable organization. . . .

In other words—there would be no trouble—if the tax credit method is adopted either party could reach its statutory limit on what it could spend by just going through the factories and mines and industries of the country and getting people to sign up, because they could possibly work it so that of their withholding tax $20 would be turned over to the Democratic Party or the Republican Party or the Vegetarians or the Prohibitionists or whoever else is in the act.

There is no pain to the giving. The man's take-home pay is just the same. He probably does not even have to know about it. . . .

SENATOR CANNON. Now, Senator Mansfield's bill would provide for the giving of up to $1 million to each of the major parties for TV and radio only.

Would you favor that type of an approach or do you feel that that is not a good approach?

SENATOR MORTON. Well, I do not think we should give anything for any purpose to the political parties from the Federal Treasury other than the loss of taxes by virtue of making a reasonable contribution as tax exempt.

But if such a provision were enacted you could earmark it for television and radio, because the total cost is so much greater than $1 million. I mean, when you are desperate, as I was and as "Scoop" Jackson was for money, you will take it and use it for that purpose, and then if you have any other money you might use it for another purpose.

But I do not think that it should be done. After all, in this business we look at what is spent here at the national level. Many, many, many times that amount is spent, as you know, at the State and local level.

There is really no estimate of what a national campaign costs. If you take it all the way down to the precinct level in our quadrennial election of a President and Vice President, it certainly is in the area of $100 million. And if you give $1 million, that is 1 percent.

And you are getting into something then that would never end because then what will we do about your race and my race? What will we do about the Governor of your State and my State, the Members of Congress from your State and mine?

We can get all the way down to the justices of the peace.

SENATOR CANNON. In the light of your experience as national chairman and as a U.S. Senator, do you believe that the Federal laws governing finances are too lax?

In other words, do you believe that the Corrupt Practices Act should be repealed or substantially revised to meet the problems of modern political campaign technique?

SENATOR MORTON. Yes, I think that it can well be reviewed and your committee is well qualified to do so. Any tightening up that might be necessary for more accurate reporting would be fine.

I also think that we ought to make more realistic these feelings. It is perfectly ridiculous in both parties, but we have had to set up other committees because of the unrealistic statutory limitation of $3 million.

Now, we have a Republican Congressional Campaign Committee, and the Senatorial Campaign Committee. In the Democratic Party, they have the same thing and that gives you $9 million.

Then, in addition to that, we both have to set up special committees. You can call them television committees or volunteers or citizens or something else. I think it ought to be a realistic figure. I do not think there is any use in going through these bookkeeping maneuvers, which are all open and aboveboard, but I think the figure of $3 million is a very archaic one, and I think that could well be broadened in terms of today's costs.

There is no question about it that the development of the electronic communication devices has jumped the cost of a national or any political campaign, but especially a national campaign tremendously.

SENATOR CANNON. Which, in your opinion, is of greater importance, strict limitation of contributions and expenditures or merely a requirement for more detailed public disclosure?

SENATOR MORTON. Well, I believe in public disclosure. I think that is important in political contributions.

If you have proper public disclosure I do not think you have to worry about any limitation on the amount that can be given. . . .

Now, if some oil baron wants to give one party or the other $100,000, let him do it, but let us know that. Let the public know that. It will be not only a restraint on him but it will be a notice that "Yes, I am trying to influence; I am trying to prevent the depletion allowance from being repealed," but let the public know it.

Public disclosure is the answer to any sort of political corruption.

SENATOR CANNON. With respect to the elections themselves, there has been a suggestion made that the election, perhaps, should cover 2 days rather than 1 to encourage greater participation.

What is your feeling on that?

SENATOR MORTON. Of course, we have the traditional Tuesday and it has become a tradition.

In many States our primaries or special elections are often held on Saturday. In Europe many of the elections, as you know, are held on Sunday.

I do not think, in the tradition of the American people, that we would ever go for Sunday elections, and I would be against that.

I think, perhaps, Saturday might be a better day than Tuesday, and it might well be considered a holiday. Actually, so few plants and industries operate on Saturday today that that might be a better day.

I hope that you could do it in 1 day. It is a long day as it is. Two days would be—I don't know whether I could live through 2 days.

I do not know, in Kentucky, until 3 days after the election whether I have been elected or not anyway. So it is 3 days with me now. Maybe it would be 5 if we had 2 days of election. . . .

SENATOR CANNON. What is your feeling as to the presidential primary in general? . . .

SENATOR MORTON. I think I am strongly opposed to it.

I think that we have got to maintain a degree of party responsibility, and I think the convention system is the way to do it.

A primary could become a popularity contest. I would hate to run against Wyatt Earp in a national presidential primary, frankly, and I think that this question of party responsibility—not that either party has any monolithic structure, not that we, as Republicans, always stick together or on the other side, the Democrats stick together but I do think there is a need in a system such as ours for a certain degree of party responsibility.

And I think that it is best achieved through the convention system.

Now, if the delegates for the convention from a State want that, have a presidential primary and, of course, you know there are 50 different laws as there are 50 different States, that is up to the people of the State.

I think it is a terribly grueling thing, all of these State primaries. I think that the job our President had to do to gain the nomination in Los Angeles was far above and beyond the call of duty and it does, for a man who is in office as he was at that time, present a very difficult challenge.

In my own State there is no primary. There are laws covering the selection of delegates by the parties themselves. I, personally, prefer that system.

I have no quarrel with a State that does have its primary but I certainly do not think we ever want it in a national primary.

CHAPTER 6

THE JUDICIARY AS AN INSTRUMENT OF GOVERNMENT

AT THE APEX of the highly elaborate and complex American judicial system is the Supreme Court. Symbol and concrete expression of the American acceptance of the rule of law, the Supreme Court, together with the Federal district and circuit courts, exercises the judicial power of the United States.

The Constitution, itself a basic law, is, as Oliver Wendell Holmes once observed, not a set of "mathematical formulas having their essence in their form"; on the contrary, "they are organic living institutions transplanted from English soil." There must be *some* way of figuring out what the Constitution means when cases arise. "Laws," remarked Alexander Hamilton in the twenty-second *Federalist* paper, "are a dead letter without courts to expound and define their true meaning and operation." If the rule of law is to govern, the judiciary must be one of the governors. The Massachusetts constitution of 1780 asserted the objective: "a government of laws and not of men." There are no laws without men, of course, so that always a government of laws is an idea beyond our grasp; yet the reach of the idea can be seen in the simple expedient of supposing all the laws of the nation suddenly abolished, and government left to men without the laws' guidance and limitation or without the climate of opinions and expectations inhering in a system where the law is deemed supreme.

In thinking of the role and functioning of the Supreme Court, the citizen may usefully hold a number of considerations in mind. As a court of last resort, the Supreme Court receives difficult and uncertain cases so that decisions understandably are often divided. What is more, the Court deals with cases and controversies; governments and people must sue or be sued because real things have been said and done and real injuries suffered before the Court can take jurisdiction. When the Court adjudicates an issue, it formulates a rule of constitutional law, as Justice Brandeis once said, no "broader than is required by the precise facts to which it is applied." Thus, rather than deciding whether motion pictures can be censored under the terms of the Constitution, the Court examines the specifics of a specific portion of a statute, the specifics of a specific act by a motion-picture exhibitor, and then decides that the circumstances warrant the conclusion, say, that the denial of a license to exhibit the film *The Miracle* because it is "sacrilegious" infringes on the constitutional protection. The Court said in concluding its opinion in *Burstyn Inc. v. Wilson* in 1952: "Since the term 'sacrilegious' is the sole standard under attack here, it is not necessary for us to decide, for example, whether a state may censor motion pictures under a clearly-drawn statute designed and applied to prevent the showing of obscene films. That is a very different question from the one now before us. We hold only that, under the First and Fourteenth Amendments, a state may not ban a film on the basis of a censor's conclusion that it is 'sacrilegious.' "

The Court spreads out its determinations in writing and so displays its evidence and its reasoning in highly public fashion. Herein lies one of its central attributes: its visibility, and, in fact, the ample basis given to those critics who seek to expound what they wish by taking off from what the Court has decided.

In a sense, it must be said, there is no such entity as the Supreme Court; instead there are individual judges who in majority or minority or concurring opinions have said their say at a particular time under particular circumstances. The Supreme Court of the 1930s, for example, was only semantically the same as the Supreme Court of the 1960s. Concurrently there is a profound sense in which the Supreme Court remains what it has been over much of the nation's history: one of the principal instruments for governing America.

Marbury v. Madison, 1803. Judicial Review Is Established

The Constitution contains no provision explicitly empowering the Supreme Court to declare that an act of Congress is in violation of the Constitution and therefore null and void. It was in *Marbury v. Madison* that the Court reasoned its way to the conclusion from which the precedent of judicial review has been solidified. Giving to the American Supreme Court political power whose magnitude is unequaled by any judiciary in the world, this case has monumental constitutional significance.

Just prior to leaving office after the elections of 1800, President John Adams made a number of judicial appointments, one of which was that of William Marbury to be a justice of the peace in the District of Columbia. The commission had been signed by the President and countersigned by the Secretary of State. However, the appointment had not been wound up because the commission had not been delivered.

When the new administration took office, the newly elected President Thomas Jefferson ignored Marbury's commission. Marbury then sued for a writ of mandamus requiring Madison, the new Secretary of State, to deliver the commission.

Several paraconstitutional phases of the Court's decision are noteworthy as examples of politics in action. In delivering the opinion, Chief

Justice John Marshall denied to the Court a trivial power, that of issuing a writ of mandamus as part of its original jurisdiction; and, in this act of apparent self-denial, he gave to the Court a power of enormous sweep, judicial review. Performing this act of political legerdemain, Marshall managed to have his judicial cake while he munched on the same moralistic cake, doing it all behind clear and transparent but shatterproof glass.

What Marshall did was to say that Marbury was entitled to his appointment as a matter of vested right, but that the Court was powerless to issue the writ of mandamus requested as a part of its original jurisdiction. Marshall pointed out that the Constitution spells out the circumstances where the Supreme Court has original jurisdiction; the power to issue the desired writ of mandamus is not included therein.

President Thomas Jefferson could and did object vigorously to the decision, but there was nothing positive he could do. For instance, he could not virtuously refuse to give Marbury the commission, for the Court had not made itself vulnerable by directing Jefferson to complete Marbury's appointment.

Stretched through the whole case was the fact that John Marshall was himself one of the judges appointed by John Adams to protect the Federalists. Capping it all was the circumstance that it was John Marshall himself who as Secretary of State under John Adams had failed to deliver the commission which would have fulfilled the Marbury appointment. There appears little doubt that under comparable conditions a member of today's Supreme Court would have disqualified himself from taking part in the determination of the case of *Marbury v. Madison.*

After finding that Marbury had a right to the commission, Marshall inquired whether the laws of the country afford a remedy to Marbury and found such remedy is available.

The opinion then proceeds:

. . . 1st. The nature of the writ. . . . This, then, is a plain case for a mandamus, either to deliver the commission, or a copy of it from the record; and it only remains to be inquired, whether it can issue from this court.

The act to establish the judicial courts of the United States authorizes the supreme court "to issue writs of mandamus, in cases warranted by the principles and usages of law, to any courts appointed, or persons holding office, under the authority of the United States."

. . . The constitution vests the whole judicial power of the United States in one supreme court, and such inferior courts as congress shall, from time to time, order and establish. This power is expressly extended to all cases arising under the laws of the United States; and consequently, in some form, may be exercised over the present case; because the right claimed is given by a law of the United States.

In the distribution of this power, it is declared, that "the supreme court shall have original jurisdiction, in all cases affecting ambassadors, other public ministers and consuls, and those in which a state shall be a party. In all other cases, the supreme court shall have appellate jurisdiction." . . . If it had been intended to leave it in the discretion of the legislature, to apportion the judicial power between the supreme and inferior courts, according to the will of that body, it would certainly have been useless to have proceeded further than to have defined the judicial power, and the tribunals in which it should be vested. The subsequent part of the section is mere surplusage—is entirely without meaning, if such is to be the construction. If congress remains at liberty to give this court appellate jurisdiction, where the Constitution has declared their jurisdiction shall be original; and original jurisdiction where the constitution has declared it shall be appellate; the distribution of jurisdiction, made in the constitution, is form without substance. . . . To enable this court, then, to issue a mandamus, it must be shown to be an exercise of appellate jurisdiction, or to be necessary to enable them to exercise appellate jurisdiction. . . . It is the essential criterion of appellate jurisdiction, that it revises and corrects the proceedings in a cause already instituted, and does not create that cause. Although, therefore, a mandamus may be directed to courts, yet to issue such a writ to an officer, for the delivery of a paper, is, in effect, the same as to sustain an original action for that paper, and therefore, seems not to belong to appellate, but to original jurisdiction. Neither is it necessary in such a case as this, to enable the court to exercise its appellate jurisdiction. The authority, therefore, given to the supreme court, by the act establishing the judicial courts of the United States, to issue writs of mandamus to public officers, appears not to be warranted by the constitution; and it becomes necessary to inquire whether a jurisdiction so conferred can be exercised.

The question, whether an act, repugnant to the constitution, can become the law of the land, is a question deeply interesting to the United States: but, happily, not of an intricacy proportioned to its interest. It seems only necessary to recognize certain principles, supposed to have been long and well established, to decide it. That the people have an original right to establish, for their future government, such principles as, in their opinion, shall most conduce to their own happiness, is the basis on which the whole American fabric has been erected. The exercise of this original right is a very great exertion; nor can it, nor ought it, to be frequently repeated. The principles, therefore, so established, are deemed fundamental: and as the authority from which they proceed is supreme, and can seldom act, they are designed to be permanent.

This original and supreme will organizes the government, and assigns to different departments their respective powers. It may either stop here, or establish certain limits not to be transcended by those departments. The government of the United States is of the latter description. The powers of the legislature are defined and limited; and that those limits may not be mistaken, or forgotten, the constitution is written. To what purpose are powers limited, and to what purpose is that limitation committed to writing, if these limits may, at any time, be passed by those intended to be restrained? The distinction between a government with limited and unlimited powers is abolished, if those limits do not confine the persons on whom they are imposed, and if acts prohibited and acts allowed, are of equal obligation. It is a proposition too plain to be contested, that the constitution controls any legislative act repugnant to it; or that the legislature may alter the consitution by an ordinary act.

Between these alternatives, there is no middle ground. The constitution is either a superior paramount law, unchangeable by ordinary means, or it is on a level with ordinary legislative acts, and, like other acts, is alterable when the legislature shall please to alter it. If the former part of the alternative be true, then a legislative act, contrary to the constitution, is not law; if the latter part be true, then written constitutions are absurd attempts, on the part of the people, to limit a power, in its own nature, illimitable.

Certainly, all those who have framed written constitutions contemplate them as forming the fundamental and paramount law of the nation, and consequently, the theory of every such government must be, that an act of the legislature, repugnant to the constitution, is void. This theory is essentially attached to a written constitution and is, consequently, to be considered, by this court, as one of the fundamental principles of our society. It is not, therefore, to be lost sight of, in the further consideration of this subject.

If an act of the legislature, repugnant to the constitution is void, does it, notwithstanding its invalidity, bind the courts, and oblige them to give it effect? Or, in other words, though it be not the law, does it constitute a rule as operative as if it was a law? This would be to overthrow, in fact, what was established in theory; and would seem, at first view, an absurdity too gross to be insisted on. It shall, however, receive a more attentive consideration.

It is, emphatically, the province and duty of the judicial department, to say what the law is. Those who apply the rule to particular cases, must of necessity expound and interpret that rule. If two laws conflict with each other, the courts must decide on the operation of each. So, if a law be in opposition to the constitution; if both the law and the constitution apply to a particular case, so that the court must either decide that case, conformably to the law, disregarding the constitution; or conformably to the constitution, disregarding the law; the court must determine which of these conflicting rules governs the case: this is of the very essence of judicial duty. If then, the courts are to regard the constitution, and the constitution is superior to any ordinary act of the legislature, the constitution, and not such ordinary act, must govern the case to which they both apply.

Those, then, who controvert the principle, that the constitution is to be considered, in court, as a paramount law, are reduced to the necessity of maintaining that courts must close their eyes on the constitution, and see only the law. This doctrine would subvert the very foundation of all written constitutions. It would declare that an act which, according to the principles and theory of our government, is entirely void, is yet, in practice completely obligatory. It would declare that if the legislature shall do what is expressly forbidden, such act, notwithstanding the express prohibition, is in reality effectual. It would be giving to the legislature a practical and real omnipotence, with the same breath which professes to restrict their powers within narrow limits. It is prescribing limits, and declaring that those limits may be passed at pleasure. That it thus reduces to nothing, what we have deemed the greatest improvement on political institutions, a written constitution, would, of itself, be sufficient, in America, where written constitutions have been viewed with so much reverence, for rejecting the construction. But the peculiar expressions of the constitution of the United States furnish additional arguments in favor of its rejection. The judicial power of the United States is extended to all cases arising under the constitution. Could it be the intention of those who gave this power, to say, that in using it, the constitution should not be looked into? That a case arising under the constitution should be decided, without examining the instrument under which it arises? This is too extravagant to be maintained. In some cases, then, the constitution must be looked into by the judges. And if they can open it at all, what part of it are they forbidden to read or to obey?

There are many other parts of the constitution which serve to illustrate this subject. It is declared, that "no tax or duty shall be laid on articles exported from any state." Suppose, a duty on the export of cotton, of tobacco, or of flour; and a suit instituted to recover it. Ought judgment to be rendered in such a case? ought the judges to close their eyes on the constitution, and only see the law?

The constitution declares "that no bill of attainder or ex post facto law shall be passed." If, however, such a bill should be passed, and a person should be prosecuted under it; must the court condemn to death those victims whom the constitution endeavors to preserve?

"No person," says the constitution, "shall be convicted of treason, unless on the testimony of two witnesses to the same overt act, or on confession in open court." Here, the language of the constitution is addressed especially to the courts. It prescribes, directly for them, a rule of evidence not to be departed from. If the legislature should change that rule, and declare one witness, or a confession out of court, sufficient for conviction, must the constitutional principle yield to the legislative act?

From these, and many other selections which might be made, it is apparent, that the framers of the constitution contemplated that instrument as a rule for the government of courts, as well as of the legislature. Why otherwise does it direct the judges to take an oath to support it? This oath certainly applies, in an especial manner, to their conduct in their official character. How immoral to impose it on them, if they were to be used as the instruments, and the knowing instruments, for violating what they swear to support!

The oath of office, too, imposed by the legislature, is completely demonstrative of the legislative opinion on this subject. It is in these words: "I do solemnly swear, that I will administer justice, without respect to persons, and do equal right to the poor and to the rich; and that I will faithfully and impartially discharge all the duties incumbent on me as ——, according to the best of my abilities and understanding, agreeable to the constitution and laws of the United States." Why does a judge swear to discharge his duties agreeably to the constitution of the United States, if that constitution forms no rule for his government? if it is closed upon him, and cannot be inspected by him? If such be the real state of things, this is worse than solemn mockery. To prescribe, or to take this oath, becomes equally a crime.

It is also not entirely unworthy of observation, that in declaring what shall be the supreme law of the land, the constitution itself is first mentioned; and not the laws of the United States, generally, but those only which shall be made in pursuance of the constitution, have that rank.

Thus, the particular phraseology of the constitution of the United States confirms and strengthens the principle, supposed to be essential to all written constitutions, that a law repugnant to the constitution is void; and that courts, as well as other departments, are bound by that instrument.

The Future of Judicial Review

Between Jefferson's reference to the judiciary as a hospital for decayed politicians and any modern designation of the Supreme Court as a bunch of Communists or the ultimate expression of American constitutionalism, the Court has been applauded, ignored, and hissed, sometimes by the same people at different times.

The following selection is designed to help the citizen understand the past, present, and future of the role of the Supreme Court. Loren P. Beth, the author, is professor of government at the University of Massachusetts and author of *The American Theory of Church and State* and *Politics, the Constitution and the Supreme Court.*

[Loren P. Beth, "The Supreme Court and the Future of Judicial Review," *Political Science Quarterly,* vol. 76, pp. 11–23, 1961.]

Seen from the vantage point of twenty years, the Supreme Court "revolution" of 1937–1940 does not seem as revolutionary as was once thought. The Court has continued to play a major role in American political affairs, and it can now be seen that far from giving up the power of judicial review, the judges preserved it intact in 1937. This has become obvious with the period of renewed judicial activism which set in with the accession of Chief Justice Earl Warren. Since 1953, the Court has performed such significant feats as the outlawing of school segregation, the limiting of state power to control subversive activities, and the limiting of powers of legislature to investigate; and it has continued its careful—if not always consistent—oversight of the way in which the states enforce their criminal law. Previous to 1953 it had drawn strict limits to the "inherent" power of the president and had attempted to define the boundaries of church-state separation. The power of military authorities to use judicial process has been challenged. The right of free speech has been adumbrated (though perhaps not clarified). The court has, in fact, been so active in so many areas that criticism of its decisions (and even of its basic function) has mounted almost to the levels of 1936.

The judges have thus succeeded in doing what no observer in 1937 would have foreseen: they have, by their decisions, again put in question the utility of the whole institution of judicial review. The judges may be able to read the history of 1937: but apparently what they find in it is not what the 1937 commentators thought was there.

The result has been a rash of new demands that the Court be curbed. Some of these may be discounted as the obvious reactions of those (especially in the South) who disagree with particular decisions so strenuously that they would destroy judicial review in order to reverse one set of decisions. But beyond this, criticisms more serious and proposals more substantial have been made. The National Conference of (State) Chief Justices, meeting in 1958, charged the Court with making too many decisions which are nonunanimous, with ignoring the principle of *stare decisis,* and (more broadly) with a lack of self-restraint in cases involving federal-state relations. Here was, in other words, the old plaint that the Court is acting as a superlegislature. The charge has been echoed by the American Bar Association and by many spokesmen for Southern interests. It has—not surprisingly—cropped up in dissenting opinions on the Supreme Court itself. Bills have been introduced into Congress which would have the effect of clipping the Court's wings in one way or another: one of them failed of passage in the 1958 Congress by only one vote.

In the light of this new controversy it seems important to try to assess the nature of the conflict, and to attempt to discern the future of this characteristic American political institution.

Background to Conflict

There is some disagreement as to the bases of this new era of conflict, but there is wide agreement on at least two fundamental causes: the changed nature of the questions coming to the Court, and the inherent nature of judicial review itself. To these we now turn.

The New Deal judges were unanimous upon one thing: that the old Court (at least its conservative majority) had been too activist in prohibiting government action in the economic realm. The conservatives had misconstrued either the Constitution or their proper functions as judges, or both. It was natural, then, that the New Deal Court would scrap the old structure: it proceeded to reverse, either explicitly or *sub silentio,* the previous course of decisions. It unanimously agreed with Chief Justice Stone that the only check on the Court was the judges' own sense of self-restraint. The judges all felt that the government could constitutionally exercise large controls over the economy. They all, therefore, were willing that the Court retire from the politico-economic battlefield. Consequently, since 1937 there has been little litigation involving the economic powers of government in the old terms. This is perhaps the chief result of the events of 1937.

But here the area of agreement between the judges ended. The events of World War II and the "cold war" which ensued brought renewed pressure by nationalistic as well as by more sober citizens for action protecting the nation against disloyalty, subversion and espionage; and (in a general way) there was equivalent pressure for social and political conformity. Such action, when taken, raised serious issues of conflict between national security and constitutional liberty. The democratic aspirations of the American people, and the aspirations of Negroes for social equality, at the same time led to increased pressure for government action in the aid of the achievement of such equality. Both in the area of security and in that of racial equality, the Supreme Court has found itself—perhaps against its own will—a major participant in the struggle.

It is on such questions that the Court has again come near to foundering on the shoals of a hostile public opinion; and conjointly the unanimity which the Court showed on economic questions after 1937 gave way to almost hopeless division on the new questions to which it had to address itself.

The lesson we may draw from the history of judicial review is a twofold one: that judicial review is used most frequently (and acts most effectively as a brake) at those times when governmental action is reaching out into new and unprecedented fields; and that the Court itself is most effective in using review when it has the support of influential political and/or social groups. Both of these lessons are in point as regards the civil liberties cases of the last ten years. Government action—as manifested in such laws as the McCarran Communist Control Act of 1950, various state loyalty oath laws, and the investigations by Congressional and legislative committees with their inseparable issues of the rights of witnesses—was unprecedented. Both the scale and the scope of such activity were new in this country. It was therefore natural that the courts, used to old ways and brought up in old conditions, would act as conservative censors on government. The Court's reaction has been somewhat inconsistent, however. During the period roughly ending with the death (in 1946) of Chief Justice Stone, it stood as a protector of liberty against the encroachments of government, except in a few prominent areas such as the Japanese exclusion cases. From 1946 to the accession of Chief Justice Warren in 1953, counsels of caution prevailed more often, and the Court usually acquiesced in government actions infringing on the old liberties. Now again, since 1953, the Court has become "activist" in such matters.

Given the pressure for repressive legislation, it is inevitable that libertarian decisions by the courts would arouse great opposition. Such opposition has been the greater—or at least has seemed greater—because there is no large "prestige" group in American society which stands to gain directly from libertarian decisions. Consequently no such group has seen fit to defend the Court. If we are correct that much of the Court's strength is dependent upon the degree to which public opinion sustains it, this lack of significant political support is an important element in the present conflict in which the judges are involved. Certainly the backing of such groups as the NAACP, the American Civil Liberties Union, or the ADA is not in itself calculated to preserve the Court's power and prestige.

On the old type of economic issue the Court had the advantage of having powerful group support on either side of most decisions. This has not been true of the civil liberties cases (in which even a President of the United States has refused to approve categorically the Court's course of action).

It is, then, in the very nature of these new kinds of questions which have been presented to the Supreme Court since 1937 that there would be loud complaints about the decisions: unless indeed the Court were to abdicate as completely its functions of review in this area as it has in the economic sphere. Such abdication, however, was not likely unless the Court were to give up its power of review absolutely, and no one on the Court has counselled such a course. A second cause of conflict, then, has its seed in the very nature of the institution of judicial review.

Fundamentally, it can now be seen that the Supreme Court lost a battle, not a war, in 1937. It retired from the economic battlefield (at least for the moment) but retained intact the power of review which had been its major weapon in that struggle. But so long as the power itself remains, there will be the urge to use it; and as long as it is used, opposition will exist. Paradoxically, it appears that the Supreme Court is least popular at times when it is most effectively using the powers which we have entrusted to it. So it has been since 1937. Despite the warning of (then) Justice Stone that "the Courts are not the only agencies that have the power to govern," and the whole thrust of Holmesian judicial philosophy (which seemed to say that the representative legislature must have its way), the post-1937 Supreme Court with Stone himself in the vanguard has not been notable for its self-restraint when questions of civil rights and liberties have been presented. And this is true even though practically every judge in the last twenty years has regarded himself in some degree as a follower of Holmes.

The nub of the matter seems to be this: that it is a rare judge who will refuse to use his power to accomplish those things which be believes the Constitution requires (or allows). And it is at the same time a rare judge who can separate his judgment as to what is right from his conclusions as to what is constitutional. Consequently almost every judge will use his power (judicial review) when his constitutional beliefs are transgressed by legislative action. Perhaps the "almost" is not needed in the above sentence, for even Holmes himself, and his leading disciple, Justice Frankfurter, have been perfectly willing to use the power of review on occasion, and Frankfurter has voted with the majority in some of its most criticized decisions.

The Court, then, must always act in the light of its duty as that duty is seen by the majority of its members; and so long as the majority's concept of duty includes the possibility of judicial review, self-restraint is an illusion when cases arise "on the frontier where a changing social necessity impinges upon the established law." Unless one wishes to challenge the whole institution of judicial review, perhaps the controversy over "activism" and "self-restraint" is largely academic; for in being "activist" the Court may be acting exactly as we wish. One is reduced, then, to criticizing the constitutional and moral rightness of particular decisions, and the argument over the proper *function* of the Court is beside the point.

To put all this into somewhat different language, we may recall that the Court has often been criticized for "legislating" and for constituting itself as "a third house of the legislature." But the question now seems to be: is not such action an inevitable accompaniment of judicial review? As we all know by now, the fundamental law under which we operate is hardly crystal clear; and all the points of major conflict involve the clauses of the greatest opacity. Decisions thus require interpretation; and interpretation inevitably means the upholding or rejecting of governmental policy made (in the first instance) by some other agency of government. The effect of judicial review is thus inevitably to make policy; it could hardly be otherwise. The only way to avoid "judicial legislation" is to banish the power of judicial review, and even then much law would be "made" in the process of statutory interpretation by the courts.

It is in argument over the nature and function of the Supreme Court in its exercise of judicial review that the New Deal and post-New Deal judges have split among themselves. So far as the conflict has been conscious and overt, it may be represented by the two powerful antagonists whose careers span the entire period from 1940 to the present. . . .

"The Legacy of Holmes and Brandeis"

Paradoxically, the opposing ideas of Justices Black and Frankfurter both find their source in the judicial theories of Oliver Wendell Holmes. But the two modern judges have seized on different aspects of Holmes' thought, and shaped these to fit their own attitudes and concepts. It is important to note that the thought of Holmes was shaped in an era when civil liberties were (except for a short period in the early twenties) distinctly secondary to economic questions coming before the Supreme Court. It is thus a question what the "Yankee from Olympus" would say to modern civil liberties issues: one may make strong assumptions, but without proof.

No study of the Supreme Court since 1937 could ignore the influence of Holmes and Brandeis, for every later judge is indebted to them for part of the law as it is and part of the theory on which his judicial actions must rest. Justice Cardozo acknowledged this debt in his usual graceful prose: "He [Holmes] is today for all students of the law and for all students of human society the philosopher and the seer, the greatest of our age in the domain of jurisprudence, and one of the greatest of the ages." While today there is a tendency to play down Holmes, nevertheless he has left a judicial heritage on which the Supreme Court is bound to live for many years into the future. The influence of Brandeis is perhaps not so obvious, though it seems to be true that Justice Black has rested his judicial philosophy on Holmes at the points where Holmes and Brandeis were in agreement; certainly his attitude resembles that of Brandeis more than that of Holmes. And Justice Douglas is said to regard himself as the personal heir of Brandeis.

Holmes is perhaps most famous as an apostle of judicial self-restraint. His reputation in this regard was made by his rejection of the concept of substantive due process of law as an interpretation of the Fourteenth

Amendment. Close reading of his opinions, however, seems to indicate that his objection to substantive due process was not due to the fact that it constituted "judicial legislation," but that it was an improper reading of the Constitution, which (he said), was "not intended to embody a particular economic theory, whether of paternalism and the organic relation of the citizen to the State or *laissez-faire*." In short, Holmes felt that the Constitution had nothing to say about economic systems, and that the Court was reading into that document something which was not there. Substantive due process might be perfectly proper in some cases, but not in those involving economic interference by the state. Holmes recorded no objection, for instance, when the Court began to use substantive due process in free speech cases during the 1920's. Nor did he object when the Court constructed the so-called "rule of reason" by which to interpret the Sherman Anti-Trust Act. He had, in other words, no basic objection to "judicial legislation" if it was exercised with restraint and in areas in which he felt it could be justified by a reasonable reading of Constitution or statute. Whatever may have been thought at the time, then, his disagreements with his "conservative" colleagues were something less than fundamental.

Nevertheless, Holmes' statements about judicial self-restraint were so felicitous and persuasive that they had an effect on later judges which perhaps went beyond what he intended by them. Judges like Stone, who used these statements as the bases for later dissents, were to find that they were complicating factors when new types of cases arose. Stone, for instance, wrote that the "only check upon the courts is our own sense of self-restraint"; and he said further that "the courts are not the only agencies of government that have the power to govern." In both instances he was writing of the Court's handling of New Deal cases. But by 1938 he was hedging, and in what must be the most famous footnote in Supreme Court history, he remarked that in First Amendment cases the same doctrine might not apply. Cardozo had made the same reservation in his well-known opinion in the Palko case.

Justice Frankfurter: Democracy and Judicial Values

Justice Felix Frankfurter has seized on the "self-restraint" aspect of this question, and made it the key point in his judicial philosophy. Frankfurter starts with the assumption that we have a democratic system of government, in which the legislatures have the power to make law relatively free from judicial interference. Echoing Holmes, he would allow the people, acting through their representatives, to make their own mistakes: for (as one of his supporters has remarked) "who are judges to deprive the community of the wisdom that comes with self-inflicted wounds, the strength that grows with the burden of responsibility?" This view regards the Court as an irresponsible and undemocratic institution (when it uses judicial review) which has no right to substitute its judgment for that of the democratic branches of government.

The flavor of Frankfurter's views can best be presented by a quotation from one of his most famous judicial opinions, the dissenting opinion in *West Virginia v. Barnette:*

> As a member of this Court I am not justified in writing my private notions of policy into the Constitution, no matter how deeply I may cherish them or how mischievous I may deem their disregard. The duty of a judge who must decide which of two claims before the Court shall prevail, that of a state to enact and enforce laws within its general competence or that of an individual to refuse obedience because of conscience, is not that of the ordinary person. It can never be emphasized too much that one's own opinion about the wisdom or evil of a law should be excluded altogether when one is doing one's duty on the bench. The only opinion of our own even looking in that direction that is material is our opinion whether legislators could in reason have enacted such a law.

It should be noted that in the above quotation Frankfurter has taken Holmes' doctrine of self-restraint and pushed it even farther; for Holmes always recognized that human beings are, after all, human, and so he knew that whatever judges should do, they would never in practice be able to achieve the inhuman objectivity for which his theory calls. Frankfurter not only seems to think such objectivity is achievable, but at times he is suspiciously close to saying that he has achieved it.

Further, if the argument appearing earlier in this article is sound, it seems to indicate that the ambiguous nature of the law to be construed actually forces the judge to fill in the written law out of his own preconceptions; we may find it interesting to discover what these are, but useless to inveigh against them.

Justice Frankfurter continued:

> When Mr. Justice Holmes . . . wrote that "it must be remembered that legislatures are ultimate guardians of the liberties and welfare of the people in quite as great a degree as the courts," . . . he went to the very essence of our constitutional system and the democratic conception of our society. He did not mean that for only some phases of civil government this Court was not to supplant legislatures and sit in judgment upon the right or wrong of a challenged measure. He was stating the comprehensive judicial duty and role of this Court in our constitutional scheme whenever legislation is sought to be nullified on any ground, namely, that responsibility for legislation lies with legislatures, answerable as they are directly to the people, and this Court's only and very narrow function is to determine whether within the broad grant of authority vested in legislatures they have exercised a judgment for which reasonable justification can be offered.

Perhaps the main difficulty here is that Frankfurter speaks of "our constitutional system" and "the democratic conception of our society" as if they were the same thing, and then goes on to define the two phrases only in terms of the latter. He speaks, therefore, of the constitution as only a "power-granting" document, and the limitations contained in the Bill of Rights become (implicitly) mere exhortations to right conduct on the part of the public; or in Learned Hand's words, "Thrown large upon the screen of the future as eternal verities, they are emptied of the vital occasions which gave them birth, and become [not law, but only] moral adjurations." The idea here seems to be that while the power-granting provisions can be enlarged by interpretation to meet later contingencies, the limitations are a time-bound strait jacket on future generations and thus should not be too actively enforced by the courts. The course of judicial decision seems to disprove this idea, since modern interpretations can be (and have been) grafted onto the Bill of Rights limitations just as easily as to other parts of the Constitution.

One might think that at base this is merely a dispute as to whether ours is a limited or a majoritarian democracy; but Frankfurter confuses the issue by admitting that there are occasions upon which the use of judicial review is proper: if we may cite Hand again this may be done not when the legislature "misappraises" values, but only when it fails to appraise them at all. How one is to decide when this occurs Judge Hand does not inform us; nor do Justice Frankfurter's decisions in actual cases seem to offer much enlightenment, for the occasions in which he is willing to use judicial review do not seem to differ fundamentally from those in which he is not. For instance, his flag opinions are statements of his principle, while his opinions in *Burstyn v. Wilson* and in *McCollum v. Board of Education* seem to be contradictions of it.

There is a dilemma of major proportions involved. Frankfurter's ideas offer no possible guide as to when, and when not, to use judicial review. Logically he seems almost to say we must give up the institution; practically he is not willing to do so. Consequently even a Supreme Court made up of nine Frankfurters would at times lay itself open to the charge of "legislating"—as indeed majorities including him have been so charged (witness the public reactions to the *McCollum v. Board of Education* and School Segregation cases) even though the whole idea is for the Court to avoid legislating.

Justice Black and "Selective Activism"

Justice Black and his followers have seized upon the other aspect of the thought of Holmes—his firm belief in civil liberties—and built on it a theory that while "self-restraint" is all very well when the powers granted to legislatures are involved, the Courts have a duty to intervene in protection of the limitations our constitutions place on government action. This involves activism in selected areas only, and thus may be called the theory of "selective activism." (One should not confuse this term with the "selective inclusion" which Justice Frankfurter uses in Fourteenth Amendment due process cases, following the so-called "Palko rule" developed by Justice Cardozo.)

This theory rests on a twofold foundation, one part of which consists of a theory about the nature of democracy while the other involves a constitutional argument. As to the nature of a democratic polity, Justice Black has felt (as did Holmes) that a democracy cannot long survive unless it does permit a wide area of liberty. The argument is the obvious one that it is only through the exercise of free expression that democracy can work. As Justice Douglas remarked in his dissent in the *Dennis* case,

> Free speech has occupied an exalted position because of the high service it has given our society. Its protection is essential to the very existence of a democracy. The airing of ideas releases pressures which otherwise might become destructive. . . . Full and free discussion keeps a society from becoming stagnant and unprepared for the stresses and strains that work to tear all civilizations apart. . . . Full and free discussion has indeed been the first article of our faith. We have founded our political system on it. . . . This has been the one single outstanding tenet that has made our institutions the symbol of freedom and equality. . . .

There is, between this and the Frankfurter view, a fundamental difference in the approach to democracy. Frankfurter's is based on the idea of legislative supremacy: the legislature stands as the only proper representative of majority opinion, and the Supreme Court with its power of judicial review is viewed almost as an undemocratic excrescence on the body politic. Black's view, on the other hand, is that democracy consists of a political method which can only be maintained through broad freedom; that the necessity for freedom is so great that legislatures have been constitutionally limited from encroaching on it. In this view the Court is—if not democratic—at least a guardian of democracy. Both approaches believe, in a way, that the people should be allowed to make their own mistakes: but to Frankfurter this means the majority acting through the representative legislature; to Black it means the people as a whole acting through freedom of discussion.

The second foundation of the Black-Douglas theory of selective activism is its belief that ours is a constitutionally limited democracy, and that in consequence the limitations which are written in the Constitution should be enforced fairly rigidly by courts. Perhaps the best statement of this point of view was made by Chief Justice Stone in his famous dissenting opinion in the first Flag Salute case, in which he said:

> The very fact that we have constitutional guaranties of civil liberties and the specificity of their command where freedom of speech and of religion are concerned require some accommodation of the powers which government normally exercises, when no question of civil liberty is involved, to the constitutional demand that these liberties be protected against the action of government itself.
>
> The framers were not unaware that under the system which they created most governmental curtailments of personal liberty would have the support of a legislative judgment that the public interest would be better served by its curtailment than by its constitutional protection. I cannot conceive that in prescribing, as limitations upon the powers of government, the freedom of the mind and spirit secured by the explicit guaranties of freedom of speech and religion, they intended or rightly could have left any latitude for a legislative judgment that the compulsory expression of belief which violates religious convictions would better serve the public interest than their protection.

Selective activism is not entirely free from ambiguity, particularly in cases where two Bill of Rights provisions come in conflict with each other.

And obviously, in view of the controversy existing it is not the only possible way of looking at the problem of freedom in a constitutional democracy. It is often criticized as allowing too great scope to the personal preferences of judges; and certainly men like Black and Douglas have a strong emotional belief in liberty which dictates their judicial conclusions in civil liberties cases. These are no doubt honest beliefs, deeply felt: but the question remains whether a judge should so consciously base his law on his preferences.

This writer believes that selective activism is a wiser approach to decision-making than Frankfurter's willingness to assume that legislatures are both democratic and reasonable. It is, nevertheless, an arguable point. It will not be finally settled in the near future; it may never be. And perhaps it is in the tension between these two dominant and admirable judges that the most viable reconciliation lies. The truth may not be a monopoly of either side, and we may come closer to a proper balance between the power of a majoritarian government and the liberties of a free people by allowing the two sides to clash than by relying on one alone.

The Future of Judicial Review

It seems, then, that the future of judicial review lies somewhere within the limited spectrum which finds Frankfurter and Black at opposite ends. It is obvious that neither school of thought wishes to abolish this uniquely American contribution to the theory and practice of government. The only foreseeable contingency that might lead to such an abolition would be an activism so unpopular that Congress (or the people, through the amending process) would act to curtail the Supreme Court's power. Almost throughout our history there have been proposals to do this, but no serious curtailments have been adopted. The events of 1937 did not—if the above discussion is accurate—mean any fundamental change in the Court as an institution, even though there was a considerable shift in the course of decision and a resultant pronounced change in the subject matter of American constitutional law. Students before 1940 studied primarily the commerce and due process clauses; contemporary students must concentrate on the Bill of Rights.

At bottom the power of judicial review—both as a general doctrine and as applied in specific cases—rests today, as it has in the past, on public acceptance. Judicial review is democratic in the sense that it is accepted by most people, if in no other way. Such an institution can only survive so long as the general public and officialdom as well accept it, both in principle and in practice. As the courts cannot enforce particular decisions by themselves, neither can they force on us an acceptance of a power we do not wish. Consequently, if the Supreme Court "gets away" with its present activist course in cases involving civil rights and liberties, this would seem to be an indication that the general public (a) still respects and is willing to follow the Court and its power; and/or (b) acquiesces in the major line of court decision.

It seems likely, in other words, that the American public (consciously or subconsciously) feels the need for some sort of "constitutional guardian" despite our general attachment to the idea of majority rule. This need is great enough to have survived tremendous public criticism and disapproval of decisions in particular cases such as *Dred Scott,* the *Sugar Trust Case,* and the New Deal cases. It seems also to be surviving the present wave of criticism, although it is perhaps too soon to make a final judgment on this question.

It is true that we are no longer as naive about judicial review as we once were; it no longer gains strength from the idea that the decisions of the Court have the authority (if sometimes also the Delphic ambiguity) of an oracle. Indeed, we now take it for granted that judges are all too human and that their decisions are inevitably suffused with their humanity; this is perhaps the great lesson taught us by Justice Holmes. And while the change may have destroyed the mystical prop on which judicial review has often been thought to depend, it may be that our more sophisticated and realistic approach today actually gives judicial review a strength which it did not have before. For we are not, today, likely to be disillusioned by individual decisions: we take it for granted that human beings even on the bench are fallible. Nor do we any longer take very seriously the charge (as made by Southerners in the school segregation situation) that a decision is "political," since we take it for granted that all constitutional decisions are inevitably political—and because we know that the opposition to particular decisions (on and off the bench) is also inevitably political. If our attachment to judicial review is no longer mystical, but realistic, it may gain strength from this fact, since it can be seen to be based on realistic reasoning and can be held without undue expectations. Perhaps we no longer expect judicial review to save us, but only to help us save ourselves.

Baker v. Carr, 1962: a Choice among Competing Theories of Political Philosophy

In six opinions that came to 165 pages, the Supreme Court decided a case in 1962 that the nation's Attorney General hailed as "a landmark in the development of representative government" and dissenting Justice Felix Frankfurter called "a massive repudiation of our whole past in asserting destructively novel judicial power" and "devoid of reality."

The ultimate impact of the decision was unclear; unquestionable were two aspects of the Court's action. Basic features of the American political scene *could* change enormously, and the changes were far more likely to be deliberate than speedy. Fused in one case were disputes about people's opportunities to influence public policy and policy makers, legislative apportionment, the urban-rural struggle with suburban ramifications, representative government, politics, the distribution of national-state governmental power—all interlaced with assertions of "judicial dictatorship" and defense of the Supreme Court as the last governmental refuge of the American citizen.

Suit had been brought to redress the alleged deprivation of Federal constitutional rights. The complaint was filed by residents of several metropolitan areas in Tennessee; each person was allegedly qualified to vote for members of the General Assembly representing his county. The appellees were the Tennessee Secretary of State, Attorney General, Coordinator of Elections, and members of the State Board of Elections. Consisting of a senate with thirty-three members and a house of representatives with ninety-nine members, the General Assembly of Tennessee had not been reapportioned since 1901. Between 1901 and 1961 Tennessee experienced substantial growth and redistribution of population, producing significant changes in the relative standings of her counties in terms of qualified voters. It was primarily the continued application of the 1901 Apportionment Act in Tennessee which gave rise to the controversy.

The complaint argued that even the 1901 statute had been arbitrary and capricious, that changing the state constitution to alter the entire mechanism for reapportionment was difficult or impossible, and concluded that "these plaintiffs and others similarly situated are denied the equal protection of the laws accorded them by the Fourteenth Amendment to the Constitution of the United States by virtue of the debasement of their votes." For example, rural Moore County had 3,454 residents and one member of the Tennessee House. Shelby County (Memphis) had eight members for 627,019 residents—about 78,000 persons per legislator. Thus a vote in Moore County was worth more than twenty-two times as much as a vote in Shelby.

After the suit had been dismissed in the Federal District Court, an appeal was brought to the United States Supreme Court. Departing from its traditional reluctance to get into issues of legislative districting as political questions, the Supreme Court in a 6-to-2 decision held that the distribution of seats in state legislatures was subject to the constitutional scrutiny of the Federal courts.

Excerpts from some of the opinions follow:

[Justice Brennan, delivering the opinion of the Court:]

In light of the district court's treatment of the case, we hold today only (a) that the court possessed jurisdiction of the subject matter; (b) that a justiciable cause of action is slated upon which appellants would be entitled to appropriate relief; and (c) because appellees raise the issue before this Court, that the appellants have standing to challenge the Tennessee apportionment statutes. Beyond noting that we have no cause at this stage to doubt the district court will be able to fashion relief if violations of constitutional rights are found, it is improper now to consider what remedy would be most appropriate if appellants prevail at the trial.

[Justice Clark, concurring:]

Although I find the Tennessee apportionment statute offends the equal protection clause, I would not consider intervention by this court into so delicate a field if there were any other relief available to the people of Tennessee. But the majority of the people of Tennessee have no "practical opportunities for exerting their political weight at the polls" to correct the existing invidious discrimination. Tennessee has no initiative and referendum. I have searched diligently for other practical opportunities present under the law. I find none other than through the Federal courts. The majority of the voters have been caught up in a legislative straitjacket. Tennessee has an informed, civically militant electorate and an aroused popular conscience of the people's representatives. This is because the legislative policy has riveted the present seats in the assembly to their respective constituencies, and by the votes of their incumbents a reapportionment of any kind is prevented. The people have been rebuffed at the hands of the assembly; they have tried the constitutional convention route, but since the call must originate in the assembly it, too, has been fruitless. They have tried Tennessee courts with the same result and Governors have fought the tide only to founder. It is said that there is recourse in Congress and perhaps that may be, but from a practical standpoint this is without substance. To date Congress has never undertaken such a task in any state. We therefore must conclude that the people of Tennessee are stymied and without judicial intervention will be saddled with the present discrimination in the affairs of their State government.

[Justice Frankfurter, whom Justice Harlan joins, dissenting:]

Disregard of inherent limits in the effective exercise of the Court's "judicial Power" not only presages the futility of judicial intervention in the essentially political conflict of forces by which the relation between population and representation has time out of mind been and now is determined. It may well impair the Court's position as the ultimate organ of "the supreme Law of the Land" in that vast range of legal problems, often strongly entangled in popular feeling on which this Court must pronounce. The Court's authority—possessed neither of the purse nor the sword—ultimately rests on sustained public confidence in its moral sanction. Such feeling must be nourished by the Court's complete detachment, in fact and in appearance, from political entanglements and by abstention from injecting itself into the clash of political forces in political settlements. . . .

One of the Court's supporting opinions, as elucidated by commentary, unwittingly affords a disheartening preview of the mathematical quagmire (apart from divers judicially inappropriate and elusive determinants), into which this Court today catapults the lower courts of the country without so much as adumbrating the basis for a legal calculus as a means of extrication. . . .

Recent legislation, creating a district appropriately described as "an atrocity of ingenuity," is not unique. Considering the gross inequality among legislative electoral units within almost every State, the Court naturally shrinks from asserting that in districting at least substantial equality is a constitutional requirement enforceable by courts. Room continues to be allowed for weighting. This of course implies that geography, economics, urban-rural conflict, and all the other non-legal facts which have throughout our history entered into political districting are to some extent not to be ruled out in the undefined vista now opened up by review in the federal courts of state reapportionments. To some extent, aye, there's the rub. In effect, today's decision empowers the courts of the country to devise what should constitute the proper composition of the legislatures of the fifty States. . . .

At first blush, this charge of discrimination based on legislative underrepresentation is given the appearance of a more private, less impersonal claim, than the assertion that the frame of government is askew. Appellants appear as representatives of a class that is prejudiced as a class, in contradistinction to the polity in its entirety. However, the discrimination relied on is the deprivation of what appellants conceive to be their proportionate share of political influence. This, of course, is the practical effect of any allocation of power within the institutions of government. Hardly any distribution of political authority that could be assailed as rendering government non-republican would fail similarly to operate to the prejudice of some groups, and to the advantage of others, within the body politic. It would be ingenuous not to see, or consciously blind to deny, that the real battle over the initiative and referendum, or over a delegation of power to local rather than state-wide authority, is the battle between forces whose influence is disparate among the various organs of government to whom power may be given. No shift of power but works a corresponding shift in political influence among the groups composing a society.

What, then, is this question of legislative apportionment? Appellants invoke the right to vote and to have their votes counted. But they are permitted to vote and their votes are counted. They go to the polls, they cast their ballots, they send their representatives to the state councils. Their complaint is simply that the representatives are not sufficiently numerous or powerful—in short, that Tennessee has adopted a basis of representation with which they are dissatisfied. Talk of "debasement" or "dilution" is circular talk. One cannot speak of "debasement" or "dilution" of the value of a vote until there is first defined a standard of reference as to what a vote should be worth. What is actually asked of the Court in this case is to choose among competing bases of representation—ultimately, really, among competing theories of political philosophy—in order to establish an appropriate frame of government for the State of Tennessee and thereby for all the States of the Union. . . .

The notion that representation proportioned to the geographic spread of population is so universally accepted as a necessary element of equality between man and man that it must be taken to be the standard of a political equality preserved by the Fourteenth Amendment—that it is, in appellants' words "the basic principle of representative government" is, to put it bluntly, not true. However desirable and however desired by some among the great political thinkers and framers of our government, it has never been generally practiced, today or in the past. It was not the English system, it was not the colonial system, it was not the system chosen for the national government by the Constitution, it was not the system exclusively or even predominantly practiced by the States at the time of adoption of the Fourteenth Amendment, it is not predominantly practiced by the States today. . . .

The practical significance of apportionment is that the next election results may differ because of it. Apportionment battles are overwhelmingly party or intra-party contests. It will add a virulent source of friction and tension in federal-state relations to embroil the federal judiciary in them. . . .

. . . the case is of that class of political controversy which, by the nature of its subject, is unfit for federal judicial action.

[Reporting the Supreme Court decision under the caption "Rural Areas Facing Loss of Political Dominance," *The New York Times* said:]

The Supreme Court's decision in the Tennessee reapportionment case is expected to shift the balance of political power gradually against the rural conservatives.

The first reaction here was that the 6-to-2 decision authorizing voters to challenge the make-up of State Legislatures in Federal courts would probably do these things:

Decrease the voting strength of rural conservatives in the many State Legislatures and increase the strength of city and suburban voters, who tend to be more sympathetic toward social change and government intervention.

Increase, over all, the power of the Democratic party, which is better organized politically in the cities and is now engaged in a major drive to extend and strengthen its party organization in the suburbs.

Expand the influence of the Federal courts as instruments of social change.

[At about the same time, Senator Barry Goldwater, Republican of Arizona, called the court's ruling "a proper decision" and said, "I know there are those who say that the conservatives' political strength will be reduced if the cities gain more representation in the legislatures. But I don't agree with that. I don't think it will make any change. There are proportionately just as many conservatives in the metropolitan as in the rural areas."]

[Several days after the Supreme Court decision, the following exchange took place during President John F. Kennedy's news conference:]

Question: Mr. President, would you comment on the Supreme Court reapportionment decision, that is to say whether there's anything the Federal Government could do to support it?

Answer: I think as you know when the matter was before the Supreme Court, the Administration made clear its endorsement of the principles implicit in the court decision as a friend of the court. . . .

Quite obviously, the right to fair representation that each vote count equally is, it seems to me, basic to the successful operation of a democracy.

I would hope that through the normal political processes these changes to insure equality of voting, especially of representation, would be brought about by the responsible groups involved in the states, in the national government.

Now, in the case that was involved here for many years it was impossible for the people involved to secure adequate relief through the normal political processes.

The inequity was built in and, therefore, there was no chance for a political response to the inequity. . . .

I would hope now the court having taken a position—I would hope that those responsible in the various states and this is not a matter confined merely to Tennessee but is true of Massachusetts and other states—I would hope because of the change in population areas that every state would re-examine this problem and attempt to insure equality of voting rights.

There is no sense of a Senator representing 5,000,000 people sitting next to a Senator representing 10,000 people and then when no relief comes to say the court is taking action where it should not.

It's the responsibility of the political groups to respond to the need, but if no relief is forthcoming then of course it seems to the Administration that the judicial branch must meet a responsibility.

CHAPTER 7

POLITICS, PARTIES, AND POLITICKING

THE WORD "POLITICS" is ordinarily used with multiple but uncertain meanings customarily evoking images of unappetizing people doing questionable things in a sleazy way for some selfish purpose. In actuality, politics is a method for deciding the objectives for which a community strives and the means for achieving the community's goals. To say that "when a group of politicians meet, all you get is the greatest common platitude" is to suggest also that in a democratic society successful politicians are those whose ideas are accepted, and successful ideas are those the citizenry will tolerate or applaud. In the United States, the citizen who derides politicians is mocking himself. When he scorns politics he rejects his own handiwork.

The American Constitution says nothing about political parties, and the framers rather anticipated that parties were a road to governmental perdition; and yet in the fullness of time it has become the political party—illustrating incidentally one aspect of the unwritten nature of our written Constitution—that has become a vital medium for enabling the American democracy to work.

It is the political party which helps make it possible for the United States to be governed: doing personnel recruiting and selection and training; identifying subjects of general concern; facilitating discussions of public affairs and arriving at approximations of agreements; giving the electorate a chance to acquire information and attitudes about important matters; joining people and their representatives into sizable aggregates of influence and so decreasing community fragmentation and governmental atomization.

As elsewhere in dealing with significant matters, the matter of semantics is a slippery thing; for example, there is a Humpty Dumpty quality to the use of the term "party" in application to the trained, disciplined conspirators in the Communist Party.

More accurate if less familiar and simple would be such designations as Communist Agency or Communist Conspiracy or Communist Corps of Disciplined Men Who Are Arms of a Foreign Government. Whatever other label is taken to be descriptive of the Communist organization, the use of "party" is misleading indeed, failing to differentiate between the American political party, an instrument for enforcing governmental responsibility, and the Communists, a very different vehicle with very different methods and objectives.

When the Labor-Management Relations Act of 1947 was challenged because the law required union leaders to file affidavits that they were not members of the Communist Party, the Court upheld the statutory requirement, and Justice Jackson spelled out the Party's distinguishing characteristics:

1. The goal of the Communist Party is to seize powers of government by and for a minority rather than to acquire power through the vote of a free electorate.

2. The Communist Party alone among American parties is dominated and controlled by a foreign government.

3. Violent and undemocratic means are the calculated and indispensable methods to attain the Communist Party's goal.

4. The Communist Party has sought to gain this leverage and hold on to the American population by acquiring control of the labor movement.

5. Every member of the Communist Party is an agent to execute the Communist program.

Stalin once remarked that "a party is a part of a class, its foremost part. Several parties, and consequently, freedom for parties, can exist only in a society in which there are antagonistic classes whose interests are mutually hostile and irreconcilable." In the U.S.S.R., he said, there are no antagonistic classes, so that "there is ground only for one party, the Communist Party." In contrast, the American assumption is that where there is freedom, there will be diverse interests and groupings, and that competing political parties are an essential medium whereby a free people can be organized to be governed.

In effect, American politics looks much less creative than it is in actuality; totalitarian politics looks more fruitful than it is in reality.

A Soviet View of American Elections

This article comes from a Soviet magazine translated into English from a Russian edition. Written in October, 1960, the article is a case study in misleading assumptions, unsupported assertions, and deceptively defined issues, all intertwined with occasional approximations of truth. For example, Joseph North is quite right in the thought that program differences between the two parties are hardly major, utterly mistaken in the inference that the two parties are therefore indistinguishable. At a particular moment one of the parties is in office, the other out of office. From this enormous difference stems the basis for a democratic society: the possibility for holding our governors responsible, for replacing the rulers we wish to reject, for free discussion of things as they are and as they ought to be.

North is a member of the editorial staff of *The Worker*, a newspaper published in the United States with the political lilt and ideological swing of *Pravda* and *Izvestia*.

[Joseph North, "On the Eve of the U.S. Elections," *International Affairs*, November, 1960, pp. 35–40.]

This is written in the closing weeks of the American presidential campaign: no man can predict the outcome. Whether the next president will be Senator John F. Kennedy of the Democratic Party or Vice-President Nixon of the Republican Party, is a moot question. The reason for that is clear. On the most vital of all issues—that of war or peace—i.e., peaceful coexistence, on which the future turns, neither man has spoken up in a way that can win the enthusiasm of the electoral mass. Few expected Nixon to do so; many hoped Kennedy would. On most issues both candidates—to date—are as alike as two peas in a pod. "Two boots" as somebody said.

This is also written during the turbulent days of the 15th United Nations Assembly. There the Socialist nations joined by the newcomers to the U.N., most of them African states, were on hand with creative proposals against imperialists and warmongers. No doubt all this will enter into the political campaign in its closing days. That question of questions—disarmament—will not down. Disarmament is the guarantee of the peace which the American people want—but they do not, as yet, see where the path to that peace lies. There are false prophets suggesting wrong roads, and that is the main question before the bepuzzled American people, today.

There is no guarantee that they will get an answer to this question during this election campaign. It is very possible that they will not. But they will demand some action—after this campaign is ended—regardless of who will be sitting in the presidential chair. And that preludes a continuing fight, one that will take different forms, doubtless, from the ones we see today. There is a high probability that the end of this campaign will see the initial stages of forming a new party, a third party, based upon a broad coalition of the people—labour, the Negro 18,000,000, the irate farmers, middle-class sectors, and possibly even some from higher brackets economically, who want to live and therefore want an end to the alarums and the preparations, nuclear and otherwise, for another world war. For one thing is clear in this campaign to date—millions of the electorate are unhappy that they have so little choice between the two candidates. . . .

This all happens in a time that is unique in American, or rather, in world history. This is a time when the fear of war is greater than it has ever been before. Most Americans by now know what nuclear war means —there were hearings before the Senate wherein scientists and other experts said the first hours of a nuclear war would mean forty million dead in the U.S.A. That fact got widespread attention, needless to say. The effect of radiation from nuclear tests is also widely known. The fear that it is getting into the milk and food already is one which many an American harbours. He knows about the effect on mankind's genes, on heredity, on the danger to the unborn as well as to those walking this earth.

This is also a time when most Americans fear the possibility of a major depression. Already it is well known that steel is functioning at less than 50 per cent of capacity and many workers in the king industry of the land are either jobless or on a three-day week. And in the automobile industry hundreds of thousands are jobless. The *Wall Street Journal* wrote late in September that a "recession" is already on. This raises questions of job and union security, pensions, etc.

This is a time, too, when the tenth man of the populace—the Negro—is on the march for full freedom now, in housing, in schools, in jobs. This is a time when he and millions of whites display interest and concern for the future of the African nations newly admitted to the U.N., and similarly, for Cuba and the fate of other Latin American lands.

These issues are real, they are omnipresent, and they will confront the next President, the next Administration, in even more specific, more powerful and insistent terms than they do today. So whether it be Kennedy, or whether it be Nixon, he will have to contend with the gravest questions of all time—the very survival, in its present form, of the nation (should the warmakers prevail), and the other questions—domestic prosperity and civic satisfaction that can only arise if the people and their various segments receive full equality with others. This is what Kennedy or Nixon face—so it would be well to take a look at the two men, and the forces, so far as can be determined, that are behind them.

Richard Nixon came to national prominence as a foremost spokesman of that red-baiting position which—in a straight line—led to the time of McCarthyism. He has tried to cast himself in the image of Horatio Alger's heroes—the poor but honest boy who rose industriously to become the bank president. This hero wants to be the president of bank presidents. Hence he has catered to the most benighted of the American public. He came in public limelight as an eager beaver member of the House Committee on Un-American Activities—the notorious un-American Committee. The hounding of men in governmental circles alleged to be Communists or "under Communist or Soviet influence" became his particular forte. Alger Hiss was one of them, and on the basis of sending him in January 1950 to a long prison term, Nixon became nationally prominent. It made him the fair-haired boy of the worst reactionary groupings in the country. He rose to the Senate in a campaign smearing his opponent in California. These shady activities earned him the soubriquet of tricky Dick, a dubious tribute to his foxy guile in being able to put his opponent in the worst public light. He was chosen President Eisenhower's running-mate by the political forces that chose Eisenhower. . . .

One can trace his political backers to the scandal of the twenty-odd thousand dollar slush fund in his campaign of 1951–1952 that was furnished by California oil men, Herbert Hoover, Jr., and assorted bankers and others. He helped draft the anti-labour "slave act" of 1947 called Taft-Hartley and he has not wavered since from a rabid, anti-labour line. . . .

Much in the personality of the Democratic candidate resembles the Republican. He too is young, in his mid-forties, a shrewd political manipulator, adept in the tactics of political gouge and kick to get where he wants to go. He makes a good appearance on the platform, has a certain political agility, as the phrase is delicately put. Born with a golden spoon in his mouth, his father, Joseph Kennedy, is one of America's ultra-rich. The *Fortune* magazine, in 1957, rated his wealth at $250 million. The *Look* magazine said the family wealth began with the presidential candidate's grandfather who owned two Boston saloons. The latter became one of Boston's Democratic Party leaders. He became big enough to enable his son Joe to marry the daughter of the reigning Democratic boss. Joe Kennedy, the father of John, was a bank president and an utilities executive in his mid-twenties, and made a big killing in real estate through his political connections. His wealth was widely distributed for investment and he got dividends from the stock market and the movies. He became U.S. maritime commissioner during the Roosevelt incumbency, and later was Ambassador to London where, it is reported he worked closely with the Anglo-German Fellowship Group. It was charged that he was a strong adherent of the Munich Pact, and his appeasement policy became notorious, so much so that he resigned his ambassadorship in the early days of the Second World War.

So father Kennedy put up the money for son Kennedy in the early days of the campaign, but stayed discreetly behind the scenes because of his political past. He staked the boy to at least a million in the early days of the electioneering. There is no clear clue to the place the rest of the money came from since. There is no doubt—in this complicated realm of American politics—that Rockefeller money is in the Kennedy campaign coffers through the Democrats' vice-presidential choice, Lyndon Johnson of Texas who is the political spokesman for the big Texas oil interests.

And when you say oil in Texas or America generally you generally find Rockefeller in it. So the moneyed interests are overlapping and undermining, wherever it suits them best. It suits them to have plenty of money on both candidates.

So behind both candidates looms the figure of the world's richest dynasty —the Rockefellers, of whom the Governor of New York State, Nelson, is the most powerful. He represents and leads that cabal of big businessmen and Pentagon–atomic energy commission (Dr. Edward Teller) who wants to pursue the cold war and heat it up. They belong to the school of let-the-third-world-war-come-quick-before-the-Russians-get-too-strong. Nelson Rockefeller financed the report that bears his name, and played a big part in the Gaither report, both of which virtually called for preventive war. Rockefeller tried to ram through a bill in the New York Assembly which would have every family in the country's most populous state building an atomic air-raid shelter beneath their homes. That was his contribution toward peaceful solutions. Fortunately even his associates in the state Republican Party knew they could not persuade the electorate to go for that, and the proposal died—but not Rockefeller's resolve to pursue the cold war.

Rockefeller diligently sought the Republican presidential nomination for himself. But evidently his confreres in top banking circles feared he would get altogether too strong for them to be able to compete to any degree, and they feared, too, that though he could manage to become Governor of New York State, his family name would work against him nationally. But his energies were not dimmed in his pursuit of an anti-Soviet reactionary policy, an effort to influence the programmes of both major parties.

How potent his force is can be seen by the switch in Nixon's position on Rockefeller's charges—joined by many Democratic leaders—that "inadequate military spending had weakened American security." Nixon for a time defended the Administration against these assaults. But on July 23, 1960, on the eve of the Republican Convention he lined himself up with Rockefeller and called publicly for a big increase in appropriations for arms to create "a nuclear retaliatory power capable of surviving surprise attack to inflict devastating punishment on any aggressor, and a modern, flexible and balanced military establishment capable of deterring or meeting any local aggression." This is the justification now offered for a further speeding up of the arms race.

Nixon and Rockefeller agreed that this demanded "more and improved bombers, airborne alert, speeded production of missiles and Polaris submarines, accelerated dispersal and hardening of bases.". . .

Needless to say neither Kennedy nor Nixon found heart-warming mass response to such a view of the nation's needs. And so the campaign has been characterized to date by a passivity, a dullness, which is apparent to any objective political analyst.

So far as Kennedy is concerned he is gambling with another factor—that of religion. He is of Irish Roman Catholic origin, which means that millions of Americans of Protestant derivation are suspicious of him. Catholic Kennedy chose the Protestant Dixiecrat Johnson as Vice-President to deflect the ill-will the South has for Catholic candidates. Many predict that the election result may well hinge on the religious factor. For Catholics constitute less than a quarter of the voting population, though they are in the major industrial areas, and are, in the main, members of the AFL-CIO. But many among the three-quarters of the people that are Protestant fear a Catholic on the grounds that he may "take orders from Rome"—i.e., the Pope, the hierarchy, will have the final and determining say in matters of state, and that the separation of church from state will become blurred to vanishing point.

This fear has enabled some of the worst fascists and crackpots to push themselves into the national scene and endanger the Democratic chances even further than they already are. These include such rabid groups as the Ku Klux Klan and other such outfits that have long traded on a traditional Neanderthal animosity based upon religion or colour. This fact has already played a part in the campaign, for it was discovered that certain organized pressures against Catholicism, pinpointing Kennedy, were being financed by certain top Republican quarters, and that Nixon had not, as yet, repudiated aid he is receiving from such circles.

In saying all this one must take into account that the policy-makers could not totally ignore the earnest wishes of the people for peace, for negotiations to arrive at improved relations with the Soviet Union. Both Nixon and Kennedy and their parties have declared themselves on record for negotiating with the Soviet Union and both have stated they stand by the goal of disarmament. The Republican platform puts it this way: "The Eisenhower-Nixon Administration has demonstrated its willingness to negotiate in earnest with the Soviet Union to arrive at just settlement for the reduction of world tensions. We pledge the new Administration to continue in the same course." The Democrats, in their platform, said to the "Communist world," "We are prepared to negotiate with you whenever and wherever there is a realistic possibility of progress without sacrifice of principle.". . .

So the lines overrun and overlap, undercut and undermine each other. Both parties are basically alike on the major issues today: the result is a very confusing and contradictory situation that leaves many voters in a high state of uncertainty, lack of enthusiasm and in many instances, confusion. Many have said they will "sit this one out." That is dangerous, for it displays a passivity which is precisely what reaction wants. Passivity suits the warmongers fine, for it would enable them to get away with their nefarious plans for a programme that would plunge this country even further along the highway toward war. It is just against such a contingency that the Communist Party of the United States warned the people.

. . . As an American newspaper wrote, "on the central issue of peace and the cold war there is no significant difference between the Republican and Democratic platforms, candidates and records." The paper showed that both are committed to militant pursuit of the cold war, substantially increased arms spending, continued nuclear arms manufacture and tests and uncompromising hostility to China and Cuba. You don't inspire a nation with a programme like that. In fact, you can't inspire even your own party, as the foregoing indicates.

It is history, now, that the reactionaries kept a firm hand on control of both parties and in their choice of candidates at the conventions, but they were obliged to make important platform concessions which can be the basis for mass movements of tremendous proportions. These concessions reflected the sharpening contradictions in American political life, and can hold the masses to the two-party system only temporarily. In the longer view, the concessions can contribute to the political enlightenment of the masses and the greater support for a potential labour-farmer-Negro people's party uniting all anti-monopoly forces.

As indicated herein at the outset, discontent with the two old party machines is widespread and it is growing. Whatever the results of this election, history will doubtless show the coalescence toward a new, broad, grass-roots people's political coalition consisting in large part of the many labour, farm, Negro and progressive organizations like the Midwest Independent Negro Voters League, the rapidly growing Negro people's movements in the South, the California Council of Democratic Clubs, the North Dakota non-partisan movement. . . .

The election campaign is a clear demonstration of the crisis of American parliamentary "democracy." The whole system of so-called "free elections" is in a blind alley: they clearly cannot in themselves determine the fate of the country and the people, not to mention the fact that the electors are in effect not being given a choice.

The election campaign has no less clearly reflected the crisis of American foreign policy: neither of the candidates is able to propose anything to replace a policy which has long been widely acknowledged to be bankrupt.

The urgent need to win the working people of America away from the baneful influences and ideological grip of both the old parties, the parties of monopoly capitalism, which are unable to meet the vital need for a genuinely "new look" in domestic and foreign policy, and for the working people to take the road of independent political development—there is the lesson of the election campaign. This is bound to be confirmed by the results of the voting.

When Is a Party System Possible?

In exploring the question of whether a party system is possible in African nations, a noted British political scientist illuminates the meanings and presumptions on which political arrangements—including those in the United States—depend.

Sir Ivor Jennings is a professor at Cambridge University and the author of many books on virtually every aspect of political science; he has served as consultant to national governments abroad.

[Sir Ivor Jennings, "Is a Party System Possible in Africa?" *The Listener,* Feb. 16, 1961, pp. 293–294.]

Every country in the Commonwealth has adopted, at least at the beginning, the principle of responsible government with adult franchise. Provided that the transition from British rule has been well prepared there is a good chance of stable government for the first eight or ten years. Experience not only in Asia but also, in the early years, in Canada and Australia, has shown that there may be difficulties. Politicians find it easy to agree when the main object is self-government or independence. They find it less easy when independence has been attained.

The disagreement may be about policies and it may be about personalities; often it is about both. There are plenty of disagreements in United Kingdom governments; but the United Kingdom system differs from that in a newly independent country because the strength of the government rests on the support of a huge party organization. It is virtually impossible to break away and form a new party unless there is a major split right down through the party, and that can happen only over an issue of fundamental importance. On any smaller issue, a dissenting Minister has either to acquiesce and carry on as Minister, or step outside the Cabinet and remain in the party as a candid but friendly critic of the administration.

In a newly independent country this sort of party organization in depth, bound together by ancient loyalties, can hardly exist, it does exist in India, but the Indian National Congress fought for self-government for forty years; and even so the Congress is much less highly organized than, say, the Conservative Party in Britain. The ordinary party in a newly independent country effectively consists only of a collection of politicians, without organization in depth. It is therefore easy to break up on policy or personality.

The first step towards military rule in Pakistan was the split in the Muslim League caused by the dismissal of Nazimuddin in 1953. The virtual dismissal of Bandaranaike in 1952 led to the defeat of the United National Party of Ceylon in 1956. The conflict between the two major parties was one of the causes of military rule in Sudan. A party split does not matter, and indeed it may be an advantage, if it results in the setting-up of an opposition and so permits something like the two-party system of the United Kingdom. It is not likely that this will be the result, at least for some considerable time. It means that there would have to be two large parties organized in depth, that one of them would have to be content to remain out of office for something like ten years, and that the party in power would have to recognize that the Opposition was rendering a valuable service to the community—so that Government and Opposition were, so to speak, working together to ensure that the Government was effectively criticized. Every one of these requirements would be difficult to attain. They would demand the sort of political maturity which usually develops only after a long experience of democratic government. Much more likely is a fragmentation of parties, producing short and unstable Coalition Governments.

One possible solution to this problem is to get nearer to the American presidential system. That system is not likely to work in its entirety, because it is based fundamentally on understandings about the relations between the President and the Congress which have developed over nearly 200 years. It is difficult, if not impossible, to put these understandings into legal form, as I discovered when I made an experimental draft in Pakistan. But it is possible to get somewhere near the American system by other means: it has been done in France and in Ghana.

These cases depended on the personalities of General de Gaulle and Dr. Nkrumah, and it is never easy to find successors of the same quality. The presidential system makes reasonably certain that for four or five years there will be stable government; but it is also necessary to ensure that the government will be responsive to public opinion. The United States narrowly limits the powers of the President by vesting powers in the Congress. That is one of the strongest legislatures in the world, and in it are two parties as highly organized as those of Great Britain. A presidential election is a conflict of organized parties, each of which nominates its candidates. So the presidential system assumes that there will be at least one party in opposition to the President, strong in the constituencies, and strong in the legislature. . . .

In any case, one ought to write into the Constitution what in other forms of drafting are called "protective clauses." This means that the draftsman must ask himself what dangers the minorities feel most strongly, and try to invent devices to meet them. It may be their lands, their language, their share of government jobs, their educational system. Lands, for instance, are dealt with at length in the Constitution of Malaya, language in the Constitution of India, appointments to the public service in most of the recent Constitutions; and the educational systems are dealt with in the Constitution of Canada.

I do not suggest that these are examples to copy; I merely say that it is not beyond the wit of man to produce formulae which will provide protection. One could even extend the examples to social customs and tribal organization, though that might be more difficult. People usually think not in terms of protective clauses but of Bills of Rights. But Bills of Rights have a different purpose, to protect the individual rather than communities. They protect the individual against harsh or unjust legislation. They are difficult to draft because, if they contain broad, general propositions, like those in the United States, they open the way to a variety of different interpretations. If, on the other hand, they go into some detail, like the Bill of Rights in India, they become antiquated quickly because their language relates to social and economic conditions at the time of passing the Bill. Also, all Bills of Rights depend on the existence of a strong judiciary whose decisions are generally acceptable.

Nevertheless, we have had considerable experience of different forms of Bills of Rights in the United States, Canada, Nigeria, India, Pakistan, and Malaya: and so it is possible to devise a Bill of Rights which suits the conditions of a particular country. Constitutional devices give protection to groups and individuals, but they cannot replace goodwill, and this means goodwill on both sides. India's greatest protection has been not the Bill of Rights in the Constitution, but the evident intention of Mr. Nehru to discourage, by all the means in his power, the sort of communal attack which was common form before 1947.

Adlai Stevenson Talks about Campaigning

Chaired by Senator John O. Pastore of Rhode Island, the Subcommittee on Communications of the Senate Committee on Interstate and Foreign Commerce held hearings to consider legislation to amend the political broadcast provisions of the Communications Act, which mandates that radio and television stations afford equal opportunities to all legally qualified candidates for any public office if the stations permit any candidate to use their facilities.

It was the Lar Daly decision of the Federal Communications Commission which led to intensive examination of the "equal time" provisions of the law. FCC actions arose from the fact that primary elections were slated to be held in Chicago early in 1959. Mayor Richard J. Daley was a candidate in the Democratic primary; Timothy P. Sheehan, a candidate in the Republican primary. Lar Daly, a perennial candidate for open public offices who habitually campaigned wearing an Uncle Sam costume, was a candidate in both primaries. Prior to primary day, Lar Daly filed a complaint with FCC alleging that Chicago television stations had, in the course of their newscasts, shown film clips of his primary opponents in connection with certain events, such as greeting a foreign dignitary. Daly had requested equal time of these stations and had been refused. FCC then ruled that Daly was entitled to equal time.

The Adlai Stevenson testimony below is part of an extensive set of hearings at which appeared television-network executives, congressmen, interest-group representatives, civil-liberties spokesmen, minor-party leaders, and others.

In the end Congress adopted a resolution waiving the "equal time" provisions of the Communications Act for the 1960 presidential election, thus making possible the Kennedy-Nixon television appearances during the campaign. Not quite the end of the issue of politicians' access to television was signified by the adoption of the 1960 resolution, for here as everywhere in American politics, there was continuing agitation for legislative and administrative changes.

[*Presidential Campaign Broadcasting Act, Hearings before the Communications Subcommittee of the Senate Committee on Interstate and Foreign Commerce,* 86th Cong., 2d Sess. (1960), pp. 3–12.]

MR. STEVENSON. Mr. Chairman and members of the committee, while I am not an expert in the field of public relations or even in campaigning, as I think my record has proven [laughter], I appreciate very much the invitation of your committee to appear here in support of a proposal, calculated, I believe, to help to furnish the American people with the knowledge which is prerequisite to an intelligent exercise of their duty as electors in a free society. . . .

I doubt if ever before in history have so many men and women, living over so wide an area, been expected to participate in choosing from among men they do not know, two national leaders to whom they will entrust such a large measure of their destiny. I doubt further if the issues with which these leaders will have to deal have ever been more complex and fateful.

To suggest comparison with the usual questions to which our forebears expected the candidates to devote hours of public debate illustrates this growing complexity. Compare the argument over free coinage of silver with today's problems of fiscal and monetary policy, or the debate over the size of the standing army or the fortification of Guam with that over the missile gap. Consider what issues faced by previous generations had the implications of nuclear arms development and distribution. And doesn't agricultural overproduction produce more baffling problems than underproduction?

To hear the candidate discuss the great issues of an earlier America, people rode all day by buggy or wagon; they waited for hours for the candidate's train; they stood in the sun and rain and listened. They wanted to know about the issues and where the candidate stood.

Today's citizens seem to have less time and taste for political controversy, but certainly the need for enlightenment and considered participation is no less. And they are entitled to demand: Who is this man? How does he look? What does he believe? What is his idea of America's future and its place in the world? How will he use the power of the Presidency, and for what ends? Does he deal in facts, and discuss issues frankly, or does he prefer generalities and platitudes? He may declare for education, but is he for better schools; for health, but does he favor medical insurance; for free enterprise, but will he seek to restrain monopoly; for prosperity, but has he a program to restore depressed areas; for peace, but will he press for negotiated settlement of differences? How deep are his convictions? How considered his views? How honest his attitudes?

All of these matters seem directly related to the bill before you, for the technology of our civilization is equal to its problems. We have the means, through television, to bring the candidates for President and Vice President face to face with virtually all Americans for the first time. They can sit down with 40 million families often enough and for long enough periods to discuss the questions which are critical to our survival and our leadership in the world. But only the Congress can make that possible.

The political parties, the Congress, and the television industry share responsibility, I suppose, for the fact that television has contributed far less than it could to the people's understanding of the issues or knowledge of the candidate's position.

Network television time has become almost prohibitively expensive. For example, one hour of prime TV time on all networks this fall may cost over $400,000, or over $6,000 a minute.

The party with the largest campaign fund will provide its candidate more time on television than his opponent. He is seen and heard more times by more people. He gains an advantage, and democracy suffers from the unequal contest.

The cost of television also produces a frantic determination to squeeze the maximum number of votes from the investment. The almost unbelievable complexity of television scheduling has long since made necessary the services of the professional advertising agency in national campaigns. Drawing on their broad experience and unquestioned success in selling soap, cereal, and deodorants, it isn't surprising that the advertising agencies recommend the jingle, the spot announcement and the animated cartoon. So the American voter, faced with issues of life and death, is solicited in song to "Vote for Dan, the man with the plan." This kind of presentation.

There are, of course, television broadcasts of speeches by the candidates in normal campaigns. These are sometimes not much more useful, however, to the voter than the jingle. Presidential campaign ritual requires that the candidate be shuttled from coast to coast as many times as possible, assuring maximum physical exhaustion, and minimum opportunity to prepare his statements. The result is the ever greater use of the ghost writer and the ever greater difficulty of knowing the candidate himself. Because his time is scheduled around personal appearances, it is the television broadcast which must be fitted in, often at the last minute and in unsuitable circumstances.

The result is that the candidate is usually seen and heard addressing a rally of the party faithful. This means a lengthy introduction of the candidate by a person whose views on his qualifications are both predictable and irrelevant, with diminished time for the candidate. It also means the audience expects that a certain amount of time be devoted to the assertion, if a Democratic rally, that the Democratic Party is the party of the people, or if a Republican rally, that Republicans are patriotic savers and Democrats socialistic spenders. . . .

Before closing, Mr. Chairman and gentlemen, I would like to discuss some of the grounds which have been suggested for opposition to, or at least apprehension about, this legislation. Some who are in complete sympathy with its purposes are concerned over the effect of the eligibility requirements on third parties. As I understand it, the bill requires that broadcasters make free time available only to the presidential candidate of a political party whose candidate in the preceding election was supported by not fewer than 4 percent of the total popular votes cast. The practical effect of this requirement is that only the candidates of the Democratic and Republican Parties would be eligible for free television time in this year's election. A third party organized this year would have to get 4 percent of the popular vote in 1960 to have its candidate eligible for free time in 1964.

I believe that this is a sensible provision. Our two-party system has evolved more than a century and a half, and the realities of our political system are such that no third party is going to elect its candidate for President in the first election after its organization. Nor is it likely to elect its candidate in the second election after its organization if in its first attempt it was supported by less than 4 percent of the popular vote. It is obviously impractical to make free time available to a dozen presidential candidates which may emerge and often have in our political past.

I believe that the results which would be achieved through this legislation can be accomplished in no other way. Representatives of the television industry have insisted that the networks are anxious to provide adequate time, and that no legislative compulsion of this kind is required. I believe this view is unrealistic.

Even if the networks are prepared to sell prime time to the political parties, which they are not obligated to do, this does not correct their unequal ability to purchase it. It does not simplify the problem of dealing with a number of networks and dozens of individual stations, nor eliminate the difficulty of scheduling anything like nationwide coverage. It does not insure the responsible use of the time purchased by the political parties. Moreover, such offers of cooperation are always made with the unstated reservation that it be on the networks' own terms. For example, I understand that one network has recently announced that it will only sell time on an exclusive basis, and not for programs to be broadcast simultaneously by a competitor.

The networks and stations are effectively prevented from making free time available to the candidates of the major parties by the provisions of section 315, that the chairman just discussed and you are all familiar with, of the Federal Communications Act, which would require that equal time be made available to any minor party which demanded it. Before time for a series of speeches or debates could be provided, this section would have to be amended to relieve them of the obligation to provide equal time to other parties. Thus, legislation would be necessary in any event. I understand that there was strong opposition in the Congress last year to a general exemption of political debates from the equal-time requirement. Even if such an exemption were confined to the presidential campaign, we would still confront a confusion of opinion about the proper form, time, and manner of using the exemption, compounded by the inevitable differences between the two parties. . . .

Finally, gentlemen, I find no criticism of this measure is more unjustified, it seems to me, than the charge that it is Government interference with free speech. Rather, it represents a guarantee of free speech. The freedom of speech which our Nation's founders fought to preserve was more than the right of a peddler on Boston Common to hawk his oysters without restraint. It was the right of public discussion of political issues. Their devotion to it was not to an abstract right, but born of conviction that full discussion of alternatives was prerequisite to an intelligent choice between them. The same conviction motivates the sponsors of this bill. They propose only to insure the free access to the means of communication which will permit that discussion to take place in the full view of all of our citizens. . . .

SENATOR MONRONEY. Governor, you have observed through the years there has been made available to the President after he is elected nationwide programs of public information and public positions; I believe your testimony would seem to indicate that the acquaintanceship and the knowledge of what a candidate stands for before election is of a similar degree of public importance to that which the networks perform regularly and at a great expense throughout the years in making time available to a President after election.

If they claim that this is a serious imposition upon the networks, would not the same argument apply about the requirement that they impose upon themselves for Presidential broadcast after a Presidential election which they voluntarily assume as a public service and they have never complained about performing?

MR. STEVENSON. Yes, sir; I hadn't thought of it exactly that way, Senator Monroney, but I think it is fair to say that it is a matter of at least as much public interest in the choice of a President as it is in the conduct of the Presidency after he is chosen, and that this period prior to an election is quite as important as most periods after an election; therefore, to give time for this purpose is a public service at least equivalent—I would be tempted to say more important than postelection, when they give very generous time. . . .

Fair Political Campaign Practices

The excerpt below is from hearings held by a committee of the House of Representatives chaired by Clifford Davis of Tennessee. Testifying is Bruce L. Felknor, the executive director of the Fair Campaign Practices Committee. All civilization produces some sewage as a by-product, and American politics is no exception to the proposition that where there is vigorous campaigning, there is also some political fall-out. Felknor's assumption is that politics constitutes a reflection of the total society.

[*Campaign Expenditures Committee, Report and Hearings of the House Special Committee to Investigate Campaign Expenditures,* 86th Cong., 2d Sess. (1960), pp. 105–109.]

MR. FELKNOR. Thank you, Mr. Chairman and gentlemen. First, may I say that your committee is to be commended for its prompt and diligent discharge of its responsibility. The election campaign is the principal single force obviously that forms the attitudes of citizens toward politics. Politics and, indeed, government is just as healthy or just as sick as the citizens require it or allow it to be.

The Fair Campaign Practices Committee believes devoutly in vigorous, colorful, argumentative, and informative election campaigns. We do not, incidentally, feel that a campaign must be insipid in order to be fair. As Viscount Morley put it 70 or so years ago, whoever would treat politics and morality apart will never understand either the one or the other.

Mr. Chairman, your gracious invitation to Charles P. Taft, chairman of our committee, to testify found him with a legal case in which he is involved in Cincinnati and found him unable to be here today. He asked me to read a brief statement of his own and to continue with an equally brief set of comments of my own. Mr. Taft's observations follow:

> The problem of the cost of national party campaigns is obviously related to the length of the campaign, but the connection is not just mathematical. The problem for the national party begins with the premise that the real base of the national party is The Organization—capitalize them if you will—in the county. I question how really effective any State organization is. Each is a collection of county satraps. Mr. Kennedy goes after Mr. Prendergast, the State chairman, and Mr. DeSapio, county chairman, by lining up the county bosses in Brooklyn and in the Bronx; and Mr. Prendergast counters by chasing the other 60. He does not automatically have them in his pocket just by being State chairman in New York.
>
> Each county satrap in the 3,000 U.S. counties is obviously concerned about his local ticket. In the big urban counties he does not care about much else. In these days of fairly pervasive civil service restrictions under the Hatch Act, the Governor of the State is much more important for volume of patronage than is the President or a Senator. So if the candidate for President wants attention to himself and the national issues, he has to set up Independents for Wintergreen or the equivalent thereof. This means a national office and a State office in order to produce local offices with glamor, noise, and impact. This costs money in a nation of our size and variety.
>
> It has to be a rush job. It cannot be permanent because the organization in each county won't permit it. You have to have paid people at all levels for this special effort, and to get good ones producing at minimum cost and to avoid the incompetent, the self-promoter, and the universal headache takes a type of knowing and effective supervision often lacking. Even if the Independents for Wintergreen have their missions well in hand, the organization wants so many dollars per precinct for election day.
>
> In my book, this very sizable sum is money down the drain, but it is always put up. I suppose the organization could cut the candidate's throat actively or by sitting on their hands but since in a close election, when the prospects look bad, the organization, even though paid money, will cut the national candidate's throat anyway to "save the ticket." Therefore, I stick by my judgment, all of which makes Independents for Wintergreen all the more necessary.
>
> Depending on the ingenuity of its national leaders and the length of the campaign, there will be attached to this ad hoc national office burgeoning

staffs with such responsibilities as for nationality groups and under various pretty and disarming titles for problems raised by the Negro and religious groups. The expense both for the main, direct, and emergency operation and for its supporting echelons will expand in proportion to campaign length, because the very existence of this special operation requires special literature, printing, and distribution. Locally the Independents for Winteergreen must have offices in prominent downtown street locations, buttons, and gimmicks, and simple, solidly effective leaflets with some variety. The longer the campaign, the more the variety, the more the expense.

If things go well, the organization will demand at least equal attention in the way of buttons and literature. That is, the county organization. The longer the campaign, the more likely are demands for the cost of letters to names on various lists and then telephone schemes, especially the canned message types. Personally, I believe only in well-thought-out telephone schemes with personal calls by professionals, but professionals cost money. The shorter the campaign, the fewer the demands.

In my view, from every angle the national campaign as it exists today is much too long. Thus, it becomes boring. The impact of a national campaign would be much more concentrated and effective in 4 weeks. In Great Britain, of course, they do it in 3, but since the country is much smaller and the transportation problem is much smaller, it would probably require an additional week here.

A short campaign offers the candidate on the national ticket a much better excuse not to have to cover every town, but it does give time to cover all the important issues.

I believe the only realistic way to cut down on the length of the campaign would be to move the national conventions to a later date. I think it is in the interest of an effective political system—parenthetically let me explain that the word "effective" in this context is with a lower case "e"—in the interest of an effective political system, it has to happen. I would love to see it happen.

This is the end of Mr. Taft's statement. Obviously, his remarks are based on his own lifetime of political experience and observation rather than upon the activities of the Fair Campaign Practices Committee, per se.

THE CHAIRMAN. Mr. Felknor, your reading of that characteristic statement of Mr. Taft's was just as colorful as his statement. I thoroughly appreciate it for myself and also I appreciate the intonations and the emphasis you gave it.

MR. FELKNOR. Thank you very much, Mr. Chairman. I worked for Mr. Taft 5 years and listened to a lot of his intonation on the telephone and across the table. Thank you, sir. I will relay those gracious remarks to Mr. Taft.

Now, if I may undertake to address your committee's area of interest from the standpoint of the Fair Campaign Practices Committee, I will speak for myself as the executive director and staff person, so to speak, of the committee. Several pertinent matters come to mind.

Now, as to the length of campaigns, from our standpoint perhaps no cam paign would be likely to be short enough to rule out the most offensive of the smear literature, for this material is usually reserved for the closing days, however long the campaign has gone on before. However, I believe that to some degree smear tactics seek to capitalize on the boredom, the satiety, the up-to-here feeling of the voters that characterizes the closing days or weeks of a long campaign. If a campaign were short enough so that it would develop new and pertinent and genuine information on the opposing stands of candidates from beginning to end, if repetitiousness did not set in weeks before election day, perhaps dirty campaigning would face stiffer competition for the eye and ear of the voter.

If, for example, in the recent campaign Nixon and Kennedy are arguing meaningfully about foreign policy, let us say, fewer voters would be distracted from the main event by the suggestion that the Pope is ordering Catholics to vote for the Senator from Massachusetts or that a deed to a former home of the Vice President proves he is anti-Semitic and anti-Negro. . . .

The Fair Campaign Practices Committee has not yet finished counting the scurrilous and borderline anti-Catholic material that was circulated in the presidential campaign. Pieces of literature we have never seen before continue now, more than a month after election day, to reach us—every 2 or 3 days. Some of this material was printed in press runs of 100,000 copies or more. Surely, no fewer than tens of millions of pieces of this kind of literature circulated around the country by hand and by mail openly and anonymously. Surely, also scores of thousands of dollars were spent on printing alone and tens or scores of thousands more on postage. . . .

I may say the job this year dwarfs our previous efforts simply because of the fantastic volume of anti-Catholic material. This added volume meant that in addition to our so-called normal load of complaints and documentation about unfair campaigning on nonreligious issues, we have an additional load equal to some 1,000 percent of our normal volume for a biennial national election. In short, we seem to have about 11 times the volume of work ahead of us in 1961 that we undertook in 1959. We certainly do not have 11 times the staff or the budget.

I should make it clear that the great bulk of unfair campaign material, the overwhelming majority of it, comes from outside the two parties. This trash originates for the most part with overzealous individuals, unauthorized partisans and with established hatemongers who see a chance to hitchhike on a campaign to advance their own pet hate.

In this connection there comes to mind the adage, the politician's plaint: I can take care of my enemies, but God help me with my friends.

Our committee enjoys the wholehearted cooperation of both the Republican and Democratic National Committees in our educational effort to help voters and future voters become able to identify smear tactics in a campaign.

Two items in our program of public education may be of interest to your committee, and I will hand copies of them to the members. One is a pamphlet for use in schools and discussion groups, called Fair Play in Politics. The other is a leaflet called Voters Checklist, intended for large-scale distribution. It enumerates briefly and illustrates with cartoons the specific smear tactics we have found to be in widest current use. I am happy to report that local, State, and National committees of both the major parties have distributed substantial quantities of both these publications to their own people.

The position of our committee is that the area of campaign ethics is a particularly difficult one to regulate by legislation. Clearly also effective legislative regulation is difficult in the realm of campaign finance. In both areas I believe the most effective approach is publicity, disclosure, exposure.

Mr. Chairman and gentlemen, I thank you.

THE CHAIRMAN. Thank you. It is refreshing to have a man of your caliber, representing a splendid organization, appear before us. You have been most helpful.

Are there any questions?

MR. CRAMER. You do not make direct contributions to candidates?

MR. FELKNOR. No, siree. We neither endorse nor oppose any candidate nor take a stand on any issue. Our total function is to try to increase public awareness and consciousness of fair and unfair campaigning. We go beyond that to recognize that this is necessarily a subjective area of judgment, and we do not put out a checklist that is so detailed that it would enumerate every possible unfair tactic. What may be perfectly proper to one man in one situation may be quite the reverse elsewhere.

Principles of Political Decency

This code was prepared by the Fair Campaign Practices Committee, located in New York City.

Using the provisions of the code as criteria, the student may be interested in assessing elections in different places or in the same place at different times.

[Code of Fair Campaign Practices, in "Ethics in Government," *Report by the Minnesota Governor's Committee on Ethics in Government,* St. Paul, Minn., 1959, pp. 34–35.]

There are basic principles of decency, honesty and fair play which every candidate for public office in the United States has a moral obligation to observe and uphold, in order that, after vigorously contested but fairly conducted campaigns, our citizens may exercise their constitutional right to a free and untrammeled choice and the will of the people may be fully and clearly expressed on the issues before the Country.

THEREFORE:

I SHALL CONDUCT my campaign in the best American tradition, discussing the issues as I see them, presenting my record and policies with sincerity and frankness, and criticizing without fear or favor the record and policies of my opponent and his party which merit such criticism.

I SHALL DEFEND AND UPHOLD the right of every qualified American voter to full and equal participation in the electoral process.

I SHALL CONDEMN the use of personal vilification, character defamation, whispering campaigns, libel, slander, or scurrilous attacks on any candidate or his personal or family life.

I SHALL CONDEMN the use of campaign material of any sort which misrepresents, distorts, or otherwise falsifies the facts regarding any candidate, as well as the use of malicious or unfounded accusations against any candidate which aim at creating or exploiting doubts, without justification, as to his loyalty and patriotism.

I SHALL CONDEMN any appeal to prejudices based on race, creed, class or national origin.

I SHALL CONDEMN any dishonest or unethical practice which tends to corrupt or undermine our American system of free elections or which hampers or prevents the full and free expression of the will of the voters.

I SHALL IMMEDIATELY AND PUBLICLY REPUDIATE the support of any individual or group which resorts, on behalf of my candidacy, to the methods and tactics which I condemn.

I, the undersigned candidate for election to public office in the United States of America, hereby endorse, subscribe to and solemnly pledge myself to conduct my campaign in accordance with the above principles and practices, so help me God.

______

Date

____

Signature

Who Votes How?

Written by George Gallup, the material below appeared as a column in newspapers across the United States under the subhead: "Republicans Show Losses in All Groups since 1956, but Have Gained Ground in Recent Months." In examining the data, the citizen should bear in mind the closeness of presidential (and other) elections in the United States. The 1960 election outcome was close indeed, with Kennedy receiving 50.2 and Nixon 49.8 per cent of the combined Democratic and Republican vote, but even "landslide" victories will find the victor with perhaps no more than 55 to 58 per cent of the vote.

The student should remember the distinction between popular vote and electoral-college vote. In 1960, for instance, the Kennedy-Johnson ticket received 332 electoral votes and the Nixon-Lodge candidacy 191, a division of electoral votes that separates the winner and the loser far more decisively than does the difference in the popular vote.

Gallup's interpretations are concerned particularly with comparisons of the voting shifts between 1956 and 1960. Another way of reading the tables sheds considerable light on another aspect of American political life: differential voting patterns within the population groups, i.e., comparisons among voters on the basis of sex, color, education, political preference, occupation, age, and religion.

["Poll Charts Shifts in Major Voting Groups since 1956," *Public Opinion News Service Release,* Oct. 7, 1960, by George Gallup, Director of the American Institute of Public Opinion.]

One of the best ways to understand present trends in the election race is to examine the shifts which have taken place within various population groups since the 1956 presidential election.

Immediately after each national election, the Gallup Poll makes a careful analysis of its election survey data to record how each major group in the population voted in that election.

Comparison of survey results of recent weeks with 1956 election figures reveals that Vice-President Nixon is polling less in all groups than Eisenhower did in 1956. Although the losses are small in most groups, in six of these groups these losses run to 10 percentage points or more.

When figures from surveys taken before the conventions are compared with post-convention figures in the Nixon-Kennedy race, shifts are small, but generally in the direction of Nixon.

In 1956, President Eisenhower received 58 per cent of the popular vote, to Stevenson's 42 per cent. In the present campaign to date, Nixon and Kennedy are each getting approximately 50 per cent of the committed vote—which means a drop of 8 percentage points from 1956 in the case of the Republican candidate, and a like gain of 8 percentage points for Kennedy over Stevenson.

The following table illustrates the shift by population groups in the vote for the 1956 and the 1960 Republican candidates:

SHIFT SINCE 1956 (*A comparison of the 1956 Eisenhower election vote with the 1960 vote*)

Population group	Eisenhower 1956 election %	Nixon 1960 standing %	Shift in points
National	58	50	− 8
Men	55	49	− 6
Women	61	51	−10
White	59	51	− 8
Non-white	39	38	− 1
College	69	62	− 7
High School	58	48	−10
Grade School	50	45	− 5
Republicans	96	95	− 1
Democrats	15	14	− 1
Independents	70	57	−13
Professional and Business	68	63	− 5
White-collar	63	55	− 8
Farmers	54	54	0
Manual Workers	50	39	−11
21–29 years	57	42	−15
30–49 years	55	47	− 8
50 years and over	61	55	− 6
Protestants	63	61	− 2
Catholics	49	27	−22
Jews	25	19	− 6

Equally revealing are the shifts which have come about in this election year. A comparison of the standings of the two candidates in "trial heats" in the six month period prior to the national conventions, and their standings in August-September surveys, shows that the conventions did little to change their relative standings.

The shifts in most groups, as the table below illustrates, are not large enough, in most cases, to have significance. Nixon, as these figures show, has gained in 14 groups, lost in four.

SHIFT FROM PRE-CONVENTION PERIOD (*A comparison of the pre-convention vote for Nixon with the later Nixon vote*)

Population group	Nixon Pre-convention figure (Based on 6 months' surveys)	Nixon Later standing (Based on Aug.–Sept., 1960, surveys)	Shift in points
National	48	50	+ 2
Men	47	49	+ 2
Women	49	51	+ 2
White	48	51	+ 3
Non-white	41	38	− 3
College	60	62	+ 2
High School	47	48	+ 1
Grade School	44	45	+ 1
Republican	91	95	+ 4
Democrat	16	14	− 2
Independent	53	57	+ 4
Professional and Business	57	63	+ 6
White-collar	45	55	+10
Farmers	49	54	+ 5
Manual Workers	41	39	− 2
21–29 years	44	42	− 2
30–49 years	43	47	+ 4
50 years and over	55	55	0
Protestant	61	61	0
Catholic	24	27	+ 3
Jews	14	19	+ 5

Experiment in Television Influence

The column below was written by George Gallup and appeared in newspapers across the nation under the caption: "Experiment in Gallup Poll Opinion Laboratory Asked Voters for Before and After Ratings." The findings here agree with other data suggesting that television was a significant factor in influencing the Kennedy-Nixon election outcome. Whether television may generally be expected to be a major political opinion determinant remains a subject of speculation. In any case, the student may bear in mind the enormous impact on political opinions of factors other than television: socioeconomic status, place of residence, and so on through a long train of other timeworn bases of political preferences.

Gallup's data may be read not only as a commentary on the types of material that are effective in persuading people to vote this way or that; the experiment is also a case study in political (and other) communication, suggesting the bland, nonintellectual subject matter that interests people the year round.

["'Test Audience' Gave Reactions to TV Debate Minute-by-Minute," *Public Opinion News Service Release,* Oct. 2, 1960, by George Gallup, Director of the American Institute of Public Opinion.]

The real "pay-off" from the first TV debate will be a gain for either Kennedy or Nixon in the number of voters won to their standard.

Gallup Poll interviewers across the country are now completing a check—started after last Monday night's debate—which will indicate whether either candidate has been able to break the virtual dead-lock in poll findings which has characterized the 1960 race for the last month and a half.

In this same study, interviewers are finding out not only how many watched the debate, but what kind of an audience it was—whether Republicans outnumbered Democrats, more younger voters than older voters, and so on. . . .

"TEST AUDIENCE" WATCHED TV DEBATE

As one means of gauging the reaction to the debate between Nixon and Kennedy, the Gallup Poll assembled 125 men and women in its test interviewing center in Hopewell, N.J. This group—representing all shades of political belief—watched the television meeting between the rival candidates.

In this experiment—which made use of new research techniques—the audience was asked for its view about the candidates both before and after the debate. Using a scale-type question called the Stapel Scale, these voters rated Kennedy and Nixon just before the debate got underway, then again immediately upon its completion. Viewers were also asked to state what they thought were the best points made by each man.

In addition, a carefully selected group of 60 "wavering" or undecided voters were asked to record their reactions on a minute-to-minute basis throughout the debate. This part of the test in the "opinion laboratory" made use of the Hopkins Televote Machine, a device by which a voter can indicate any degree of favorable or unfavorable opinion about what is being said. Opinions of the 60 voters were recorded simultaneously and fed into a central unit. Reactions were averaged and charted on a sensitized tape—providing, in effect, a profile of audience reaction to the entire debate.

WHAT THE TEST SHOWS

As might be expected, on the over-all test, there was little change in feeling among ardent Democrats and Republicans. The former, if anything, grew more convinced of the merits of Mr. Kennedy, the latter were also favorably impressed with Mr. Nixon.

Among Independent voters, however, the evidence is that Senator Kennedy scored somewhat better than did Vice-President Nixon on his performance on this occasion. Republicans may take comfort in the fact, however, that the subject of this debate, "Domestic Issues," was one on which polls have consistently noted a Democratic edge.

Before the debate, Kennedy had 32 per cent expressing a very favorable opinion of him among the Independent group; immediately after he scored 48 per cent for a gain of 16 points.

With Nixon, his "before" and "after" scores among Independents were 46 per cent and 50 per cent—a gain of 4 points.

WHY EACH MAN WAS EFFECTIVE

Each person in the test audience of 125 was asked, at the conclusion, which candidate he believed had done the better job and why he felt that he had. Among those voters who gave Kennedy the edge, these were typical reasons why:

Why Kennedy Was Favored

"Kennedy was more constructive and definitive in his program proposals . . . his rebuttals were much more to the point and dealt less in generalities. . . . Kennedy had confident, organized, composed command of specific information . . . he replied more rapidly and forcefully—he seized challenges. . . . Kennedy was more alert and ready, particularly in rebuttal . . . he showed more poise."

Among voters who thought Nixon turned in a better performance, these were typical responses:

Why Nixon Was Favored

"Nixon's policies and proposals were more sound . . . he made more concrete suggestions for the future. . . . Nixon was more specific, factual and logical. . . . Nixon had a program with an explanation, Kennedy did not have an explanation for his. . . . I liked the positive approach Nixon used rather than the derogatory approach which Kennedy employed. . . . Nixon was more capable and more practical—his promises could be kept."

TELEVOTE REACTIONS

An examination of the electronically recorded "profile" of the debate shows these highlights about the reactions of the "Televote Audience"—persons who were wavering or undecided about their preferences:

* Kennedy's average rating was slightly higher than Nixon's when the total one-hour record is considered. The Senator's opening speech of 8 minutes was particularly effective; Mr. Nixon's rating during his 8-minute opening was generally lower.

* Both men tended to bring forth better reactions when they were speaking in an inspirational, more generalized manner.

Kennedy, for example, scored well on such phrases as: "If we fail, then freedom fails," or "I think it's time America started moving again," or "I want them to say these were the years when the tide came in; these were the years when the United States started to move again."

Nixon elicited favorable reactions with comments such as: "A record is never something to stand on. It's something to build on," or "No President should ever allow anybody else to make the major decisions," or "I stand for programs that will mean growth and progress."

* Both men tended to "lose" their audience—that is, provoke negative reaction—when they went into recitations of facts and figures—citing statistics about gross national product, growth, salaries, and so forth.

* The audience also reacted favorably when it seemed to them that either man was countering effectively. Nixon's highest point, for example, came when he commented that "it is very difficult to blame the four Republicans for the eight Democrats not getting something through that particular committee"—in answer to Kennedy's statement that Republicans were responsible for nothing getting done in the special session of Congress.

Kennedy, on the other hand, was effective in talking about education. His highest single point came when he remarked: "I think we should have an educational system second to none."

CHAPTER 8

AMERICAN FREEDOM: IDEAS AND PRACTICES

THE CITIZEN who seeks to think creatively about freedom in America will find it useful to linger on the meaning of freedom, the necessity for limitations, the values and the drawbacks of maximizing the liberties of a society, the ways and the consequences of drawing lines between the permissible and the prohibited in speech and behavior in concrete circumstances.

Define freedom as the absence of restraint and it becomes immediately clear that freedom is incompatible with civilization. There must be limits, there must be lines drawn beyond which the community will permit no man to go; else, there can be no stability for the social order, no protection for the common man.

For example, we may readily agree that freedom of religion is desirable, that all men ought to be free to practice their religion as they see fit. Having established that all men should have freedom of religion, we will nevertheless qualify such freedom and limit some forms of religious practices. Even though the individual claims that he is helping to dispatch people to heaven as a part of his religious observances, or even if he claims that his religion mandates him to marry at least four women, we shall prohibit these activities and jail the people who violate the law, no matter that their defense be freedom of religion.

We may assert adherence to the principle of free speech, and yet we shall not permit any man to say anything he may choose at any time and at any place. Meaningful freedom can exist only where freedom is trammeled. In partial limitation of freedom lies the expansion of effective freedom. Without qualifications, liberty must transform a civilization into a jungle.

In trying to figure out reasonable ways in which to set limits on freedom, the American civil libertarian has sought to maximize the area of permitted talk and action. The ground has been expressed in a thousand eloquent ways exemplified by the statement of Oliver Wendell Holmes, "The best test of truth is the power of the thought to get itself accepted in the competition of the market."

Not everybody has been impressed by the Holmes declaration. Thus, a Soviet journal quotes Holmes and goes on to say, "It is clear that this interpretation of truth is itself the best way to bar the rights of truth to those scientific ideas that fail to survive in the process of competition" where the instruments of communication, money, prestige, power, and education are subjected to the utter control of the capitalist. "Open competition of ideas," says the Soviet writer, "does not correspond to capitalist reality," but "in the conditions of modern capitalism" is "one of the forms of organization of bourgeois ideology, one of the forms of pressure by bourgeois ideology.". . .

American students (and their professors as well) are likely to have difficulty in appreciating the Soviet judgment of American freedom. Nor are Americans likely to share Khrushchev's disdain for "the author's right to commit mistakes and to suffer failures." On the contrary, said Khrushchev, "the people have deprived the author not only of the right to write badly but primarily of the right to write wrongly."

Freedom is a subtle concept whose realization is replete with obstacles. Even the American is more apt to laud the principle of free speech than to praise its application to particularized circumstances. Nations without experience as a free people would seem to have inadequate insights into the meaning and values of freedom, would appear probably to reach for whatever they prize in place of liberty or to equate "true liberty" with whatever strikes the leadership as pleasant to have and to do.

In the selections that follow three kinds of material are included to assist the student to develop deeply rooted understandings about freedom. First is an excerpt from a superb statement of the essence and values of liberty; second is a group of Supreme Court decisions illustrating the American application of freedom in cases involving Negroes; third are Supreme Court decisions involving subversives and excerpts from a television script dramatizing aspects of contemporary concern to keep the United States free.

A. THE REGION OF HUMAN LIBERTY

The following excerpts are from a classic work that has appeared in numerous editions. Concerning the book, John Stuart Mill tells of the day he was in Rome, climbing the steps of the Capitol, and thinking about the tyrants of the past and the persecutions of the present. He suddenly saw how a short essay he had written the year before, on liberty, could and should grow into a volume: "So many things might be brought into it and nothing seems more to be needed—it is a growing need too, for opinion tends to encroach more and more on liberty, and almost all the projects of social reformers of these days are really liberticide."

Mill's book appeared in 1859; more than a century later it remains one of the great commentaries on a subject of unending importance and eternal relevance.

On Liberty

[John Stuart Mill, *On Liberty*, 1859.]

This, then, is the appropriate region of human liberty. It comprises, first, the inward domain of consciousness; demanding liberty of conscience in the most comprehensive sense; liberty of thought and feeling; absolute freedom of opinion and sentiment on all subjects, practical or speculative, moral, or theological. The liberty of expressing and publishing opinions may seem to fall under a different principle, since it belongs to that part of the conduct of an individual which concerns other people; but, being almost of as much importance as the liberty of thought itself, and resting in great part on the same reasons, is practically inseparable from it. Secondly, the principle requires liberty of tastes and pursuits; of framing the plan of our life to suit our own character; of doing as we like subject to such consequences as may follow; without impediment from our fellow-creatures, so long as what we do does not harm them, even though they should think our conduct foolish, perverse, or wrong. Thirdly, from this liberty of each individual, follows the liberty, within the same limits of combination among individuals; freedom to unite, for any purpose not involving harm to others: the persons combining being supposed to be of full age, and not forced or deceived.

No society in which these liberties are not, on the whole, respected is free, whatever may be its form of government; and none is completely free in which they do not exist absolute and unqualified. The only freedom which deserves the name is that of pursuing our own good in our own way, so long as we do not attempt to deprive others of theirs, or impede their efforts to obtain it. Each is the proper guardian of his own health, whether bodily, or mental and spiritual. Mankind are greater gainers by suffering each other to live as seems good to themselves, than by compelling each to live as seems good to the rest. . . .

Let us suppose that the government is entirely at one with the people, and never thinks of exerting any power of coercion unless in agreement with what it conceives to be their voice. But I deny the right of the people to exercise such coercion, either by themselves or by their government. The power itself is illegitimate. The best government has no more title to it than the worst. It is as noxious, or more noxious, when exerted in accordance with public opinion, than when in opposition to it. If all mankind minus one were of one opinion, and only one person were of the contrary opinion, mankind would be no more justified in silencing that one person, than he, if he had the power, would be justified in silencing mankind. . . .

But, indeed, the dictum that truth always triumphs over persecution is one of those pleasant falsehoods which men repeat after one another till they pass into commonplaces, but which all experience refutes. History teems with instances of truth put down by persecution. If not suppressed for ever, it may be thrown back for centuries. . . . It is a piece of idle sentimentality that truth, merely as truth, has any inherent power denied to error of prevailing against the dungeon and the stake. Men are not more zealous for truth than they often are for error, and a sufficient application of legal or even of social penalties will generally succeed in stopping the propagation of either. . . .

The real advantage which truth has, consists in this: that when an opinion is true, it may be extinguished once, twice or many times, but in the course of ages there will generally be found persons to rediscover it, until some one of its reappearances falls on a time when from unfavourable circumstances it escapes persecution until it has made such head as to withstand all subsequent attempts to suppress it. . . .

There have been, and may again be, great individual thinkers in a general atmosphere of mental slavery. But there never has been, nor ever will be, in that atmosphere an intellectually active people. Where any people has made a temporary approach to such a character, it has been because the dread of heterodox speculation was for a time suspended. Where there is a tacit convention that principles are not to be disputed; where the discussion of the greatest questions which can occupy humanity is considered to be closed, we cannot hope to find that generally high scale of mental activity which has made some periods of history so remarkable. Never when controversy avoided the subjects which are large and important enough to kindle enthusiasm, was the mind of a people stirred up from its foundations, and the impulse given which raised even persons of the most ordinary intellect to something of the dignity of thinking beings. . . .

He who knows only his own side of the case, knows little of that. His reasons may be good, and no one may have been able to refute them. But if he is equally unable to refute the reasons on the opposite side; if he does not so much as know what they are, he has no ground for preferring either opinion. . . .

Such being the partial character of prevailing opinions, even when resting on a true foundation; every opinion which embodies somewhat of the portion of truth which the common opinion omits, ought to be considered precious, with whatever amount of error and confusion that truth may be blended. No sober judge of human affairs will feel bound to be indignant because those who force on our notice truths which we should otherwise have overlooked, overlook some of those which we see. Rather, he will think that so long as popular truth is onesided, it is more desirable than otherwise that unpopular truth should have onesided asserters too; such being usually the most energetic, and the most likely to compel reluctant attention to the fragment of wisdom which they proclaim as if it were the whole. . . . Truth has no chance but in proportion as every side of it, every opinion which embodies any fraction of the truth, not only finds advocates, but is so advocated as to be listened to.

We have now recognised the necessity to the mental well-being of mankind (on which all their other well-being depends) of freedom of opinion, and freedom of the expression of opinion on four distinct grounds; which we will now briefly recapitulate.

First, if any opinion is compelled to silence, that opinion may, for aught we can certainly know, be true. To deny this is to assume our own infallibility.

Secondly, though the silenced opinion be an error, it may, and very commonly does, contain a portion of truth; and since the general or prevailing opinion on any subject is rarely or never the whole truth, it is only by the collision of adverse opinions that the remainder of the truth has any chance of being supplied.

Thirdly, even if the received opinion be not only true, but the whole truth; unless it is suffered to be, and actually is, vigorously and earnestly contested, it will, by most of those who receive it, be held in the manner of a prejudice, with little comprehension or feeling of its rational grounds. And not only this, but fourthly, the meaning of the doctrine itself will be in danger of being lost or enfeebled, and deprived of its vital effect on the character and conduct: the dogma becoming a mere formal profession, inefficacious for good, but cumbering the ground, and preventing the growth of any real and heartfelt conviction, from reason or personal experience.

B. THE NEGRO, THE WHITE MAN, AND THE CONSTITUTION

The Fourteenth Amendment, enacted in 1868, the Plessy decision made in 1896, and the Brown case of 1954 represent landmarks in the continuing struggle for freedom by Negroes and white people in the United States. In examining the two judicial determinations that follow, made possible by the Fourteenth Amendment, the citizen may usefully bear in mind five considerations beyond the judicial ingredients of these cases.

First, Plessy and Brown are rich sources of understandings, but there have been many additional adjudications involving segregation and other Negro-white social, political, and economic relationships in the United States; the student will not acquire all that is to be known about race and the Constitution simply from two cases.

Secondly, Negroes and whites engage in numerous and various extra-constitutional efforts to carry forward and to frustrate their objectives: the economic boycott and the bomb are but two of the more prominent tools.

Thirdly, prejudice is not peculiar to the United States; where there are people, there is bias, and where the bias is not governmentally limited, it takes especially virulent forms. Any other nation that flings accusations at the United States also suffers from some approximation of American interpersonal ailments.

Fourthly, color problems in the United States are obvious and highlighted for many reasons that in part embody a principal glory of America. We are free to organize, to agitate, and to do a thousand things resulting, among other by-products, in considerable attention to the occasions when violence or persuasion helps to realize or hamper some objective. The fact that there is a spotlight on color is itself evidence that the United States is free, that any concrete racial act or thought is a point on a continuum of changing ideas and practices. (In somewhat comparable fashion in another setting, the existence of strikes in America is evidence that working people are free; equally, the absence of strikes elsewhere is insufficient proof that everybody is happy there.)

Fifthly, the biased American is buffeted by differing forces: his respect for law and the habits and customs which prompt him to behave in illegal ways to circumvent a decision which affronts his social and emotional heritage.

In sum, analysis of the Plessy and Brown cases is best done in a context which takes full cognizance of a familiar phenomenon: rightly considered, the American Constitution is what the American people are.

Plessy v. Ferguson, 1896: the Doctrine of "Separate but Equal" Appears

A Louisiana law required railroads carrying passengers within the state to provide "equal but separate" facilities for white and colored persons. Plessy was a passenger who was said to have been one-eighth Negro, an estimate whose arithmetic is more plausible than its sociology. Imprisoned for sitting in an area reserved for white people, Plessy brought suit, mainly citing the protection of the Fourteenth Amendment. The case was ultimately adjudicated by the Supreme Court in the following decision, subsequently modified in later determinations, notably *Brown v. Board of Education.*

The majority decision was written by Justice Brown, a Yale graduate from Michigan; the minority decision was rendered by Justice Harlan, a Centre College graduate from Kentucky. Evidently, not all men's opinions are precisely predictable from the traditions in which they have been reared. Individual judges have ample room within the broad confines of law to fit the values that mesh with their personalities.

[Justice Brown, delivering the opinion of the Court:]

. . . By the Fourteenth Amendment, all persons born or naturalized in the United States, and subject to the jurisdiction thereof, are made citizens of the United States and of the State wherein they reside; and the States are forbidden from making or enforcing any law which shall abridge the privileges or immunities of citizens of the United States, or shall deprive any person of life, liberty or property without due process of law, or deny to any person within their jurisdiction the equal protection of the laws. . . .

The object of the amendment was undoubtedly to enforce the absolute equality of the two races before the law, but in the nature of things it could not have been intended to abolish distinctions based upon color, or to enforce social, as distinguished from political equality, or a commingling of the two races upon terms unsatisfactory to either. Laws permitting, and even requiring, their separation in places where they are liable to be brought into contact do not necessarily imply the inferiority of either race to the other, and have been generally, if not universally, recognized as within the competency of the state legislatures in the exercise of their police power. The most common instance of this is connected with the establishment of separate schools for white and colored children, which has been held to be a valid exercise of the legislative power even by courts of States where the political rights of the colored race have been longest and most earnestly enforced.

One of the earliest of these cases is that of Roberts v. City of Boston, 5 Cush. 198 (1849), in which the Supreme Judicial Court of Massachusetts held that the general school committee of Boston had power to make provision for the instruction of colored children in separate schools established exclusively for them, and to prohibit their attendance upon the other schools.

. . . Similar laws have been enacted by Congress under its general power of legislation over the District of Columbia . . . as well as by the legislatures of many of the States, and have been generally, if not uniformly, sustained by the courts. . . .

The distinction between laws interfering with the political equality of the negro and those requiring the separation of the two races in schools, theatres, and railway carriages has been frequently drawn by this court. Thus, in Strauder v. West Virginia, 100 U.S. 303, it was held that a law of West Virginia limiting to white male persons, 21 years of age and citizens of the State, the right to sit upon juries, was a discrimination which implied a legal inferiority in civil society, which lessened the security of the right of the colored race, and was a step toward reducing them to a condition of servility. Indeed, the right of a colored man that, in the selection of jurors to pass upon his life, liberty and property, there shall be no exclusion of his race, and no discrimination against them because of color, has been asserted in a number of cases. . . .

It is claimed by the plaintiff in error that, in any mixed community, the reputation of belonging to the dominant race, in this instance the white race, is property, in the same sense that a right of action, or of inheritance, is property. Conceding this to be so, for the purposes of this case, we are unable to see how this statute deprives him of, or in any way affects his rights to, such property. If he be a white man and assigned to a colored coach, he may have his action for damages against the company for being deprived of his so called property. Upon the other hand, if he be a colored man and be so assigned, he has been deprived of no property, since he is not lawfully entitled to the reputation of being a white man.

In this connection, it is also suggested by the learned counsel for the plaintiff in error that the same argument that will justify the State legislature in requiring railways to provide separate accommodations for the two races will also authorize them to require separate cars to be provided for people whose hair is of a certain color, or who are aliens, or who belong to certain nationalities, or to enact laws requiring colored people to walk upon one side of the street, and white people upon the other, or requiring white men's houses to be painted white, and colored men's black, or their vehicles or business signs to be of different colors, upon the theory that one side of the street is as good as the other, or that a house or vehicle of one color is as good as one of another color. The reply to all this is that every exercise of the police power must be reasonable, and extend only to such laws as are enacted in good faith for the promotion of the public good, and not for the annoyance or oppression of a particular class. . . .

So far, then, as a conflict with the Fourteenth Amendment is concerned, the case reduces itself to the question whether the statute of Louisiana is a reasonable regulation, and with respect to this there must necessarily be a large discretion on the part of the legislature. In determining the question of reasonableness it is at liberty to act with reference to the established usages, customs and traditions of the people, and with a view to the promotion of their comfort, and the preservation of the public peace and good order. Gauged by this standard, we cannot say that a law which authorizes or even requires the separation of the two races in public conveyances is unreasonable, or more obnoxious to the Fourteenth Amendment than the acts of Congress requiring separate schools for colored children in the District of Columbia, the constitutionality of which does not seem to have been questioned, or the corresponding acts of state legislatures.

We consider the underlying fallacy of the plaintiff's argument to consist in the assumption that the enforced separation of the two races stamps the colored race with a badge of inferiority. If this be so, it is not by reason of anything found in the act, but solely because the colored race chooses to put that construction upon it. The argument necessarily assumes that if, as has been more than once the case, and is not unlikely to be so again, the colored race should become the dominant power in the state legislature, and should enact a law in precisely similar terms, it would thereby relegate the white race to an inferior position. We imagine that the white race, at least, would not acquiesce in this assumption. The argument also assumes that social prejudices may be overcome by legislation, and that equal rights cannot be secured to the negro except by an enforced commingling of the two races. We cannot accept this proposition. If the two races are to meet upon terms of social equality, it must be the result of natural affinities, a mutual appreciation of each other's merits and a voluntary consent of individuals. As was said by the Court of Appeals of New York in People v. Gallagher, 93 N.Y. 438, 448, "this end can neither be accomplished nor promoted by laws which conflict with the general sentiment of the community upon whom they are designed to operate. When the government, therefore, has secured to each of its citizens equal rights before the law and equal opportunities for improvement and progress, it has accomplished the end for which it was organized and performed all of the functions respecting social advantages with which it is endowed." Legislation is powerless to eradicate racial instincts or to abolish distinctions based upon physical differences, and the attempt to do so can only result in accentuating the difficulties of the present situation. If the civil and political rights of both races be equal one cannot be inferior to the other civilly or politically. If one race be inferior to the other socially, the Constitution of the United States cannot put them upon the same plane. . . .

The judgment of the court below is, therefore,

Affirmed.

[Justice Harlan, dissenting:]

The white race deems itself to be the dominant race in this country. And so it is, in prestige, in achievements, in education, in wealth and in power. So, I doubt not, it will continue to be for all times, if it remains true to its great heritage and holds fast to the principles of constitutional liberty. But in view of the Constitution, in the eye of the law, there is in this country no superior, dominant, ruling class of citizens. There is no caste here. Our Constitution is color-blind, and neither knows nor tolerates classes among citizens. In respect of civil rights, all citizens are equal before the law. The humblest is the peer of the most powerful. The law regards man as man, and takes no account of his surroundings or of his color when his civil rights as guaranteed by the supreme law of the land are involved. It is, therefore, to be regretted that this high tribunal, the final expositor of the fundamental law of the land, has reached the conclusion that it is competent for a state to regulate the enjoyment by citizens of their civil rights solely upon the basis of race. . . .

The sure guarantee of the peace and security of each race is the clear, distinct, unconditional recognition by our governments, National and State, of every right that inheres in civil freedom, and of the equality before the law of all citizens of the United States without regard to race. State enactments, regulating the enjoyment of civil rights, upon the basis of race, and cunningly devised to defeat legitimate results of the war, under the pretence of recognizing equality of rights, can have no other result than to render permanent peace impossible, and to keep alive a conflict of races, the continuance of which must do harm to all concerned. . . .

The arbitrary separation of citizens, on the basis of race, while they are on a public highway, is a badge of servitude wholly inconsistent with the civil freedom and the equality before the law established by the Constitution. It cannot be justified upon any legal grounds.

If evils will result from the commingling of the two races upon public highways established for the benefit of all, they will be infinitely less than those that will surely come from state legislation regulating the enjoyment of civil rights upon the basis of race. We boast of the freedom enjoyed by our people above all other peoples. But it is difficult to reconcile that boast with a state of the law which, practically, puts the brand of servitude and degradation upon a large class of our fellow-citizens, our equals before the law. The thin disguise of "equal" accommodations for passengers in railroad coaches will not mislead anyone, nor atone for the wrong this day done. . . .

I do not deem it necessary to review the decisions of state courts to which reference was made in argument. Some, and the most important, of them are wholly inapplicable, because rendered prior to the adoption of the last amendments of the Constitution, when colored people had very few rights which the dominant race felt obliged to respect. Others were made at a time when public opinion, in many localities, was dominated by the institution of slavery; when it would not have been safe to do justice to the black man; and when, so far as the rights of blacks were concerned, race prejudice was, practically, the supreme law of the land. Those decisions cannot be guides in the era introduced by the recent amendments of the supreme law, which established universal civil freedom, gave citizenship to all born or naturalized in the United States and residing here, obliterated the race line from our systems of governments, National and State, and placed our free institutions upon the broad and sure foundation of the equality of all men before the law. . . .

For the reasons stated, I am constrained to withhold my assent from the opinion and judgment of the majority. . . .

Brown v. Board of Education, 1954: "Separate Educational Facilities Are Inherently Unequal"

In this unanimous decision of the Supreme Court, written by Chief Justice Earl Warren, the "separate but equal" doctrine of the *Plessy v. Ferguson* case was upset. Holding that racial segregation in the public schools violates the Constitution, the Supreme Court then ordered desegregation with "all deliberate speed." Reactions to the decision were, and remain, intense.

Testifying before a congressional committee, Representative Frank E. Smith of Mississippi declared that the Supreme Court, repudiating the construction placed upon the Fourteenth Amendment through the preceding eighty-six years, had usurped the power to amend the Constitution, and so the Court had itself repudiated the integrity of the law. Speaking before the same congressional committee, Judge Leander H. Perez of Plaquemines Parish, Louisiana, connected the Court's decision with communism. He remarked that the psychological and sociological purported authorities cited by the Court were similar to the data in the official files of the House Un-American Activities Committee and the Attorney General, that the so-called authorities on psychology and sociology adopted by the Court in its decision included dozens of people who had been officially cited by the U.S. Attorney General and the House Un-American Activities Committee as being members of scores of pro-Communist and subversive organizations dedicated to the overthrow of our Constitution and government. The Judge emphasized: "The NAACP and Communist fronts know that under the present system in the South Negroes under the 'separate but equal rule' can obtain a satisfactory education. The question in these cases is how to employ the coercive power of the Federal Government to produce racial integration in the South—or how to produce turmoil, chaos, and national disunity in the Communist cause."

When the executive director of the American Veterans Committee testified before the committee, he took quite another tack: "We think it is time that the Congress went on record by referring to Supreme Court decisions in the field of civil rights as the law of the land. We think that this will be of great assistance to people throughout the United States in understanding that the Supreme Court decision in the Brown case, eliminating segregation in schools, for example, is the law of the land, and a part of the Constitution."

A New York congressmen talked about what "is popularly called civil rights but which is freedom rights." Equally outspoken, a Mississippi congressman testified against the "drive for these civil wrongs proposals."

The court had been unanimous in its adjudication, and supporters applauded the conclusion while disputing the technical merits of the decision. One leading commentator called the opinion "short, lucid"; another authority said the decision "does not seem in perspective to have been very well thought out." Another view was that "by all standards," the decision was "a great decision. The *opinion,* on the other hand, was not a great opinion."

Characterizing every judgment, whether favoring or attacking the judicial opinion, was the speaker's assertion that what he was saying and doing cohered with the American Constitution and, in the final analysis, was good for the American Negro.

These cases come to us from the States of Kansas, South Carolina, Virginia, and Delaware. They are premised on different facts and different local conditions, but a common legal question justifies their consideration together in this consolidated opinion.

In each of the cases, minors of the Negro race, through their legal representatives, seek the aid of the courts in obtaining admission to the public schools of their community on a nonsegregated basis. In each instance, they had been denied admission to schools attended by white children under laws requiring or permitting segregation according to race.

This segregation was alleged to deprive the plaintiffs of the equal protection of the laws under the Fourteenth Amendment. In each of the cases other than the Delaware case, a three-judge Federal District Court denied relief to the plaintiffs on the so-called "separate but equal" doctrine announced by this court in Plessy v. Ferguson. . . .

Under that doctrine, equality of treatment is accorded when the races are provided substantially equal facilities, even though these facilities be separate. In the Delaware case, the Supreme Court of Delaware adhered to that doctrine, but ordered that the plaintiffs be admitted to the white schools because of their superiority to the Negro schools.

The plaintiffs contend that segregated public schools are not "equal" and cannot be made "equal" and that, hence, they are deprived of the equal protection of the laws. Because of the obvious importance of the question presented, the Court took jurisdiction. Argument was heard in the 1952 term, and reargument was heard this term on certain questions propounded by the Court.

Reargument was largely devoted to the circumstances surrounding the adoption of the Fourteenth Amendment in 1868. It covered, exhaustively, consideration of the Amendment in Congress, ratification by the states, then existing practices in racial segregation, and the views of proponents and opponents of the Amendment.

This discussion and our own investigation convince us that, although these sources cast some light, it is not enough to resolve the problem with which we are faced.

At best, they are inconclusive. The most avid proponents of the postwar Amendments undoubtedly intended them to remove all legal distinctions among "all persons born or naturalized in the United States."

Their opponents just as certainly were antagonistic to both the letter and the spirit of the Amendments and wished them to have the most limited effect. What others in Congress and the State legislature had in mind cannot be determined with any degree of certainty.

An additional reason for the illusive nature of the Amendment's history, with respect to segregated schools, is the status of public education at that time. In the South, the movement toward free common schools, supported by general taxation, had not yet taken hold. Education of white children was largely in the hands of private groups. Education of Negroes was almost nonexistent, and practically all of the race was illiterate. In fact, any education of Negroes was forbidden by law in some states.

Today, in contrast, many Negroes have achieved outstanding success in the arts and sciences as well as in the business and professional world. It is true that public education has already advanced further in the North, but the effect of the Amendment on Northern States was generally ignored in the Congressional debates.

Even in the North, the conditions of public education did not approximate those existing today. The curriculum was usually rudimentary; ungraded schools were common in rural areas; the school term was but three months a year in many states; and compulsory school attendance was virtually unknown.

As a consequence, it is not surprising that there should be so little in the history of the Fourteenth Amendment relating to its intended effect on public education.

In the first cases in this court construing the Fourteenth Amendment, decided shortly after its adoption, the court interpreted it as proscribing all state-imposed discriminations against the Negro race.

The doctrine of "separate but equal" did not make its appearance in this court until 1896 in the case of Plessy v. Ferguson . . . involving not education but transportation. . . .

. . . American courts have since labored with the doctrine for over half a century. In this court, there have been six cases involving the "separate but equal" doctrine in the field of public education.

In Cumming v. County Board of Education, 175 U.S. 528, and Gong Lum v. Rice, 275 U.S. 78, the validity of the doctrine itself was not challenged. In most recent cases, all on the graduate school level, inequality was found in that specific benefits enjoyed by white students were denied to Negro students of the same educational qualifications. . . .

. . . In none of these cases was it necessary to re-examine the doctrine to grant relief to the Negro plaintiff. And in Sweatt v. Painter . . . the court expressly reserved decision on the question whether Plessy v. Ferguson should be held inapplicable to public education.

In the instant cases, that question is directly presented. Here, unlike Sweatt v. Painter, there are findings below that the Negro and white schools involved have been equalized, or are being equalized, with respect to buildings, curricula, qualifications and salaries of teachers, and other "tangible" factors.

Our decision, therefore, cannot turn on merely a comparison of these tangible factors in the Negro and white schools involved in each of the cases. We must look instead to the effect of segregation itself on public education.

In approaching this problem, we cannot turn the clock back to 1868, when the Amendment was adopted, or even to 1896, when Plessy v. Ferguson was written. We must consider public education in the light of its full development and its present place in American life throughout the nation. Only in this way can it be determined if segregation in public schools deprives these plaintiffs of the equal protection of the laws.

Today, education is perhaps the most important function of state and local governments. Compulsory school attendance laws and the great expenditures for education both demonstrate our recognition of the importance of education to our democratic society. It is required in the performance of our most basic public responsibilities, even service in the armed forces. It is the very foundation of good citizenship.

Today, it is a principal instrument in awakening the child to cultural values, in preparing him for later professional training, and in helping him to adjust normally to his environment.

In these days, it is doubtful that any child may reasonably be expected to succeed in life if he is denied the opportunity of an education. Such an opportunity, where the state has undertaken to provide it, is a right which must be made available to all on equal terms.

We come then to the question presented: Does segregation of children in public schools solely on the basis of race, even though the physical facilities and other "tangible" factors may be equal, deprive the children of the minority group of equal educational opportunities? We believe that it does.

In Sweatt v. Painter . . . in finding that a segregated law school for Negroes could not provide them equal educational opportunities, this court relied in large part on "those qualities which are incapable of objective measurement but which make for greatness in a law school."

In McLaurin v. Oklahoma State Regents . . . the court, in requiring that a Negro admitted to a white graduate school be treated like all other students, again resorted to intangible considerations: ". . . his ability to study, engage in discussions and exchange views with other students, and, in general, to learn his profession."

Such considerations apply with added force to children in grade and high schools. To separate them from others of similar age and qualifications solely because of their race generates a feeling of inferiority as to their status in the community that may affect their hearts and minds in a way unlikely ever to be undone.

The effect of this separation on their educational opportunities was well stated by a finding in the Kansas case by a court which nevertheless felt compelled to rule against the Negro plaintiffs:

> Segregation of white and colored children in public schools has a detrimental effect upon the colored children. The impact is greater when it has the sanction of the law; for the policy of separating the races is usually interpreted as denoting the inferiority of the Negro group.
>
> A sense of inferiority affects the motivation of a child to learn. Segregation with the sanction of law, therefore, has a tendency to retard the educational and mental development of Negro children and to deprive them of some of the benefits they would receive in a racially integrated school system.

Whatever may have been the extent of psychological knowledge at the time of Plessy v. Ferguson, this finding is amply supported by modern authority.

. . . Any language in Plessy v. Ferguson contrary to this finding is rejected.

We conclude that in the field of public education the doctrine of "separate but equal" has no place. Separate educational facilities are inherently unequal. Therefore, we hold that the plaintiffs and others similarly situated for whom the actions have been brought are, by reason of the segregation complained of, deprived of the equal protection of the laws guaranteed by the Fourteenth Amendment. This disposition makes unnecessary any discussion whether such segregation also violates the Due Process Clause of the Fourteenth Amendment.

Because these are class actions, because of the wide applicability of this decision, and because of the great variety of local conditions, the formulation of decrees in these cases presents problems of considerable complexity. On reargument, the consideration of appropriate relief was necessarily subordinated to the primary question—the constitutionality of segregation in public education.

We have now announced that such segregation is a denial of the equal protection of the laws. In order that we may have the full assistance of the parties in formulating decrees the cases will be restored to the docket, and the parties are requested to present further argument. . . .

C. SUBVERSION AND AMERICANISM

The American struggle against communism has extended into every significant institution and process that American governments and nongovernmental groups can control. At the middle of the twentieth century, Maine alone among the states was without a law designed specifically to repress or combat subversive organizations or groups. Noting that more than three hundred state statutes were directed at subversion, one political scientist has added that a reasonable man may well think of this what Justice Holmes thought of three generations of imbeciles: it's enough.

Part of the national effort to cope with subversives was exemplified in the Taft-Hartley Law requiring union officers to file non-Communist affidavits to avail themselves of the services of the National Labor Relations Board; part of the attempt was seen in *The New York Times* announcement that it would not knowingly employ a Communist on its news or editorial staff; and yet another aspect was imbedded in a community leader's declaration about schools and colleges that "the time has come to clean out these institutions of all Communist influences and the crazy idea of commingling of the races which was sponsored in this country by the Communist party."

Illustrating the ideological and behavioral patterning that makes any society coherent were the uncounted instances where people ostracized a suspected neighbor and where individuals and groups assailed and assaulted physically and in other ways those persons and associations they thought were subversive.

Some observers suggested that the Communist movement had a dual nature, that it was both a political movement and a conspiracy. Thus, when the American Civil Liberties Union testified before a Senate committee concerned with government security, the ACLU asserted that Communist Party members were entitled to "all the rights of members of other parties" to the extent that the movement is "political agitational," although Communist Party members "may in some particulars be restricted by law" to the degree that the movement is a part of the Soviet conspiracy. While commentators saw the ACLU distinction as an exercise in semantic fancies, everybody agreed on the objective: the reconciliation of security and liberty.

The four readings below, concerned with subversion and patriotism, are designed to provide for student analysis two kinds of material. In one category are the three major judicial decisions exhibiting, among other characteristics, the blurs, the problems, and the accommodations in figuring out what the Constitution says. The other kind of material, a dramatization of patriotism, bears intimate relation to the cases, being another manifestation of the same ultimate source from which the issues of constitutional law come: the nature of the American people and the character of the American society, both so enormously variegated as to permit great variations in the expressions of American freedom at a particular time and place.

Schenck v. United States, 1919: the "Clear and Present Danger Test" Is Formulated

Schenck, the general secretary of the Socialist Party, sent out approximately 15,000 leaflets to men who had been drafted, urging them to oppose the Conscription Act. He was indicted and convicted in a Federal district court of violating the Espionage Act of 1917, by causing and attempting to cause insubordination in the armed forces of the United States when the United States was at war with Germany. Schenck's defense was that the Act abridged his freedom of speech and press in violation of the First Amendment.

The first instance of the use of the "clear and present danger test," this case is a watershed in the development of civil liberties thinking in the United States.

Among the questions which the student may raise for himself is whether the expansiveness of the "clear and present danger test" is more apparent than real; one may wonder whether Schenck and his cohorts represented a danger to the nation which was either clear or present, whether here is an instance of a beautiful criterion not applied to the instant case. One may wonder about the utility or the relevance of the famous Holmes dictum in the decision: "The most stringent protection of free speech would not protect a man in falsely shouting fire in a theatre and causing a panic."

For, in the kind of issue which comes before the Court, the questions would arise as to how false the shout has to be to be classified as false, just what is meant by fire, whether the situation would change if only one or two people were in the theater or perhaps none at all. The free-speech problem in specific circumstances is a matter of degree and nuance and is not apt to be resolved by reference to a figure of speech.

Following is Justice Holmes's opinion, beginning with his description of the Socialist Party leaflets.

. . . The document in question upon its first printed side recited the first section of the Thirteenth Amendment, said that the idea embodied in it was violated by the Conscription Act and that a conscript is little better than a convict. In impassioned language it intimated that conscription was despotism in its worst form and a monstrous wrong against humanity in the interest of Wall Street's chosen few. It said "Do not submit to intimidation," but in form at least confined itself to peaceful measures such as a petition for the repeal of the act. The other and later printed side of the sheet was headed "Assert Your Rights." It stated reasons for alleging that any one violated the Constitution when he refused to recognize "your right to assert your opposition to the draft" and went on "If you do not assert and support your rights, you are helping to deny or disparage rights which it is the solemn duty of all citizens and residents of the United States to retain." It described the arguments on the other side as coming from cunning politicians and a mercenary capitalist press, and even silent consent to the conscription law as helping to support an infamous conspiracy. It denied the power to send our citizens away to foreign shores to shoot up the people of other lands, and added that words could not express the condemnation such cold-blooded ruthlessness deserves, &c., winding up "You must do your share to maintain, support and uphold the rights of the people of this country." Of course the document would not have been sent unless it had been intended to have some effect, and we do not see what effect it could be expected to have upon persons subject to the draft except to influence them to obstruct the carrying of it out. The defendants do not deny that the jury might find against them on this point.

But it is said, suppose that that was the tendency of this circular, it is protected by the First Amendment to the Constitution. Two of the strongest expressions are said to be quoted respectively from well-known public men. It well may be that the prohibition of laws abridging the freedom of speech is not confined to previous restraints, although to prevent them may have been the main purpose, as intimated in Patterson v. Colorado, 205 U.S. 454, 462. We admit that in many places and in ordinary times the defendants in saying all that was said in the circular would have been within their constitutional rights. But the character of every act depends upon the circumstances in which it is done. Aikens v. Wisconsin, 195 U.S. 194, 205, 206. The most stringent protection of free speech would not protect a man in falsely shouting fire in a theatre and causing a panic. It does not even protect a man from an injunction against uttering words that may have all the effect of force. Gompers v. Bucks Stove & Range Co., 221 U.S. 418, 439. The question in every case is whether the words used are used in such circumstances and are of such a nature as to create a clear and present danger that they will bring about the substantive evils that Congress has a right to prevent. It is a question of proximity and degree. When a nation is at war many things that might be said in time of peace are such a hindrance to its effort that their utterance will not be endured so long as men fight and that no Court could regard them as protected by any constitutional right. It seems to be admitted that if an actual obstruction of the recruiting service were proved, liability for words that produced that effect might be enforced. The statute of 1917 in §4 punishes conspiracies to obstruct as well as actual obstruction. If the act (speaking, or circulating a paper), its tendency and the intent with which it is done are the same, we perceive no ground for saying that success alone warrants making the act a crime. Goldman v. United States, 245 U.S. 474, 477. . . .

Judgments affirmed.

Dennis v. United States, 1951: American Government Need Not Wait for a Putsch

The Federal effort to deal with subversion through the Smith Act of 1940 was tested in the Supreme Court for the first time in the Dennis case. Eugene Dennis and ten other defendants comprised the "board of directors," the eleven top leaders of the Communist Party in the United States. Symptomatic of the uncertainties involved in the American concern to embrace both liberty and security at the same time was the course of events in the genesis, evolution, and conclusions of the case. Although the legislation was enacted in 1940 and evidently directed particularly against the Communists, it was not until 1948 that an indictment was brought against Dennis and his colleagues; and through the Courts until 1951 wound the prosecution and appellate process. In the decision itself five opinions were written embodying various interpretations of the meaning of "clear and present danger." The student may figure out for himself whether every judge who talked about "clear and present danger" was talking about the same idea and with the same understanding of the same data. Similarly, he may wonder about the relation between the famous phrase and the eleven-year span between legislation aimed chiefly at the Communists and final conviction of the principal people who had violated the law.

It would be easy to argue that the period of time between the beginning and the end of the legal effort here exemplified the bumbling slowness with which Americans dealt with an urgent conspiratorial problem; yet it would not be difficult to defend the position that America's tenderness and slowness in dealing with the Communist leaders was powerful international (and domestic) propaganda to demonstrate our interest in maintaining freedom. All could agree that the United States had not yet happily squared the liberty-security circle. Few commentators went so far as Eugene Dennis, the convicted general secretary of the Communist Party, who charged that the "Truman court majority" had voted to substitute thought control for the free-speech amendment to the Constitution. Agreeing with Dennis, the chairman of the Communist Party of Illinois, Gilbert Green, declared: "It is a sad day for America when the high court proceeds to make a cynical mockery of the Bill of Rights." The decision, he said, constituted "a danger to the peace and liberty of the American people" and the Communist Party would grow stronger when the public learned of "the miscarriage of justice."

In the Dennis decision, Chief Justice Vinson spoke for the Court in an opinion in which Justices Reed, Burton, and Minton joined. The decision considered two questions: (1) whether section 2 or 3 of the Smith Act, inherently or as construed and applied in this case, violates the First Amendment and other provisions of the Bill of Rights; (2) whether section 2 or 3 of the Act, inherently or as construed and applied in this case, violates the First and Fifth Amendments because of indefiniteness.

The decision continued, citing sections 2 and 3 of the Smith Act.

[Chief Justice Vinson, delivering the opinion of the Court:]

. . . "Sec. 2

"(a) It shall be unlawful for any person—

"(1) to knowingly or willfully advocate, abet, advise, or teach the duty, necessity, desirability, or propriety of over-throwing or destroying any government in the United States by force or violence, or by the assassination of any officer of such government;

(2) with intent to cause the overthrow or destruction of any government in the United States, to print, publish, edit, issue, circulate, sell, distribute, or publicly display any written or printed matter advocating, advising, or teaching the duty, necessity, desirability, or propriety of overthrowing or destroying any government in the United States by force or violence;

(3) to organize or help to organize any society, group, or assembly of persons who teach, advocate, or encourage the overthrow or destruction of any government in the United States by force or violence; or to be or become a member of, or affiliate with, any such society, group, or assembly of persons, knowing the purpose thereof. . . .

. . . "Sec. 3. It shall be unlawful for any persons to attempt to commit, or to conspire to commit, any of the acts prohibited by the provisions of . . . this title."

The indictment charged the petitioners with wilfully and knowingly conspiring (1) to organize as the Communist Party of the United States of America a society, group and assembly of persons who teach and advocate the overthrow and destruction of the Government of the United States by force and violence, and (2) knowingly and wilfully to advocate and teach the duty and necessity of overthrowing and destroying the Government of the United States by force and violence. The indictment further alleged that Sec. 2 of the Smith Act proscribes these acts and that any conspiracy to take such action is a violation of Sec. 3 of the Act. . . .

The obvious purpose of the statute is to protect existing Government, not from change by peaceable, lawful and constitutional means, but from change by violence, revolution and terrorism. That it is within the power of the Congress to protect the Government of the United States from armed rebellion is a proposition which requires little discussion. Whatever theoretical merit there may be to the argument that there is a "right" to rebellion against dictatorial governments is without force where the existing structure of the government provides for peaceful and orderly change. We reject any principle of governmental helplessness in the face of preparation for revolution, which principle, carried to its logical conclusion, must lead to anarchy. No one could conceive that it is not within the power of Congress to prohibit acts intended to overthrow the Government by force and violence. The question with which we are concerned here is not whether Congress has such power, but whether the means which it has employed conflict with the First and Fifth Amendments to the Constitution.

One of the bases for the contention that the means which Congress has employed are invalid takes the form of an attack on the face of the statute on the grounds that by its terms it prohibits academic discussion of the merits of Marxism-Leninism, that it stifles ideas and is contrary to all concepts of a free speech and a free press. . . .

. . . The very language of the Smith Act negates the interpretation which petitioners would have us impose on that Act. It is directed at advocacy, not discussion. Thus, the trial judge properly charged the jury that they could not convict if they found that petitioners did "no more than pursue peaceful studies and discussions or teaching and advocacy in the realm of ideas." He further charged that it was not unlawful "to conduct in an American college and university a course explaining the philosophical theories set forth in the books which have been placed in evidence." Such a charge is in strict accord with the statutory language, and illustrates the meaning to be placed on those words. Congress did not intend to eradicate the free discussion of political theories, to destroy the traditional rights of Americans to discuss and evaluate ideas without fear of governmental sanction. Rather Congress was concerned with the very kind of activity in which the evidence showed these petitioners engaged. . . .

. . . the basis of the First Amendment is the hypothesis that speech can rebut speech, propaganda will answer propaganda, free debate of ideas will result in the wisest governmental policies. It is for this reason that this Court has recognized the inherent value of free discourse. An analysis of the leading cases in this Court which have involved direct limitations on speech, however, will demonstrate that both the majority of the Court and the dissenters in particular cases have recognized that this is not an unlimited, unqualified right, but that the societal value of speech must, on occasion, be subordinated to other values and considerations.

No important case involving free speech was decided by this Court prior to Schenck v. United States, 249 U.S. 47 (1919). . . . Writing for a unanimous Court, Justice Holmes stated that the "question in every case is whether the words used are used in such circumstances and are of such a nature as to create a clear and present danger that they will bring about the substantive evils that Congress has a right to prevent.". . .

. . . The rule we deduce . . . is that where an offense is specified by a statute in nonspeech or nonpress terms, a conviction relying upon speech or press as evidence of violation may be sustained only when the speech or publication created a "clear and present danger" of attempting or accomplishing the prohibited crime, e.g., interference with enlistment. . . .

Speech is not an absolute, above and beyond control by the legislature when its judgment, subject to review here, is that certain kinds of speech are so undesirable as to warrant criminal sanction. . . .

. . . In this case we are squarely presented with the application of the "clear and present danger" test, and must decide what that phrase imports. We first note that many of the cases in which this Court has reversed convictions by use of this or similar tests have been based on the fact that the interest which the State was attempting to protect was itself too insubstantial to warrant restriction of speech. . . . Overthrow of the Government by force and violence is certainly a substantial enough interest for the Government to limit speech. Indeed, this is the ultimate value of any society, for if a society cannot protect its very structure from armed internal attack, it must follow that no subordinate value can be protected. If, then, this interest may be protected, the literal problem which is presented is what has been meant by the use of the phrase "clear and present danger" of the utterances bringing about the evil within the power of Congress to punish.

Obviously, the words cannot mean that before the Government may act, it must wait until the putsch is about to be executed, the plans have been laid and the signal is awaited. If Government is aware that a group aiming at its overthrow is attempting to indoctrinate its members and to commit them to a course whereby they will strike when the leaders feel the circumstances permit, action by the Government is required. The argument that there is no need for Government to concern itself, for Government is strong, it possesses ample powers to put down a rebellion, it may defeat the revolution with ease needs no answer. For that is not the question. Certainly an attempt to overthrow the Government by force, even though doomed from the outset because of inadequate numbers or power of the revolutionists, is a sufficient evil for Congress to prevent. The damage which such attempts create both physically and politically to a nation makes it impossible to measure the validity in terms of the probability of success, or the immediacy of a successful attempt. In the instant case the trial judge charged the jury that they could not convict unless they found that petitioners intended to overthrow the Government "as speedily as circumstances would permit." This does not mean, and could not properly mean, that they would not strike until there was certainty of success. What was meant was that the revolutionists would strike when they thought the time was ripe. We must therefore reject the contention that success or probability of success is the criterion. . . .

Chief Judge Learned Hand, writing for the majority below, interpreted the phrase as follows: "In each case [courts] must ask whether the gravity of the 'evil,' discounted by its improbability, justifies such invasion of free speech as is necessary to avoid the danger.". . . We adopt this statement of the rule. As articulated by Chief Judge Hand, it is as succinct and inclusive as any other we might devise at this time. It takes into consideration those factors which we deem relevant, and relates their significances. More we cannot expect from words.

Likewise, we are in accord with the court below, which affirmed the trial court's finding that the requisite danger existed. The mere fact that from the period 1945 to 1948 petitioners' activities did not result in an attempt to overthrow the Government by force and violence is of course no answer to the fact that there was a group that was ready to make the attempt. . . .

. . . We hold that sections 2(a)(1), 2(a)(3) and 3 of the Smith Act, do not inherently, or as construed or applied in the instant case, violate the First Amendment and other provisions of the Bill of Rights, or the First and Fifth Amendments because of indefiniteness. Petitioners intended to overthrow the Government of the United States as speedily as the circumstances would permit. Their conspiracy to organize the Communist Party and to teach and advocate the overthrow of the Government of the United States by force and violence created a "clear and present danger" of an attempt to overthrow the Government by force and violence. They were properly and constitutionally convicted for violation of the Smith Act. The judgments of conviction are

Affirmed.

[Justice Frankfurter, concurring:]

In enacting a statute which makes it a crime for the defendants to conspire to do what they have been found to have conspired to do, did Congress exceed its constitutional power?

Few questions of comparable import have come before this Court in recent years. The appellants maintain that they have a right to advocate a political theory, so long, at least, as their advocacy does not create an immediate danger of obvious magnitude to the very existence of our present scheme of society. On the other hand, the Government asserts the right to safeguard the security of the Nation by such a measure as the Smith Act. Our judgment is thus solicited on a conflict of interests of the utmost concern to the well-being of the country. . . .

. . . "The law is perfectly well settled," this Court said over fifty years ago, "that the first ten amendments to the Constitution, commonly known as the Bill of Rights, were not intended to lay down any novel principles of government, but simply to embody certain guaranties and immunities which we had inherited from our English ancestors, and which had from time immemorial been subject to certain well-recognized exceptions arising from the necessities of the case. . . . Absolute rules would inevitably lead to absolute exceptions, and such exceptions would eventually corrode the rules. The demands of free speech in a democratic society as well as the interest in national security are better served by candid and informed weighing of the competing interests, within the confines of the judicial process, than by announcing dogmas too inflexible for the non-Euclidian problems to be solved.

But how are competing interests to be assessed? . . .

. . . Primary responsibility for adjusting the interests which compete in the situation before us of necessity belongs to the Congress . . . we must scrupulously observe the narrow limits of judicial authority even though self-restraint is alone set over us. Above all we must remember that this Court's power of judicial review is not "an exercise of the powers of a super-legislature.". . .

. . . There is ample justification for a legislative judgment that the conspiracy now before us is a substantial threat to national order and security. If the Smith Act is justified at all, it is justified precisely because it may serve to prohibit the type of conspiracy for which these defendants were convicted. . . .

. . . The phrase "clear and present danger," in its origin, "served to indicate the importance of freedom of speech to a free society but also to emphasize that its exercise must be compatible with the preservation of other freedoms essential to a democracy and guaranteed by our Constitution.". . .

. . . The defendants have been convicted of conspiring to organize a party of persons who advocate the overthrow of the Government by force and violence. The jury has found that the object of the conspiracy is advocacy as "a rule of principle of action," "by language reasonably and ordinarily calculated to incite persons to such action," and with the intent to cause the overthrow "as speedily as circumstances would permit."

On any scale of values which we have hitherto recognized, speech of this sort ranks low.

Throughout our decisions there has recurred a distinction between the statement of an idea which may prompt its hearers to take unlawful action, and advocacy that such action be taken. . . .

. . . It is true that there is no divining rod by which we may locate "advocacy." Exposition of ideas readily merges into advocacy. The same Justice who gave currency to application of the incitement doctrine in this field dissented four times from what he thought was its misapplication. As he said in the Gitlow dissent, "Every idea is an incitement.". . . Even though advocacy of overthrow deserves little protection, we should hesitate to prohibit it if we thereby inhibit the interchange of rational ideas so essential to representative government and free society.

But there is underlying validity in the distinction between advocacy and the interchange of ideas, and we do not discard a useful tool because it may be misused. That such a distinction could be used unreasonably by those in power against hostile or unorthodox views does not negate the fact that it may be used reasonably against an organization wielding the power of the centrally controlled international Communist movement. The object of the conspiracy before us is clear enough that the chance of error in saying that the defendants conspired to advocate rather than to express ideas is slight. Mr. Justice Douglas quite properly points out that the conspiracy before us is not a conspiracy to overthrow the Government. But it would be equally wrong to treat it as a seminar in political theory.

These general considerations underlie decision of the case before us. . . .

. . . A public interest is not wanting in granting freedom to speak their minds even to those who advocate the overthrow of the Government by force. For, as the evidence in this case abundantly illustrates, coupled with such advocacy is criticism of defects in our society. Criticism is the spur to reform; and Burke's admonition that a healthy society must reform in order to conserve has not lost its force. Astute observers have remarked that one of the characteristics of the American Republic is indifference to fundamental criticism. . . . It is a commonplace that there may be a grain of truth in the most uncouth doctrine, however false and repellent the balance may be. Suppressing advocates of overthrow inevitably will also silence critics who do not advocate overthrow but fear that their criticism may be so construed. No matter how clear we may be that the defendants now before us are preparing to overthrow our Government at the propitious moment, it is self-delusion to think that we can punish them for their advocacy without adding to the risks run by loyal citizens who honestly believe in some of the reforms these defendants advance. It is a sobering fact that in sustaining the conviction before us we can hardly escape restriction on the interchange of ideas.

We must not overlook the value of that interchange. Freedom of expression is the well-spring of our civilization—the civilization we seek to maintain and further by recognizing the right of Congress to put some limitation upon expression. Such are the paradoxes of life. For social development of trial and error, the fullest possible opportunity for the free play of the human mind is an indispensable prerequisite. . . .

. . . It is not for us to decide how we would adjust the clash of interests which this case presents were the primary responsibility for reconciling it ours. Congress has determined that the danger created by advocacy of overthrow justified the ensuing restriction on freedom of speech. The determination was made after due deliberation, and the seriousness of the congressional purpose is attested by the volume of legislation passed to effectuate the same ends.

Can we then say that the judgment Congress exercised was denied it by the Constitution? Can we establish a constitutional doctrine which forbids the elected representatives of the people to make this choice? Can we hold that the First Amendment deprives Congress of what it deemed necessary for the Government's protection?

To make validity of legislation depend on judicial reading of events still in the womb of time—a forecast, that is, of the outcome of forces at best appreciated only with knowledge of the topmost secrets of nations—is to charge the judiciary with duties beyond its equipment. . . .

. . . Civil liberties draw at best only limited strength from legal guaranties. Preoccupation by our people with the constitutionality, instead of with the wisdom of legislation or of executive action, is preoccupation with a false value. Even those who would most freely use the judicial brake on the democratic process by invalidating legislation that goes deeply against their grain, acknowledge, at least by paying lip service, that constitutionality does not exact a sense of proportion or the sanity of humor or an absence of fear. Focusing attention on constitutionality tends to make constitutionality synonymous with wisdom. When legislation touches freedom of thought and freedom of speech, such a tendency is a formidable enemy of the free spirit. Much that should be rejected as illiberal, because repressive and envenoming, may well be not unconstitutional. The ultimate reliance for the deepest needs of civilization must be found outside their vindication in courts of law; apart from all else, judges, howsoever they may conscientiously seek to discipline themselves against it, unconsciously are too apt to be moved by the deep undercurrents of public feeling. A persistent, positive translation of the liberating faith into the feeling and thoughts and actions of men and women is the real protection against attempts to strait-jacket the human mind. Such temptations will have their way, if fear and hatred are not exorcized. The mark of truly civilized man is confidence in the strength and security derived from the inquiring mind. We may be grateful for such honest comforts as it supports, but we must be unafraid of its uncertitudes. Without open minds there can be no open society. And if society be not open the spirit of man is mutilated and becomes enslaved. . . .

[Justice Jackson, concurring:]

This prosecution is the latest of never-ending, because never successful, quests for some legal formula that will secure an existing order against revolutionary radicalism. It requires us to reappraise, in the light of our own times and conditions, constitutional doctrines devised under other circumstances to strike a balance between authority and liberty.

Activity here charged to be criminal is conspiracy—that defendants conspired to teach and advocate, and to organize the Communist Party to teach and advocate, overthrow and destruction of the Government by force and violence. There is no charge of actual violence or attempt at overthrow.

The principal reliance of the defense in this Court is that the conviction cannot stand under the Constitution because the conspiracy of these defendants presents no "clear and present danger" of imminent or foreseeable overthrow. . . .

Communism . . . appears today as a closed system of thought representing Stalin's version of Lenin's version of Marxism. As an ideology, it is not one of spontaneous protest arising from American working-class experience. It is a complicated system of assumptions, based on European history and conditions, shrouded in an obscure and ambiguous vocabulary, which allures our ultra-sophisticated intelligentsia more than our hard-headed working people. From time to time it champions all manner of causes and grievances and makes alliances that may add to its foothold in government or embarrass the authorities.

The Communist Party, nevertheless, does not seek its strength primarily in numbers. Its aim is a relatively small party whose strength is in selected, dedicated, indoctrinated, and rigidly disciplined members. From established policy it tolerates no deviation and no debate. It seeks members that are, or may be, secreted in strategic posts in transportation, communications, industry, government, and especially in labor unions where it can compel employers to accept and retain its members. It also seeks to infiltrate and control organizations of professional and other groups. Through these placements in positions of power it seeks a leverage over society that will make up in power of coercion what it lacks in power of persuasion. The Communists have no scruples against sabotage, terrorism, assassination, or mob disorder; but violence is not with them, as with the anarchists, an end in itself. The Communist Party advocates force only when prudent and profitable. Their strategy of stealth precludes premature or uncoordinated outbursts of violence, except, of course, when the blame will be placed on shoulders other than their own. They resort to violence as to truth, not as a principle but as an expedient. Force or violence, as they would resort to it, may never be necessary, because infiltration and deception may be enough. . . .

. . . The United States, fortunately, has experienced Communism only in its preparatory stages and for its pattern of final action must look abroad. Russia, of course, was the pilot Communist revolution, which to the Marxist confirms the Party's assumptions and points its destiny. But Communist technique in the overturn of a free government was disclosed by the coup d'état in which they seized power in Czechoslovakia. There the Communist Party during its preparatory stage claimed and received protection for its freedoms of speech, press, and assembly. Pretending to be but another political party, it eventually was conceded participation in government, where it entrenched reliable members chiefly in control of police and information services. When the government faced a foreign and domestic crisis, the Communist Party had established a leverage strong enough to threaten civil war. In a period of confusion the Communist plan unfolded and the underground organization came to the surface throughout the country in the form chiefly of labor "action committees." Communist officers of the unions took over transportation and allowed only persons with party permits to travel. Communist printers took over the newspapers and radio and put out only party-approved versions of events. Possession was taken of telegraph and telephone systems and communications were cut off wherever directed by party heads. Communist unions took over the factories, and in the cities a partisan distribution of food was managed by the Communist organization. A virtually bloodless abdication by the elected government admitted the Communists to power, whereupon they instituted a reign of oppression and terror, and ruthlessly denied to all others the freedoms which had sheltered their conspiracy.

The foregoing is enough to indicate that, either by accident or design, the Communist stratagem outwits the anti-anarchist pattern of statute aimed against "overthrow by force and violence" if qualified by the doctrine that only "clear and present danger" of accomplishing that result will sustain the prosecution.

The "clear and present danger" test was an innovation by Mr. Justice Holmes in the Schenck case, reiterated and refined by him and Mr. Justice Brandeis in later cases, all arising before the era of World War II revealed the subtlety and efficacy of modernized revolutionary techniques used by totalitarian parties. . . .

. . . I would save it, unmodified, for application as a "rule of reason" in the kind of case for which it was devised. When the issue is criminality of a hot-headed speech on a street corner, or circulation of a few incendiary pamphlets, or parading by some zealots behind a red flag, or refusal of a handful of school children to salute our flag, it is not beyond the capacity of the judicial process to gather, comprehend, and weigh the necessary materials for decision whether it is a clear and present danger of substantive evil or a harmless letting off of steam. It is not a prophecy, for the danger in such cases has matured by the time of trial or it was never present. The test applies and has meaning where a conviction is sought to be based on a speech or writing which does not directly or explicitly advocate a crime but to which such tendency is sought to be attributed by construction or by implication from external circumstances. The formula in such cases favors freedoms that are vital to our society, and, even if sometimes applied too generously, the consequences cannot be grave. But its recent expansion has extended, in particular to Communists, unprecedented immunities. Unless we are to hold our Government captive in a judge-made verbal trap, we must approach the problem of a well-organized, nation-wide conspiracy, such as I have described, as realistically as our predecessors faced the trivialities that were being prosecuted until they were checked with a rule of reason.

I think reason is lacking for applying that test to this case.

If we must decide that this Act and its application are constitutional only if we are convinced that petitioner's conduct creates a "clear and present danger" of violent overthrow, we must appraise imponderables, including international and national phenomena which baffle the best informed foreign offices and our most experienced politicians. . . .

. . . The authors of the clear and present danger test never applied it to a case like this, nor would I. If applied as it is proposed here, it means that the Communist plotting is protected during its period of incubation; its preliminary stages of organization and preparation are immune from the law; the Government can move only after imminent action is manifest, when it would, of course, be too late.

The highest degree of constitutional protection is due to the individual acting without conspiracy. But even an individual cannot claim that the Constitution protects him in advocating or teaching overthrow of government by force or violence. . . .

. . . What really is under review here is a conviction of conspiracy, after a trial for conspiracy, on an indictment charging conspiracy, brought under a statute outlawing conspiracy. With due respect to my colleagues, they seem to me to discuss anything under the sun except the law of conspiracy. One of the dissenting opinions even appears to chide me for "invoking the law of conspiracy." As that is the case before us, it may be more amazing that its reversal can be proposed without even considering the law of conspiracy. . . .

. . . I do not suggest that Congress could punish conspiracy to advocate something, the doing of which it may not punish. Advocacy or exposition of the doctrine of communal property ownership, or any political philosophy unassociated with advocacy of its imposition by force or seizure of government by unlawful means could not be reached through conspiracy prosecution. But it is not forbidden to put down force or violence, it is not forbidden to punish its teaching or advocacy, and the end being punishable, there is no doubt of the power to punish conspiracy for the purpose.

The defense of freedom of speech or press has often been raised in conspiracy cases, because, whether committed by Communists, by businessmen, or by common criminals, it usually consists of words written or spoken, evidenced by letters, conversations, speeches or documents. Communication is the essence of every conspiracy, for only by it can common purpose and concert of action be brought about or be proved. . . .

. . . When our constitutional provisions were written, the chief forces recognized as antagonists in the struggle between authority and liberty were the Government on the one hand and the individual citizen on the other. It was thought that if the state could be kept in its place the individual could take care of himself.

In more recent times these problems have been complicated by the intervention between the state and the citizen of permanently organized, well-financed, semisecret and highly disciplined political organizations. Totalitarian groups here and abroad perfected the technique of creating private paramilitary organizations to coerce both the public government and its citizens. These organizations assert as against our Government all of the constitutional rights and immunities of individuals and at the same time exercise over their followers much of the authority which they deny to the Government. The Communist Party realistically is a state within a state, an authoritarian dictatorship within a republic. It demands these freedoms, not for its members, but for the organized party. It denies to its own members at the same time the freedom to dissent, to debate, to deviate from the party line, and enforces its authoritarian rule by crude purges, if nothing more violent.

The law of conspiracy has been the chief means at the Government's disposal to deal with the growing problems created by such organizations. I happen to think it is an awkward and inept remedy, but I find no constitutional authority for taking this weapon from the Government. There is no constitutional right to "gang up" on the Government.

. . . Communism will not go to jail with these Communists. No decision by this Court can forestall revolution whenever the existing government fails to command the respect and loyalty of the people and sufficient distress and discontent is allowed to grow up among the masses. Many failures by fallen governments attest that no government can long prevent revolution by outlawry. Corruption, ineptitude, inflation, oppressive taxation, militarization, injustice, and loss of leadership capable of intellectual initiative in domestic or foreign affairs are allies on which the Communists count to bring opportunity knocking to their door. Sometimes, I think they may be mistaken. But the Communists are not building just for today—the rest of us might profit by their example.

[Justice Black, dissenting:]

. . . Public opinion being what it now is, few will protest the conviction of these Communist petitioners. There is hope, however, that in calmer times, when present pressures, passions and fears subside, this or some later Court will restore the First Amendment liberties to the high preferred place where they belong in a free society.

[Justice Douglas, dissenting:]

If this were a case where those who claimed protection under the First Amendment were teaching the techniques of sabotage, the assassination of the President, the filching of documents from public files, the planting of bombs, the art of street warfare, and the like, I would have no doubts. The freedom to speak is not absolute; the teaching of methods of terror and other seditious conduct should be beyond the pale along with obscenity and immorality. This case was argued as if those were the facts. The argument imported much seditious conduct into the record. That is easy and it has popular appeal, for the activities of Communists in plotting and scheming against the free world are common knowledge. But the fact is that no such evidence was introduced at the trial. There is a statute which makes a seditious conspiracy unlawful. Petitioners, however, were not charged with a "conspiracy to overthrow" the Government. They were charged with a conspiracy to form a party and groups and assemblies of people who teach and advocate the overthrow of our Government by force or violence and with a conspiracy to advocate and teach its overthrow by force and violence. It may well be that indoctrination in the techniques of terror to destroy the Government would be indictable under either statute. But the teaching which is condemned here is of a different character.

So far as the present record is concerned, what petitioners did was to organize people to teach and themselves teach the Marxist-Leninist doctrine contained chiefly in four books: *Foundations of Leninism* by Stalin (1924), the *Communist Manifesto* by Marx and Engels (1848), *State and Revolution* by Lenin (1917), *History of the Communist Party of the Soviet Union* (B) (1939).

Those books are to Soviet Communism what *Mein Kampf* was to Nazism. If they are understood, the ugliness of Communism is revealed, its deceit and cunning are exposed, the nature of its activities becomes apparent, and the chances of its success less likely. That is not, of course, the reason why petitioners chose these books for their classrooms. They are fervent Communists to whom these volumes are gospel. They preached the creed with the hope that some day it would be acted upon.

The opinion of the Court does not outlaw these texts nor condemn them to the fire, as the Communists do literature offensive to their creed. But if the books themselves are not outlawed, if they can lawfully remain on library shelves, by what reasoning does their use in a classroom become a crime? It would not be a crime under the Act to introduce these books to a class, though that would be teaching what the creed of violent overthrow of the government is. The Act, as construed, requires the element of intent—that those who teach the creed believe in it. The crime then depends not on what is taught but on who the teacher is. That is to make freedom of speech turn not on what is said, but on the intent with which it is said. Once we start down that road we enter territory dangerous to the liberties of every citizen. . . .

. . . Intent, of course, often makes the difference in the law. An act otherwise excusable or carrying minor penalties may grow to an abhorrent thing if the evil intent is present. We deal here, however, not with ordinary acts but with speech, to which the Constitution has given a special sanction.

The vice of treating speech as the equivalent of overt acts of treasonable or seditious character is emphasized by a concurring opinion, which by invoking the law of conspiracy makes speech do service for deeds which are dangerous to society. The doctrine of conspiracy has served diverse and oppressive purposes and in its broad reach can be made to do great evil. But never until today has anyone seriously thought that the ancient law of conspiracy could constitutionally be used to turn speech into seditious conduct. Yet that is precisely what is suggested. I repeat that we deal here with speech alone, not with speech plus acts of sabotage or unlawful conduct. Not a single seditious act is charged in the indictment. To make a lawful speech unlawful because two men conceive it is to raise the law of conspiracy to appalling proportions. That course is to make a radical break with the past and to violate one of the cardinal principles of our constitutional scheme. . . .

. . . There comes a time when even speech loses its constitutional immunity. Speech innocuous one year may at another time fan such destructive flames that it must be halted in the interests of the safety of the Republic. That is the meaning of the clear and present danger test. When conditions are so critical that there will be no time to avoid the evil that the speech threatens, it is time to call a halt. Otherwise, free speech which is the strength of the Nation will be the cause of its destruction.

Yet free speech is the rule, not the exception. The restraint to be constitutional must be based on more than fear, on more than passionate opposition against the speech, on more than a revolted dislike for its contents. There must be some immediate injury to society that is likely if speech is allowed. . . .

. . . The nature of Communism as a force on the world scene would, of course, be relevant to the issue of clear and present danger of petitioners' advocacy within the United States. But the primary consideration is the strength and tactical position of petitioners and their converts in this country. On that there is no evidence in the record. If we are to take judicial notice of the threat of Communists within the nation, it should not be difficult to conclude that as a political party they are of little consequence. Communists in this country have never made a respectable or serious showing in any election. I would doubt that there is a village, let alone a city or county or state which the Communists could carry. Communism in the world scene is no bogey-man; but Communists as a political faction or party in this country plainly is. Communism has been so thoroughly exposed in this country that it has been crippled as a political force. Free speech has destroyed it as an effective political party. It is inconceivable that those who went up and down this country preaching the doctrine of revolution which petitioners espouse would have any success. In days of trouble and confusion when bread lines were long, when the unemployed walked the streets, when people were starving, the advocates of a short-cut by revolution might have a chance to gain adherents. But today there are no such conditions. The country is not in despair; the people know Soviet Communism; the doctrine of Soviet revolution is exposed in all of its ugliness and the American people want none of it.

How it can be said that there is a clear and present danger that this advocacy will succeed is, therefore, a mystery. Some nations less resilient than the United States, where illiteracy is high and where democratic traditions are only budding, might have to take drastic steps and jail these men for merely speaking their creed. But in America they are miserable merchants of unwanted ideas; their wares remain unsold. The fact that their ideas are abhorrent does not make them powerful.

. . . The First Amendment provides that "Congress shall make no law . . . abridging the freedom of speech." The Constitution provides no exception. This does not mean, however, that the Nation need hold its hand until it is in such weakened condition that there is no time to protect itself from incitement to revolution. Seditious conduct can always be punished. But the command of the First Amendment is so clear that we should not allow Congress to call a halt to free speech except in the extreme case of peril from the speech itself. The First Amendment makes confidence in the common sense of our people and in their maturity of judgment the great postulate of our democracy. Its philosophy is that violence is rarely, if ever, stopped by denying civil liberties to those advocating resort to force. The First Amendment reflects the philosophy of Jefferson "that it is time enough for the rightful purposes of civil government for its officers to interfere when principles break out into overt acts against peace and good order." The political censor has no place in our public debates. Unless and until extreme and necessitous circumstances are shown our aim should be to keep speech unfettered and to allow the processes of law to be invoked only when the provocateurs among us move from speech to action.

Vishinsky wrote in 1948 in the *Law of the Soviet State*, "In our state, naturally there can be no place for freedom of speech, press, and so on for the foes of socialism."

Our concern should be that we accept no such standard for the United States. Our faith should be that our people will never give support to these advocates of revolution, so long as we remain loyal to the purposes for which our Nation was founded.

Yates v. United States, 1957: Philosophy Is Not Illegal

As the Supreme Court moved through the changing specifics of concrete circumstances brought to it in the form of cases in the context of national and international changes, one thing of which the citizen could be sure was that exact forecasting of future constitutional developments was impossible; that after the Yates case would come other judicial determinations (and legislative and executive and paraconstitutional actions) that would sharpen and alter the civil liberties *status quo*. Commenting on the Yates case, the American Civil Liberties Union said that the decision was "of special importance because of the court's view that philosophical advocacy of violent overthrow of the government, unrelated to any advocacy of action to accomplish this objective could not be held illegal." The ACLU called the decision "spectacular" and added that in this case the Supreme Court "placed itself squarely on the side of the individual citizen's rights of free speech and association."

The decision is not easy reading for the student; it may be a small comfort for him to know that one political scientist has commented, "The division of the Justices in this case was extremely complex"; another said, "Perhaps the viewpoint expressed in the Court's opinion is more significant than the actual decision. The tone is hostile to the theory of the prosecution." In a dissenting opinion, Justice Clark, who thought that the Yates case should have been dealt with on the same basis as the Dennis case, referred to the majority decision's "artillery of words."

Yates was one of fourteen Communist Party leaders and organizers who had been convicted by a Federal district court in California of conspiracy to (1) teach and advocate the violent overthrow of the United States and (2) organize the Communist Party, a society of persons teaching or advocating violent overthrow of the government.

Justice Harlan delivered the opinion of the Court, taking the unprecedented step for five of the fourteen Communists of ordering their acquittal. In the case of the other nine, the convictions were reversed and the way left open for a new trial. The Federal government, however, did not prosecute any of these people.

One portion of Justice Harlan's opinion rested on the interpretation of the word "organize," so as to exclude evidence of actions involving the "organizing" of the Communist Party in 1945 and earlier; the effect was to bar this part of the indictment, returned in 1951, under the statute of limitations.

In part, the decision, continuing, said:

. . . Petitioners contend that the instructions to the jury were fatally defective in that the trial court refused to charge that, in order to convict, the jury must find that the advocacy which the defendants conspired to promote was of a kind calculated to "incite" persons to action for the forcible overthrow of the Government. It is argued that advocacy of forcible overthrow as mere *abstract doctrine* is within the free speech protection of the First Amendment; that the Smith Act, consistently with that constitutional provision, must be taken as proscribing only the sort of advocacy which incites to illegal *action;* and that the trial court's charge, by permitting conviction for mere advocacy, unrelated to its tendency to produce forcible action, resulted in an unconstitutional application of the Smith Act. The Government, which at the trial also requested the court to charge in terms of "incitement," now takes the position, however, that the true constitutional dividing line is not between inciting and abstract advocacy of forcible overthrow, but rather between advocacy as such, irrespective of its inciting qualities, and the mere discussion of exposition of violent overthrow as an abstract theory. . . .

There can be no doubt from the record that in so instructing the jury the court regarded as immaterial, and intended to withdraw from the jury's consideration, any issue as to the character of the advocacy in terms of its capacity to stir listeners to forcible action. Both the petitioners and the Government submitted proposed instructions which would have required the jury to find that the proscribed advocacy was not of a mere abstract doctrine of forcible overthrow, but of action to that end, by the use of language reasonably and ordinarily calculated to incite persons to such action. The trial court rejected these proposed instructions on the ground that any necessity for giving them which may have existed at the time the Dennis case was tried was removed by this Court's subsequent decision in that case. . . .

. . . We are thus faced with the question whether the Smith Act prohibits advocacy and teaching of forcible overthrow as an abstract principle, divorced from any effort to instigate action to that end, so long as such advocacy or teaching is engaged in with evil intent. We hold that it does not. . . .

. . . The legislative history of the Smith Act and related bills shows beyond all question that Congress was aware of the distinction between the advocacy or teaching of abstract doctrine and the advocacy or teaching of action, and that it did not intend to disregard it. The statute was aimed at the advocacy or teaching of concrete action for the forcible overthrow of the Government, and not of principles divorced from action.

The Government's reliance on this Court's decision in Dennis is misplaced. The jury instructions which were refused here were given there, and were referred to by this Court as requiring "the jury to find the facts essential to establish the substantive crime.". . . It is true that at one point in the late Chief Justice's opinion it is stated that the Smith Act "is directed at advocacy, not discussion," but it is clear that the reference was to advocacy of action, not ideas, for in the very next sentence the opinion emphasizes that the jury was properly instructed that there could be no conviction for "advocacy in the realm of ideas.". . .

In failing to distinguish between advocacy of forcible overthrow as an abstract doctrine and advocacy of action to that end, the District Court appears to have been led astray by the holding in Dennis that advocacy of violent action to be taken at some future time was enough. It seems to have considered that, since "inciting" speech is usually thought of as calculated to induce immediate action, and since Dennis held advocacy of action for future overthrow sufficient, this meant that advocacy, irrespective of its tendency to generate action, is punishable, provided only that it is uttered with a specific intent to accomplish overthrow. In other words, the District Court apparently thought that Dennis obliterated the traditional dividing line between advocacy of abstract doctrine and advocacy of action. . . .

. . . The essence of the Dennis holding was that indoctrination of a group in preparation for future violent action, as well as exhortation to immediate action, by advocacy found to be directed to "action for the accomplishment" of forcible overthrow, to violence "as a rule or principle of action," and employing "language of incitement," is not constitutionally protected when the group is of sufficient size and cohesiveness, is sufficiently oriented towards action, and other circumstances are such as reasonably to justify apprehension that action will occur. This is quite a different thing from the view of the District Court here that mere doctrinal justification of forcible overthrow, if engaged in with the intent to accomplish overthrow, is punishable per se under the Smith Act. That sort of advocacy, even though uttered with the hope that it may ultimately lead to violent revolution, is too remote from concrete action to be regarded as the kind of indoctrination preparatory to action which was condemned in Dennis. . . .

. . . In light of the foregoing we are unable to regard the District Court's charge upon this aspect of the case as adequate. The jury was never told that the Smith Act does not denounce advocacy in the sense of preaching abstractly the forcible overthrow of the Government. We think that the trial court's statement that the proscribed advocacy must include the "urging," "necessity," and "duty" of forcible overthrow, and not merely its "desirability" and "propriety," may not be regarded as a sufficient substitute for charging that the Smith Act reaches only advocacy of action for the overthrow of government by force and violence. The essential distinction is that those to whom the advocacy is addressed must be urged to do something, now or in the future, rather than merely to *believe* in something. . . .

Thunder on the Right

Real and fancied threats to freedom have been with us since the birth of the nation; likewise, we have always had men who have courageously defended Constitutional liberties. Stretching from the "witch hunts" before the United States was formed and through several centuries of governmental and nongovernmental efforts to cope with recurring crises in freedom, and up to yesterday's episode in libertarian good or evil, America has survived to see each antidemocratic "ism" become a "wasm."

Long ago, the Federalists asserted that "Government should be a terror to evil doers"; today, we can go along with that conclusion, even though we may be somewhat disquieted by the dramatic language. In any case, we remain puzzled as to just how to react to the activities of people who set out to catch Communists while they spurn the requirements of constitutional niceties.

In the quest for appropriate attitudes and behavior to adopt toward anticommunism and antianticommunism, the citizen will take some of his cues from the mass communications media. Vivid, attention-arresting and attention-holding, the television documentary program is potentially one of the most powerful instruments for stimulating thinking about and discussion of public affairs. Accordingly, we have thought it useful to reproduce the following excerpts from a Columbia Broadcasting System script whose subject matter is concerned with significant phases of American political life.

[CBS Reports "Thunder on the Right" as broadcast over the CBS Television Network, Feb. 22, 1962. Narration written by Eric Sevareid, Bill Leonard, and Jack Beck; producer: Jack Beck; executive producer: Fred W. Friendly.]

SEVAREID: A conservative spokesman has said: "The big problem for the responsible conservative today is to disassociate himself from the extremists."

MINUTEMAN: We'll set up an ambush form at the gap.

SEVAREID: The Right Wing is a spectrum that ranges all the way from these Minutemen vigilantes prowling for Communists on the banks of a Midwest river to the more responsible Senator Barry Goldwater, whom many of them consider pretty far to the left of the Right, and who is more worried about Harvard eggheads like Arthur Schlesinger, and the graduated income tax.

GOLDWATER: "The problems are intricate and cannot be fully understood even by the intelligent minority." Now, this is Harvardese for "the people are too damn dumb," and you recall that. This is the attitude that we face in Washington daily, and I mean this sincerely.

SEVAREID: In between Goldwater and the Minutemen, whom he dislikes, are a broad range of people who have been called everything from super-patriots to cranks and crackpots. Captain Eddie Rickenbacker, who would build a statue to another hero:

RICKENBACKER: Some day, and I hope to live to see it, the American people will erect a monument to the memory of the late Senator Joe McCarthy for his heroic efforts to awaken the American people to the danger that this country, its people, and generations to come, would have to face.

SEVAREID: General Ed Walker, who wants to be Governor of Texas:

WALKER: The time to save America is now. Our symbol is the American eagle, devoid of and unscathed by partisan politics. Super-patriots have led many squads in platoon. They have died in the assault. Fear and moderation have made followers and not leaders. . . .

ANNOUNCER: CBS Reports: "Thunder on the Right." Here is CBS News Correspondent Eric Sevareid.

SEVAREID: A political democracy can't fly on one wing. Ours has two, the Right and the Left, with the main body politic in the middle. Right now, the flapping of the Right Wing is setting up the most vibrant vibrations in the national air. This report deals with the Right Wing. For years, political liberals have complained that Right Wingers see only one kind of feather on the Left Wing, and think that all liberals are Socialists, all Socialists are

Communists, and all Communists are spies. Now, conservatives complain that many liberals see only one kind of feather on the Right Wing, and confuse a Russell Kirk, writer of philosophy, with Gerald L. K. Smith, thumper of tubs. The word "extremist," according to Webster's, means "ultra," or "radical," or "very far out." It depends, of course, on where you stand yourself. From where most of us stand, the Minutemen are way out yonder. They seem itching to shoot at something red, hoping it's not a deer hunter's cap. Near Norborne, Missouri, cameraman Wendell Hoffman joined them on their prowl for any dialectical materialism that might come down the paths.

HOFFMAN: Well, we spent two days with Robert DePugh and the Minutemen, and they simulated that field exercise. It wasn't a regular training period. The whole thing took place just south of Norborne, Missouri, and supposedly the Russian gunboats they're talking about were spotted on the Missouri River.

FIRST MINUTEMAN: Now, there's a patrol boat going down the river.

SECOND MINUTEMAN: Well, they're headed for Cruzey's Landing.

HOFFMAN: It was supposed that Mrs. DePugh telephoned an alarm. You can see that in the pictures.

MRS. DE PUGH: Band 4—Cruzey's Landing—scramble immediately.

HOFFMAN: And Minutemen in the surrounding area snatched up their rifles—some of them had telescopic sights—and converged at Cruzey's Landing. Actually, the rifles being snatched were filmed in a cabinet in DePugh's home. Presumably, under the right circumstances, a coded telephone signal would go out—the Minutemen would grab their weapons and melt into the woods to carry on a guerrilla war. The trench mortar was filmed just outside Bill DePugh's home on a farm near Norborne. Bill is Robert's brother. That had to be postponed one day because the mortar was locked in the trunk of Robert DePugh's car, and nobody could find the key. I saw correspondence indicating that the Minutemen is a secret organization. When you become a member, your name is replaced with a number, and Robert DePugh, at least part of the time, uses a number as a signature.

SEVAREID: Not as exotic as the Minutemen but a steadier star in the constellation of the Right is an Australian citizen who came to America to sound his warning against communism. Dr. Fred C. Schwarz had his greatest success in Los Angeles, California, and he still cherishes that memory.

SCHWARZ: We beat "The Untouchables." We beat "Wagon Train." It was a tremendous experience. I couldn't go out in the streets hardly without being mobbed. You'd walk into a restaurant—everybody'd—or restaurant—everybody would stand up and start clapping and cheering. You'd open the door at the hotel and the maid would almost faint. "Oh, can I have your autograph?" This, in Southern California.

SEVAREID: From Los Angeles, Dr. Schwarz's travels took him to another haven of the retired—St. Petersburg, Florida. CBS News Correspondent Bill Leonard spent a week with Schwarz's traveling troupe.

GROUP: I pledge allegiance to the flag of the United States of America.

LEONARD: We shared with St. Petersburg the impact of a week under the spell of Dr. Schwarz, one of his rare excursions east of the Mississippi—by no means the most successful of his exhibitions, but nevertheless, a fair sample of the man *Time* magazine calls "the hottest thing around" in a world of mass-meeting, group-action anti-communism.

SCHWARZ: I then proceed to say, "Communism has a system of thought, an interpretation of being, a book of rules known as its philosophy."

LEONARD: Fred Schwarz, with careers in medicine, psychiatry and fundamentalist preaching behind him, now devotes full time and talent to the Christian Anti-Communist Crusade, which he founded, and the anti-Communist school, a traveling institution of learning and inspiration, of which he is dean, star lecturer and fund raiser. Whether his mood is angry or coy, confidential or coercive, you get your money's worth.

SCHWARZ: The philosophy of communism is, of course, dialectical materialism. D-i-a-l-e-c-t-i-c-a-l—dialectical materialism. The Communists shorten it to the term "dia-mat." They say, "History's working for them. Nothing I can do can change the tide." Are they right? Are they right? Oh, it's easy to get people disturbed. It's easy to get them convinced. The problem is to get them to do something about it that really costs them something. They said, "Dr. Fred Schwarz, whose friends say he's a dedicated anti-Communist and his enemies say he's a spellbinding pitchman who only stops shouting long enough to take up a collection." All our books are audited. We publish the audit, and in Los Angeles we made a profit of two hundred thousand dollars. How dreadful! How wonderful. How wonderful! We're proud of it. Now, I'm no martyr. I've got enough. It's not my ambition to be the richest man in the Communist liquidation line.

LEONARD: But there is no arrow in the Schwarz quiver that he shoots with more zip and relish than the closing commercial.

SCHWARZ: Now, don't go yet. I've come to the commercials. We've always got to come down to the mountains, to the valleys and what we want you to do. Now, we're going to culminate this school in a great victory banquet. These are thrilling experiences. You'll hear stories to warm your hearts. You'll have the matchless privilege of giving a big offering. What a favor we do you. Now—so get your banquet ticket. They're five dollars outside. You've never seen me take an offering. You come and watch on—but bring your checkbook on Friday night. Now, if you know anyone with a good checkbook, bring them along. It'll be my responsibility after that. We've got all sorts of programs. Now, the next thing is, get the literature.

LEONARD: To qualify for these graduation exercises, students enlist for all or part of the anti-Communist curriculum—five dollars a day or twenty dollars for the full five-day course—which in St. Petersburg, and typically elsewhere, consisted of six lectures and a film each day.

SCHWARZ: "Insurance Against Communism." "Communism, a Disease." "What Can Students Do?" "The Heart, Mind and Soul of Communism" have been translated into many languages. It'll show you why the Communists propose as their loving duty to put you somewhat brutally to death. Now, we come down to the only three major books we've got. Now, these are not the only books, but I don't believe in having too many books. Only confuses you.

Now, people always say, "I want to study communism. Where do I start?"

Here, of course, is where I come into this fundamental conflict between honesty and humility. I always say, "Begin with my books." I speak first. But here is the book—"You Can Trust the Communists." It's had a tremendous reception. Many of the lectures I give in the morning, you'll find in this. "You Can Trust the Communists" has the chapter, "The Difficult, Devious and Dangerous Dialectic." That costs you three dollars. Cleon Skausen's "The Naked Communist." This costs, I think, five. J. Edgar Hoover's "Masters of Deceit." This one's only fifty cents, so you've now got a ten-minute interception to buy the literature, drink your coffee, order the tapes, get your banquet tickets, and come back. . . .

SEVAREID: Robert Welch has said that Los Angeles, California, and Houston, Texas, are the two strongholds of his Birch Society. He became wealthy selling candy. He has now become notorious selling the thought that Chief Justice Warren deserves impeachment and that the last three presidents of the United States leaned toward communism.

HOLCOMB: On this one where you say that Eisenhower—you never called him a card-carrying Communist.

WELCH: I did not, but I am not answering any questions.

HOLCOMB: Well, in your writing, didn't you call him a dedicated, conscious agent of the Communist conspiracy?

WELCH: I told you—no interview—no comment. Now, get out of here!

HOLCOMB: Well, now, why won't you answer our questions? We're legitimate reporters representing a legitimate news agency.

SEVAREID: For the kind of charges he levels, Mr. Welch is very shy of reporters—likes to dictate the circumstances in which he will be photographed, and often refuses to answer questions about his indictment of public officials.

HOLCOMB: Didn't you call him that?

WELCH: Who's in charge here? Is anybody in charge?

HOLCOMB: No. This is a free press group, Mr. Welch. Every one of us here . . .

SEVAREID: More and more conservatives are denouncing Welch as a fanatic, a radical of the Right.

CHAIRMAN: I welcome you to a meeting of the John Birch Society.

SEVAREID: The more eager Birchers have put pressure on school superintendents and editors, sometimes by mail or telephone campaigns. Some have asked children to spy on their teachers. Some have talked about arming themselves for the "day when." Other chapters, including this one in Los Angeles, have milder objectives, although they usually open with the latest instructions from Belmont on the matter closest to the heart of Robert Welch:

CHAIRMAN: . . . is to work for the impeachment of Earl Warren. Somehow there's been criticism in many circles, most of them leftist circles, of the campaign to impeach Earl Warren, and I wish somebody would please advise me, if I don't know my constitutional rights, if it is not part of the law that we have a right to request impeachment of a public official.

SEVAREID: Next item on the agenda, from Birch headquarters:

CHAIRMAN: . . . as requested, here in our bulletin, is the sale of slave labor merchandise. Personally, we are helping to maintain the slaves and to keep people in slavery behind the Iron Curtain every time we buy something that is made on the other side of the Iron Curtain. Indirectly, we're doing just as much to keep those people in subjugation as their slave masters are. "Hams from Poland."

FIRST WOMAN: We had, I think it was, three dozen Christmas ornaments. They were beautifully made, and on the box we noticed MADE IN POLAND.

SECOND WOMAN: I think it's shocking that we should be compelled to buy ornaments and things made by atheists. It just doesn't make sense. . . .

SEVAREID: "Where there is lightning there is thunder" can be inverted to show that thunder on the Right (or Left) can create lightning. This is the bombed home of the Reverend John G. Simmons, Pastor of St. Matthews Lutheran Church in North Hollywood, California. Those who support the anti-Communist crusades ask: "What harm can come from alerting the nation to the danger of subversion?" The Reverend Simmons can attest to the emotional climate generated thereby. His home was bombed while he was addressing a forum about extremists in the Right Wing movement. Paul Udell of CBS talked to him.

UDELL: Reverend, how would you evaluate the danger to this country from far-Right groups?

SIMMONS: I think it serves to divide us, because it makes those who are thinking people, who are afraid, or who are intimidated by threats of violence, or things like happened in our home last night and the home of Reverend Walker, that we will be frightened into silence; and I think that the threat to our country from the outside, from the Soviet and the satellites, and from the People's Republic of China, that we will begin to be attacking ourselves, and this is, of course, precisely what Lenin suggested would happen, that we would not be able to agree within our own country, and therefore, we would become divided, and when you divide, you conquer. If you can silence enough people who are responsible, by threats to their family, by using the tactics of the Communist, then your country will be undermined from within.

UDELL: Do you consider that these people are members of the Birch Society or another far-Right group?

SIMMONS: No, I don't believe that, myself, that the Society or groups like this as such, would do this. I think that what they are saying, incites people who are emotionally upset, disturbed, who are mentally ill, in my judgment, to acts of violence, on the theory that it's a holy war, that it's something which is God's will, to protect us, which is a form of nationalism with a halo; and this kind of thing, I think, is the result. I don't think the societies or groups, as such, are involved in anything like this. . . .

SEVAREID: The views of the extreme Right range over everything from social security to recognition of the Soviet Union—library books, mental health programs and the United Nations. In every case, their position is against some existing institution or practice. Finding one candidate to cover this range of dissent is a problem. Many of these groups seem to feel that the man who shares more of their views than any other man, with some chance of being effective, is Senator Barry Goldwater of Arizona.

Senator Goldwater, Mr. Nixon, General Eisenhower, various others, including the Hearst press now, the Right Wing writers, like George Sokolsky and others, have in effect renounced and criticized these extreme Right groups. You do not wish, then, to make any statement renouncing the support . . . ?

GOLDWATER: I have gone just as far as any of those gentlemen long before they did. For instance, when they suggested they impeach the Chief Justice, I can't buy that. Now, you are going to find, though, in this particular case of the Birch Society that there is one man that's responsible for all of this—it's not the organization. Mr. Welch is the one that keeps making these statements about impeaching Earl Warren, and that the State Department is filled with Communists. These are statements that are made in an irresponsible way, in my mind, and I think that it would be to the Birch Society's betterment if Mr. Welch removed himself from the active head of it. In my home town, I don't know all of the members of the Birch Society, but I know the leaders, and I can't condemn them. They're just fine Americans who are concerned. They believe that communism is a threat to the world, and they've conducted several seminars in Phoenix, open to the public; with one, a former Chief Justice of our Supreme Court; another one, one of our top businessmen in the state. These aren't crackpots. I don't know—all of a sudden it's become popular in this country to downgrade a man's patriotism. If this is the frustrated American's way of showing his frustration, there's no law against it; but if they become harmful, I'll be the first one to speak out about it. I wish they'd get rid of Mr. Welch, and I think their troubles would go away. . . .

CHAPTER 9

PUBLIC OPINION, PRESSURE GROUPS, AND PROPAGANDA

To KNOW AMERICAN GOVERNMENT is to know far more than merely the make-up and functioning of the three governmental branches. Modern research on government has made use of nomenclature, categorization, and concepts that have a strange sound to the citizen accustomed to approaching government as a problem in making laws, carrying them out through an executive arm, and resolving judicial problems through a court system. When the new research talks of "input functions" and "output functions," the reference is to analysis of political systems stretching far beyond the observation of what has sometimes been called government by the lawyer.

There are political and parapolitical and extrapolitical organizations and processes that wind to, through, around, and among the Congress, the Executive, and the Supreme Court. No man can comprehend the government of the United States unless he has thought about major aspects of interrelations between American governing agencies and communications: the ways in which public opinion operates in this country, the means used by interest groups to articulate their goals and combine to achieve their purposes and receive and disseminate propaganda, the media through which ideas, information, and attitudes are carried, and the concepts implicit in assessing public opinion.

The result is to make the study of American government an area open at its middle and at all its ends to the other social sciences, to produce an interpretation of government that peers behind, under, and around the solemn declarations of a document or the charismatic assertions of an officeholder.

What happens in government is a function of the ideas and activities of the politician, the businessman, the farmer, the union or the military leader, or any group in a position to influence the opinions and behavior of the community's decision makers, or perhaps even to exercise power directly themselves by heading public agencies, writing legislation, or in other ways. In modern America individuals and groups are likely to wield their governing authority through persuasion, through access to the means of communicating ideas and manipulating the symbols and instruments of government to guide the flow of benefits from the public purse and the distribution of purposes for which public moneys are to be expended.

Not always intentional and organized, persuasion through propaganda has taken on special meanings these days; the burning of a bus to protest desegregation or the picketing of a public official to protest nuclear explosions may (or may not) be designed simply to influence American public policy, but each has repercussions on the rest of the world, and so on America again in somewhat circuitous and heightened fashion. The form, nature, and impact of propaganda on the nation's internal affairs are closely bound up with its character and operations in the country's international relationships.

Great questions are involved here: the role of American government in telling the world about America, the effectiveness of truth in international propaganda, the relative susceptibility to skillfully presented propaganda of literate Western-politics-style peoples, literate one-party-style peoples, and populations in underdeveloped and developing areas. Permeating these questions is one of the principal handicaps facing the United States in its international propaganda: the fact that our democratic ideas are complicated and subtle (not every man will see immediately that strikes are concomitants of a free society), that the ideas require a considerable basis in experience for their understanding, that America's extraordinarily high standard of living works in part to block the foreigner's appreciation of the United States (and the American's appreciation of the foreigner as well).

It can be argued that the foreigner has difficulties in seeing America's art and literature through such gloss as America's shower curtains and bathtubs, that our material accomplishments are a prod to other people to find tarnished places in our chrome exterior despite our propaganda. At the same time one of the reasons Americans are likely to be less than perfect in the image they display to the world is that Americans are truly less than perfect. America has a magnificent revolutionary past and an impressive set of reasons for adjusting creatively to the emerging world, but again and again Americans are likely to exhibit difficulties in understanding people who use their "streets" as toilets, who live in mud huts, who have a long history of deprivation and oppression and hunger, who have never thought of freedom as other than a farm to own and cultivate right now, who speak a different "language."

The material below assumes that anybody who talks intelligently of propaganda talks necessarily about public opinion, and about ways of figuring out the state of public opinion; polls are hardly the only way of assessing people's judgments, but their comprehension does offer an opening to analysis of characterizations of the state of public opinion anywhere.

A. PUBLIC OPINION

Role of Public Opinion

Concern with the views of the man on the street is as old as the street, and leaders have given thought to the opinions of their followers ever since there have been followers. "The voice of the people is the voice of God" is a cry that can be traced back to the ancient Hebrews; it embodies an idea whose approximations and relationships are threaded everywhere that people are found. "Public opinion" is a phenomenon and a process that ramifies to any place and time where people had something to get done.

It is no accident, however, that the term "public opinion" was not used until the eighteenth century. For the rise to power and status of the ordinary man was a correlative of the rise of the middle class, the expansion of institutions for making the hitherto-unimportant man's voice heard, the appearance and the spread of literacy, and the extraordinary growth and development of means of communication both within and between nations. Considered below are the rationale and operation of public opinion in the American democracy.

[Norman John Powell, *Anatomy of Public Opinion,* © 1951, Prentice-Hall, Inc., Englewood Cliffs, N.J. Reprinted by permission.]

There is a greater welter of conflicting judgments as to the place of public opinion in a democratic government, as to the limits of competence of that opinion, as to the proper and possible objects of its concern. The issue of the role of public opinion penetrates deep into our social fabric; it determines how we shall allow our governors to rule; how we shall establish and shape political and social and economic institutions; how we shall have the community function and change with changing circumstances and needs. On the definition of the role of public opinion depend the distribution, forms, and expressions of power and freedom in any society, in any place, and at any time.

We are concerned here with public opinion in a democracy, and we interpret democracy as a form of government whose central characteristic is ultimate responsibility to that section of public opinion represented by qualified voters who go to the polls. Distinction is sometimes made between economic and political democracy, economic democracy being taken to refer to approximate equality of income for individuals, or the right of every man to a job, or security against sudden deprivation of his means of sustenance. If economic democracy be any of these, the instrument for enforcing responsibility is, anyway, the vote. The economic equality or right or security is safeguarded in the long run only through the political apparatus built on democratic political theory. Through the vote, the electorate may bring into being or expansion systems of government intervention in the economy that provide particular goods for the individual. Without political democracy, "rights" are at the mercy of power groups—to be withdrawn or constricted without defense by the individual. With political democracy, the individual sets up the final safeguard of whatever mode or degree of economic democracy his representatives contrive. In the end, the root of economic democracy is politics and the fruit of political democracy is the tendency toward economic democracy.

For example, a totalitarian state may provide for its population a species of apparent economic democracy in respect to job security or pay rates. The system, let us say, is working out badly in the opinion of most individuals. They cannot change the system peacefully, for without political democracy they are without voice in its fundamental arrangements. They cannot, in fact, be "secure" in their security, for it may be rescinded or modified in its application to an individual with no possibility for him of rejecting the change. Imprisonment or death is the alternative to acceptance; individuals have no way to hold governors responsible for their acts under totalitarian government. There are not two kinds of democracy, but one—political democracy. The only method thus far developed in the history of all civilization for effectively enforcing the responsibility of the rulers to the mass of the governed is the vote of the general electorate itself, the unfolding of the democratic process where there is access to competing sources of information, freedom of discussion, and the politician is not all-powerful.

In totalitarian governments the pyramid stands on its point; the public is responsible to its rulers. Duties is the catchword instead of rights. The candidate for membership in the Hitler Youth was required to declare his support of a formula represented by the twin cores, "The Leader is always right," and "The program is your dogma, it demands your complete surrender to the cause." In effect, then, as the Nazi organization expanded and took deeper hold on what it seized, the general public expressed its opinions through all the institutions of the community in accordance with the theme enunciated by the leadership. The role of the citizenry's participation in economic, religious, political, or other affairs was the bending of efforts to support *the* program and *the* leader. Power became homogeneous and single; it was totalitarian. "Freedom" was the duty to strive mightily to sustain and further an already given dogma and to follow an already established leadership.

In a democracy, power has heterogeneous expressions and the opinions of the general public are manifested in different institutional forms, each competing with the others, the political power being one among an array. Each is split; there are, for example, different religions, different kinds of groups in power in differing governmental units, opposing economic aggregates. Each sets and seeks differing objectives. Who would be a democrat is hydra-headed and multiple-bodied.

The differentiation between the operation of public opinion in a democracy and in a totalitarian nation is not that the one is omnipotent and the other impotent. It lies in the way public opinion is formed, in how it is evidenced, in the extent to which it can choose and replace leadership. One is formed in an environment of conflicting propagandas, is manifested freely in variegated publics and institutional expressions, and is able to select and replace leaders. The other is determined in a monistic propaganda environment, effected in institutions all of which have one political nucleus, and is constrained to be content with those in office.

In particular application to a democracy the basic questions relating to the configuration of public opinion power are four: Is man-in-the-street opinion competent to rule? Is rule by "the majority" compatible with continued freedom? Does "the majority" rule? What conditions make for an optimum public opinion power pattern? There can be no effective government of or through fools, but even if competent, public opinion may not produce just results.

Not only capability, but morality and justice and practicality must be considered in interrelations of public opinion and government. In part these are matters to be settled on the basis of the individual's value system. In part, on the other hand, they are issues to be decided on the grounds of empirical and rationalistic data.

COMPETENCE OF PUBLIC OPINION

Let us take the question of public opinion competency and focus the discussion on America. At one extreme is the view represented by the declaration of Alexander Hamilton, "The voice of the people has been said to be the voice of God; and however generally this maxim has been quoted and believed, it is not true in fact. The people are turbulent and changing; they seldom judge or determine right." At the other is the statement of any man who, running for national office in the middle of the twentieth century, heaps encomiums on the wisdom and nobility of the average American.

The fundamental issue of the competence of public opinion arises in the area of politics. The relevant public here is the qualified voter, for he, multiplied by 50 million, is the means through which responsibility in a democracy is implemented. Judgments of ability are, of course, relative to the talents of the general public as compared with special publics—politicians, businessmen, public administrators, trade union or agricultural leaders, and others. In this context of relativity, we shall analyze the four main categories into which the competency of the electorate subdivides itself: intelligence, information, interest, and emotionalism. Analysis of each factor follows:

Intelligence

Are the American people intelligent? It may be that this question is suggestive of the "How high is up?" dilemma. Nevertheless, the frequent charge has been made that people are too stupid to rule their rulers. The evidence? Data like intelligence test results; the popularity of nonintellectual and trivia-laden newspapers, radio programs and movies; the number of mediocre, and worse, politicians who are elected; the occasional instance of widespread apparently feebleminded behavior, such as the popular reaction to the newspaper advertisement that stated "Last day to send in your dollar." To the box number that accompanied the announcement were sent many thousands of dollars; or the county election at which the majority of the electorate turned down one lever to vote for an increase in pay for a particular office, and turned down another to vote for abolition of that office.

Not only are the masses enormously unintelligent, is the allegation, but they become more stupid with succeeding generations. For the more intelligent tend to rise from their lowly origins to take their place in the upper social and economic groups, reducing further the average intelligence of the stupid many.

Let us take these criticisms in turn. The intelligence test result most often cited is that of World War I, where the average army recruit was found to have a mental age of about 14 years. But the deduction is not necessarily that people are stupid. The average score obtained by soldiers on the Army Alpha intelligence test was a certain number of items correct. Fourteen-year-old children, on the average, received similar marks. Presumably the average fourteen-year-old has a mental age corresponding to his chronological age of fourteen. The average soldier, whose score approximated that of the typical fourteen-year-old, has been said, therefore, to have a mental age of fourteen. But the test consisted of questions in arithmetic, vocabulary, numerical relations, reading, and other items of the kind that the test-makers, educated people accustomed to pencil and paper situations, would be expected to write.

Another meaning that may be attached to the findings emerges from consideration of the differing histories of the youngster and the grown-up. It is that fourteen-year-olds have the same capacity to learn as the adult, but the adult has, merely by virtue of his maturity, learned more about practical matters than the child. He has been in a greater variety of situations, has had more opportunity to engage in trial-and-error learning, and has far more experience in dealing with adult problems. He has, not the greater capacity for profiting by his encounters with life, but the greater know-how, because he has those encounters as part of his experiential background. The psychologists themselves, it should be said, have all but abandoned the practice of interpreting adult test scores in terms of mental age, on the ground that the mental age concept is inappropriate for the grown-up. Modern psychological write-ups of adult intelligence refer to statistical differentiations; thus, scores may be said to be in the upper five, twenty or other per cent of the total distribution of all marks earned by persons taking the test.

Whether intelligence test results demonstrate that people are dunces or not appears to be highly questionable. Nor does the alternative proof seem to be weightier. The specific newspaper, radio program, or movie selected by the member of the general public is in part a function of his educational level and of the availability of other recreational and communication instruments, and is the consequence of drives arising from such varied sources as his home life and his social satisfactions. It is an index not of his intelligence necessarily, but of his needs and his upbringing.

Do people elect mediocrities to public office? Those who framed the American Constitution were themselves men with deep distrust of the common men whose expression is public opinion. Roger Sherman, a signer of both the Constitution and the Declaration of Independence, said: "It would be as unnatural to refer the choice of a proper character for chief magistrate to the people, as it would be to refer a trial of colors to a blind man." It is the most superficial of parallels to cite Hitler's similar figure of speech: "It is easier for a camel to pass through the eye of a needle than for a great man to emerge from a popular election." Hitler's solution was simple: regiment the population. The solution of the American Constitution-makers was far more complicated and held steadily to the end of securing liberty and great, but bounded, political power.

Unquestionably, mediocrities have been elected to public office in America; undoubtedly, too, first-rate men have also been elected. And there is no research that indicates that the average democratically selected political leader is inferior to the one chosen by any other means. Studies of our legislators show them, on the average, to be comparatively well-educated men of relatively good achievement. A top political office that has numbered among its occupants men of the stature of Washington, Jefferson, Jackson, Lincoln, Cleveland, Wilson, and the two Roosevelts, has certainly not been bare of eminent capabilities and talents. . . .

Whether the many are extraordinarily unintelligent appears to be a contestable proposition. Are they becoming more stupid with time because they are steadily deprived of their better minds? The claim of diminishing mass intelligence assumes that intelligence is an inherited unitary characteristic. Neither psychological nor biological research supports this assumption. . . .

The sum of these arguments is certainly not that Americans are a moronic lot. Some people, evidently, are not bright, others are brighter, and what they or their progeny become is not readily predicted from their mental age.

The student should remember that in any case, abstract intelligence as such, associated with both education and economic status, is likely to result only in the individual's voting in a conservative direction. Poll the members of *Who's Who* and you find a politically conservative majority. The implication is that intelligence as such is no guarantor of "rightness" in politics, but tends, instead, correlated as it is with many other facets of the individual, to produce "rightist" political valuations.

Information

The prime question here is whether people are so uninformed as to be unable to hold their governors responsible. In analyzing this issue, we shall touch on the matter of popular ignorance, attempt to account for it, and estimate the likelihood of increase of popular information. Then we shall assess the extent to which public opinion can, in democratic government, determine public policy, and end by indicating the limits within which freely formed public opinion can hold political power responsible. The relations between informed and uninformed public opinion and democracy are not summed up in the point that public opinion is informed or not; they are epitomized in the kind of information needed and used to effectuate democratic responsibility.

Public opinion surveys have revealed great areas of ignorance on the part of Americans. Relatively few know what the Bill of Rights is; many do not know the names of their representatives or senators; many have vague geographical concepts; United Nations is little more than a name to many; and the ideas of most about great issues and problems and projects are uninformed and blurred. . . .

Such data do not dim the faith of those who quote findings of opposite meaning. The people, says Gallup, citing his own surveys, correctly appraised the value of air-power before many of the experts themselves. Most persons were urging military conscription many months before political leaders or Congressmen advocated the plan. For at least four years before Pearl Harbor the people were opposed to the shipment of American oil, scrap, and war materials to Japan.

The fact is that the community and the communications machinery in America are so organized as to make it monumentally difficult and inconvenient for people to be well informed on the details, or even the outlines of many major problems of the day. One aspect of the situation is seen in a remark of John Adams: "Public information cannot keep pace with the facts." But, says political scientist Richard S. F. Eells, at the time of the adoption of the Constitution, the means of communication in the United States were practically the same as they were in England in the Middle Ages, a fact that accounted for Americans' lack of information on public affairs. "The growth and transmutation of political ideas during the colonial period," Eells points out, "were the result of personal correspondence, journals, and treatises by the leading men in the different localities."

In the 150-year period since colonial days, the new and expanding communications instruments generated by a forward-leaping technology have, it is claimed, made it possible for Adams' objection to be met: public information can now keep up with the facts. To this reasoning, two points can be made in reply. One is that in actuality public information remains sparse and faulty. Poll results show that. The air-power, conscription, and similar opinion figures cited by Gallup can hardly be classified as evidence of intelligent possession of information by the general public; they would seem much more nearly to fall into the category of glandular responses to difficulties. Planes sailing off into the empyrean to secure America and to win a war are an imagination-firing notion; that the notion turned out to possess considerable validity is testimony only to the fact that dreams and fears sometimes come true.

For it is inevitable in a technological society that public opinion is a substantially uninformed opinion. The explanation lies not in the public's congenitally defective mental equipment but in the nature of the operating environment. Some portions of the world are too much with us to allow more than scanty attention to others of the world's aspects. The man whose judgment and attitudes go to make up public opinion must earn his living, he must accompany his wife to a bridge game or to the movies, children must be fed and their noses wiped, the shopping must be done and the house must be cleaned. Leisure has increased, but the competing demands on that leisure have widened. Recreational and other outlets for the consumption of time have multiplied even more rapidly than non-working time has increased. As John Dewey says, "Man is a consuming and sportive animal as well as a political one. What is significant is that access to means of amusement has been rendered easy and cheap beyond anything known in the past." People are just too busy to acquire much information about abstractions and matters that do not lie immediately under their noses.

Simultaneous with the extension of pressures on the public's time has been the swelling flood of information, misinformation, and evaluation emanating from the communications media. Simultaneous also has been the accelerated proliferation and increased tempo of change of problems. . . .

In public affairs, now it is an event in China or Britain or Korea or elsewhere over the whole of the globe, then it is a domestic development in taxation, or the tariff, or education, or housing, or inflation or disinflation or deflation or reflation, or a nearly infinite number of other political, economic, or social segments. At the same time there is too much information to cull out and digest, there are too many and too complex issues to follow and grasp, and there is not enough time to acquire what knowledge may be necessary for opinion to be informed. People are not well informed and, if the preceding argument is valid, they cannot be well informed.

Suppose this rationalization to be persuasive. Does it follow that public opinion is so ill informed as to be without value? That has been one inference, the result of which is the belief that government should be carried on by the so-called great and by the wise men.

Another interpretation is possible. It is that the public does not know enough to identify significant problems or to initiate sensible programs of action, does not know enough, perhaps, even to be aware that policies are working well or badly, but does know enough to make a competent selection every so often among competing personalities seeking public favor. The life experiences of the adult give him a ready-made ground from which he can appraise real people, not abstruse programs. After all, in American elections, candidates' programs proclaim as their objectives the attainment of all goods for all men. Particularly at local levels of government are different political parties opposed, not in principles or in behavior, but in being outs and ins. Sometimes there may be ideological or behavioral distinction between two sets of ideas or acts, promised or performed—say, the extent to which government should intervene in the national economy in order to promote some purpose, or whether a tax or a foreign relations policy is working out effectively. Under these circumstances, it should be remembered first that even the specialists disagree: the possession of much information does not lead automatically to the correct answers. Second, as democracy works in America, the people are not given formal opportunity in elections (saving instances of referenda) to vote for or against government extension or other specific policies; people vote for or against candidates. Not even the candidates are chosen by the people; those who run for public office are the men who have been designated after the elaborate operation of a highly involved political process, so remote in reality from the general public that few people are able to describe its functioning.

Walter Lippmann sums up this view: ". . . by their occasional mobilizations as a majority, people support or oppose the individuals who actually govern." This personality function would appear to be the frame of action within which public opinion is informationally competent and within which it actually works. "It is on the men inside, working under conditions that are sound, that the daily administration of society must rest," says Lippmann, proceeding to delineate a public opinion range of action wider than choice between candidates: "The general public outside can arrive at judgments about whether these conditions are sound only on the result after the event, and on the procedure before the event."

Do people know enough to judge results and to identify acceptable procedures in such cases? How, for example, could the people judge whether American policy toward the Soviet Union is sound or not? Only the most palpable and dramatic of results would become general and accurate knowledge—war, revolution, or other impressive, overt phenomena—although, when practicable, there would undoubtedly be debate as to responsibility for the event. Public opinion is informed sometimes about grievances, almost never about remedies. It is not the general public that requires knowledge of the factual data, but the competing experts who supply the competing politicians with the information they require. Only access to the factual data is required for the general public, because that is a basic condition for the existence of the freedom that makes possible competition between the experts and the politicians. The value of factual information as such is easily overrated.

Such data are useful in informing us about the consequences of acts and the ways in which acts can be performed, but they do not tell us what acts to perform. Satisfaction with things as they are depends ultimately on a value system rather than an informational complex.

The foregoing discussion departs greatly from what has become American folklore: that public opinion is competent to and does determine general public policies indirectly through its designated representatives. It is the designated representatives who determine policy without the influence of general public opinion, if with the assistance and intrusion of the more articulate and well-informed persons who combine themselves into competing pressure groups. We have labeled as folklore the thought that the people decide public policy; what they do is to choose between politicians (using the term in no invidious sense) and to vent their spleen or express their approbation of a status quo. Political scientist Gabriel A. Almond, particularizing for foreign policy, suggests that the criteria for popular control are met as long as there are competing groups of experts and as long as the ultimate electoral power is reserved for the rank and file. Almond's additional requirement of "an attentive public" is discussed below under the head of interest.

That the public does not determine policy is clear once we look at the facts rather than the stereotype. Candidates commonly run on similar promises that are identical in their broad statement. Suppose even that a man in the street agrees with one part of a set of promises, rejects a second, and is indifferent to a third. Limited to "Yes," "No," or abstention, the voter can only make a selection between candidates. Similarly, he cannot approve some acts performed by an incumbent and disapprove others as good or bad policy, effectuated well or badly; he can only vote for or against the person in office. Just how meaningless is the vote as an expression of policy preference may be seen in two respects. One: following an election, debate frequency arises as to what the public has mandated. After Truman's election in 1948, widespread newspaper comment held that he had no sizable popular support for seeking the enactment of a greatly revised labor relations policy. It was argued that Truman had been elected despite his labor stand, that he had been elected because people admired his courage, or for other reasons. Two: announced promises bear no necessary relation to subsequent operating policies. Lincoln undertook during his campaign to keep slavery as an institution; Wilson said he would keep America out of war; Franklin Roosevelt in 1932 stated he would reduce government expenditures. The list can be extended at Federal, state, and local government levels. The five-cent subway fare, traditional in New York City, was not even discussed in 1945 during the mayoralty campaign. Two years later, the silence was broken, tradition was shattered, and the fare was doubled.

Public policy is not and cannot be fixed by public opinion; what is more, there is sound rationale for not so establishing it. For the public lacks necessary information and is unable to acquire it; the broad mass of public opinion expresses itself on infrequent, isolated occasions and continuous policy-making and adjusting is vital; public opinion can only nod or shake its head or be still; it cannot, like its representatives, conciliate and compromise and make the second choices demanded in practical situations. In substance, all that public opinion can and does is to size up those who seek office; it neither initiates nor defines public policy; it is no positive, creative agency. What it can and does is to express its dissatisfaction or satisfaction with a status quo by voting for or against an incumbent. It is only in this most oblique, negative fashion that the general public affects policy, although it does hold the policy-makers responsible through its votes. . . .

Interest

The bases for believing that people are uninterested in public affairs are several: the extent of nonvoting, the relatively small audience for serious materials, the slender circulation of informative periodicals and books, the difficulties of reaching people in informational campaigns, and the like. . . .

What is the impact of this fact of public indifference on the determination of the role of public opinion? We may note first the idea that some apathy is a healthy phenomenon. Incidence of voting, suggests political scientist Francis G. Wilson, may be like a fever chart. Were all of us to be vitally concerned with voting in the "right" man, were all of us acutely interested in the election, it might mean that we regarded our stake in the result as so momentous that political unity would be endangered. Elections since the Civil War have ended in average winning percentages of about 52 per cent of the total vote for the victor in national campaigns. That means that the other 48 per cent have had to go along and abide by the results. Were the 48 per cent intensely aroused, the probability would be increased that bullets might supplement ballots.

This is not to say that indifference cannot be excessive. Too much nonvoting could well mean untrammeled manipulation of public affairs by a minority, victorious not on merit but on the basis of "clever" manipulation.

Indifference can be too little or too great. Certainly it is not too little in America. Is it too great? "Yes" seems a fair answer, where 30 million voters absent themselves from the polls on the quadrennial occasion of the selection of a president. Nonvoting in state and local elections is proportionately even greater. Yet almost 50 million persons voted in the 1948 elections; many millions vote in the state and local elections. Active electors in such great numbers, although the number should be greater, would hardly seem to argue that apathy is nearly so complete as to signify an almost inert public. Political interest is still considerable enough to prompt half or more of the potential electorate to exercise its franchise, and is sufficient to stimulate the birth and growth of diversely oriented pressure groups. . . .

Tentatively, we may say that too many nonvoters must spoil the democratic broth, but too few may foreshadow political struggles where ballots are spiked with savagery and burnished with violence and fury. We may try to educate the nonvoter, but equally, we may recognize that the nonvoter is a result of government, whether by Democrats or Republicans, that is good enough to keep our political temperatures at about normal.

Emotionalism

The charge is that people think with their hearts and stomachs. A slogan is a more effective organ of persuasion than a rational argument; saluting the Statue of Liberty verbally is more appealing than mundane presentation of undramatic matters. . . . Assume that sometimes, but not always, rampant emotionalism controls most people's judgments and attitudes. Side by side with this statement must be set down the observation that sometimes the judgments and attitudes of the intellectual and informational elite are likewise emotionally rooted. The basic issue is not that of the emotional many vs. the unemotional few. The question is just how often emotionalism governs the two groups and what form the emotionalism takes. Franklin Roosevelt may be a name to send a highly educated few into a paroxysm of fury as it may send an uneducated many into a frenzy of enthusiasm. Maybe some, more sophisticated than others, have no adrenal response to the Constitution and perceive that even a mother is a mortal creature, unendowed with all virtue. Perhaps, however, the person who is sophisticated with regard to the Constitution or motherhood can be reached in other emotion-centered ways. It can undoubtedly be said of some that their blood pressure rises and their pulse rate quickens in an emotional response to what most would regard as abstractions: a gold standard, reorganization of a public agency, scientific method. Not every man has his price, but almost every man has his emotion-bespattered object. The variables are intensity of attachment or aversion, the objects of the emotionalism, and the frequency with which the nonintellectual apparatus of the individual or group may function. About these particularized matters, empirical research has furnished no adequate base for a judgment. Certainly, the data on opinion formation and propaganda effects imply no readiness for the man in the street to jump attitudinally at the propagandist's call. What appears tentatively reasonable is the generalization that all men are emotional and that the differences among individuals and groups are not inevitably of a character to lend credence to an all-embracing conclusion of emotionalism for the many and intellectualism for the few.

Is public opinion competent? An absolute answer seems to be impossible. One comparative characterization seems admissible: public opinion is quite hopelessly incompetent with respect to specific issues: it is most competent in determining the relative virtues of opposing candidates, rather than contrasting ideas or philosophies. In any case, the position that people are gross incompetents possesses no overwhelming evidentiary strength, although the reverse stand that people are equipped with vast political insight is equally challengeable.

PUBLIC OPINION AND GOVERNMENT

Is the Power of "the Majority" Compatible with Continued Freedom?

In political affairs, the question concerns itself with the consequences for minority groupings of having the majority of the electorate constitute the ultimate governor. The additional question of the merits of the select few as against the common multitude is a familiar one and has, in a measure, been considered in the previous discussion. Brief if inadequate further mention of the issue requires citation of the principal arguments for vesting ultimate control of the community in the elite few: they are endowed with superior special talents in mind and in spirit. The counter-argument has been stated by John Stuart Mill: speaking of a "completely popular government," Mill says:

> . . . [its] superiority in reference to present well-being rests upon two principles. . . . The first is, that the rights and interests of every or any person are only secure from being disregarded when the person interested is himself able and habitually disposed to stand up for them. The second is, that the general prosperity attains a greater height, and is more widely diffused in proportion to the amount and variety of the personal energies enlisted in promoting it.

Is there, however, a limit beyond which the result of majority rule is the denial of freedom? Henry Steele Commager speaks of "Majority Rule and Minority Rights"; Lord Acton held that "The most certain test by which we judge whether a country is really free is the amount of security enjoyed by minorities." Referring to a legislative body, Thomas Jefferson stated that "173 tyrants can be as tyrannical as one." Can we not also talk of tyranny by the majority of the persons in a democracy? Acton's logic with respect to an ancient democracy may be applicable to modern democracies:

> . . . the possession of unlimited power, which corrodes the conscience, hardens the heart, and confounds the understanding of monarchs, exercised its demoralising influence on the illustrious democracy of Athens. It is bad to be oppressed by a minority, but it is worse to be oppressed by a majority. For there is a reserve of latent power in the masses which, if it is called into play, the minority can seldom resist. But from the absolute will of an entire people, there is no appeal, no redemption, no refuge but treason.

The lesson, said Acton, of the Athenians' experience

> . . . endures for all times, for it teaches that government by the whole people, being the government of the most numerous and powerful class, is an evil of the same nature as unmixed monarchy, and requires, for nearly the same reasons, institutions that shall protect it against itself, and shall uphold the permanent reign of law against arbitrary revolutions of opinion.

Here, then, is the base for believing in trammeling the will of the majority: its absolute power must, in the end, be corrupted and become inflexible. In opposition is the thought that no effective alternative to the will of the majority exists for the definition of justice, that corruptibility and inflexibility are not unique traits of the majority, but may, likewise, characterize minorities of any nature or number.

The dilemma, however, persists; it remains possible that the majority will conform to the Acton thesis. The ideal is to avoid tyranny by the majority, to escape oppression by a minority, and yet to protect the minority and to free the majority. It is a dilemma that can easily lead to endless wandering in a rationalistic labyrinth. Let the majority be at liberty to do what it wills, except that it may not invade certain rights of the minority. Then both are free and both are protected. The question, then, is about deciding the rights of the minority. Only two possibilities are present. Those rights may be defined by the majority or by a minority. Defined by the minority those rights may invade the liberties of the majority. Set up by the majority, those rights may curtail the freedom of the minority.

Proposed as a solution to the majority rule–minority rights problem is a line marking the outer boundary of the rights of the majority by the guarantee of civil liberties. The majority may do what it pleases except to deprive either itself or the minority of freedom of speech and the dependent liberties, such as freedom of religion, the press, and petition. For the majority to abrogate freedom of speech is to deny to the minority opportunity to become a majority, and to deprive later generations of the chance to choose for themselves their own governing forms.

Where freedom exists, there is no such classification as *the* majority; there are, instead, many majorities varying with the issue at hand. The dominant political party is one species of majority and the most numerous economic class is another and—here is a second fact—every person is a member of majority and minority groups. He may be white and rich, Protestant and Negro, a citizen and a labor union member. Highly relevant, also, is the third point: majorities and minorities on socio-economic-political matters are in perpetual flux. So, neither Democrats nor Republicans are always in the majority and individuals pass from one economic category to another. As a result, majorities must trade with each other and with minorities and thus compromise to win their goals; awareness of membership in particular minority groups is a check on the activities of those in majorities. Examples are the continual efforts of political parties to obtain the support of special groups like labor unions and agricultural organizations.

This reasoning assumes no natural rights on the part of any persons, no inborn rights anterior to those of society. The rationale is simply that liberty is an end in itself. The argument for the civil liberties boundary line is the support for freedom of speech itself. Minorities may be right in whole or in part; such freedom promotes technical and cultural progress and is the prerequisite for the use of scientific method; it challenges majorities to rethink through and maintain understanding of their procedures and doctrines; it compels discussion and consultation before decisions are made and unmade; it assumes that which is reasonable: that majorities are not infallible.

What actual resolution of the majority rule–minority rights issue is embodied in the American Constitution? Fearing both majority and minority, the men who wrote the Constitution, who were not ardent democrats and who respected men of property and the lessons of experience, set out to control both the majorities and the minorities, both the governed and the governors. The governors were segmented horizontally and vertically through separation of powers and through Federalism. Controlling any majority were the indirect system of electing the president and the Senate, and of designating the Supreme Court; the representative arrangement itself; the Constitutional prohibition upon certain acts, as impairing contracts and enacting ex post facto legislation; the extraordinary difficulty of amending the Constitution and the extraordinary majorities required for certain purposes, as to impeach the president and to make treaties; the great expanse of the nation; the variety of possible majorities that could be formed by people in association with one another. All the devices, of course, that serve to control the majority likewise exercise constraint over the minority.

The Constitution, independent of majorities and minorities both, is thus a document purporting to embody justice as a principle. Usage and judicial interpretation as well as formal amendment have modified the original Constitution in the general direction of enabling the majority more directly and readily to express its will, although the delicately worked-out Constitutional machinery retains many of its slowing-up-the-majority characteristics. To minorities, the formal and informal government processes in and around the Constitution have resulted in binding the majority to guarantee to the minority a variety of civil liberties.

Civil rights, guaranteed by the Constitution, can in theory be rescinded by amending the Constitution, by being chipped away through Supreme Court decision, or by being disregarded by the national or state governments or other agents without corrective action by competent bodies. Two points must be noted. One is that it would be an extraordinarily difficult undertaking to effect the rescission legally, involving as it does two-thirds and three-quarters majorities and a most remarkable set of political and administration conditions. The second is that legal and Constitutional limitations are no more powerful than the mores, sentiments, and will of the people allow. . . . Constitutions and laws exert pressure on the expression and formation of opinions, but the essential restraint, if restraint there is, comes not from the legal instrument but from the values, custom, tradition, and folkways that breathe life and meaning into statute and charter. At bottom, the limits of majority action are set by the accretion of custom. What public opinion is habituated to do and allow is the final guarantee of what the community will do and allow.

The argument is that the continued power of general public opinion is compatible with continued freedom, that the limiting conditions for their compatibility can be set theoretically by rational analysis and by law, that in practice the limits will be fixed at whatever place the community leadership (acting for the public) permits in the light of the community's heritage and habits.

Does "the Majority" Rule?

The ceiling of what public opinion should be empowered to do appears in the Constitution and is supported by the nation's folkways. But, below this ceiling, is "The Sovereign Citizen" an accurate description of a member of the public in America? Is public opinion actually sovereign, whether or not it should be? Thomas A. Bailey, the historian, quotes Charles Dudley Warner's judgment: "Public opinion is stronger than the Legislature, and nearly as strong as the Ten Commandments." In reality, says Bailey, "it is often stronger than the Ten Commandments." The evidence? Government may be influenced positively or negatively. "The classic example of positive action may be found in 1898, when the masses rose and cried out for war against Spain with such overwhelming insistence that the amiable McKinley dared not deny their demands." Bailey also gives a negative example:

> When the United States minister to Mexico City, James Gadsden, was negotiating in 1853 for the strip of southwestern territory that bears his name, he suggested that the State Department supply him with money for bribing certain Mexican officials. He was informed from Washington that such funds could be provided only by Congressional action, and that the resulting stench would be undesirable.

A more recent example of the power of public opinion cited by Bailey is the failure of Franklin Roosevelt to force a major policy upon the American people, as he attempted to do in the famous Quarantine Speech.

Does Bailey's evidence collide with the previously stated position that, by and large, public opinion exercises its control by choosing between ins and outs, that it is informed only on the most momentous of events, that it neither can create nor choose between policies, except under the most extraordinary conditions? Yes, is one answer; the data are self-evident.

Another view is that Bailey's data are compatible with the apparently antithetical position. For instance, Charles Beard said of the "classic" case of 1898, that it was "a combination of economic interest, appealing humanity, 'good journalism' and popular tumult which drove the United States steadily toward war." Certain it is that a complicated array of circumstances, not wholly described by "overwhelming insistence" of "the masses" led to the Spanish-American War. What is significant in any case is that war and atrocities, as in this example, are exactly the obvious and dramatic stuff that the public is likely to be informed and have an opinion about. . . .

The fundamental task of the citizen in a democracy is not to direct foreign policy (or any other large and intricate area of public affairs), but to choose between candidates who will direct policy, and to make a decision as to whether or not incumbents' acts in prices, housing, international relations, and other areas of importance to him have been so handled as to merit re-election of those incumbents. The role of public opinion in a democracy is not to fashion or administer public policy, but to hold the policy-makers and directors responsible. In practice, "the majority" governs at the polls by supporting one rather than another personality. In practice, between elections, "the majority" is the aggregate of informal and formal opinion leaders who can persuade public officials that their views are supported by effective voting power or persuasive evidence or both. Almond remarks that "One might almost say 'who mobilizes elites, mobilizes the public.' " Public opinion is neither nearly as strong nor stronger than the Ten Commandments; it is the Ten Commandments. Public opinion, as man-on-the-street opinions, fixes the very broad, very generally stated boundaries within which public policy is defined and carried out. Public opinion, as elite opinions and those organized by elites, is precise and intense in its impact on specific issues.

Conditions of Democratic Public Opinion Power Pattern

These have already been considered; here they are merely assembled for the convenience of the reader. . . . The root fact is that public opinion in a democracy reigns primarily through the political process. Accordingly, the following statement is in terms of the effective foundation and structure of public opinion power for the end of furthering political responsibility—for making those who wield political power accountable to the general public for their activities.

1. No one institution of the community is dominant; the state and the community are not one. That is to say that the power of government (or any other single expression of or influence on public opinion) is not so great as to be able to annihilate the sum total of the other agencies of the community. This serves as a check on the tendency of all power to expand, to become total, and to be corrupted.

2. Government and politics are so organized as to make it possible for individuals to identify those who are the largely responsible political agents for whatever consequences have ensued.

3. The suffrage is widespread, preferably universal, and a sizable section of the electorate goes to the polls. Control over the government is thus increased, and itself controlled. Not participation, but control is the essential. In Nazi Germany there was extensive action by the citizenry in implementing the decisions made by the governing few; so vast and elaborate was the organization of participation that virtually everyone, youngsters included, had a role to play. But the role was that of executing mandates from the gov-

ernment, that of facilitating control from the top of the political hierarchy, rather than controlling the hierarchy. Yet a certain amount of citizen participation in political matters is vital as an expression of interest, a means of acquiring information about politics, and a base for making accountable those who formulate and carry out public policy.

4. Education is qualitatively adequate and quantitatively extensive. Otherwise, access to and use of competing ideological data is necessarily limited.

5. There is adequate economic organization of the community; the standard of living is relatively acceptable to the mass of the citizenry. This tends to be accompanied by greater toleration of political opposition, and diminishes the possibility that liberty will be exchanged for a specious but attractive economic good.

6. The citizenry have free access to sources of information. If the government is to be responsible, the citizen must be enabled to find out what government has done, can do, is likely to do, what it should have done, and so on.

7. Competition exists among the sources of information and argument available to the citizen.

8. Those holding political office may be displaced by opposing individuals and groups; the decision as to whether or not top political policy makers are to be retained is made by the majority of the general electorate through the vote.

9. Elite groups are relatively numerous and in competition with one another.

10. Those who oppose the existing government or other political instrumentalities may organize to seek popular support. All organization demands leadership that must, by the very nature of complex organization, operate on a day-to-day basis substantially without the assistance of most people. But all must be free to lead, in a democracy, hampered only by their personal and situational limitations and the opposing organization. Otherwise, entrenched power cannot be rooted out.

11. The understandings whereby the victorious political power does not forcibly extinguish its opposition are imbedded deep in the traditions and propaganda conventions of the nation. Similar bases hold for the agreements whereby the defeated and minority groupings use non-violent propaganda rather than force as their means for winning political victory.

The essence of these 11 items may be variously viewed. Thus, accent on their generalized result results in thinking of democracy as a way of life. Attending particularly to the value system permeating them leads to interpreting democracy as institutionalized respect for individual persons. Accenting the political phases gives rise to thinking of democracy as a way in which the governed control those who govern.

All 11 items have a single kernel: freedom of speech and organization. Given freedom of the individual and the group to talk and listen, a freedom reflected in institutional and propaganda arrangements and grounded in community mores, valuing the individual as a dignified human being, the political power established by the operation of public opinion becomes responsible.

B. PRESSURE GROUPS

Advertising an Idea

Interested in combating the possibility of extension of the Tennessee Valley Authority idea to other great river basins, the Electric Companies Advertising Program (ECAP) studied public opinion systematically to guide its advertising campaign. Polls revealed that 63 per cent of a cross section of the American people approved TVA, 10 per cent disapproved, and 27 per cent had no opinion. Support for TVA was not limited to special segments of the community; approval was shown by 65 per cent of upper-income people, 55 per cent of Republicans, 83 per cent of editors and educators. Apparently there was broad support for TVA and an effective propaganda offense against the idea was going to be difficult.

Other poll results furnished to ECAP a public relations cue. The question was asked, "Would socialism be a good thing or a bad thing for the United States?" Answers were: 69 per cent "bad"; 10 per cent "good"; 21 per cent "no opinion."

ECAP identified the necessary tie:

> It is apparent that to link our fight to the TVA question would run into a lot of opposition. . . . But to link our fight to socialism is something else again. The people do not want socialism.
>
> We're on favorable ground there. ECAP advertising in magazines and on the radio will stress the fight against the socialistic state more in the future.

The following item, describing the ECAP campaign, is taken from *Editor and Publisher,* the organ of the American newspaper publishers and editors.

[Robb M. Winsborough, "A Case Study of Successful Public Relations Advertising," *Editor and Publisher,* Feb. 21, 1953, p. 54.]

Necessity, it seems, has fathered nearly as many public relations programs as it has inventions since the early 30's—that era when public confidence in business leadership reached an all-time low. But few, if any, depression born programs to build good will have had a record equal to the Electric Companies Advertising Program. Certainly, none devoted exclusively to the use of advertising has had a more interesting record. Now in its 12th year, it is well worth careful review.

The necessity for ECAP, as the Electric Companies Advertising Program is widely called, was expressed in 1941 by one of its founders this way: ". . . we believe that unless a majority of the public is sold on private operation of public utilities, we will lose our business to government operation no matter what kind of public relations we have with our own customers. The decision is going to be made in Washington and that action will be greatly influenced by public opinion."

The federal government had recently introduced TVA and similar government power programs which met with widespread approval by the public and by the press. The executives of several private electric light and power companies met in Chicago and agreed that theirs was a national problem and that they must answer it on a national level.

To carry the unified voice of the electric industry, national advertising (via N. W. Ayer & Son, Inc.) was clearly indicated as the best means of mass communication. It has these advantages: 1) It can be controlled; 2) It is responsible; 3) It is economical.

However, these electric company presidents recognized that many of them would want to go further than this and include ECAP messages as a part of their own company's local advertising, so, ECAP made provisions for newspaper mats and radio commercials on suggested ECAP subjects.

The purpose agreed upon was and still is: "To present the facts about the business of producing and distributing electricity so that the people may become better informed as to the public benefits which result from efficient business management of the electric companies of America."

Objectives growing out of the purpose: 1) To improve the public attitude toward the business-managed electric companies; 2) Through such improvement of public opinion, to discourage further government encroachment in the electric business.

Next, the electric companies had to decide two basic questions: 1) Who did they want to reach, and; 2) What did they want to say?

The first question was relatively easy to answer. They wanted to reach all eligible voters and young people about to become voters. A big audience. Within it, they recognized a smaller group of influential people who represented, for them, a special audience. It included editors, educators, ministers, lawyers, legislators, and others having special influence.

For reaching the basic audience—the electorate—they determined that nationally circulated magazines and network radio were best suited for the job.

They decided that the advertising would be human, calm and reasonable. It would be based on the interests of the reader or listener. It would be factual, and the facts would prove that electricity is a big value: that electric companies are good citizens; that they give good service; that they are constantly expanding and developing to give still better service; and that the electric industry is not the "power trust," but is owned by all sorts of people.

But how did these men know that their plan was sound or that it would work? They had to answer these questions: "Can the job be done? Can we actually exert any influence that will help us? Will the money we spend do enough to justify the expenditure?"

The men who started ECAP were mostly engineers, and they undertook a cooperative advertising program to test, scientifically, the possibility of converting unfavorable public opinion by presentation of the facts.

A scientific procedure was followed on a national scale. Misinformation was found concerning service, rural electrification, rates, ownership and other subjects. Magazine advertising was prepared to deliver the facts about these subjects. ECAP radio commercials paralleled these efforts.

Meanwhile, the companies were keeping a finger on the pulse of public opinion. Starting in 1943, ECAP commissioned the Opinion Research Corporation of Princeton, N.J., to conduct public attitude surveys at two-year intervals. These surveys covered the entire nation. The sixth such survey is now underway and the results will be published about mid-Summer. They have shown definite improvement in favor of the private companies.

Using percentage figures as a basis for extension, Opinion Research Corporation estimates that approximately 8,000,000 fewer people favor some sort of government ownership of the electric business today than did in 1943.

From the 1949 Survey, the electric companies learned that the large majority of the public had come to oppose socialism—69 per cent said socialism would be a "bad thing" for the U.S.

But people did not recognize the socialistic implications of government in the power business. For when they were asked, "should the federal government produce and sell all electricity in the country?" only 46 per cent opposed it.

And here was an important opportunity. Magazine advertisements were prepared on this subject, and many of the radio commercials were patterned upon the same theme—that government in the electric business is creeping socialism at work.

The response was tremendous.

During 1950, '51 and '52 the campaign bore down consistently on the creeping socialism story. It was attacked and criticized by public power proponents in high places. But, according to one ECAP spokesman, nobody has been able to criticize the program because of any inaccuracy or any untruthful statement. It has also been quoted widely and has attracted numerous important allies to the side of the electric industry.

One hundred and thirty electric companies now support ECAP. These companies serve nearly 60 per cent of the nation's electric users.

In 1953 ECAP had a budget of nearly $2,000,000.

One unique fact is that every dollar of this money—as it does every year—goes into the advertising effort. ECAP has no headquarters, no offices, no executive or traveling secretary, not even any letterheads.

Nor does it have any bosses. It belongs to the participating companies and they direct it in meetings to which all participants are invited. In this regard, what was first thought of as a weakness of the electric industry—its diversity—has actually emerged as a strength. ECAP includes companies in all parts of the U.S., in towns and cities of all sizes. These companies have operating heads who are confronting practically every situation there is and who have had experience with all phases of this problem. When you assemble these people you have a counseling staff that could hardly be equaled. No decision of importance is ever reached before the original thinking has been hammered out on the anvil of open debate. In a nationwide group of this sort this is a minor miracle. It's gone on this way for nearly 12 years and no one man or group has gained control of ECAP or dominated the discussion. It's still a completely democratic process.

Participation in this national program has undoubtedly resulted in stronger local programs on these same issues.

On an average, three newspaper advertisements (in various sizes) are sent to the companies each month. One of these is usually an adaptation of the current magazine advertisement; the other two are specially prepared for mat service use. Since 1941, 396 advertisements have been prepared. And companies have ordered over 195,000 mats. This last figure, of course, does not include the many advertisements that were slightly revised but were based on ECAP's mat service messages.

On an average, eight suggested radio announcements are sent to the companies each month. Sometimes more than this number are sent when special occasions or timely events warrant special messages.

But membership in ECAP has helped local efforts to a greater extent, perhaps, than can be measured in these mat service statistics. It would be hard to calculate how many companies have been able to strengthen and improve their own local advertising and public relations activities as a result of the discussions and experiences they share at ECAP meetings—where attention is focused on problems of advertising and public relations currently important to the electric industry.

There is good reason to believe that this public relations program of advertising has contributed much to the progress of the electric industry—and perhaps to all business and industry. If it pursues its course with vigor and courage—and there is assurance that it will—ECAP can be expected to challenge and exploit even greater opportunities.

Agriculture, Business, and Public Affairs

As a preliminary to the analysis of the two excerpts below from the *Congressional Record,* dealing respectively with the interest of farmers and businessmen in protecting and advancing their status, the citizen will find it useful to know something of general public opinion in relation to the merits and behavior of these interest groups.

In one study, this question was put: Which group do you think tries to put the most pressure on Congress to get what it wants, labor unions, businessmen, or farmers? In percentages, answers were:

Labor unions	43.9
Businessmen	24.3
Farmers	6.2
All equal (volunteered)	6.0
Don't know	19.6

When another question was put dealing not with effort but effectiveness (Which group do you think Congress pays the most attention to, labor unions, businessmen, or farmers?), no great difference was found; activity was pretty well equated with success. The figures were substantially changed, however, when the question was centered on the merits of the several groups: Which group do you think Congress should pay most attention to, labor unions, businessmen, or farmers? Answers in percentages were:

Labor unions	14.7
Businessmen	10.3
Farmers	22.1
All equal (volunteered)	36.8
Don't know	16.1

Any effort to interpret these data, relating them to the descriptions and prescriptions below, should recognize that agriculture and business are summary references to people and activities that are hardly homogeneous in size, power, make-up, methods, and objectives.

[Hon. H. Carl Andersen, "How to Get Congressional Support for Agriculture," *Congressional Record,* July 27, 1961, pp. A5761–5762. (Speech before the 45th Annual Conference of the American Association of Agricultural College Editors.)]

. . . Ladies and gentlemen and distinguished guests, it is a great honor and a privilege to meet with you today. Last March when your program chairman, Mr. Ward, invited me to speak, he asked that I speak to you on the important job of getting congressional support for agriculture.

From my association with farm editors, county agents, and extension workers over a span of 40 years or more, and especially from 20 years of service on the Appropriations Subcommittee for Agriculture, I would say that you are about as expert in that field as any group to my knowledge. You have rendered great service to agriculture and to farm people; and in so doing you have drawn highly favorable attention to our programs.

Contrary to some popular misconceptions, the Congress is genuinely interested in the programs for which it legislates. Perhaps some of you have attended sessions of the House or Senate, and you may have remarked upon the limited attendance in the Chambers. It is quite possible that you found the debate of little interest or of minor importance. If you judge the Congress by these impressions you miss completely the responsible manner in which the House and Senate meet their constitutional obligations.

Perhaps you have heard of the midwest farm family who came to Washington, D.C., as tourists to visit the Nation's Capital. They attended a session of the Congress and as the Chaplain opened the day's session of the Congress with the customary prayer, the farmer's small son said, "Daddy, why does the Chaplain pray for the Congress?" The father said, "Son, he doesn't pray for the Congress; he takes one look at the few Congressmen present and then he prays for the people."

The important work of the Congress is done in the committees where literally thousands of individual bills introduced each year are studied, debated, and a limited few chosen for consideration by the Congress as a whole. Over 8,300 bills have been introduced in the House of Representatives since

January 1 of this year. Because the work of the committees is so important, let me take a few minutes to describe for you the process by which the annual appropriation bill for agriculture, for example, is developed.

Early in each session of Congress the President sends us his budget estimates together with a voluminous document of explanation and justification. The estimates for agriculture are referred to our Subcommittee on Agricultural Appropriations, and we begin a series of daily hearings which continue for many weeks. The seven men who serve so faithfully on that subcommittee are in effect the board of directors for the multibillion dollar agricultural programs. This seven-man committee is composed of the following: Jamie L. Whitten, of Mississippi, chairman; myself, H. Carl Andersen, of Minnesota; Walt Horan, of Washington; William H. Natcher, of Kentucky; Robert H. Michel, of Illinois; Alfred E. Santangelo, of New York; John M. Slack, Jr., of West Virginia.

In the course of our hearings, we have all of the top administrative staff of the U.S. Department of Agriculture before us, and we make a searching examination of their conduct in the past and their plans for the future. Because we have the responsibility for decisions on the spending of billions of dollars of public funds, we make certain that every dollar we recommend is required for the public good, so far as we can judge.

After we have heard witnesses from the Department on every phase of the budget, we hear other Members of Congress and outside witnesses. While the Government witnesses testify in support of the precise amounts requested in the budget estimates, many Members of Congress and most of the outside witnesses come before us to ask for increases in items of particular interest to them. It is rare indeed that we receive a constructive proposal for economy from any source.

When our hearings have been concluded, the subcommittee meets in executive session to decide as to the exact amounts for the hundreds of individual items, together with language changes from previous appropriations bills. This is known as the markup.

Decisions are made by majority vote and in all of the years I have been on the subcommittee, we have had few differences which could not be reconciled, and they were usually of relatively minor importance.

The next step in the process is to take our recommended bill to the full Committee on Appropriations where 50 of the most responsible Members of Congress sit in judgment upon our findings. It is a compliment to our subcommittee that few changes have been made in our recommendations during the last 20 years, and they too, have generally been of minor significance.

With the approval of the full committee, our bill is then reported out and programed for consideration by the House of Representatives. Congressman Whitten is in charge of the debate on his side of the political aisle, and I am in charge on my side. We members of the subcommittee discuss, in turn, the details of the measure, and then it is thrown open for amendments. As a measure of the confidence the House has in our work, very few amendments of any consequence have been adopted on the floor.

On some occasions our bill has been approved without serious debate or suggested amendment.

After the House has completed action, the bill goes to the Senate and the whole process is repeated. The Senate usually makes a number of changes—we on the House side call it the upper body because it generally "ups" the appropriations—and then the bill goes to a conference committee, composed of conferees from both the House and the Senate, to reconcile the differences in the bill.

From this description of the legislative process, you can see that the important work of Congress is done in committee. One good Congressman strategically placed on the right committee or subcommittee is actually worth more than a score of high-paid lobbyists when it comes to influencing the course of national legislation.

The seven Congressmen who sit in judgment on our farm programs, as members of the Agricultural Appropriations Subcommittee, have contributed far more than their personal or political interests dictate. Only two of us have farm backgrounds. Three are attorneys who grew up in cities. The other two have business and Government experience. They are all stanch and stalwart friends of agriculture.

From the administration of Lincoln, which created the Department of Agriculture, to the administration of Roosevelt which established the principles of price supports and production controls, the cause of agriculture has prospered.

But the Congress as a whole has changed greatly since I first took the oath of office, a little more than 23 years ago. When I came to Washington the farm bloc was still a power to be reckoned with. All we needed was agreement among farm members on legislation to assure its enactment. Today all that is changed.

There is no farm bloc in the Congress today. Redistricting following the population census of 1940 and again in 1950, saw many of the seats formerly held by farm Congressmen move into urban control. Redistricting in accordance with the 1960 census will further diminish rural influence in the Congress. After the next election, the once powerful voice of agriculture will be little more than a whisper.

This, alone, is a great handicap. But in addition to reduced numbers, we are today sharply divided and the minority of agricultural representation is further diminished by an almost complete lack of unanimity on the part of farm Congressmen.

First, we are almost always divided along partisan lines—something that seldom occurred a generation ago. We find further divisions along sectional and commodity lines to the point that overall farm leadership as such no longer exists to any effective degree in the Congress of the United States.

With farm population reduced to about 9 percent of our total population, and with rural voting strength in the Congress ebbing fast, those of us concerned with the future of agriculture and farm programs must face up to the realities of our predicament. We must look increasingly to our urban friends and neighbors for support.

My friends, there is a compelling need for—and we must have—public understanding of our problems.

The statistics of agriculture—by its demonstrated efficiency—proves the success of the efforts of leaders like you in the farm communications field, to educate farm people. But just what can we—you the agricultural editors, you the research and extension workers—and our small, ever dwindling group of farm Congressmen—do to secure public and congressional understanding of our problems? How can you, the agricultural editors, influence urban Members of Congress?

Far be it from me to compare in any way Congressmen to the stubborn mule. But there is a popular misconception in some segments of our press that the average Congressman is a selfish, hard-boiled, unapproachable individual. In reality, Congressmen on an average are kind, modest, and sympathetic people. In your efforts to win their cooperation for agriculture, you may want to be guided by the old story of the gentle mule the preacher sold to the farmer. He explained to the new owner that the mule was unaccustomed to rude or violent treatment and that he would work his heart out if kindly and properly treated.

A few days later the preacher came by and found the farmer out in the field pleading with the balky mule who refused to work. The frustrated farmer explained that he had been kind and gentle with the animal and had employed no harsh language as was customary with mules in those days, but the beast would not budge.

The preacher walked over to the edge of the field, picked up a two-by-four and struck the mule right between the eyes, knocking him to the ground. When the mule got up, he leaned into the harness and went to work.

"You must be kind and gentle with him," the preacher said, "but first you must establish an understanding."

Yes, I repeat—there is a compelling need for—and we must have—congressional and public understanding of our problems.

In 30 years, cotton yields have increased almost threefold. Research and education made that possible.

In 30 years, wheat yields have almost doubled and so have tobacco.

Call the roll of commodities and you will find that farmers have doubled and trebled their production within the lifetimes of most of us, and research and education have accomplished all of this.

Control programs have also contributed greatly to increased efficiency in agriculture. You may recall the story of the county agent who went out to see a farmer to teach him better farming methods. The farmer said: "Young fellow, I'm already not farming half as good as I know how." When we cut that farmer's acreage, he showed us how well he could farm the remaining acreage. As planted acres went down, yields per acre went up, and the treadmill moved another turn.

It is tragic but true that farm people and certainly farm programs are in national disrepute today.

It is a paradox of our times that the people and the segment of our economy that have contributed more than any other to the strength of our Nation have shared the least in its abundance.

Look with me for a moment at some of the ailments of agriculture. Vertical integration with all of its implications. Twenty-five-cent eggs and 10-

cent chickens. Dollar corn, 60-cent oats, and 80-cent barley. Fifteen-dollar hogs and $20 cattle. Fifteen-dollar lambs and 15-cent broilers. Twenty-cent turkeys and 80-cent rye. Annual per capita income from farming of $675 compared with nonfarm per capita income of $2,282. Eroding soil and falling water tables. Mountainous surpluses of corn, wheat, sorghums, and other commodities.

These are the symptoms of a sick agricultural economy. They strike bitterly at the heart of rural America and their impact is felt in the steel mills of Pittsburgh, the automobile plants of Detroit, and throughout our entire economy.

Can a nation which splits the atom not find a solution to this problem? Can a nation considering a flight to the moon not meet the challenges of inequity here at home? Can a nation dedicated to Christian principles fail to overcome economic injustice?

I say that we have the capabilities to solve all of these problems if we have but the will to do so. I say also that new legislation and dynamic new programs will be required because farmers cannot by themselves solve problems over which they exercise no control.

It is shortsighted in the extreme for advocates of free enterprise to condemn, as they do, our efforts to foster and preserve the very foundation of free enterprise—the family-farm system in America.

And the cruelest blow of all which farm people have had to sustain is the manner in which they and their rights and interests have been made a political football in recent times.

America needs to know that economic injustices prevail in our rural areas.

America needs to be reminded that the farms of this great land furnish the raw materials and the manpower to make our Nation the greatest industrial giant in the annals of history and that the farmers who have made all of this possible are entitled to a fair return for their investment and labor.

America must be told the truth about farm problems and educated to the peril to the national interest if solutions are not provided.

I was invited here today to give you my viewpoint on "How to Get Congressional Support for Agriculture." I hope you recognize from my brief discussion of the subject that it is a task of monumental proportions. I trust you also agree that the job must be done if we are to preserve in this great land a free agriculture and a system of family farms which is unequaled in the history of mankind.

You have always had the responsibility to help farm people appraise their problems and evaluate the proposed solutions. This you have done, and done well. Through your access to news media reaching the eyes and ears of our people, and through your personal contacts, you have performed a commendable job in directing your efforts to the 9 percent who comprise our farm population.

But today the challenge of our times is the urgent need for broadened understanding on the part of the other 91 percent of our people—the nonfarm people.

The future well-being of all agriculture, and of farm people, will rest in the hands of the Congressmen who will be the elected representatives of these nonfarm people. These Congressmen will be asked to support or reject farm legislation and agricultural appropriations of every kind. If the job of educating and informing the urban Congressmen and the nonfarm people is not done promptly and effectively, the cause of agriculture will surely suffer at the hands of an unsympathetic Congress.

I submit to you—that it is the job of you—and all of us—to establish an understanding, among nonfarm people—of the problems of agriculture. This, more than anything else, will light the way to support for agriculture in the Congress of the United States.

This job is staggering in its proportions and in my opinion is impossible if we are to look to a mere handful of farm Congressmen to do the missionary work. But it is not nearly so formidable if placed in the capable hands of such people as you, throughout the Nation.

God bless you. Keep up the good work.

[Charles R. Barr, "Businessmen's Responsibility in Public Affairs," *Congressional Record,* Aug. 1, 1961, pp. A5910–5912. (Speech by an executive of the Standard Oil Company of Indiana before the 74th Annual Convention of the Michigan Savings and Loan League.)]

Today I want to talk about the political responsibilities and obligations of a particular group of our citizens. I want to talk about that group classified as businessmen and their participation in public affairs. Businessmen have a long tradition of participating in the field of public affairs of our country. Our founders for the most part, were business and professional men like Washington, Jefferson, Franklin, Adams, and Hamilton, who risked and pledged their lives, their liberty, and their honor to achieve their goals. The men who subsequently led in the development of our great political system, were also by and large, men of similar background, dedicated to the development of our Nation. Tragically, some 25 or 30 years ago, there began to be some evidence that a large number of members of the business community were leaving political affairs "up to George." George often seemed to have ideas that were not compatible with the continued development and enhancement of the principles which made our country the envy and the model of the free world. Because of the forfeiture and neglect of accepting political responsibility on the part of more and more businessmen, our political system has more and more fallen into the hands of those who seem to worship principles and ideologies contrary to those which made this country's high standards possible. Too often high ideals and purposes have been neglected and political interest and activity has been aimed primarily for the selfish benefit of special groups with the goal of what they could take out of government. If this trend continues, then our free political system and all that it means in the way of freedom and of a sound economic system will soon perish. Anyone who has taken time to read a little history must be aware of the tragic roles of other democracies and republics long demised, where high principles gave way solely to the pursuit of selfish interests by myriads of solely self-seeking interests. Our forefathers were aware of this danger. Benjamin Franklin was acutely aware of it when, after the signing of the Declaration of Independence he said, "We have given you a republic if you can keep it."

We have kept and developed that Republic amazingly well to date. But now we see more and more attempts to take liberty and rights from our people in return for a dole or a subsidy. We see more and more of the fruit of our efforts taken from us by the tax collector and all about us we see evidence of the degeneration of large segments of our population whose particular goal in life appears to be to live off the fruits of other people's efforts by using their vote solely to gain economic advantages for themselves. There is substantial evidence that certain groups are using their franchise as a method of confiscating property and rights from others via the route of taxation. The ones whose labors are being robbed increasingly year by year with the meeting of every Congress and legislature, are those who produce the goods and services of this Nation, all of whom I would classify as businessmen, whether they work at a lathe or whether they manage the plant. Why then the lack of resistance? I believe that there are several answers to this question:

1. Many of us have come to take our way of life for granted and have forgotten "the price of liberty is eternal vigilance."

2. Because of insidious propaganda emanating from many sources and because our system has not reached perfection, many members of the business community apparently have lost faith in themselves and their system.

3. In the race for competitive advantage among businessmen, they have tended to avoid anything controversial for fear that it may affect sales. Politics is controversial and no one can indulge in it to any extent for any period of time without getting a bloody nose.

Our forefathers risked everything they had to develop this country but today we find all too many people unwilling to risk criticism or the loss of a customer or client in order to stand up for principles which make their business possible in the first place. Many businessmen have developed a tendency to hide behind and to use specialists such as lawyers, public relations people, and lobbyists to do work which they ought to be doing themselves to a large extent. This is not to say that these specialists are not necessary and desirable in our complex society, but they need help and they need it badly. Too often we seem to think that because we belong to an association whose job it is to protect our particular industry, we don't have to do anything more, or that because we have created an advertising and public relations program which has developed a good image of our own particular group, we have nothing to worry about.

Sound government is created at the grassroots. Grassroots are the precincts where you and I live. This is where votes are decided upon, where they are cast and where they are counted. There is probably not a precinct in America that is not populated by a substantial number of businessmen and their families. Until such time as these people are willing to sell the principles of sound government to their neighbors and friends, to take responsibility and leadership in their own communities, it is not going to be possible to have a sound political system. If our political system becomes unsound, our economic system is going to fail. We are going to lose our rights and liberties and as surely as night follows day, we will follow Rome and ancient Greece into the ashes of history.

Now, what specifically can we as businessmen do? I have some suggestions:

1. We must rededicate ourselves to the ideals and principles of our forefathers. We must match the diligence and spirit which sustained them.

2. We must take our share of leadership in our own communities in the political party of our choice by giving of our time, our talent, and our substance. We must encourage others to follow our example.

Now, assuming that some of you gentlemen decide to do this, what are some of the problems that you may expect to find? First, I am sure that you will find a lot of apathy. Second, you will probably find in many instances that political participation is not the social "thing to do." This is one of the greatest hurdles to overcome and it is only through leadership of responsible people like yourself that this stigma can be overcome. If political participation ever becomes popular and the "thing to do," then our battle is at least half won. Third, you will be surprised at how many people fail to register and vote. Some of these people fail to vote because they are apathetic or lazy, or just do not know why they should vote. Many people in the business community are unable to vote because of their transitory nature, from one community to another. All people should be interested in modernization of the laws to reduce the number of those people who are disenfranchised because of the transitory nature of our society. Let me spell out in some detail what you can do to be politically effective as a leader in your community.

1. Join a party and become identified with it; find out who the local leaders are, such as precinct captains, judges of election, local officeholders, etc. They are all neighbors of yours and probably you know most of them.

2. Voluntarily ask them what you can do to help and, if they are doing a good job, encourage them and let them know you appreciate their efforts.

3. If an opportunity comes to serve in your capacity in their political organization, accept it—don't sluff it off on George. Encourage others to do the same thing.

4. Be willing to give some time, talent, and money to this effort.

Once you have done this, then you will have the right and probably an opportunity to be heard in higher councils and to become a real influence for good, sound government. Enter politics and work for sound, general principles, and not merely for narrow interests which may affect you personally, because then you only become another special interest working for self-gain.

I think it is important that anybody entering this area get a proper perspective and put first things first. Few will quarrel with me when I say that first, we should all serve our God and stand only for those principles and rules which have been developed through a long period of His teaching; second, I think you will agree, is our obligation to our country, and we should never knowingly stand for any principle contrary to its best interests, followed closely by our interest and loyalty to those principles which will preserve and develop our families. Then, perhaps, we can think about the special problems that concern our own method of livelihood. If we really work and achieve sound principles for God, country and family, we are seldom going to have to worry very much about good economic principles for our own business enterprises. I suppose what I am really advocating is for each of us to start our own do-it-yourself program in public affairs.

Finally, as businessmen, we can all do a job of selling our political and economic system to our employees, to our associates and our friends. There are millions of people that no one has ever taken the trouble to tell where they fit into the scheme of things and how they benefit from this great country of ours. Liberty is like water. Too often we don't miss it until the well goes dry.

Let us stand up and speak up for what we believe.

We should not be like the parrot whose story so well illustrates the points that I have been trying to make. A merchant had long desired to own a fine parrot. One day, as he was walking to work, he noticed a fine parrot in a pet shop window. He entered the store and asked the manager about the bird and was told that it was an extraordinary bird and could speak seven different languages—the finest bird that he had ever seen. The businessman asked the price and after some negotiation, bought the bird and a cage for $35 and had it delivered to his home. When he returned that evening and met his wife at the door, he asked if his parrot had arrived and she said that it had. He asked where it was and she advised him that it had been in the oven for about 30 minutes and would be ready to be served in another hour. The husband shouted, "My good woman. That was a very expensive and talented bird that could speak fluently in seven different languages. Why in the world are you baking it?" To which his wife replied, "Well, why didn't he speak up?"

Unlike the parrot, the businessmen of America had better speak up.

Don't leave the preservation of this country up to others, but as I said before, start a do-it-yourself program of your own for the benefit of yourself and the generations to come. I am sure that you will get a great deal of personal satisfaction from it and you will leave a heritage far greater than the wealth of the Andes.

We must act. We must speak out.

Congress Reports on Lobbying

The report below constitutes the conclusions of an extensive investigation by a committee of the House of Representatives into the status, finances, and methods of private persons and groups and by agencies of the Federal government, "intended to influence, encourage, promote, or retard legislation." The committee, chaired by Representative Frank Buchanan of Pennsylvania, produced a considerable number of publications in the form of hearings and reports; in coherence with the American emphasis on the informational spotlight as the means for understanding and controlling lobbying activities, no fundamental legislative changes were enacted as a result of this or later investigations.

[*General Interim Report of the House Select Committee on Lobbying Activities,* H.R. Rep. No. 3138, 81st Cong., 2d Sess. (1950), pp. 62–67.]

. . . Practical Causes of Lobbying

For all the high gloss with which discussions of lobbying are usually adorned, it remains a very practical problem with a number of very practical causes. First among these is our long and splendid tradition of free association. Americans are free to band together as they choose, subject only to the requirements of public safety. This tradition, compounded with the high degree of group consciousness and organization typical of any modern industrial society, has provided the raw materials from which our present system of lobbying has been built.

The tools with which this system was built were the constitutional guarantees of political freedom, especially the right of petition, of which lobbying is usually regarded as the most important expression.

The conditions in which a highly developed system of pressure politics could flourish were provided by two other unique features of our governmental arrangements. First, our political parties have grown progressively more loosely controlled and undisciplined. Pressure groups thrive on the inability or unwillingness of political parties to exercise the powers of government which they have lawfully gained at the polls. The advantages of this situation to the lobby group are obvious: lack of cohesion in the parties enables well-organized private interests to secure some of the advantages of political power without having to submit to the democratic electoral process by which this power is usually attained.

The necessarily complex structure of our Government, with its separation of powers, checks and balances, and bicameral legislature, has also contributed to the growth of lobbying. Complex government inevitably means government with bottlenecks at which pressure can be quietly and effectively applied. Thus the great pressure campaigns of recent years have relied heavily on the tactics of attrition and delay at every critical spot in the legislative process. The prevention of governmental action, and this is the aim of many lobbies, is relatively easy under these circumstances.

Finally, lobbying has reached its present proportions because our Government has always been sensitive to private demands. One successful piece of special pleading bred another and the entire system developed gradually but with irresistible momentum.

Theory of Lobbying

While these practical causes are paramount, there are several theoretical considerations which underlie the present high level of lobbying activity. We lack and have always lacked any established theory as to the proper relationship and balance between private power and the power of government. Lacking such an established theory, we have rested our thinking about lobbying on two premises: first, that lobbying is not a problem of who is to exercise political power, but is, rather, a matter of expressly granted individual rights; and, second, that lobbying is no problem in a free society because one interest can be depended upon to "cancel out" another. This process of cancellation and compromise, it is said, should produce responsible public policy.

As to the first premise, the right of petition is cited as both the cause and justification of lobbying, and rightly so. Organized groups of interested citizens have an important informational and representative role to play in our kind of government. Citizens can and should exercise their right of petition individually and through organized groups. Without this constitutionally guaranteed right of petition, our kind of free government could not exist. But we often fail to recognize that while lobbying is a necessary right which should not in any way be restricted or abridged, it is a right which is not exercised for itself alone. People and groups seek to influence legislative policy because they hope to gain thereby and not because they want to keep their rights from becoming flabby for want of exercise.

So it is that, in their public utterances, lobbyists show the utmost attachment to constitutional rights. Privately, however, they often admit that rights to them are only a means to an end and not an end in themselves. As one of the most expert of them said, ". . . organized power is the only thing that Government can take into account."

It is also a bitter paradox that the right of petition, one of the highest rights which democracy can bestow on a free people, is sometimes put to its most effective use by persons who are far from devoted to the principles of democracy. "I do not believe in democracy. I think it stinks," wrote Herbert U. Nelson, of the National Association of Real Estate Boards. Yet Mr. Nelson's organization was and is spending hundreds of thousands of dollars for lobbying, something which can only be done in a democracy such as ours.

The second major premise, that one interest will cancel out another, has been a staple of American political thinking since James Madison wrote his *Federalist* Paper No. 10. Unfortunately, Madison's prophecy has never matured; instead of canceling out, the pressures on Government have become cumulative. We referred earlier to the growing joint effort in lobbying, the long-run tendency of which is to break down the barriers against private domination of State power. Even if pressure groups did compete instead of join forces, the advantage in lobbying would always lie with those interests which were best organized, best financed, and had the easiest access to mass media of communication. Organized business has always gained the most from lobbying because it has had the best organization, the most money, and the readiest access to publicity. It has had, in addition, the great advantage of seeking generally to prevent rather than encourage action by broadly based popular government. Given the strategic bottlenecks of our legislative procedure, it is far easier to obstruct than it is to create.

Could responsible public policy result from this theoretical canceling of group interests? It is not likely. While this process seems neat and automatic, it simply does not operate as it is supposed to. Even if it did, it would represent a degrading conception of democratic politics in which the highest function of government would be to yield to the strongest pressure. Absolute responsiveness to group interests is one thing, but truly responsible representative government is quite another.

All of these questions inhere in the traditional American approach to lobbying. We raise them only to indicate that while lobbying is natural in our system, and should not be curbed, the outer limits beyond which lobbying is an offense against the welfare of the whole community have not begun to be charted.

The Costs of Lobbying

We seldom stop to consider the legislative costs of lobbying, perhaps because it is difficult to say when a measure is the product of lobbying and when it is an accurate reflection of real public need. Still 150 years of congressional history provide dozens of clear cases in which well-organized pressures have been instrumental in the enactment of ill-considered, inequitable, or vastly unpopular legislation. In many other cases, private pressures have been responsible for the defeat, delay, or emasculation of measures having overwhelming public support. With Congress daily assuming new and complex responsibilities, the dangers of increased pressure on the legislative process are very real.

What might be called the social costs of lobbying are even more serious, although just as seldom recognized. Our leadership in a troubled world demands clear thought and common effort; but can we maintain this leadership in the face of the social tension, the group conflict, the "me first" attitude of which mass lobbying is both a cause and a symptom? The lobby-as-usual philosophy which prevailed in some quarters during World War II should serve as a grim reminder that even the deadliest of national perils does not put an end to selfish interest. As we enter the new world crisis, this experience is both a sobering lesson and an ugly portent.

The lobbying situation is basically a reflection of the state of our economy. As the management of this economy has drifted into fewer and fewer hands, so too has pressure on the legislative front been sharply intensified. The giant concentrations of corporate wealth which the Temporary National Economic Committee found to dominate the prewar economy have developed since at an accelerated pace. It is inevitable that such great concentrations of economic power should seek to extend their power to the political field as well, and we count this fact as one of the most serious problems which large-scale lobbying poses for our kind of easygoing institutional structure. Economic power provides one of the essential raw materials for successful pressure politics; the greater the power, the larger are the possibilities of success. And so to the extent that some groups are better endowed than others, there is a disparity in the pressure which these groups can exert on the policy-making process. As we said earlier, "lobbying for all," may be a sacred right but it is a right which some men can make more meaningful than others. It is said, for example, that the individual consumer and the billion-dollar corporation have equal rights before the law, but are they equal before the lawmakers?

This, then is the problem: the great political imbalance between tightly organized economic power blocs, such as big labor, big business, and big agriculture, and more casually organized interests and a loosely patterned state. This imbalance is reflected in lobbying activities as it is in other aspects of our national life.

We also count as "social costs" of lobbying the ideological conflict and public confusion which has already begun to result from the growing use of a charged public opinion as an instrument of pressure. Men need slogans, catch-phrases, and generalizations to reduce their experience to understandable terms. But these slogans should not be a substitute for thought; when they are, men have lost the first part of their ability to govern themselves. Yet this is precisely what the pressure groups and their public relations experts are about. Organizations seeking to protect a privileged status for their members at the expense of the general welfare of all Americans use terms like "socialism," "statism," and "welfare state" to forestall rational analysis of legislative proposals which they oppose. We are prepared to risk our national existence against totalitarianism, yet there are those among us who live by the totalitarian principle of the great distortion, endlessly repeated. Political freedom cannot live in an atmosphere of such hysterical oversimplification.

There are finally the economic costs of lobbying to be considered, and these are staggering. The costs of 150 years of relentless raiding of the Public Treasury are beyond estimate, but we do know that the present demands of the great interests total far more than the Nation can afford. The people must also bear the costs of lobbying as well as pay for its end results. It is ultimately the people who pay for the big front and the high-pressure campaigns that the pressure boys put forward. They pay Mr. Rumley's commissions on all receipts of the Committee for Constitutional Government; they pay for the National Association of Home Builders' round-robin telephone conferences; they pay Mr. Purcell L. Smith the $65,000 salary which he draws as Washington representative for the private utilities; they pay the $2,000,000 which the American Medical Association has spent in its effort to defeat national health insurance. Pressure groups are quite free-handed with both their own and with other peoples' money. The circle of lobbying is endless, and endlessly expensive.

The Alternatives

We have sought to express above our conviction that the present system of pressure politics has assumed extraordinary proportions. We have also tried to show that this system must continue to expand, and that this expansion may challenge the existence of representative government as we have known it. What is to be done? The constitutional right of petition must be preserved, and no restriction should be imposed on legitimate lobbying.

A number of approaches to the problem have been suggested. Some of the more important of these are discussed below.

(1) It has been suggested, seldom with any clear outline for practical implementation, that Government should support those important interests which do not have adequate resources so that they can contend on an equal basis with better-financed groups. This approach might help solve the problem of the present imbalance between various groups, but it would ultimately result in more rather than less pressure on policy-making; we are not persuaded that this would be desirable. There is, in addition, the difficulty of selecting some reasonable criteria on which such support could be based.

(2) Suggestions are frequently made that organized groups be given some formal place in the policy-making process. We already achieve something of this kind in the advisory councils to numerous administrative bodies and in the invitations extended to interested groups to appear before congressional committees on most major legislation. But we do not believe it would be wise to go beyond these steps. Again, there is a problem of choosing the criteria on which formal group representation should be based. In this respect, the experience of various European countries with official economic councils is not very encouraging. Would this not also be yielding to pressures rather than coping with them? Popular, geographic representation is basic in our system of government.

(3) Streamline the legislative and administrative process, for pressures thrive on Government when it becomes too complex for ordinary citizens to understand. This may point to at least a partial answer, and the Legislative Reorganization Act of 1946 and the work of the Hoover Commission indicate that useful first steps have already been taken in this direction. There still remains, of course, a considerable need for further improvements.

(4) We need stronger political parties and party discipline. This is basic. Much of the current onus placed on partisanship in politics overlooks the fact that if the parties don't accept responsibility the pressure groups will move in by default. Lobbying is no serious problem in a society where the parties can make up their minds and live up to their commitments. A stronger sense of party cohesion may be difficult to achieve in the United States, for most Americans seem to like their parties as they are. Ultimately, however, responsible parties are an essential requisite of responsible government.

(5) We need more information on lobbying and lobbyists. This, at the moment, is the most feasible approach. Every group has the right to present its case, but at the same time Congress and the public have a right to know who they are, what they are doing, how much they are spending, and where the money is coming from—in a word, full disclosure of the relevant facts. Such disclosure is thoroughly in accord with our system and principles and has already received legislative recognition in the Regulation of Lobbying Act. What is needed is that this act be equipped to fulfill more effectively the purposes for which it was designed. We shall offer elsewhere a series of detailed recommendations and amendments by which we believe that the act can be brought to a higher level of efficiency. The act as it stands is a workable and valid piece of legislation. Our recommendations will be

designed to eliminate some of the misconstructions that have hampered the operation of the act. The act does not seek to regulate but to inform. It works on the simple premise that Congress and the public have the right to full information on those who actively attempt to influence the decisions of government.

No one of these approaches alone is equal to the magnitude of the problem we face; but together, they are the first steps which must be taken if special interest groups are not to ride roughshod over a public interest which may often be inarticulate.

There is a final catalyst which can cement these various approaches together into a solid and meaningful program. Prof. Stephen K. Bailey expressed it splendidly when he testified before the committee:

> . . . moral judgments constitute the real answer to the existence of lobbyists. No registration law, no listing of connections and salaries in the *Congressional Record,* no system of party responsibility, by itself, can scratch the surface of the problem of controlling pressure politics. In the long run, a civilized morality is the sole key to the survival of democracy.

C. PROPAGANDA

Edward R. Murrow and the United States Information Agency

Not every man who enters American public service comes from a job paying an annual salary of reportedly somewhere around $200,000; even more rare is the new appointee who has been a television luminary. Just before the beginning of the excerpt below, Senator Bourke B. Hickenlooper had asked whether Murrow had separated himself from any business or financial connections with the Columbia Broadcasting System and had been assured that all such arrangements had been terminated. Murrow's nomination was subsequently approved by the Committee, then by the Senate, all to a resoundingly favorable press.

[*Nomination of Edward R. Murrow (United States Information Agency), Hearings before the Senate Committee on Foreign Relations,* 87th Cong., 1st Sess. (1961), pp. 13–21.]

. . . SENATOR HICKENLOOPER. Mr. Murrow, what do you consider the primary overall objective of the job as Director of the United States Information Service? In other words, is it a propaganda agency, is it an objective reporting agency, or just what do you consider the major area of operation?

MR. MURROW. I regard it as primarily an objective reporting agency. I feel that part of its obligation is to destroy and expose the lies that are constantly circulated about us.

I think its objectives should be to reflect the culture and the civilization of this country to indicate that we share the aspirations of those who desire freedom and, in general, to operate as an accurate reflection of a free and pluralistic society.

SENATOR HICKENLOOPER. Do you believe there is a place in the United States Information Agency for exposing the fallacies or falsehoods that are circulated about the West and the western countries and about the United States, in particular, because we are the main target of Communist propaganda?

MR. MURROW. Most certainly.

Presentation of the United States Image

SENATOR HICKENLOOPER. In the presentation of the image of the United States and our ideals and in connection with an objective presentation of those, do you believe that we should indulge in self-examination as well as in the presentation of what we believe to be our strong points and our most appealing points to those people and nations who are seeking for the truth?

MR. MURROW. If, by self-examination, you mean should we reflect in our broadcasts and in our literature significant controversy on matters of importance in the country, I feel that within limits we should.

SENATOR HICKENLOOPER. Could you clarify the definition of "within limits." What do you mean by that?

MR. MURROW. I think we should not reflect or deal with the trivial or unimportant controversies. I feel that we should not reflect controversies that are purely regional, local in interest.

What I mean by reflecting controversy was when it occurs on matters of national importance we should reflect the controversy with restraint.

Iowa Documentary Produced by Mr. Murrow

SENATOR HICKENLOOPER. Now, I think you are aware of the area that I am going to discuss with you now because you and I discussed this in my office the other day, so this will be nothing new to you. I am not attempting to slip up on your blind side, Mr. Murrow—not that you have a blind side; I probably shouldn't have used that wording—but you have been engaged over the past in the presentation of various so-called documentaries of certain issues in the United States, I believe. That is correct, is it not?

MR. MURROW. Yes, sir.

SENATOR HICKENLOOPER. In the presentation of those documentaries there have been those who have felt that you have overemphasized what you believed to be the less attractive side of our society, or particular segments of our economy, to the exclusion of the more hopeful side of those things. What I say is that there are those who believe that you have done that.

Now, because one of these instances affected my home State I would like to take you back just a few years when you presented the documentary, I believe, that was entitled "The Farm Problem: The Crisis of Abundance," where you went to Corning, Iowa, in Adams County, and produced a documentary film there. Many people—and I am frankly stating that I am one—seemed to feel that in this portrayal you created ideas that the Iowa farmer was a peon, that he was starving to death, and that he was being put upon by rapacious landlords or by other things of that kind.

I just wonder whether you had anything to do with the active production of this from a discretionary standpoint or from the editing of that film?

MR. MURROW. Yes, sir; I did.

SENATOR HICKENLOOPER. Now, were there any parts of that film that were what we might call faked or put in for color or for emphasis but which were not fully factual or truthful?

MR. MURROW. I did not witness all of the filming myself. I did the editing. I am responsible for the program. So far as I know there was not a scene that was faked or staged.

SENATOR HICKENLOOPER. An investigation was made into the background of that situation there and, as I recall it, one of the prominent features of the film was a young farmer who was portrayed as having been driven off his farm and being forced to migrate because of the very low economic state which he had reached. And, frankly, our investigation and conversations with this young farmer indicated that he was not driven off his farm at all; that he had sold out in a regular springtime sale because his wife wanted to move to California. She thought they would like it better out there, and he had an opportunity to get a job in California and so he went. But his picture was taken as a vicious example of the economic destruction which was being visited upon that area. Do you recall that young farmer?

MR. MURROW. Yes, sir; I do.

SENATOR HICKENLOOPER. I believe he made a written statement that he was not being forced off the farm, that he had had a reasonably successful year, everything considered, and that the decision to leave was purely a personal one and based on a desire on the part of his family to move to California to join his brother who was out there and having a very satisfactory time. Do you remember any details about that?

MR. MURROW. I remember what he said to the cameras, and it is not uncommon to have one thing said to the cameras and something else later on.

SENATOR HICKENLOOPER. Well, then the responsibility, of course, in putting out information about the United States should probably demand a fairly intensive examination as to what the facts of the matter are, don't you think, before it is put out as true?

MR. MURROW. Certainly.

SENATOR HICKENLOOPER. Do you recall one scene in that documentary that depicted the sale of a baby crib with the connotation that they even had to sell the crib in which the little baby was supposed to rest; do you happen to recall that particular scene?

MR. MURROW. I remember that we showed the sale of a crib and other household products; yes, sir.

SENATOR HICKENLOOPER. I believe the man whose farm was referred to was named Peterson. Are you aware that that sale had been planned for some months before the time of the filming and that this baby crib had not been in use for several years—they did not have a baby of that age. And only a part of the household furniture was sold in this moving operation; yet this situation was depicted as one of the distressing results of the economic situation at that time?

MR. MURROW. I did not know the timetable, Senator. But I do know that the crib was shown along with other household effects that were put up for sale.

SENATOR HICKENLOOPER. Do you know Lawrence Soth, a very prominent editor in this country? He is editor of the Des Moines Register. I believe you are acquainted with him?

MR. MURROW. I know his name; I do not believe I have met him personally, sir.

SENATOR HICKENLOOPER. Well, Mr. Soth is quite a well-known editor of the most prominent newspaper in the State of Iowa, and one of the most prominent in the United States.

Are you familiar with what Mr. Soth wrote about that particular situation? I am quoting now out of context a short statement which Mr. Soth wrote to the effect that the beginning of the show was—

> unfortunate since it gave a general impression of distress and hardship which does not reflect the general situation in the country.

Were you aware of this, sir?

MR. MURROW. I do not remember as of now; no, sir.

SENATOR HICKENLOOPER. Also Mr. Soth had this to say, and I quote:

> The show was somewhat overdramatized. Murrow overplayed the distressed farm sale theme, and made it appear to be a dominant element of the farm situation.

Do you have any comment on that particular observation as to the opinions of people who were out there in Iowa and who really knew the basic circumstances?

MR. MURROW. It was not designed so to do. The reaction to documentaries as well as other stories varies.

SENATOR HICKENLOOPER. Well, now, Mr. Murrow, I bring this up only because the presentation of the United States through the Information Agency, in my view, should be an objective presentation of our strong points and our virtues as well as an honest discussion when the occasion arises of some of the things that are criticizable in the United States.

In your documentary of this farm review, did you show the economics of the farm problem? Did you show any of our prosperous farms in Iowa and the modern conveniences that are enjoyed by a great many of our farmers there, and the things that they have, or did you just show only the seamy side of the agricultural situation at that time?

MR. MURROW. Senator, I have not reviewed that program recently. My memory is that certainly we showed some of the more prosperous farms in Wisconsin. Whether we did in Iowa, I cannot now recall.

SENATOR HICKENLOOPER. Well, the Senator from Wisconsin is a member of this committee, and I will let him defend the Wisconsin situation. I will stick to Iowa.

We have a very substantial agricultural plant there which, in my view, should be shown along with the occasional bad side. Of course, we do have things that may from time to time be criticizable, but we have a great many things that need presentation in their better light and they far overshadow the bad things.

Question of Emphasis in U.S.I.A. Portrayal of U.S. Image

I just wondered if your management of this American information program would be such that you would follow a policy of portraying only the criticizable parts of the United States and our system. Or would you expect to emphasize the desirable and the hopeful and progressive parts of the American system?

MR. MURROW. I would expect certainly to do the latter. If I may be permitted to comment on the program to which you are referring and others that we discussed—

SENATOR HICKENLOOPER. Yes.

MR. MURROW (continuing). Were designed for domestic consumption, were done in an effort to widen the area of both concern and discussion.

SENATOR HICKENLOOPER. But don't you believe that in the area of concern and discussion a commensurate amount of time should be devoted to discussing the strength of the U.S. system, to discussing the prosperous situations that we have in this country rather than devoting that time to what might be called destructive or depressing discussion?

MR. MURROW. In theory that is true. It is a matter of editorial balance.

SENATOR HICKENLOOPER. Well, of course, the meat of the whole situation is editorial discretion, editorial balance in the presentation of the picture of America abroad, particularly to the neutral nations, especially those who are on the fence.

Communist Propaganda Successes

Now, you said in your statement here, and I quote:

> We cannot imitate the tactics or the techniques of the dictatorships that now ride the backs of the most of this planet's people.

Do you believe, Mr. Murrow, that the propaganda of the Communists is having a substantial effect in many parts of the world?

MR. MURROW. Yes, sir.

SENATOR HICKENLOOPER. Do you believe that our information program has not had the effect in the past that it should have had?

MR. MURROW. I do.

SENATOR HICKENLOOPER. Well, if the Communists are having success with their propaganda, and we are failing in ours, what lesson, if any, would you take from their book to get us on the success side rather than on the losing side?

MR. MURROW. Their success, in part, has been due to the fact that they have been persuasive with many of their lies in the underdeveloped areas, partly because in the field of books and radio, particularly, they have spent infinitely more money than we have been willing to spend. They have trained skilled technicians and linguists to a greater extent than we have.

SENATOR HICKENLOOPER. Well, are you aware of any consistent pattern of self-depreciation on the part of the Communists in their propaganda?

MR. MURROW. No, sir.

SENATOR HICKENLOOPER. On the other hand, don't you agree that their propaganda is almost entirely, in fact I think entirely, devoted to what we believe to be exaggerated claims of their success and the success of their system?

MR. MURROW. That is true.

SENATOR HICKENLOOPER. And by promoting and advancing what they claim to be the attractive parts of their system they have had success in their propaganda, have they not?

MR. MURROW. This is not the sole reason for their success, but they have had success.

SENATOR HICKENLOOPER. Well, speaking of the sole reason for their success, I would agree there are many details in their propaganda system that one could say are somewhat flattering, such as their training programs and those things. But basically their propaganda is to advance what they claim to be the strength and the success of the Communist system; is that not correct?

MR. MURROW. Yes, sir.

Salesmanship

SENATOR HICKENLOOPER. Now, do you agree that we have very often in our information programs discussed problems that in many countries will depreciate Americans?

MR. MURROW. I do not know in detail, but I should think that is true.

SENATOR HICKENLOOPER. Well, do you believe that a salesman can be very successful, as such, if he goes around to his prospective customers and keeps telling them that "this machine I am trying to sell you doesn't work in certain particulars. Take it, but parts of it break down and it won't work." Do you believe that is a basic successful policy for salesmanship?

MR. MURROW. I should think not.

SENATOR HICKENLOOPER. When we go out and emphasize to the world the deficiencies of our system and do not sufficiently emphasize the overpowering strengths of our system, how can we have success in convincing people that we do have a good system?

MR. MURROW. May I suggest that one of our dilemmas arises from the fact that we are operating a different system, an open pluralistic society, where we cannot conceal our difficulties or our controversies, even though we would, and if we do not report them responsibly and accurately, they will be reported by other sources and, perhaps, distorted.

SENATOR HICKENLOOPER. Well, is that any excuse for us to go around first and say, "Well, we have certain weaknesses; therefore, we will advertise them to the world before somebody else talks about them"?

Do you think that there is any necessity for us to be zealous in attempting to point out our weaknesses?

MR. MURROW. No, sir. I do not.

SENATOR HICKENLOOPER. I have heard many discussions in various countries in the world; for example, I have heard many discussions about the racial problem in this country which, of course, is one of concern to all of us. We do not minimize the need for its solution, and we do not try to minimize here the abuses that exist. But don't you believe also that we should at least be as equally zealous in pointing out the strength of our system and the fact that legal equality is granted to everyone, and that people do have opportunity which they do not have in other countries; that there are strengths in our system, and it is not all one-sided?

MR. MURROW. I do, certainly.

SENATOR HICKENLOOPER. Well, do you believe that the amount of information put out on the opportunities that racial groups have in this country has been commensurate with the criticisms that have been put out?

MR. MURROW. I do not know the answer to that in detail, sir.

SENATOR HICKENLOOPER. Well, now I can only say, Mr. Murrow, that I think you are a man of great ability. I told you that personally, and I am perfectly willing to say it publicly. Frankly, I have the impression, as I have told you personally, that you have in a number of documentary presentations emphasized either the deficiencies or isolated instances of irregularities to the exclusion of the strength of our system, and I merely question any salesmanship based on that kind of business. And I submit that our information program, if it has deficiencies, and undoubtedly it does, should really begin to devote its time to selling the strength of the free system, to selling the good things about it, and let somebody else try to prove the bad things about it, as much as possible.

I am not so sure that we gain anything when we indulge in beating ourselves about the head, and putting sackcloth and ashes on, and mourning about some of the few things that are criticizable in this country, while depreciating or failing to emphasize fully the great strength of the American system, what we have here and what we hope the rest of the world will appreciate so far as human dignity and opportunity for the rights of man are concerned. . . .

The Soviets View America and Themselves

Americans talking about Americans are not always aware of how closely their words—and actions—are followed by other nations. One thinks of the foreigners' assertion, "American politics is too important to be left to the Americans."

How the Soviets see the need for controlling their communications is stated in a Soviet publication: "The Soviet press has a tremendous role in carrying out the great program of communist construction, in the rise and strengthening of communist social relations, in educating the new man, and in the struggle for a durable world peace and for the triumph of communism."

The American is apt to see the *Pravda* item below as something out of the McGuffey readers. For example, the rewards of honesty were shown in a story from the *Third Eclectic Reader,* 1879 edition:

A poor widow, in a great need, approaches a merchant and asks for five dollars. The merchant gives her a check for the amount, which the widow presents at the bank for payment. When the banker pays out fifty dollars, the widow protests. The banker carries the story back to the generous merchant, who then gives the widow five hundred dollars, "for such honesty is poorly rewarded by even that sum."

If the Izvestia excerpt is to be classified as "reporting," the term is used in a fashion so as to warrant its enclosure in quotation marks. Interestingly, the item is no tissue of fabrications; rather it illustrates in part one of the aspects of propaganda as a highly selective array of ingredients only a little warped here and there, but organized and combined to produce a misleading effect.

["American Society Is Rotten Through and Through—Americans Themselves Say So" (*Izvestia,* June 23, 1961). Translated in *The Current Digest of the Soviet Press,* published weekly at Columbia University by the Joint Committee on Slavic Studies appointed by the American Council of Learned Societies and the Social Science Research Council, July 19, 1961, pp. 28–29.]

. . . The attention of the American public is now fixed on a number of scandals involving political figures, businessmen and even athletes. These scandals provide illustrations of recent statements by Robert Kennedy, the U.S. Attorney General, and others to the effect that the moral foundations of the United States are becoming more and more shaky.

The *New York Times* on June 20 carried front-page reports about three scandals, one of them national and the other two local, in New York and Massachusetts.

The Massachusetts scandal was covered in a series of three articles by Anthony Lewis, this newspaper's Boston correspondent, who wrote: "A wave of public resentment against corruption in the government is rising in Massachusetts. An impending wave of protest against the policy of the authorities can be clearly sensed." [In the *Times:* "There is a tangible feeling in the air of revulsion toward politics."]

The journalist wrote further that venality and corruption have been evident in the awarding of contracts for the construction of a highway and other public works in the state of Massachusetts, President Kennedy's home state. He cites numerous instances of collusion between businessmen and corrupt authorities of the state of Massachusetts and the city of Boston. . . .

The scandal that caused a stir in New York, which is reported on the front page of the *New York Times,* is similar in character. It involves officials of the city government who accepted bribes from businessmen desirous of obtaining contracts for school construction. William Correale, former construction chief of the New York City Board of Education, admitted that he had accepted bribes from businessmen in the form of money, alcoholic beverages, etc. He and other officials of the Board of Education also admitted that they had extorted contributions for the campaign fund of the Democratic Party from architectural firms working for the city of New York.

The third scandal reported in the *New York Times* on June 20 concerns American basketball players on the teams of various American universities. These basketball players had received bribes from those who made it their occupation to place bets on athletic matches. . . .

In addition to these three scandals, extensively treated on the front page of the *New York Times,* the inside pages of this and other newspapers are telling about other episodes reflecting a profound moral disintegration in the United States.

For example, the *New York Times* reports that in White Plains, a wealthy suburb of New York, the college student Charles Messina pleaded guilty in court to having sold narcotics to high school students. He declared that he had hoped to collect money in this way to pay for his university education. . . .

When the news of the basketball scandal became public knowledge a few days ago, Bob Cousy, a well-known American professional basketball player, noted with sorrow that the basketball players involved in this scandal were merely typical representatives of the society in which they live. "Our American society," he said, "is rotten through and through."

> ["This Is How Soviet People Act" (*Pravda,* June 21, 1961). Translated in *The Current Digest of the Soviet Press,* published weekly at Columbia University by the Joint Committee on Slavic Studies appointed by the American Council of Learned Societies and the Social Science Research Council, July 19, 1961, p. 29.]

Ulyana Nikitichna Brynko, a charwoman in a housing operations office of Housing Operations Administration No. 3, Bauman Borough, Moscow, while cleaning under a staircase, found a bundle containing a large sum in foreign currency, which had been hidden there by a currency speculator.

Despite the fact that this currency speculator attempted to buy off Comrade Brynko by promising her 10,000 rubles (old currency) for the bundle, Ulyana Nikitichna turned in her find to the U.S.S.R. State Bank, thereby setting an example in the fulfillment of civic duty.

Later, Comrade Brynko helped the agencies of the State Security Committee to unmask the criminal.

By order of A. N. Shelepin, Chairman of the U.S.S.R. Council of Ministers' State Security Committee, Ulyana Nikitichna Brynko has been thanked for her help in the struggle against currency speculators and has been rewarded with a valuable gift.

D. FIGURING OUT PUBLIC OPINION

A Senator Looks at Political-Opinion Polls

Understandably irritated by early polls in 1960 which appeared to indicate that Richard M. Nixon was likely to become President of the United States, Democratic Senator Albert Gore of Tennessee rose to join a long line of others who over a period of years had vigorously attacked polls, polling, and pollsters. On one previous occasion a President of the United States had talked of "sleeping polls"; another presidential candidate had declared, "Give Gallup enough Roper and he'll hang both of them." The pollsters themselves said mildly that polls had a probable error of 3 or 4 per cent.

John F. Kennedy had made use of a polling organization as he steered his way through the presidential primaries and the campaign of 1960. On the day after Election Day, the results showed that in predicting the outcome of the election, Gallup had come within two-tenths of 1 per cent and Roper had come within three-tenths of 1 per cent.

With a statistical sliver separating the winner from the loser, Gallup had forecast Kennedy as the winner, and Roper had picked Nixon while he remarked that the election "can go either way."

[Comments by Senator Albert Gore on "Political Public Opinion Polls," *Congressional Record,* Aug. 22, 1960, pp. 15775–15780.]

MR. GORE. Mr. President, I am concerned with the significance which a considerable number of people attach to political polls. It is because so many people think they are important that they have become an unduly significant factor in our national politics.

This undue influence, as I see it, is the only really important fact about political public opinion polls. But this is important. It is important because our democratic processes are involved, and to some extent prejudiced.

Insofar as accuracy in depiction or prediction of the way the mass of our people will vote in a national election is concerned, I consider most of the political polls, including the Gallup poll, as almost meaningless and in many instances misleading. This conclusion is the result of considerable observation and study over a period of 6 months.

Yet I found some Republicans quite gleeful and some Democrats virtually wringing their hands when the Gallup poll published August 17, 1960, showed Senator Kennedy trailing Vice President Nixon 50 percent to 44 percent. I think such an influence is entirely unjustified, and to the extent that it affects or may affect the judgment of the people or the attitudes of our leaders, it is a disservice to our elective process to attach such importance—indeed, any measurable importance—to such a political poll.

The public statements of Senator Kennedy's press secretary, Mr. Pierre Salinger, tend to give the poll some credence. He is quoted as saying:

> Polls are not an absolute science; they are an indication.

With respect to Senator Kennedy, Mr. Salinger added, "He's been behind before."

Now, whether Senator Kennedy is behind or out in front cannot be proven by the meager Gallup sample.

I say meager because, in a letter to me on January 3, 1960, which I inserted in the *Congressional Record,* Dr. Gallup wrote:

> Our national sampling unit is made up of 1,500 adults.

Now, this amounts to less than two hundredths of 1 percent of the adult citizens of the United States, and, for example, about 1 person, man or woman, well- or ill-informed, in every third county in Tennessee.

It is interesting that Dr. Gallup would find only 6 percent of the people undecided this far from election day. This is particularly interesting in view of the fact that on November 3, 1952—one day before election day—Dr. Gallup showed 13 percent of the people undecided. Now, I have no national poll to prove how many people are now undecided as to how they will ultimately vote in November, but I venture the suggestion that 16 percent or even 26 percent would be more realistic than 6 percent at this date. Indeed, I am reliably informed that another recent poll taken since the two political conventions with a considerably larger sample than Dr. Gallup's meager 1,500, showed 24 percent undecided. . . .

Incidentally, Dr. Gallup has a remarkable record of inaccurate prediction. As an example, I should like to read the first four paragraphs of a column written by George Gallup appearing on the front page of the *Washington Post* on November 3, 1952. The headline is "Nip-and-Tuck Race Tuesday Indicated in Final Survey":

> Princeton, N.J., November 2.—Final poll results, based upon interviewing through Thursday, show Dwight D. Eisenhower and Gov. Adlai E. Stevenson coming down the homestretch in a tight race for the popular vote majority.

That is quite a prediction, is it not, Mr. President? In his letter to me Dr. Gallup claimed he predicted the Eisenhower victory in 1952. Let us see what he said. He said:

> [They were] . . . coming down the homestretch in a tight race for the popular vote majority.
>
> Latest figures show the race has narrowed since the last report. Continuation or acceleration of the trend to Stevenson, reported in earlier surveys, would give him a majority of the popular vote on election day.

This is his prediction of the Eisenhower victory. I continue to read:

> The electoral vote, which will decide the winner, depends upon four key States—New York, Illinois, Ohio, and California—where latest figures show the candidates running virtually even.

His latest figures, according to the column, indicated the candidates were running virtually even in New York, in Illinois, in Ohio, and in California. When the real poll was taken the next day General Eisenhower received 59½ percent of the total of Eisenhower and Stevenson votes in New York and Governor Stevenson received 40½ percent. In Illinois General Eisenhower received 55 percent and Stevenson 45 percent. In Ohio Eisenhower received 56.8 percent and Stevenson received 43.2 percent. In California Eisenhower received 56.9 percent and Stevenson 43.1 percent. This was the real poll.

I have read from the column and the poll by which Dr. Gallup claims he predicted the Eisenhower victory. If Senators can find such a prediction in it, I shall be pleased for one of them to point it out.

MR. LONG of Louisiana. Mr. President, will the Senator yield?

MR. GORE. I yield.

MR. LONG of Louisiana. If I correctly understand the Senator's point, he is saying that not only was the Gallup poll incorrect in 1948, but also in 1952, only 4 years later, after the pollsters had undertaken to correct the mistakes which were apparent in 1948. Dr. Gallup predicted a nip-and-tuck race, pinpointing the four major States, and insofar as the general experience in those States was concerned the victory was a landslide victory on that occasion for President Eisenhower.

MR. GORE. The Senator is correct.

MR. LONG of Louisiana. Four years previous the poll had predicted a landslide for Mr. Dewey, and Mr. Truman was elected.

MR. GORE. The Senator is correct. Despite this, many people continue to attach great importance to the Gallup poll. I think it is wholly unjustified. It is virtually meaningless. . . .

. . . there is 1948, when all the polls elected the wrong man. Dr. Gallup predicted that President Truman would receive only 44.5 percent of the popular vote. He missed it by 12 percent—5.4 divided by 44.5. Yet in his booklet entitled "The Story behind the Gallup Poll," Dr. Gallup claims to have missed it by only 5.4 percent. This is twisted arithmetic. By the same calculation, he claimed that he missed the vote for Henry Wallace by only 1.6 percent. He predicted that Mr. Wallace would receive 4 percent of the popular vote. Actually he received only 2.4 percent. Now this is a 40 percent error. But by the Gallup computation method of "percentage points" this margin of error is reduced from 40 percent to 1.6 percent.

We recall that in 1956 T. Coleman Andrews, former Commissioner of Internal Revenue, was a candidate for President with a third party nomination. Dr. Gallup predicted that he would receive 1 percent of the vote, or more than 600,000 votes. Actually Mr. Andrews received only 134,000 votes. Yet by the Gallup computation of margin of error he missed the T. Coleman Andrews vote by less than seven-tenths of 1 percent. What a convenient method of calculating one's error. My banker will not let me get by with it.

MR. LONG of Louisiana. Mr. President, will the Senator yield for an observation at that point?

MR. GORE. I yield.

MR. LONG of Louisiana. If the margin of error were computed in the manner in which I or any layman would compute it, Dr. Gallup missed his prediction by a margin of 4 to 1. He missed it as 1 is to 4. While he predicted that a candidate would receive 600,000 votes, the candidate received only 134,000—one vote for every four that Dr. Gallup predicted. Mr. Andrews had been paying for this service and the poll taker predicted he would get four times the number of votes which he actually received, he would not hire that group to take any more polls for him, even though the poll taker might think he was within his margin of error.

MR. GORE. According to Dr. Gallup's computation, if T. Coleman Andrews had received twice the number of votes that Dr. Gallup predicted, Dr. Gallup's percentage of error would have been only 1 percent. If he had received no votes at all he would have been only 1 percent wrong, which is remarkably twisted arithmetic.

This is a publicity guessing game. In addition to its prejudice of our elective process, I am concerned that so many publishers of great newspapers, at a time when world tension and national and international affairs compete for space on the printed pages to inform our people, large areas of printed space on the front pages of our daily newspapers are devoted to this worthlessness. . . .

The fact that political polls are accurate or inaccurate is not the important element to which I wish to call the attention of the Senate. It is not their accuracy or inaccuracy that urges me to take the time of the Senate to speak upon this subject. They have become political phenomena. The Gallup poll has become a political event, largely, I believe, because so many newspapers give the poll such wide publicity.

Such polls interfere with our elective processes. Not only do they exercise an influence upon the voters, but we observe events such as occurred recently in connection with Governor Rockefeller of New York. I remember that a story was written after the Governors' conference in Puerto Rico, to the effect that Governor Rockefeller would determine whether he would enter the race for President upon the basis of his standings in the political polls.

When it comes to pass that the Governor of the largest State in our Union can base a major political decision as to whether he will seek the Presidency of the United States upon political polls, then I think it is time for the Senate and the Subcommittee on Privileges and Elections to take a look at political polls.

The danger is that they will be used to influence public opinion, rather than to reflect it. No pollster is held to task for any poll except his last one before election day, and some of them tend, as Dr. Gallup clearly did before the 1952 election, to crowd the middle. . . .

. . . Dr. Gallup has a sample poll of 1,500. Mr. Elmo Roper has a sample of 3,000. Other pollsters have more, some less. Dr. Gallup and other pollsters contend that the size of the sample is far less important in achieving reliable and valid results than several other factors. I concede there may be some truth in this statement, particularly since I have considerable misgivings about some of the other factors connected with political polling, to which I shall later refer. Still I feel the size of the sample merits close scrutiny. As a layman, I would question that a straw poll of less than 1 percent of the people could under any reasonable circumstances be regarded as a fair and meaningful cross section test. This would be something more than 500 times as large a sample as Dr. Gallup takes.

In 1944 a committee of the House of Representatives, headed by the then Representative and now the junior Senator from New Mexico, Clinton P. Anderson, conducted a study of political polls. The committee appointed a technical committee to examine the data and statements submitted by Dr. Gallup. The committee was composed of representatives from the Bureau of the Budget, the Bureau of the Census, and the Bureau of Agricultural Economics, which, of course, engage in considerable statistical analyses. Upon examination of Dr. Gallup's testimony and statistics, the technical committee stated in its report:

> The size of the samples used for many of the States was not large enough, even if properly drawn, to insure reliable individual State estimates based solely on polls of the voting population. The use of a size of sample adequate to insure reliable results for individual States might have involved more expense than the Gallup organization could afford.

Mr. President, this was in 1944. I recognize that, especially because of the historic 1948 miscalculation, polling organizations have made some alterations in their polling methods. I believe, though, that the committee very properly questioned the adequacy of the sample size in 1944. I would still question it today. . . .

Handling the Undecided Vote

There undoubtedly has never been a time when every person polled had his mind made up as to who his favorite candidate is. We had such an experience in the experimental poll conducted in Washington. It is the undecided vote and how to handle it in the tabulations that poses a major problem for all pollsters. Once more the element of judgment on the part of the pollster enters in deciding how to handle the undecided responses. It is the view of many that the silent vote swung last year's British elections, in which most polls failed to predict the decisiveness of the sweeping Conservative victory. A normal method is to split the undecided vote according to the percentages of the decided vote in the poll. This method, however, has been seriously questioned on the ground that the undecided people are in many ways unique and their mental processes differ from those with strong party or candidate affiliation. There is, therefore, no reason to assume that they will make up their minds and split their votes in the same way as do the "decided" voters. A few percentage points off either way in the tabulation could make a substantial difference in the predicted outcome. . . .

Even if the pollsters could come up with a valid poll, we cannot escape the possibility that political polls may be subject to manipulation and misuse. Mr. Roper, in speaking of the political poll, has told me:

> I feel the tool with which we're working is a potentially very valuable one, but like many other thoughtful people, I have misgivings about its possible misuse.

I certainly concur in that statement.

I go back once more to the 1944 investigation. Dr. Gallup has said that—

> From the Gallup Poll started in 1935, we have always regarded ourselves as fact-finders—or, in a sense, as score keepers.

In spite of this statement, however, it appears that upon occasion Dr. Gallup, and possibly other pollsters, has exceeded the "fact-finders" limit in reporting the poll results. At one point during the 1944 Presidential campaign, Dr. Gallup subtracted 2 percentage points from the Democratic Party total for what he said was an anticipated low turnout. On this point, I refer again to the report of the House Technical Committee:

> The manner of handling the adjustment of anticipated low election turnout, which resulted in a 2-percentage-point subtraction from the estimated Democratic vote as reported in the actual canvass of the voting population for the three polls published prior to October 27, is subject to criticism. While it is at least debatable whether or not such subtraction was justified in the publication of the early polls, the publication of the estimates, without specific mention of the character and magnitude of the subtraction, may be questioned. This is particularly true, inasmuch as turn-out adjustment had such an important effect in the early Gallup predictions for the 1944 election. Moreover, the adjustments were made on a rough appraisal basis rather than on any basis of precise quantitative measurement, and the same percentage was applied uniformly to the States without regard to local variations.

. . . it is my hope that some curiosity—and, indeed, some concern—has been aroused about political polling procedure, and especially about some of the pitfalls and some of the dangers to our democratic system that I have mentioned. I submit, however, that concern is of no significance unless the published results of political polls have an influential effect in our election processes or upon our leaders. From my study, I have concluded that polls do, in fact, have an influence which is entirely unjustified.

Most pollsters firmly maintain that there is little evidence that published results of their polls even weeks or months before an election have a "band wagon" effect, pulling voters to the candidate which polls show is in the lead. They point to the miscalculated 1948 campaign, and state that if the desire to be with the winner had operated, Dewey would have won by the greatest majority of the century. Reasoning, however, does not permit dropping from our consideration the "band wagon" possibility. The operation of the "band wagon" effect does not necessarily have to lead to an out-and-out victory for the candidate who polls erroneously predict is in the lead. . . .

Polls may have a very great influence months ahead of a political campaign. They may discourage campaign contributors. They may affect morale of campaign workers. They may influence local political leaders who wish to be with the winner to make an alinement, which they may maintain through the campaign.

The influence of polls in the early stages of the campaign may be more effective than very near the end of the campaign, when some pollsters crowd the middle line in order to protect themselves, as I have said.

There is reason to believe that, especially in the case of early polls, when the minds of many voters have not been made up, published results of polls do exert an influence. Even if such an influence amounts to only 1 percent, the damage to our election processes has been done. That might be the margin between victory and defeat of a good man.

The danger is that polls will be used to influence public opinion rather than reflect it. To the extent that the public considers the polls seriously meaningful, this danger is magnified. . . .

A Pollster Looks at the Polls

Louis Harris, the author of the following selection, has served as a private polling organization to President John F. Kennedy. It should be noted that public-opinion measurement makes use of varied methods, that what is customarily called polling is but one way of assessing and analyzing public opinion, that many social scientists regard polling as a great contribution to modern social science sampling and interviewing techniques, that many political scientists regard quantitative measurements of public opinion as grossly inaccurate efforts that actually tend to subvert the democratic process by assuming for public opinion a role not at all commensurate with its capacities.

[Louis Harris, "A Pollster Defends the Polls," *The New York Times Magazine,* Nov. 5, 1961, pp. 29, 128.]

The business of political polling at times can be likened to Russian roulette. Our own organization has just pulled the trigger in the polls we are doing in the current New York mayoral election. Polling has become a built-in part of the mechanics of modern campaigns. But this doesn't mean that polls are always "right"—whether they are "public" polls, whose results are published or broadcast, or "private" polls, taken for a candidate's own guidance and paid for out of his own pocket.

When polls figure largely in the outcome of a major victory, such as that of Mayor Robert F. Wagner in the New York City Democratic primary or President Kennedy's West Virginia primary win in May, 1960, then the poll-taker becomes a kind of political miracle worker. But when the polls go astray, as in President Truman's 1948 upset over Thomas E. Dewey, then the poll-taker is a false prophet devoid of all honor.

Much has been made of the accuracy of polling, but the preciseness of a poll is exactly where its value does not rest. A poll can describe to the candidate the shape and nature of concerns the voters have. It forces him to make decisions.

So point No. 1 about political polling is this: the precise percentage point standing is far less important than the extent to which the poll clearly shows an understanding of the dynamic elements at work in the election itself.

Here, in my judgment, the widest gap exists between public and private polls. Part of the problem for public polls is that newspaper editors are far more interested in the game of political Russian roulette (is the poll right and, if so, within how many percentage points?) than in a comprehension of the "whys" behind the voter's decision. Part, too, is the fact that no newspaper can afford the space to carry a 7,000-word to 10,000-word report, which often is required to interpret truly what is happening to an electorate.

The published polls usually have statistical validity, but often lack the full reporting that gives a reader an understanding of what forces really are at work in an election. Technically, private and public polls are likely to differ little. The private poll, however, will have concentrated more on probing the reasons that lie behind the voters' choices. It will leave far more room for free expression.

But the biggest difference lies in the analysis itself. The private poll must lay out the anatomy of an election and provide the candidate with a guide to tactics. The public poll is far more interested in a series of relatively isolated headlines.

This leads us to a second point: to understand properly the issues in a campaign, political polling must be taken and reported in depth, and this means it must come from the mouths of the voters themselves, in their own words, their own language.

Elections do have meaning for the voters. While much rationalization takes place in voters' minds as election day approaches, there are perceptible combinations of reasons for their behavior. Many of these reasons are predictable long before an election has been joined (such as that Negroes and Jews are likely to vote Democratic by at least 2 to 1, or that Swedish and German farmers and small-town people are likely to vote heavily Republican), but the marginal difference in an election is likely not to be predictable without a poll.

A normal poll in a state will survey a sample no larger than 1,000 voters. The sample is drawn on a probability basis, meaning that each adult in the population has an equal opportunity of being interviewed. A national cross section of 3,000 voters will usually be sufficient.

In conducting a private poll, we send out as many as fifty to sixty trained interviewers in a state. The analyst himself also must do a substantial number of interviews to obtain an accurate feel of the popular mood. Verbatim records are kept of each interview, and these are tabulated on electronic equipment in the home office. Then the analyst must "sweat out" his data to extract its meaning.

To determine the crucial issues in any election, voters must be interviewed in depth. People can tell you what is meaningful to them, but only if they are allowed to talk.

Several years ago, the National Opinion Research Center received wide attention by asking people if they approved or disapproved of the Government's Metallic Acts Corporation. The results indicated overwhelming approval, although no such corporation ever existed. The experiment was widely taken to mean that people in a poll can be made to answer anything. To the poll-taker, the lesson was obvious: beware putting words into the mouths of the people polled.

Thus began what has come to be known as non-directive interviewing, under which people are encouraged to express themselves freely in their own language. If the same topics are probed repeatedly in various ways in the course of the same interview, and if, in the analysis of an interview, replies are taken as a whole (a process called "flow coding"), then it is likely that, at the end of a fifty-minute interview, a skilled analyst will know more about the probable political behavior of an individual than that individual himself might.

When these free-response replies of voters are carefully codified, punched onto tabulating cards and compared statistically against past voting patterns, the poll-taker has gone a long way toward uncovering what is making an electorate move toward a decision.

Much has been made of issues in elections, but far too often the issues on the minds of campaign strategists and candidates are totally remote from the people. For example, in the 1960 election, control of nuclear testing never aroused more than 2 per cent of the electorate and was simply not decisive as an issue. Similarly, the problem of Communists in the United States in the same election never stirred more than five out of every hundred voters and was equally nondecisive.

By contrast, medical care for the aged and extension of Social Security benefits deeply affected a full three voters in every ten and was a major issue working in Mr. Kennedy's behalf. Aid to education was an issue that affected one voter in four and also worked for the Massachusetts Senator. However, waste and spending in Government affected one in ten and worked powerfully for Richard Nixon.

Issues can swell or shrivel rapidly. An example is the conquest of space: for about three months after the Russians put the first sputnik into orbit, space and missile development were important issues to people; after that, they were no longer vote determinants.

Closely akin to their picture of the issues is a third important point about political polls: they can clearly show what the electorate really thinks of the candidates as individuals, where their personal strengths and weaknesses rest.

As a people, we are probably shrewder in assessing public figures than in delineating issues. When a public official has been weak and vacillating, the public spots it. When a Senator is a stuffed shirt, people know it almost immediately. When a Mayor is shorttempered, people will object. Almost invariably the people will strike down an "actor" politician in short order.

This leads to a fourth important point about polls: they can accurately locate the moving part of an electorate—that part which so often provides the margin between victory and defeat in an election.

Roughly three-quarters of an electorate does not change its voting pattern from election to election. The remaining 25 per cent creates all the havoc.

A poll can spot the people who are deviating from past voting patterns—those who voted twice for Eisenhower, for example, but this last time switched to Kennedy. Equally important, a poll can size up just what is keeping the hard core of a Democratic or Republican vote in line in an election. Often, the appeal of a candidate to a hard core may be not at all the same as the reasons that move "switchers."

The candidate must make his own assessment of what issues to emphasize with whom. The polls can tell him accurately just which groups, affected by what, can make up his majority.

Properly taken, opinion surveys can supply these vital directions to a candidate, but polls have two serious shortcomings which have not yet been solved: One is that a poll taken at a single point in time is not reflective of changes which may be occurring. Thus a poll can make a candidate in the lead overconfident or prove unnecessarily discouraging to a candidate who is behind.

A poll taken in August, 1960, showed Nixon with a clear lead over Kennedy. Approximately one month later, the Nixon lead was wiped out. In October, Kennedy held a clear lead. Yet by Election Day, Kennedy's lead had slipped away again, and the election was as close to a stand-off as one could be.

Ideally, polls should be continuing. They should go back to the same voters to observe changes and to watch the undecided vote crystallize.

This is easier said than done. Up to now, such polling has been done only during election campaigns of short duration and of a highly special nature, such as the West Virginia Kennedy primary. Generally, funds simply are not available for such continuous polling efforts. Furthermore, most polls still do not account for last-minute shifts in the vote.

A second shortcoming is that polls have not really unlocked the riddle of who will vote and who will not, thus leaving the poll-taker at the mercy of the vagaries of selective turnout on election day.

Polls sometimes are limited to those who have voted in past elections. Even then, a certain proportion of this seemingly "sure to vote" group will not turn out. And such a screening will consistently underestimate the new vote, which can be crucial.

The most critical aspect of political polling remains interpretation. Simply obtaining the facts does not necessarily mean that the answers are obvious. The task of the analyst is to apply judgment, based on experience, insight and discipline, to the data in order to make a meaningful interpretation. His is a systematic process, but one that calls for a creative sense.

Once an analysis is clear to the analyst, there remains the difficult problem of communicating the results either to the general public or to the candidate. We have learned that candidates find especially helpful separate sections called "observations"—i.e., suggestions derived from the results of the poll.

Poll-takers have created one problem that has constantly come back to plague them. They have made enormous strides in applying systematic and scientific methods to data involving human behavior. But the implication that polls are wholly scientific has led laymen to expect more precision than is possible. Involved are some measurable and some unmeasurable errors, along with a good-sized dose of judgment. A fair statement is that polls today are a hybrid between science and art—not unlike, one might add, the practice of medicine.

There have been many charges and countercharges about the moral implications of political polling. Public polls have been accused of creating a bandwagon effect for the candidate running in the lead. This must be patent nonsense, or else Thomas E. Dewey would have been elected by a landslide in 1948.

Private polling for candidates has been subjected to quite a different attack. Private polls have been accused of making candidates into personalities they wouldn't be otherwise. The answer to this is that disaster awaits the candidate who tries to be something he isn't. The public will spot him quickly—and decisively.

In addition, private polls are accused of sometimes forcing a man out of a race when he should stay in. Gov. Nelson Rockefeller's decision not to run in 1960 against Mr. Nixon is most often cited. Such a claim is equal nonsense, for it is well known that in 1958, when Mr. Rockefeller entered the race for Governor of New York, his own polls showed him running 40 to 60 per cent behind the incumbent Governor, Averell Harriman.

Private polls are supposed to persuade Senators and Governors to steer clear of unpopular issues and causes. This is nonsense as well, for when a man in public life is blessed with the rare courage to stand for an unpopular position he is highly unlikely to let anything dissuade him.

Finally, private polls are accused of influencing delegates to conventions to support one candidate over another. If the polls are accurate, and if the poll-taker and the candidate are willing to run the risk of being challenged in an open primary, then why shouldn't delegates be told what a cross-section of their own constituency prefers?

These criticisms, it seems to me, miss an essential point. Political polls are collections of information, and, when done objectively and soundly, they provide a factual basis for action. As with all facts, they do not wear a partisan label. A poll done for a Democrat should contain the same set of facts as though it were done for a Republican. The pursuit of information has been a mark of all civilized societies. The poll-taker is not a magician, but rather a gatherer and interpreter of intelligence.

To object to political polling is to argue that politicians and the general public should be more poorly informed. This is to argue that politicians are better, more courageous, sounder, more clear-headed, wiser when less well-informed about their constituencies. Such talk is patent nonsense and belongs back in the dark ages when knowledge was feared, rather than cherished and put to constructive purpose.

CHAPTER 10

THE UNITED STATES IN THE WORLD CONTEXT

ELITE OPINION becomes more significant in influencing public policy generally as the matter under consideration is the more abstract, the more remote from everyday experience, the more technical, the more intellectually complex. By and large, similarly, the able citizen is the more influential as the subject matter requires more time to comprehend, necessitates more effort and organization and knowledge to take appropriate action, involves the application of continuous attention over a lengthy period of time, and embraces awareness of avenues of access to the people and the methods needed to accomplish desired objectives. These are precisely the characteristics of foreign-policy questions and information, and they are also the matters on which the opinions of educated people can be especially valuable.

In all the reaches of public affairs, the competent citizen searches for evidence and turns all data round and round in the effort to evaluate their probative value, to see whether asserted conclusions follow from sound data, whether declared interpretations accord with facts, whether facts are what they are represented to be. Good thinking in international affairs, like good thinking anywhere, or for that matter anything that is worthwhile, is achieved only by sweat and strain. It is vital that the citizen, the reader, the listener, work at understanding and analysis, that he adopt a questioning and curious attitude, that he set out to weigh and to examine.

Command of principal substantive ideas in foreign relations can be obtained only after wide reading, much thought, and extended discussions. One writer has commented wryly that a student of international relations is "a person who regrets that he does not better understand psychology, economics, diplomatic history, law, jurisprudence, sociology, geography, perhaps languages, comparative constitutional organization, and so on down a long list." Another analyst, discussing the politics of the developing areas, says, "The magnitude of the formal and empirical knowledge required of the political scientist of the future staggers the imagination and lames the will."

As a developing member of the elite, the student is in the position of a foreign-policy consumer; he does not and cannot ordinarily have the detailed information and insights in depth of the "producer" in international relations. When the experts talk about the necessity for knowing almost everything about almost everything in and around social science, they are talking about the researchers, the analysts, the teachers, the writers, and the decision makers.

As an intelligent consumer, the citizen's task is more nearly to choose between the data and the appraisals of rival sources, to make a selection between the claimants of prescience and omniscience rather than himself to devise the package in which he can wrap the answers to all questions.

Specific details of international relations are constantly changing, and it would seem most useful for the student to examine case materials that deal with major matters of continuing significance. The articles and excerpts below are organized around the main headings: (A) The New World; (B) Overall Views of America in Its International Relations; (C) Soviet-Chinese-American Ideas and Relations.

A. THE NEW WORLD

Revolutions and their progeny are everywhere, and Americans have been trying to work out appropriate behavioral and attitudinal reactions. Long ago, Thomas Jefferson said kind things about revolutions. He declared that "a little rebellion now and then is a good thing, and as necessary in the political world as storms in the physical." He asserted that the mass of mankind "was not born with saddles on their backs, and for a favored few, booted and spurred, ready to ride them by the grace of God," and capped his statements by saying, "The American Revolution is intended for all mankind."

In the continuing sweep of time, American political leaders have taken the occasion to compare foreign anticolonial revolutionary leaders with Washington and Lincoln. In the twentieth century too the Daughters of the American Revolution said seriously that the American Revolution was not really a revolution at all; it was a revolt.

One view of the American's difficulties in coping with the present-day "Age of Revolution" was exemplified by the occasion when real estate men from all over the nation attended their annual convention at Miami Beach during the winter of 1961. Running the convention was the National Association of Real Estate Boards, an organization said in a *New York Times* dispatch to rank well to the "right" of the American Bar Association and the American Medical Association. To educate the members in anticommunism and to persuade them to conduct similar activities in their home communities, the NAREB exhibited diverse materials, including films, pamphlets, and other items, such as automobile stickers bearing legends like "Join the American Revolution . . . Freedom Forever under God." When the slogan on the sticker drew a puzzled query from a real estate man who wondered if it was not a mistake to use the word "revolution" in the service of a patriotic group, he was informed that others had also objected, but the statement was all right, for "the meaning was safely conveyed by the additional words, 'under God.' "

The Age of Revolution

Henry L. Wriston, author of the following article, is president of the American Assembly of Columbia University, president emeritus of Brown University, former consultant for various public agencies, including the Department of State, and author of many articles and books, including *Strategy of Peace* and *Diplomacy in a Democracy.*

[Henry M. Wriston, "The Age of Revolution," *Foreign Affairs,* vol. 39, pp. 533–548, 1961. Copyright by the Council on Foreign Relations, Inc., New York.]

I

Of the many roads by which a private citizen may approach consideration of international relations, three are worthy of particular mention: knowledge, emotion, imagination. The last of these—imagination—deserves special thought, for it offers extremely useful help in dealing with a turbulent world, and above all the acutely disturbed new and underdeveloped nations.

Knowledge is the first method of approach; the process for its creation is scholarship. This is the way to develop the specialist, a man who knows a great deal about some aspect of policy in time or space or thought—or all three. Such work is essential to progress in the quest for peace. Without specialists statesmen would lack access to essential knowledge. Not all citizens can be scholars; they have other preoccupations. But all citizens can profit by the research of scholars, for the work of many is summarized and synthesized by secondary writers. Essential knowledge is made available in palatable form, and every citizen should learn as much as possible. Above all, he should think about what he knows. One historical fact, in particular, should enter his consciousness and become firmly fixed: there never was a golden age when men lived happily, securely, without tensions.

When we read history, events are foreshortened. A century or more of progress may be covered in a sentence or two. Thus it seems as though the meaning of events must have been obvious to those who lived among them. But that is a rare occurrence; the normal rule is that only in the long perspective does the significance of the age become clear. A verse in Ecclesiastes reminds us how old is this problem: "For man also knoweth not his time: as the fishes that are taken in an evil net, and as the birds that are caught in the snare; so are the sons of men snared in an evil time." One of the fundamentals a citizen must grasp is that every age has had its problems, its dangers, even its moments of desperation.

The second approach to foreign affairs is emotional. This road is hard packed, for it has been well traveled by idealists. No one with any sensitiveness can look out upon the world without acute awareness of the prevalence of hunger amounting to starvation, poverty almost beyond belief, disease, misery, degradation of life itself. These things prevail among the vast majority.

Those whose responses are primarily emotional will be tempted to make a direct, naive assault upon these evils. Such sentimentalism is self-defeating;

it retards reform by offending those whom it is intended to help. None the less, all impulse to action has its roots in the emotions. As the citizen who tries to be effective in shaping public opinion must seek knowledge, so also he must draw inspiration to action from emotion.

Imagination is the third method by which a citizen can be effective in forming sound public opinion regarding foreign relations. Imagination is not dreaming; by definition dreams are unreal. Imagination can be, and must be, disciplined. Those who wish to strengthen their imaginative powers will draw not only on knowledge, but also upon idealism, the urge "to do something about it." They will go further; imaginative citizens will remember that a stranger's pattern of thought and action, even his value judgments, are largely inherited. They may be modified by skill and patience, but the process cannot be hurried.

Patience must, therefore, be a principal ingredient in the discipline of the imagination. Only by the cultivation of almost infinite patience can the citizen escape the defeatism that arises when the initial effort fails to produce perfection. Such lack of patience tends to be characteristic of journalists; it explains their prevailing pessimism. They look for "news," particularly "hard" news, something dramatic, decisive. They do not usually observe the slow process of evolutionary change because their perspective is too short. Even if they could catch the drift, they would not think it worth a line of type because it lacks "impact." Thus much of the solid progress of the world goes unreported.

The man of disciplined imagination will be happy with progress which, though small, astonishes the scholar, while its slow pace will dismay the sentimentalist. Ignorance, disease, poverty, hunger are not the fruits of imperialism, nor colonialism, nor the industrial revolution. They are as old as mankind and will not be banished easily or swiftly. That is not pessimism; it is a summons to patience.

In the discipline of imagination, persistence comes next to patience. As patience realizes that great results will not be easy, persistence appreciates that even slow progress will grind to a halt unless effort is vigorous and continuous.

II

If the idea be accepted that a vivid and disciplined imagination is a valid instrument by which the private citizen can think constructively about foreign affairs, we can offer six illustrations of how it can be applied to our relationships with the newly independent, the anciently ignorant, the shockingly poor and the sadly diseased nations of the world.

The first necessity is to rid ourselves of nervousness when "revolution" is mentioned. Politicians often shy like skittish horses at the mere word. That is nonsensical. Thomas Jefferson once wrote in a letter: "What country before ever existed a century and a half without a revolution? . . . the tree of liberty must be refreshed from time to time with the blood of patriots and tyrants. It is its natural manure."

The slightest acquaintance with history makes it clear that revolutions are as old as recorded history—and as current as today's news. The Cromwellian era in Britain was revolutionary; that should remind us that even the most stable institutions have from time to time been shaken to their foundations. The United States broke its ties with the mother country by revolution, and far from being ashamed of the fact, our forefathers made it a matter of pride. Our Civil War was long and costly in life as well as treasure.

Since the eighteenth century, revolution has been endemic in France. In the latest successful instance, when de Gaulle swept into power, legal forms were meticulously followed and violence was latent rather than overt, but the substance of the change was revolution. A series of revolutions occurred in Italy and in Germany, in both the nineteenth and twentieth centuries, and the same has been true in Russia. If the well-developed, relatively stable parts of the world have experienced so many explosive changes, there is no reason to be astonished that revolution is not merely endemic but epidemic in Asia, Africa and Latin America.

It is easy to assert that all changes in government should be achieved by ballots instead of bullets, but the realities of human experience make that a mere wish-fancy which a well-disciplined imagination must reject. So common has been revolutionary change that there is a considerable body of literature in its defense. The United States is the source of some of the most eloquent pleas for the legitimacy of revolution. Even a state we regard as conservative, New Hampshire, put this passage in its Constitution of 1792: "The doctrine of nonresistance against arbitrary power and oppression is absurd, slavish, and destructive of the good and happiness of mankind." Read again the Declaration of Independence where, among the "causes" of our revolution, appears this statement: "That whenever any form of government becomes destructive of these ends it is the Right of the People to alter or to abolish it, and to institute new Government, laying its foundation on such principles and organizing its powers in such form as to them shall seem most likely to effect their Safety and Happiness."

It would be difficult to find more persuasive defenses of revolution. Such statements, too often forgotten or neglected in the United States, are quoted frequently in the new nations. Read aright, our Declaration of Independence makes us kin to all the new nations which have escaped from the status of wards and attained the stature of independence.

Our own interest in revolution did not wane when we achieved independence, nor did we regard it is a blessing appropriate to ourselves alone. From the days of Washington almost to the presidency of Wilson our recognition policy reflected that interest. Jefferson put it in these words: "We surely cannot deny to any nation that right wherein our own government is founded—that one may govern itself according to whatever form it pleases and change these forms at its own will . . . the will of the nation is the only thing essential to be regarded."

We rejoiced in Kossuth's effort to make Hungary free in 1849. At that time Daniel Webster said the United States could not be indifferent to "the fortunes of nations struggling for institutions like our own. Certainly the United States may be pardoned . . . if they entertain an ardent affection for those popular forms of political organization which have so rapidly advanced their own prosperity and happiness." In our current mood his words seem bombastic, but at the time they evoked passionate approval, for they expressed a profound urge to see the whole world free. Abraham Lincoln spoke for all Americans when he spoke of the Declaration of Independence as "a stumbling block to tyrants" and giving "hope to the world for all future time. It was that which gave promise that in due time the weight would be lifted from the shoulders of all men." It would be easy to compile a long list of instances when, with public support, the Government of the United States welcomed and encouraged revolution.

Familiarity with our own record will end much of the difficulty in understanding current revolutions. For 1961 is still part of the Age of Revolution that was launched in 1776. Once the citizen has become accustomed to this idea, there will be no temptation to bewail all violent political change. The first essential in an imaginative approach to new governments, therefore, is to realize that revolution is normal, sanctified by experience and by theory.

III

The second step in the imaginative understanding of new governments is a realization that they will be unstable, that there will be keen competition to govern. The reasons lie plain upon the surface. During a struggle for independence all patriots can unite upon that one common goal, subordinating their differences to the single paramount objective. Deficiencies that have existed in the public service, of whatever sort, can be attributed to the imperial power, taxes can be blamed upon the distant rulers, and every burden can be described as "exploitation." Our Declaration of Independence contained a whole catalog of abuses.

Once independence is achieved, all that is changed. Unity of purpose can no longer be attained by fighting against an outsider; no distant devil can be blamed. There must now be purpose for, not against, and every man is likely to have his own program.

Again our own history illustrates the problem perfectly. Thomas Paine, one of the authors of our Revolution, whose "Appeal to Reason" was such a potent force, was as one with George Washington throughout the war. But in 1796, Paine wrote in a pamphlet entitled "Letter to George Washington":

> There was a time when the fame of America, moral and political, stood fair and high in the world. The luster of her revolution extended itself to every individual and to be a citizen of America gave a title to respect in Europe. Neither meanness nor ingratitude had then mingled itself into the composition of her character. . . . The Washington of politics had not then appeared. . . .
>
> And as to you, sir, treacherous in private friendship . . . and a hypocrite in public life, the world will be puzzled to decide, whether you are an apostate or an impostor; whether you have abandoned good principles, or whether you ever had any.

The rift after our Revolution was not merely personal; it was revealed in the structure of government. The colonies, having become states, set up a central government, but they had been resisting centralized control and saw to it that it was weak. "The Articles of Confederation" were slow in the drafting (17 months), tardy in acceptance (over three years), feeble in action. Our first national government was a failure.

From the Declaration of Independence to the establishment of our second government in 1789, nearly 13 years elapsed. Even then we had not fully faced reality. The new Constitution made no reference to parties, which Washington and others denounced, calling them factions. Yet between the ideas of Jefferson on the one hand and Hamilton on the other there was a great gulf which neither all the efforts nor all the persuasion nor all the prestige of Washington could bridge. Parties proved to be essential to the operation of the government.

If, with all the inheritance from British constitutional tradition and all the training in self-government which our forefathers possessed, they could not remain united, how can we expect these new nations, most of whom have no such sound inheritance, to do better? At the end of 13 years of declared independence, our government was virtually bankrupt. Even after the new government was set up and fiscal order restored, as late as 1800 Aaron Burr was almost able to steal the presidency from Thomas Jefferson. Few Americans now recall that Jefferson finally won only on the 36th ballot. It took a constitutional amendment to prevent a recurrence of so scandalous a gambit—and to admit thereby how essential a role parties play.

Yet we tend to feel upset if, though none are yet so old as we were in 1789, new nations and new governments show evidences of instability, rivalry among leaders, fiscal disorder—in short the same symptoms we exhibited in our own infant days. In summary, the second point which the imaginative approach must stress in thinking about new nations is that instability is inherent in post-revolutionary states.

IV

A third characteristic of new governments, which imagination should help us understand, is the relationship of the new rulers to their political opponents. During our political campaigns, candidates denounce each other on the hustings; election over, they meet amiably. The transition from one administration to another is extraordinarily smooth. We take it for granted that foreign ambassadors will maintain social relations with leaders of opposition parties, and if, before our election, the British Ambassador had not known Adlai Stevenson, Lyndon Johnson and Sam Rayburn, we would have felt he was not up to his job. Similarly, our Ambassador in the United Kingdom as a matter of course knows Hugh Gaitskell and Harold Wilson.

In revolutionary situations, different rules apply, for the opposition is not a "loyal opposition" or merely a political competitor; it is the enemy. The defeated opponent is likely to be plotting the overthrow of the government and may be assembling clandestine armed forces. In these circumstances, a revolutionary leader will not look with calm upon social or personal relations between foreign ambassadors and his opponents. The effort to maintain such contacts may well lead to the diplomat being declared persona non grata.

Again our own history should assist in understanding this problem. When these new governments curb such normal social contacts on grounds of "internal security," we should recall the dismissal of Citizen Genêt by Washington. We should remember, also, the Alien and Sedition Acts during the administration of John Adams. Like much legislation in today's new states, those acts were aimed at suppressing political opposition. We hope we have outgrown such manoeuvres, but the feelings which motivated them survive in the United States today.

It required all our political sophistication to treat Khrushchev when he came for the first time, not as the author of savagery in Hungary, but as the leader of a great power with whom the realities of international life required us to deal. His second trip produced many hostile manifestations. If it is so hard for us to exhibit restraint, we ought to be able to understand the oversensitiveness of weak, new governments menaced by an opposition ready to resort to bullets at the first hope of success.

An imaginative approach should help us grasp a fourth fundamental point about revolutions. Revolution, as the word itself suggests, is like turning a wheel. Start a wheel and momentum takes over to some extent; it rarely stops—except in closely controlled circumstances—just where you want it to.

Even revolutionary leaders who are pure in heart, dedicated in purpose, democratic in ideals cannot make the wheel spin and stop exactly 180 degrees from the starting point. Their energies may prove deficient and move the wheel not at all—or only 90 degrees. The wheel may turn full circle—360 degrees—which, in another context, is one revolution. The French Revolution spun all the way from the Bourbons clear around to Napoleon. Revolutions develop a dynamic of their own, and no one can predict just how far they will go. The righteousness of the initial impulse does not always govern the result.

Victory is heady wine. One who has ever lived upon a college campus understands this, for he has observed the behavior of students at the moment of a football victory—exuberant, irrational, abandoned. It is the more intense when the team's record has not been good, and when some break in the game or a dramatic surge has brought victory when defeat seemed imminent. The emotional release is violent. If, with the long tradition of sportsmanship which exercises rigid control over normal behavior, so much ungoverned emotional energy is loosed over what is, relative to the great events of the world, so minor an occasion, how much more readily can we understand the intoxication that follows success in bringing an end to tyranny at imminent risk of life. No wonder it often produces wild excesses.

V

The fifth aspect of revolution we can also apprehend imaginatively: victors do not take kindly to advice. In gaining independence, they were "do-it-yourself" men. Many leaders in the world today, and virtually all the revolutionaries, have been in prison, in exile or in great personal danger: Bourguiba, Nkrumah, de Gaulle, Adenauer, Gomulka, Tito, Nasser, Diem, Nehru, Sukarno, Castro—and many more. Most of them owe no thanks to armchair critics that they are now in power rather than in graves.

The colonial revolutionaries, especially, feel no gratitude to outsiders. Indeed, did we not do business with their late masters and so "help the enemy"? We gave money and military goods to many of the former rulers, and though our motives were pure and we did not intend to help hold colonies in subjection or suppress revolution, the net result of our aid often was to strengthen the metropolitan power or the predecessor government. And despite our historic anticolonialism, we have not been wholly free, since we became a world-wide power, to exhibit our real feelings. Our relations with Europe—the necessity for maintaining alliances—sometimes conflicted with our desire for the liquidation of colonialism in Asia and Africa. We urged the Netherlands so strongly to give independence to Indonesia that we strained our relations with that key nation in Europe, yet our diplomatic pressure was neither so overt nor so dramatic as aid to the Netherlands through the Marshall Plan and NATO. Sukarno was aware of our tangible help to his enemy; our intangible diplomatic pressure was not so visible.

Moreover, revolutionary leaders are under severe domestic pressures. In rallying their own people to make sacrifices for the revolution, they made promises, explicit or implicit. They cannot now exercise power without making major changes. It may well be that the first need of the new country is wiser use of the land, improved breeds of hens to lay more eggs, better cows to give more milk. But that does not mean that such programs will have priority, for they are not dramatic and their results appear too gradually to satisfy people whose expectations have been inflated. Having achieved something great and dynamic in the moment of revolution, the new leader cannot ask his people to wait for evolutionary processes to mature over a long period of time. He is the symbol of action, not of more eggs! He will resent counsel to move slowly. As a man of wide experience has put it, we must expect that "new governments may sometimes insist on types of growth which have more to do with prestige than need." The "revolution of rising expectations" has often, therefore, more to do with the dramatic than the necessary.

Independence, we must remember, means freedom to do the wrong thing as well as the right. That ought not to be a difficult concept to grasp, for we have pursued farm policies, for example, which pile up bigger and bigger food surpluses and higher and higher costs and deficits. Those policies add up to economic folly, but have been thought to be politically profitable. Clearly, we are in no position to be overly censorious of those who, with less experience, less training and fewer resources, make mistakes which seem to us serious.

The argument that the development of new nations should be left to private capital—or to "free enterprise"—will fall on deaf ears. The word "socialism," far from holding terrors for them, has deep attraction. The leaders of new states know that most of the free nations of the world have now, or have had, socialist governments. Many of them are more aware than we appear to be that our own economy is a mixture—that government plays a large role in our economic life. The Tennessee Valley Authority is one of our most conspicuous exports. Our railroads were built with heavy government subsidy, and many want more now. Our canals and waterways are all public enterprises, and in most free nations so are railroads and telephones—and the universities.

These men who engineered revolution want now to manage the economy. They remember that the hated imperial control followed in the train of private trade and investment. We tend to think that the normal sequence is for trade to follow the flag, but their own history tells them that it was often the other way round. The Belgian Congo started as a private speculation of King Leopold, who became fabulously wealthy without notable benefit to the Africans. The Indonesians saw the Dutch grow rich, while they remained poor. This experience, many times repeated in many places around the world, created the image—still dominant today—of capitalism as exploitation. They view with deep suspicion, therefore, great capitalistic enterprises coming from abroad. Having once found that process a prelude to colonialism, they are doubly shy.

Many of the new nations fear the rule of prices by a free market, for they are producers of raw materials—tin, rubber, coffee, tea, cocoa, jute, and so on. Asians can point to a United Nations calculation that in recent experience their reduced incomes from such exports, occasioned by falling prices in free markets, just about offset the grants-in-aid. They are also aware that the United States puts quotas on oil, zinc, copper, sugar, and that it deliberately sets out to defeat the free market in agriculture by government intervention. Why, they ask, should we be critical when they follow the same pattern of political suppression of economic forces?

Moreover, many new nations have not the wealth to support free enterprise. There is no accumulation of domestic capital with which to finance industrial development. Poverty is so intense that domestic savings can be found only, as in Russia in Stalin's day or now in Red China, by grinding the faces of the poor and letting millions starve. If, therefore, the nation is not to become totalitarian, the money must come from abroad. But so sensitive are the new leaders that they will regard any advice, any cautionary devices connected with aid, as "strings."

The ordinary requirements which we all accept when borrowing money, they resent. They see them as manifestations of economic—and ultimately political—imperialism, and having just escaped from one form of dependence they do not want to fall into another. Our history ought to remind us that this is the normal mood of debtors. The resentments of our Western states at what was regarded as "Wall Street control" are classic. When mortgages were being foreclosed, the great Senator from Missouri, Thomas Hart Benton, exploded: "A lump of butter in the mouth of a dog, one gulp, one swallow, and all is gone." Many a Westerner in the mid-nineteenth century regarded that as the restrained statement of a moderate.

These things partially explain why our foreign aid program is not uniformly a "success." We need to do many things better, but the point is missed completely by those who feel that, if only we had a different organizational structure or more money or made this, that or the other change in procedure, our troubles would disappear. There is no simple, easy way to achieve the desirable ends. We must do the best we can, profiting by experience, not endlessly repeating the same errors, but accepting, nevertheless, the inevitability of failure to attain Utopia in a short time. The growth of economic freedom, as of political freedom, is a slow process, with many painful setbacks.

VI

Appreciation of the fact that each individual nation has a unique perspective upon history is a sixth way in which imagination can help the citizen grasp the realities of a revolutionary world. Depending upon the national points of view from which it is observed, the same historical event carries wholly different significances; what seems trivial to one appears vital to the other. Each nation tends to regard its version as "truth," overlooking the validity of other viewpoints.

When this national emphasis is forgotten, present difficulties are too often attributed to current or recent episodes, whereas the roots of trouble frequently lie deeper in divergent national interpretations of history. Such difficulties will not disappear rapidly, or be eliminated by some change in the style of our diplomacy. In South America, in Africa and in Asia many nations feel that we are obsessed with the menace of Communism. We can justify that concern to ourselves, for we have experienced the retreat from Wilson's vision of a world safe for democracy, and have seen the rise of Soviet confidence that Marxism-Leninism will embrace the entire world.

The historical tradition of many nations makes other menaces—such as imperialism, economic or political—seem much more real. Their experience has not sensitized them to the Communist danger. When we try to transfer our justified alarm to them, they not only do not accept the warnings, they resent them. Our interest in their development is seen as an effort to draw them into a power struggle which they regard as irrelevant to their concerns.

One of the most striking instances of different national perspectives upon history—as a cause of profound misunderstanding—is the Monroe Doctrine. It has customarily been treated in our histories as a wholly defensive concept. From the standpoint of the United States, it was an anti-imperialist pronouncement designed to let the nations of this hemisphere develop without external interference. The angle of vision of Latin countries is different. When we undertook to speak on behalf of this hemisphere, it is undeniable that we "took Latin America for granted," since no nation had given us authorization to speak on its behalf. From the Latin point of view, we were at least impinging upon the policy formation of independent nations; to that extent we committed a trespass upon their sovereignty. It was a manifestation of the unconscious arrogance that arises from the consciousness of power. Inconceivable as it may seem to us that Monroeism could be identified with imperialism, for some Latin nations that identification seems natural.

Once this divergence in perspective is grasped imaginatively, many episodes which appear as almost insignificant in our history are seen to loom decisively large in theirs. To us Cuba is a small nation in which we have taken an avuncular interest. Cubans read history differently; for a century our statesmen spoke of the acquisition of the island as inevitable. Even after we decided against annexation, we retained control through the Platt Amendment, which limited the power of Cuba to act as a sovereign state and authorized intervention by the United States. We exercised that right from time to time, treating the Cubans as wards and determining who should govern them. The liquidation of the Platt Amendment did not occur until 1934. Cuban history stresses the reality of our control rather than the philanthropic purpose which our histories emphasize.

Mexicans recall our war with them in 1846–1848, as a consequence of which we took California, New Mexico and parts of three states. President Polk asked authority to occupy Yucatan; President Pierce arranged the Gadsden Purchase; President Buchanan proposed intervention and the occupation of two Mexican states. Even after the Civil War there were considerable periods when Mexico lived in perpetual fear of imminent invasion. Woodrow Wilson twice invaded Mexico, and sought to determine who should be its president.

The United States acquired as many of the Caribbean islands as possible and wanted more. The purchase of the Virgin Islands was negotiated by Seward, and consummated in this century. We took over Puerto Rico from Spain. President Grant's acquisition of the Dominican Republic was defeated by the Senate, but later the finances of that republic were supervised by the United States, and it was militarily occupied and governed by us for some years. In 1915, during occupation by Marines, a virtual American protectorate was established over Haiti by treaty; it went further than the Platt Amendment in establishing American control. Fiscal independence for the two republics was conceded only 20 years ago.

In 1879 President Hayes called the proposed Isthmian Canal "virtually part of our coastline." To us that seemed logical enough; to others it looked like imperialism. The British commented that the President's view would deny the states in the vicinity of the Canal "as independent a position as that which they now occupy." A Republican Secretary of State, James G. Blaine, spoke of "a long-established claim of priority on the American continent," and a Democratic Secretary of State, Richard Olney, announced that the United States was "practically sovereign on this continent and its fiat is law upon the subjects to which we confine our interposition." Later Secretary Philander Knox spoke of the area as "a portion of the world where the influence of the United States must naturally be preeminent." The word "naturally" was galling in the extreme as were the earlier statements based upon our overwhelming power.

When Theodore Roosevelt said, "I took Panama," it seemed to us merely a brash statement about a regrettable episode. For Colombia and Panama it was an event decisive in their history, one which has bedevilled our relationships ever since.

The Roosevelt corollary to the Monroe Doctrine assigned the United States an international police power; we were to determine unilaterally when, where and how much we should intervene. From the Latin point of view, we were saying: "Might makes right." The gospel of the corollary was followed by three administrations, the most extreme of which was that of Woodrow Wilson. He set out to "instruct" the Latin American republics in democracy. He held it "our peculiar duty" to teach them "to elect good men" and establish "order and self-control." He was willing to act in some cases "even if the sovereignty of unwilling nations be outraged in the process." Under the impulse of these dogmas, he violated the sovereignty of several nations, occupying some and controlling others.

The principal historian of the Monroe Doctrine has recorded that by 1915 Monroeism had "been deeply charged with an assumption of the right of control, of superior power, of hegemony over the other states of the New World." How better describe imperialism?

To use a current term, we made satellites of a number of nations. From our standpoint, American imperialism was distinctive: we did not intend our control to be permanent but a transient phase during which the people for whom we accepted responsibility gained experience in self-government. In the second place, the element of exploitation inherent in classic imperialism, though not wholly absent, was subordinated to philanthropic purpose. The recipients of our unwelcome attentions, however, resented our assumption of superior virtue and did not accept at face value our protestations of good intentions. The management of satellites proved unrewarding; it did not produce desired results and it deeply implanted fear of "Yankee imperialism" throughout Latin America.

There is, indeed, a whole literature in Latin America which interpreted Monroeism as imperialism. As a consequence, when Cleveland intervened in the Venezuelan boundary dispute, his initiative, instead of evoking support, was viewed with grave suspicion in Mexico, Chile and Argentina. An Argentinian statesman, later president of that republic, championed Spain against the United States in 1898. When we presented resolutions in Pan American conferences, they often met with suspicion that we were seeking hegemony rather than defense of common interests. During the First World War the Mexican Government was sympathetic to Germany.

We see the episodes mentioned and many others as marginal incidents in our history, and, in any event, part of a closed book. From our point of view, we have exchanged the expansive and imperialist dreams of earlier times for the status of counselor and friend, though our relationship to events in Guatemala in 1954 seemed to Latins to go much further. The one who exercises power and the one upon whom it is exercised almost always have a different interpretation of the motives involved. The slightest hint of condescension, even in connection with economic aid, is sure to evoke deep resentment. If we approach the matter imaginatively, we will not be surprised at the lingering fears of the Colossus of the North, or at the persistent suspicion that we have not wholly abandoned imperialist ambitions.

We think we have learned at great cost that we must not let dislike of political and social retrogression induce us actively to manage other people's affairs. We may use such diplomatic instruments as are available, but beyond that it is unwise to go, except in concert with other nations through the Organization of American States or the United Nations. Otherwise, we set ourselves up as moral imperialists, seeking to choose not only our own course of action but also to direct the lives of other nations.

Latin America illustrates the need imaginatively to remain constantly alert to the different historical perspectives of other people as we attempt to understand their prejudices and fears. What we sometimes take for jealousy of our might and our wealth is, to some extent, a reaction to unconscious arrogance when we speak all too glibly of "our position of leadership." Leadership should be a combination of wisdom, courage and persuasiveness. The more fully we appreciate the folly of mistaking dominance for leadership, the sooner will the underdeveloped nations accept the sincerity of our purpose.

VII

There has been a growing feeling that the problems of foreign affairs have become so complicated that the private citizen cannot be expected to understand them, much less make a positive contribution to their resolution. Concurrently there has been a surfeit of demands that Washington officials should develop "bold, new, imaginative policies and plans." This is tantamount to asking that those eminently desirable ends should be achieved in a vacuum. That is not only undesirable, it is impossible. We do not have a government of experts, and if we were to try to form one it would be utterly disastrous to the whole concept of democracy to which we are deeply committed. The expert has an essential but none the less a subordinate role to play; he can advise, but he cannot take the place of political leadership. By its very nature political leadership loses its effectiveness unless there is a significant degree of public consensus behind proposals for action. Many a novel and constructive idea, possibly conceived by experts but responsibility for which was accepted by a political leader, has come to nought for lack of intelligent popular support.

So long as the United States remains committed to the democratic process, there can be no substitute for effective citizenship. The development of that effectiveness with regard to foreign affairs depends to a great extent upon the application of imagination to help in achieving an understanding of events in the world. Long ago Aristotle argued that citizens need not be experts in order to exercise a sound judgment in public affairs. Time has proved him right. In practice, freshness of official thought is often stimulated by imaginative suggestions from individuals or groups of citizens. They are then ready to rally support for courageous alterations in old policies that time has made sterile.

B. OVERALL VIEWS OF AMERICA IN ITS INTERNATIONAL RELATIONS

American Foreign Policy

The following excerpts are taken from hearings conducted before congressional committees and from a Senate committee report.

Secretary Dean Rusk discusses United States interests in a dynamic peace; Secretary Robert S. McNamara talks about military assistance to other countries and its relations to American security; General Lemnitzer considers civil defense; General Trudeau examines military research and space; major administrators Talbot and Grantham of the State Department and the Defense Department talk with Senators about the question of whether American aid should be limited to democracies. Taken as a whole, the materials give a picture of much of the essence and rationale of America's foreign policy.

Four points should be noted at the outset: (1) The great expanse of foreign affairs is illustrated, including economic, military, and other phases. Beyond these wide-ranging examples, the observer must bear in mind that large sectors of America's relations to the rest of the world are not covered. For literally everything is related to foreign affairs: the fact that the President's wife is attractive and is able to make a speech in Spanish to a Latin American audience; or the contribution of an American ambassador who with his large family joins enthusiastically and intimately in the life of the nation where he is serving; or the strengthening of the United States occasioned by the forward leap of its productivity.

(2) The American top officials represented in the excerpts from the documents below are obviously intelligent, well-informed, articulate, quick-thinking people. Whether they are typical of Federal officials is a judgment the citizen can make for himself in the light particularly of the high visibility of such personnel. One would suppose in any case that it is unlikely that a foolish or otherwise defective man could survive for long in the heat of the foreign-affairs scrutiny of the press, interest groups, and every other organized grouping of power in our society.

Currently it has become fashionable for interested people to set out to educate the community by attention-arresting efforts like placing newspaper advertisements with some such message as "Let's prevent war rather than build air-raid shelters; shelters are no more than incinerators" or "You can't buy friends" or "Communism is an idea and you can't fight an idea with armies." None of these is a subtle concept difficult to grasp. All are at least partially wrong or at least incomplete and misleadingly simplistic.

The quality of the testimony below suggests the improbability that such notions are flashes of truth that have not been considered by America's foreign-policy makers and executives. Shouting a slogan directed at an unreal problem or a fanciful solution is not the equivalent of an effective criticism of foreign policy. For example, you cannot reasonably object to a shelter program on the ground that shelters will not protect people from the blast effect of a thermonuclear attack; informed persons claim no such protection for shelters. When General Lemnitzer talks about the values of a civil defense program, he refers to fall-out shelters. Valid criticism, if any, would have to be directed at the idea of fall-out shelters, not at an idea which has not been proposed. Similarly, the thought that we ought to try to prevent war, rather than burrowing under the ground, embraces a deceptive pair of options. For the choice is not between trying to prevent war and building shelters. Always reasonable men seek to prevent war; the search can continue with or without shelters.

Sensible discussion would focus on essential questions; whether shelters in the United States will shrink the possibility of war and whether shelters further American security.

(3) American foreign policy assumes a long-time conflict with communism, is aware that the conflict covers every aspect of our society, and involves the participation and oversight of a good many executive agencies, as well as a substantial role by the Senate and the House of Representatives, and by nonpublic agencies.

(4) Early in their commentaries, Secretary Rusk and Secretary McNamara quote President Kennedy on various aspects of international affairs. The citation is not accidental and illustrates the fact that it is the President of the United States who carries the ultimate responsibility for initiating and working out foreign-policy proposals.

[Dean Rusk, Secretary of State, testifies before the Senate Committee on Foreign Relations on "A Bill to Promote the Foreign Policy, Security, and General Welfare of the United States by Assisting Peoples of the World in Their Efforts towards Economic and Social Development and Internal and External Security, and for Other Purposes," May 31, 1961:]

Every age, historians remind us, is an age of transition. But some ages are surely more transitional than others. I cannot but feel that ours is preeminently such an age; and that here, just beyond the middle of the 20th century, humanity stands, for better or for worse, on the threshold of a new historic epoch. . . .

Our decisions by themselves can have only a partial effect on the rest of the world. Yet this effect, if limited, may also in many parts of the world provide indispensable margin which makes the difference between a peaceful order and the law of the jungle. That is why President Kennedy has rightly called the economic measures here under consideration "the single most important program available for building the frontiers of freedom."

The frontiers of freedom, we hope, will be the symbols of the new international order which it is our purpose to promote. What will the characteristics of this international order be? What kind of world are we Americans striving for?

We want, of course, a world of peace and progress under law. And I would lay particular stress on the word "progress." For there can be no greater error than to regard peace as a permanent ratification of an unacceptable status quo. Peace in such terms would be quickly shattered by the explosive forces of change. The object of peace is not to bring change to an end; it is to provide peoples the opportunity to achieve essential change without war.

We seek, in short, not a static but a dynamic peace. We hope for a world in which frontiers will mark national identity and not national self-assertion; in which peoples can peacefully revise their own institutions to meet their own national needs; in which nations differing in their internal forms of organization will dwell together in mutual self-respect and freely exchange goods and persons and ideas; in which competition among national states will lose its cutting edge as nations work together in the common interest of mankind; in which the dignity of the individual will be securely established on the basis of social justice, civic freedom, and international order.

We seek, above all, a world of free choice in which a great diversity of nations, each faithful to its own traditions and its own genius, will learn to respect the ground rules of human survival. We do not wish to make the world over in our own image—and we will not accept that the world be made over in the image of any society or dogmatic creed. Against the world of coercion, we affirm the world of choice. We believe that the revolution of human liberty will never come to an end.

The world today is a very different world from what it was at the end of World War II. The Soviet Union has grown in economic, technical, and military strength. Western Europe, with its astonishing economic recovery, has resumed its place as a potent factor in international affairs. The nations of Latin America, of Asia and of Africa, rising on the tide of nationalist aspiration, are demanding their places in the sun.

Such a world contains contradictions, perplexities, and dangers. Wider distributions of power increase the hazards of world affairs in a nuclear age. At the same time, this new world offers exceptional opportunities for positive, flexible, and imaginative effort. Wise policy in this new world requires a number of things from the United States.

It requires a sufficiency of military force to restrain nations from aggression—and sufficiently diversified military capabilities to deter or meet aggression at every level, from the thermonuclear holocaust to assassination in the jungle.

It requires, equally, a strong and sincere determination to advance the cause of disarmament—to do everything possible to establish the conditions under which nations may reduce their military establishments and know that, in doing so, they are not exposing themselves to enemy attack.

It requires, too, an active and affirmative policy of building the social, economic, and moral strength of independent nations so that they will have the capacity within themselves to throw off the virus of totalitarianism and pursue national objectives in a climate of expanding freedom.

The first thing I would say about the programs under consideration today is that they reflect to a degree our own national experience. We were once an underdeveloped country ourselves. We grew through a combination of foreign assistance, public aid, and private investment and enterprise. We know that a free society under representative institutions can achieve extraordinary economic growth. Our opportunity today—and our obligation—is to assist other nations to reach a stage of secure national independence and self-sustaining economic development.

The need today is for the United States and other developed nations to open to the emergent societies of Latin America, Asia, and Africa opportunities for a continuous and concurrent growth of independence, of democracy, of industry and agriculture, of social justice, and of the institutions and ideals which express and safeguard the dignity of man.

The battleground of freedom, as the President said last Thursday, is the whole southern half of the globe. Here over 40 new nations have attained independence since the war, 19 since the beginning of last year. Here nations, old and new, are struggling to convert formal independence into true nationhood. Everywhere people are awakening from the stagnation of centuries. They decline any longer to regard poverty and oppression and squalor as the law of nature. They are determined to have for themselves and their children the food they need, housing fit for human habitation, the benefits of their farming, schools, sanitation and medicine, and honest, responsible government. They are determined to claim these benefits of modern life without delay.

And, if the democratic world cannot satisfy this passion for modernization, then the Communists can leap aboard this great revolution of freedom, seize it, direct it to their own ends and make it the instrument of their own limitless imperialist ambitions. We would be false both to our own national interest and to our obligations to others were we to allow this to happen.

Our task is made more difficult because the Sino-Soviet bloc has systematically focused its political, economic, and propaganda assault on the underdeveloped world in the last half dozen years. They have exploited their capabilities with considerable effect. They have spread the illusion that rapid development is their monopoly. They have shown speed and flexibility, a minimum of red tape, a readiness to make long-term commitments, and a willingness to accept goods in repayment for loans. They are competing hard, with mixed results, but with an energy which ought to concern those committed to freedom.

But this competition or national self-interest alone is not the essence of the program we are discussing. We need no other reason to support these measures than the profound and overriding fact that they are right.

It is right to do these things because peoples are in need of help and we are able to help them to help themselves; because their children sicken and die while we have the science to save them; because they are illiterate while we have the means of education and knowledge; because their agricultural methods and tools win them an annual income of $50 from the soil while we have the technical skill and capital to help them live like human beings.

Nor is the assurance that this aid will save the underdeveloped world. But those who opposed foreign aid must accept the consequences of their opposition. They must understand that, if they succeed, they deny the people in the emergent societies their last great hope for independent development and therefore condemn them to the high probability of Communist servitude—and us to Communist world encirclement.

[Robert S. McNamara, Secretary of Defense, testifies with especial reference to the utility of American programs giving military assistance to other countries, June 14, 1961:]

As I have become acquainted with the workings of the military assistance program, I have been impressed with its contribution, both actual and potential, to the flexibility of our military planning. . . . Although my appearance before you is properly confined to military assistance, I wish to make it clear that I fully support the economic aid program as well. The two parts of the legislation and the two programs are in fact indispensable to each other; they are not competitive but complementary one to the other.

The role of military assistance was well defined by President Kennedy in his March 22 message to Congress. At that time he said that:

> The economic programs I am recommending in this message cannot succeed without peace and order. A vital element toward such stability is assurance of military strength sufficient to protect the integrity of these emerging nations while they are advancing to higher and more adequate levels of social and economic well-being.

Military assistance has always had to do a variety of jobs. As you know, the program began with President Truman's decision in 1947 to furnish military aid to Greece and Turkey without which, I think we can agree, these countries would have succumbed to Soviet aggression and Communist subversion.

Thereafter, military aid played a key role in the development of the first reasonably adequate NATO forces. As the NATO area became more secure, higher proportions of the program were devoted to Far East areas in jeopardy—Japan, Korea, the Republic of China, and southeast Asia—and to areas south of the USSR which historically have been the objects of Russian expansionism, notably Iran and Pakistan.

Today, as we consider the reasons which dictate continuance of the military assistance program, we look out upon a world still convulsed by rapid change and watched over by strong, resourceful, unscrupulous adversaries ready to take advantage of any show of weakness, indecision, or timidity. . . .

As President Kennedy pointed out on his return from Vienna:

> In the 1940's and the early 1950's the great danger was from Communist armies marching across free borders. . . . Now we face a new and different threat. We no longer have a nuclear monopoly. Their missiles, they believe, will hold off our missiles, and their troops can match our troops should we intervene in their so-called wars of liberation.
>
> Thus the local conflict they support can turn in their favor through guerrillas or insurgents or subversion. A small group of disciplined Communists could exploit discontent and misery in a country where the average income may be $60 or $70 a year and seize control, therefore, of an entire country without Communist troops ever crossing any international frontier.

President Kennedy went on to point out:

> The future for freedom in these areas rests with the local peoples and their government. Our historic opportunity [is] to help these countries build their societies until they are so strong and broadly based that only an outside invasion could topple them.

. . . We attach great importance to the proper coordination of the program with our overall defense effort. From the President's messages to Congress you will have noted the new emphasis on strategic forces which can ride out a nuclear attack, emphasis on command and control of nuclear weapons, on increased and more mobile non-nuclear forces, and on the problem of how best to assist those jeopardized by internal aggression.

Our projected military assistance programs are a necessary, integral part of this conceptual framework. Through the assistance planned we anticipate an improvement in our ability to deal with aggression in its incipient phases, to furnish help for friends and allies which will be more consistent with the kind of threat they face, and to maintain the facilities abroad required for the quick and effective deployment of appropriate U.S. forces.

We do not claim that what we propose is a cure-all for the complex, variegated threat the forces of freedom confront around the world. In the current situation surprises are frequent; the future is unpredictable. But the program we now propose we believe will give us additional flexibility and permit us to respond rapidly to a large variety of situations.

Turning now from the general relationship of military assistance to the overall defense effort and objectives, we consider the program should serve a threefold purpose. It must be more active than ever in enabling free and independent nations to protect their internal security. It must continue to make "local war" clearly unprofitable, and thus to deter such wars, or the mere threat of such wars, which may be a very vital part of the subversive effort. And it must play its part, especially in NATO in deterring any resort to general war.

Along these lines we have grouped the countries covered by the fiscal year 1962 program in three categories—categories which, though not precise or mutually exclusive, provide a useful key to the program.

The three categories are: 1) those countries who in the main face only the threat of internal aggression—the now familiar pattern of penetration, infiltration, subversion, dissidence and guerrilla warfare; 2) those countries who face the threat of direct military aggression in addition to internal aggression; and 3) the very special situation in the NATO area.

In the first category, which may be called the single-threat countries, belong the underdeveloped nations of Asia, the Middle East, Africa, and Latin America that are not contiguous to the Sino-Soviet bloc but which Communist words and actions have shown to be targets for indirect aggression. In these areas we recognize as the primary requirement the need for economic and social progress and the cooperation of governments and peoples in striving for a better life. Through economic programs we seek to contribute to this development. An essential component of their progress, however, is the maintenance of internal stability, and in this function the role of the Military Establishment and other security forces is essential. Military aid to such countries involves primarily the provision of small arms, transport, communications and training. Our objective here is to provide the means for local military establishments, with the support and cooperation of local populations, to guard against external covert intrusion and internal subversion designed to create dissidence and insurrection. . . .

We cannot, of course, dictate to recipient nations how they shall use their armed forces. This type of activity—what we are coming to call "civic action"—must be compatible with the military missions of these forces; this is not a covert use of the military channel for economic purposes. But where the mission is, wholly or in large part, one of internal security, we know, as a matter of common sense as well as from such experiences as that of the Vietnam armed forces dealing with the Communist guerrilla menace, that armed forces will do a better job if they are identified with civic progress.

This emphasis is just beginning. It is not primarily a matter of money. Properly guided, we think it can be a major factor in the security of the free world, while at the same time making a contribution to economic progress.

In the second category, which may be called the double-threat countries, belong those nations contiguous to or near the Sino-Soviet bloc that face a direct threat from without and an indirect threat from within. Vietnam today is a classic example of how these threats feed on and reinforce each other. The twofold threat requires dual-purpose forces in terms of arms, equipment, and personnel. Our military assistance programs play an essential role in furnishing arms and equipment, and in teaching troops to operate, maintain, and use them. Because of this twofold threat the military aid we plan to give them is proportionally high. We recognize the inadequacy of their forces to cope with an outright Communist invasion, yet with our assistance we count on their courage and ability to deal with large-scale guerrilla warfare. Should they suffer an open attack across their borders, we look for local forces to resist the initial thrust until such time as free world forces may come to their support. In these areas the capability of our own forces to deploy quickly against aggression is heavily dependent upon the development and maintenance of base facilities or military infrastructure on the spot or in the vicinity. Military assistance is a key factor in constructing new facilities, improving existing facilities and insuring their availability when required.

The third category of NATO is a special case because of our particularly close relationship to our NATO allies, the continuing and direct Soviet military threat against Europe, and the importance of increasing the effectiveness of NATO shield forces to deter this threat in the changing circumstances with which NATO is confronted. . . .

The military assistance program has frequently been misunderstood. Some of its opponents have called it a giveaway program and have referred to it as foreign military aid—as though it were something given to other countries without return. Nothing could be further from the truth. In fact, this program reflects a realistic hardheaded, commonsense approach to our very difficult security problems—problems which also confront the other free nations of the world.

I should like to emphasize this point, because it is an important one. The security problems of the free world are truly mutual. The military assistance program is a reflection of this basic fact—a reflection of the global nature of the Communist threat which faces the United States and its allies and the need to meet that threat on a worldwide basis. Without any question, the assistance we have provided and continue to provide our allies—in the form of training and equipment—has been a major factor in thwarting Communist aggression. It will continue to be a major factor for the foreseeable future.

I look upon military assistance to our allies as adding strength and depth to the military posture of the United States. It enables our allies to organize, train and equip units which enhance the capability of the free world to meet the challenge of Communist aggression and subversion. No amount of money spent on our forces could give the United States a comparable asset of trained, well-equipped forces, familiar with the terrain, and in suitable position for immediate resistance to local aggression.

[General Lyman L. Lemnitzer, U.S. Army, at the time Chairman of the Joint Chiefs of Staff, testifies on the values of a civil defense program, Aug. 1, 1961:]

I shall address three aspects of the civil defense problem: First, the interrelationship between civil defense and military strength; Second, the contribution of civil defense to deterrence; and Third, the importance of both active and passive defense measures.

In regard to the interrelationship between civil defense and military strength it is important to remember that the basic objective of any nation's security policy is to protect its people. Throughout history, nations have relied on armed might as a primary means to attain such an objective. In warfare, nations almost invariably sought destruction of enemy armed forces for the purpose of forcing enemy capitulation. To facilitate defeat of enemy forces, those parts of the enemy's economy which provided the tools of war were also attacked. It was during World War II, for the first time, that populations, as an essential aspect of a nation's economy, were taken under attack. Today, with both range and destructiveness of weapons vastly increased, a deliberate attack on populations—or a threat of such an attack—might well become the primary means selected by an aggressor to force surrender of his victim. Even if civilian populations were not primary targets, the inadvertent or incidental loss of life among noncombatants in a general war as the result of fallout could achieve unprecedented proportions. Thus, today, all who are charged with national security responsibilities, must give close attention to one of the most elemental of our security objectives—preserving the lives of our people.

There is a very important way in which an effective civil defense program would support our military capabilities. Ultimate victory or defeat in general war would depend upon our ability to recover from the effect of nuclear attack and to conduct such operations as may be necessary to lead to a successful termination of hostilities.

As regards the contribution of civil defense to deterrence: The extent to which we have the ability to defend against an attack, particularly the initial attack, or to minimize the effects of an attack, is an essential element of our overall deterrent. Any doubt in the mind of a potential enemy with respect to his capability to deal us a decisive blow makes less likely the possibility that he will initiate a nuclear attack against us. This, then, is the important way in which civil defense contributes to deterrence. It provides further unmistakable evidence of serious determination on our part.

Finally, there is the matter of the importance of both active and passive defense measures. An active defense comprises weapons systems and allied communications and early warning systems which can, together, detect, engage, and destroy incoming enemy bombers or missiles.

By "passive measures" I mean civil defense, which is designed to reduce or minimize damage to our civilian population from enemy weapons which penetrate our active defenses. These passive measures, such as a trained population—and I wish to emphasize strongly the importance of such training—fallout shelters, properly identified and stocked, identification and warning systems, plus an effective organization for assuring adequate control, are prudent steps to take in the light of the risks our population may be exposed to. Further, Government leadership as evidenced by this program will serve as incentive for an expanding future civil defense effort.

To summarize, civil defense bears an essential relationship to military strength in assuring continued national security.

Civil defense should be considered an integral part of the overall deterrence.

Finally, the civil defense program presented to you today will serve effectively to complement our active military defense measures and thus provide additional protection to the American people against the dangers of nuclear attack upon this country.

[General Arthur G. Trudeau, Chief of Research and Development, Department of the Army, testifies with especial relation to space programs:]

I should like to emphasize here that the sum total of our research and development programs must contribute to our national objectives of countering any real and serious threat to our Nation. This includes programs that utilize the space environment. Let me underscore the phrase "space environment."

The Armed Forces have roles and missions to perform requiring operations in or on the long-established media of land, sea, and air. Now we have a new environment—space—erroneously considered by some to be a completely separate entity and as erroneously by others to be integral with the atmosphere. While a thoughtful appraisal of this situation reveals that it certainly is neither, space can be considered as a medium in which, or through which, military systems of the various services can operate to achieve military objectives in support of currently assigned roles and missions. Thus, space is not to be considered unique as the exclusive territory of operations of a particular service, but it is indeed a most useful and potent new environment to better support recognized military missions for each and all services. . . .

There also seems to be confusion about the distinction between near space and deep space. They are not in the same category at all. Near space is of utmost importance to us now, as we strive to solve the problem of operating vehicles—satellites at the present time—in this strange environment. And these satellites will eventually become components of a system based on Earth to assist us to better support our assigned missions. Communications, detection of ICBM's and geodesy are examples of a few of these conventional missions.

Deep space has little bearing now on our primary objectives for national security. Interplanetary travel, for instance, may uncover a host of new requirements for the military, but at this time it should be viewed from a total long-range defense outlook, not from the standpoint of individual service roles and missions. . . . Again, I come back to the necessity of an integrated defense effort for military space investigations so that we will be prepared for the surprises that await us whenever we deal with the unknown.

[The question of whether American aid should go only to democracies was discussed on June 15, 1961, by Phillips Talbot, Assistant Secretary of State for Near Eastern and South Asian Affairs, Senator Lausche, Chairman J. W. Fulbright of the Senate Foreign Relations Committee, and Admiral Grantham, Director, Near East, South Asia, and African Region, Office of Assistant Secretary of Defense.]

SENATOR LAUSCHE. Should we adopt a policy that we will, in all circumstances, help only the democracies, and that we will separate ourselves fully from the dictatorships?

MR. TALBOT. Well, sir, I found it in Asia very difficult to distinguish between what we would regard as a pure democracy or what we would regard as a pure dictatorship.

The countries which are most effectively governed in Asia these days are those that have strong leadership. Whether the leader is Jawaharlal Nehru who, by his personality and force and conviction in the country mobilizes enough political opinion so that he can act in many ways more or less as he wishes to, or whether the leader has come up through the military ranks, it seems to me that there is a key point here as to whether there is evidence of public consent and support of a government.

When that public consent and support begins to disintegrate, then it seems to me that a country is in trouble, and our relationship to the governing group needs reexamination quite extensively.

SENATOR LAUSCHE. I will just give you my opinion. I do not think we are in a position any longer where we can choose only democracies. We have tried to impose democracy upon people who are utterly unfit to exercise democracy. To be brief in answer to my own question, I would say that if

South Korea, as a democracy, was a worthy ally it does not follow that when it becomes a dictatorship such as it is now, it is utterly and absolutely worthless to us.

CHAIRMAN J. W. FULBRIGHT. I would agree with that, Senator, as a proposition. But we profess all the criticism of countries which are not being democratic.

The point I was trying to make is that this military program makes it very difficult to maintain political democracy if we profess that as our objective. Maybe we ought to straighten out our approach.

SENATOR GORE. [Deleted.]

ADMIRAL GRANTHAM. May I make a comment on that? . . . Senator Gore's premise is that military assistance is responsible for the development of military dictatorships. It is not necessarily true, sir.

You might have the same development in the total absence of any military assistance from the United States.

The United Nations

With the growth of the United Nations from fifty-one to more than a hundred members, the increasing influence of developing countries, and the unceasing lacerations of foreign-policy problems, there has come continuing questioning of the point of the United Nations. Thus, on one occasion the press carried a full-page advertisement asking readers to contribute money to support the distribution of a report telling of the atrocities of the United Nations forces in the Congo; accompanying the advertisement were photographs of dead children, "victims of the war." Another form of the criticism of the United Nations was the action of the mayor of Northampton, Massachusetts, in ordering the lowering of the United Nations flag from the front of the City Hall. His reasons: the United Nations has given the United States nothing but the Korean war, large debts, an eroded currency, and an uneasy peace.

Other views of the United Nations are set forth in the following excerpts from statements by American political leaders.

[Dean Rusk, Secretary of State, testifies at hearings before the Senate Committee on Foreign Relations, Feb. 6, 1962:]

We cannot too often recall the purposes of the United Nations, as set forth in the preamble to the charter:

to save succeeding generations from the scourge of war . . .
to reaffirm faith in fundamental human rights . . .
to establish conditions under which justice and respect for the obligations arising from treaties and other sources of international law can be maintained . . .
to promote social progress and better standards of life in larger freedom

Peace. Human dignity. The rights of the individual. The rule of law. Social well-being in larger freedom. These are the purposes of the United Nations.

They are not, of course, specifications for institutional machinery. They do not add up to a blueprint or a master plan for resolving all the inherited quarrels and sins of the centuries. Much less do these words provide any way to predict future problems or solve them automatically when they arise.

The preamble to the charter of the United Nations is simply a statement of goals derived from the idea that man is born free, capable of exerting conscious thought and free will toward the mastery of his physical and social environment.

That being said, it is true that we live in a world in which nobility of purpose is not yet the determinant factor in world affairs. It therefore is in the context of an imperfect real world that we must assess the relevance and utility of the United Nations to U.S. foreign policy.

[Adlai E. Stevenson, United States Representative to the United Nations, testifies at hearings before the Senate Committee on Foreign Relations, Feb. 7, 1962:]

. . . the United Nations in terms of our foreign policy is, to begin with, a standard—a statement of the basic aims which the United States holds in common with most of the nations of the world—however much we may differ with some of these nations on other questions. . . .

Secondly, the United Nations is itself one means for carrying those aims into effect. It is not the sole means. Indeed, the Charter itself is full of references to others. Article 33 calls for bilateral negotiation, arbitration, judicial settlement, and so forth, as the first obligation of nations involved in a dispute.

Article 51 safeguards the inherent right of nations to individual and collective self-defense. Articles 52 and 54 deal with regional arrangements. Similarly the articles dealing with economic and social matters, and with the administration of non-self-governing territories, constitute among other things pledges by the members themselves, simply as individual signatories of the Charter, to follow certain standards of conduct and to promote certain aims.

But the United Nations organization is the instrument specifically created to work full time for the achievement of the Charter's purposes. The General Assembly, the Security Council, the Economic and Social Council, the Trusteeship Council, the Secretariat, and the International Court of Justice—these basic organs and their various subsidiary bodies are designed for those purposes and no other.

[Senator Henry M. Jackson, "The United States in the U.N.: an Independent Audit," Address before the National Press Club, Mar. 20, 1962, *Congressional Record,* Mar. 21, 1962, pp. 4277–4278.]

The United Nations is, and should continue to be, an important avenue of American foreign policy. Yet practices have developed which, I believe, lead to an undue influence of U.N. considerations in our national decisionmaking. Indeed it is necessary to ask whether the involvement of the U.N. in our policymaking has not at times hampered the wise definition of our national interests and the development of sound policies for their advancement.

The test of the national security policy process is this: Does it identify our vital interests and does it develop foreign and defense policies which will defend and promote these interests? In our system, two men must bear the heaviest responsibility for giving our national security policy focus and structure. One is, of course, the President. The other is his first adviser, the Secretary of State.

The United Nations is not, and was never intended to be, a substitute for our own leaders as makers and movers of American policy. The shoulders of the Secretary General were never expected to carry the burdens of the President or the Secretary of State. But do we sometimes act as though we could somehow subcontract to the U.N. the responsibility for national decisionmaking?

At the founding of the United Nations there was the hope that all its members shared a common purpose—the search for a lasting peace. This hope was dashed. . . .

We must realize that the Soviet Union sees the U.N. not as a forum of cooperation, but as one more arena of struggle.

The maintenance of peace depends not on the United Nations as an organization but on the strength and will of its members to uphold the charter.

The truth is, although we have not often spoken it in recent years, that the best hope for peace with justice does not lie in the United Nations. Indeed, the truth is almost exactly the reverse. The best hope for the United Nations lies in the maintenance of peace. In our deeply divided world, peace depends on the power and unity of the Atlantic community and on the skill of our direct diplomacy.

In this light, some basic questions need to be asked:

First, are we taking an exaggerated view of the U.N.'s role?

In one way and another the conduct of U.N. affairs absorbs a disproportionate amount of the energy of our highest officials. . . .

The Secretary of State has called the United Nations a forum in which almost every aspect of our foreign policy comes up. The fact is correctly stated, but does it reflect a desirable state of affairs? Should we take a more restricted view of the organization's capacity for helpfulness?

I think we should. The cold war may destroy the United Nations, if that organization becomes one of its main battlegrounds, but the United Nations cannot put an end to the cold war.

As a general rule, might it be more prudent, though less dramatic, not to push the U.N. into the fireman's suit unless we are sure the alternatives are worse and, above all, that we are not seeking to evade our own responsibilities?

I believe the United Nations can best gain stature and respect by undertaking tasks which are within its capabilities, and that its usefulness will be diminished if it is impelled into one cold war crisis after another and asked to shoulder responsibilities it cannot meet. . . .

Second, may not the most useful function of the United Nations lie in serving as a link between the West and the newly independent states?

Most international business is best handled through normal bilateral contacts or through regional arrangements among the states concerned.

However, the United Nations provides a useful meeting ground for many new governments with other governments. These relationships may be of mutual benefit.

The U.N. affords good opportunities to explain Western policies, to correct misrepresentations of the Western position, and to expose the weaknesses in the Soviet line. In fact, the Soviet singing commercials themselves offend the most hardened ear. They inspire a healthy skepticism about Russian three-way cold war pills—guaranteed to end the arms race, relieve colonial oppression, and ease poverty, if taken regularly, as directed.

The U.N. and its specialized agencies may be of great usefulness in supplying technical assistance for economic development, in providing financial aid, and in preparing international development programs.

The organization may sometimes be helpful in reaching peaceful settlements of certain issues and disputes of concern to the newly independent States—especially if it is used to seek out areas of agreement rather than to dramatize conflicts of interest.

In this connection there has been too great a tendency to bring every issue to a vote. Indeed, there are too many votes on too many issues in the U.N.—and too much of the time and energy of every delegation is spent in lobbying for votes.

A vote requires a division of the house, a sharpening and even an exaggeration of points at issue, and it emphasizes the division of opinion rather than the area of agreement. Not every discussion needs to end in a vote. The purposes of the members might be better served if the U.N. forum becomes more often a place where diplomatic representatives quietly search for acceptable settlements of issues between their countries. . . .

Third, in our approach to the U.N., do we make too much of the talk and too little of the deed?

New York City is the foremost communications center of the United States, if not of the world. Once the decision was made to locate the headquarters of the United Nations in New York, it was inevitable that what went on there would receive attention disproportionate to its significance. Newsmen and photographers have to produce news stories and pictures, and politicians from any land rival the celebrities of stage and screen in their hunger for free publicity. . . .

If the U.N. were used less for drumbeating on every nerve-tingling issue, and if its energies were quietly devoted to manageable problems, there might be fewer headlines from the U.N. but more contributions to the building of a peaceful world.

Everyone talks too much. It is a world-wide disease. Sometimes it seems that the appropriate legend to place above the portals of the U.N. might be:

"Through these doors pass the most articulate men and women in the world.". . .

The effect of decisions on something called our relations in the U.N. may receive more weight than their effect on, say, the strength and unity of the Atlantic community. The result may be a weakening or dilution of policy positions in deference to what is represented in New York as world opinion.

The concept of world opinion has been, I fear, much abused. Whatever it is and whatever the importance that should be attached to it, I doubt that it can be measured by taking the temperature of the General Assembly or successfully cultivated primarily by currying favor in New York. To hide behind something called world opinion is all too often the device of the timid, or the last resort of someone who has run out of arguments. . . .

I close as I began: The United Nations is, and should continue to be, an important avenue of American foreign policy. But we need to revise our attitudes in the direction of a more realistic appreciation of its limitations, more modest hopes for its accomplishments, and a more mature sense of the burdens of responsible leadership.

[During a news conference (Mar. 21, 1962), a reporter asked President Kennedy for his view on Senator Jackson's alleged point that "this Administration and the last have been putting too much stock in the United Nations" and that "a strong Atlantic community" offered the best avenue to peace. The President replied:]

I see nothing contradictory in a strong Atlantic community and the United Nations. Nor is there anything contradictory in a strong Organization of American States and the United Nations.

In fact, the United Nations in—when it was written in 1945, gave room for these regional organizations of which there are a great many and of which the United States is a member.

I support the United Nations very strongly and I think the American people do—not because its power is unlimited and not because we commit our policy to the United Nations so much as because we believe that it serves the interests of the United States, and the interests of the United States are in an association of free people working together to maintain the peace.

Now I would be very unhappy if the United Nations were weakened or eliminated. You would have a great increase in the chances of a direct concentration in some place—like the Congo—between the great powers. It might involve the United States directly, and perhaps the Soviet Union on the other side. The United Nations serves as a means of channeling these matters, on which we disagree so basically, in a peaceful way.

But that doesn't suggest that we have to choose between the Atlantic community and the United Nations.

We believe in the Atlantic community. We are committed to strengthening it. We are attempting, for example, in a number of ways—and in fact our association is constantly growing more intimate, and we also support the United Nations.

Senator Jackson is a very valuable Senator. He's done very effective work and anything that he says deserves a good deal of attention.

I do want to point out that on this matter, certainly, there's no disagreement between us.

[Senator Jacob Javits commented on Senator Jackson's speech, *Congressional Record,* Mar. 21, 1962, pp. 4278–4279.]

. . . it does seem to me that a speech of this character, the key to which is, let us not rely too heavily on the U.N., is unfortunate. . . .

I do not believe it is necessary that we should try to relegate the U.N. to second place and say that we are going to rely primarily in first place on our military alliances. It is unfortunate, therefore, that this speech should concern itself with the supposition that we are placing too much reliance on the U.N.

I refer now to two speeches which were made in the great bipartisan tradition of our country, by President Eisenhower and President Kennedy, both of whom addressed themselves specifically to the same subject to which the Senator from Washington addressed himself. President Eisenhower, in a speech to the U.N. General Assembly, said:

> The first proposition I place before you is that only through the United Nations organization can humanity make real and universal progress toward the goal of peace with justice. I believe that to support the United Nations organization and its properly constituted mechanisms and selected officers is the road of greatest promise in peaceful progress. To attempt to hinder or stultify the United Nations or to deprecate its importance is to contribute to world unrest and, indeed, to incite the crises that from time to time so disturb all men. The United States stands squarely and unequivocally in support of the United Nations and those acting under its mandate in the interest of peace.

In almost the same historic commitment, just about 1 year later, on September 21, 1961, President Kennedy, also addressing the U.N., said:

> That is why my Nation—which has freely shared its capital and its technology to help others help themselves—now proposes officially designating this decade of the 1960's as the United Nations decade of development.

. . . Senator Jackson's speech is a provocative and thoughtful one. . . . The difficulty, however, that I find with the speech is that it is likely to be taken in the context of today as a depreciation of the importance of the United Nations as a world force. I believe it would be most unfortunate if we were to try to assign number one importance or number two importance to it, because the fact is that the U.N. is the world forum which is the world's great hope for peace.

Again, it is not necessary to say that it should be secondary to our alliances, upon which we will primarily rely. The fact is that our alliances are there, and they are important and we do rely on them. I yield to no one in my support of NATO, and everything that that support means, including economic and other forms of cooperation. But it is not necessary to apply to NATO a number one or a number two label—or to the U.N. either. The U.N., I say, can stand on its own. We have every interest in supporting it strongly.

It would be most unfortunate if the Russians should get the idea that the U.N. was to be written down somewhat in importance in this country, and that thereby the door would be opened for them to step in, because the Russians would gladly, I believe, take over the role of preeminence in the U.N. held by the United States. . . .

By placing the U.N. in the frame of reference of its world importance of maintaining the peace we enable it to stand on its own, we respect fully the historic pledges of support we have made to it, and we give the proper assurance of substance and authority to the many nations—especially the newer and smaller nations—to which the U.N. represents their major participation in world affairs.

[Senator Thomas J. Dodd commented on the United Nations, *Congressional Record,* Mar. 22, 1962, p. 4425.]

It is understandable, Mr. President, that the Western Nations should be worried over the present situation in the General Assembly, and even more worried over the prospect for the immediate future. It is understandable that doubts should now be expressed about a voting procedure that gives an African nation of 500,000, still emerging from tribalism, precisely the same vote as the United States and the Soviet Union. In this grotesque United Nations calculus, one African bushman becomes the equivalent of 100 Frenchmen or 400 Americans. And although many plans have been advanced for weighting votes by population and other factors, there is not the remotest chance that the jealous, sensitive nations of Asia, Africa, and Latin America will agree to anything less than the present formula of "one nation, one vote." . . .

[Richard N. Gardner, Deputy Assistant Secretary of State for International Organization Affairs, testified at hearings before the Senate Committee on Foreign Relations, Feb. 19, 1962.]

The question was asked, Mr. Chairman, about the Soviet position on the United Nations, whether it really wants to make the United Nations succeed. I think the answer to that would have to take account of the fact that the United Nations is in fact three things—a place for debate, a place for negotiation, and a place for action. Even in his speech attacking the United Nations 2 years ago, Mr. Khrushchev said that as far as the Soviet Union was concerned, the first two functions were perfectly valid; that is, he supported the United Nations as a place for debate and as a place for negotiation. What he objected to was the third function of the United Nations, the role of the United Nations as an action agency.

I think this is precisely the issue—that the Soviet Union does not want the United Nations to do things, either in the field of economic developmeant or in keeping the peace, whereas the United States does.

We feel that the capacity of the United Nations to act serves the national interest of the United States, and the cause of freedom around the world.

C. SOVIET-CHINESE-AMERICAN IDEAS AND RELATIONS

Lenin on State and Revolution

When the eleven American Communist Party leaders were brought to trial for violating the Smith Act by conspiring to teach and to advocate the violent overthrow of the American government, they were convicted after the lengthy prosecution in what is known as the Dennis case. The doctrine with which the Communist leaders were concerned was contained chiefly in four books: the *Communist Manifesto,* by Marx and Engels (1848), *State and Revolution* (1917), *Foundations of Leninism* (1924), and *History of the Communist Party of the Soviet Union* (1939).

In his dissenting opinion in the Dennis case, Justice Douglas said: "Those books are to Soviet Communism what *Mein Kampf* was to Nazism. If they are understood, the ugliness of Communism is revealed, its deceit and cunning are exposed, the nature of its activities becomes apparent, and the chances of its success less likely. That is not, of course, the reason why petitioners chose these books for their classrooms. They are fervent Communists to whom these volumes are gospel. They preached the creed with the hope that some day it would be acted upon."

Lenin imputed a rather more aesthetic and valid character to his own writing than did Justice Douglas. Irritated in September 1918 at a letter published in *Pravda* by the German Marxist writer Karl Kautsky, Lenin urged the publication "as soon as possible and in German of my book *State and Revolution*" with a foreword stating that it was vital the volume appear at that moment particularly to correct Kautsky's "base social liberalism."

The student of American government and politics who reads Lenin to deepen and widen his understanding of both domestic politics and international relations encounters obstacles.

Part of the difficulty is the language and the accent. Lenin spends no little time taking pot shots at people and ideas he rejects, and does his name-calling in quite extreme style. The result for the American reader is material that is both unexpectedly and unaccustomedly personalized and abstract. Any time you get five Marxists together, you get six splinter groups and seven interpretations of Marx—provided that each is free to say what he thinks. What is more, Lenin wrote so much over so long a period of time in so sweeping a manner that he could well have stated, "I am not a Leninist," just as Marx had previously said, "I am not a Marxist," in referring to the varied interpretations of his doctrine.

In any case, the reader may attempt to judge for himself the impact of such writing as the extract below from Lenin's *State and Revolution* on Americans and on other people as well. It is easy (and correct) to point out deficiences in Lenin's theses in application to this country, such as: a great pile of evidence substantiates the conclusion that the state Americans know is an instrument of conciliation, not oppression; the lot of the submerged many has been improving, not deteriorating; Americans have been utilizing instruments alternative to violent revolution to effect basic social and economic changes, despite the Leninist assumption that the power holders will never let go peacefully; "dictatorship of the proletariat" is far more accurately "dictatorship over the proletariat"; the modern state expands in size and scope, nowhere does it wither away.

What remains for explanation is the meaning and ramifications of the fact that in about half the human race what appears below is taken as insightful political analysis. Lenin has been called "the most influential man in human history since Jesus Christ and Julius Caesar," and Mao Tse-tung has talked reverentially of "the universal truth of Marxism-Leninism which is applicable everywhere" and how in consequence "the face of China changed."

[V. I. Lenin, *State and Revolution,* 1917, chap. 1.]

1. *The State as the Product of the Irreconcilability of Class Antagonisms*

What is now happening to Marx's doctrine has, in the course of history, often happened to the doctrines of other revolutionary thinkers and leaders of oppressed classes struggling for emancipation. During the lifetime of great revolutionaries, the oppressing classes have visited relentless persecution on them and received their teaching with the most savage hostility, the most furious hatred, the most ruthless campaign of lies and slanders. After their death, attempts are made to turn them into harmless icons, canonise them, and surround their names with a certain halo for the "consolation" of the oppressed classes and with the object of duping them, while at the same time emasculating and vulgarising the real essence of their revolutionary theories and blunting their revolutionary edge. At the present time, the bourgeoisie and the opportunists within the labour movement are co-operating in this work of adulterating Marxism. They omit, obliterate, and distort the revolutionary side of its teaching, its revolutionary soul. They push to the foreground and extol what is, or seems, acceptable to the bourgeoisie. All the social-chauvinists are now "Marxists"—joking aside! And more and more do German bourgeois professors, erstwhile specialists in the demolition of Marx, speak now of the "national-German" Marx, who, they aver, has educated the labour unions which are so splendidly organised for conducting the present predatory war!

In such circumstances, the distortion of Marxism being so widespread, it is our first task to resuscitate the real teachings of Marx on the state. For this purpose it will be necessary to quote at length from the works of Marx and Engels themselves. Of course, long quotations will make the text cumbersome and in no way help to make it popular reading, but we cannot possibly avoid them. All, or at any rate, all the most essential passages in the works of Marx and Engels on the subject of the state must necessarily be given as fully as possible, in order that the reader may form an independent opinion of all the views of the founders of scientific Socialism and of the development of those views, and in order that their distortions by the present predominant "Kautskyism" may be proved in black and white and rendered plain to all.

Let us begin with the most popular of Engels' works, *Der Ursprung der Familie, des Privateigentums und des Staats,* the sixth edition of which was published in Stuttgart as far back as 1894. We must translate the quotations from the German originals, as the Russian translations, although very numerous, are for the most part either incomplete or very unsatisfactory.

Summarising his historical analysis Engels says:

> The state is therefore by no means a power imposed on society from the outside; just as little is it "the reality of the moral idea," "the image and reality of reason," as Hegel asserted. Rather, it is a product of a society at a certain stage of development; it is the admission that this society has become entangled in an insoluble contradiction with itself, that it is cleft into irreconcilable antagonisms which it is powerless to dispel. But in order that these antagonisms, classes with conflicting economic interests, may not consume themselves and society in sterile struggle, a power apparently standing above society becomes necessary, whose purpose is to moderate the conflict and keep it within the bounds of "order"; and this power arising out of society, but placing itself above it, and increasingly separating itself from it, is the state.

Here we have, expressed in all its clearness, the basic idea of Marxism on the question of the historical role and meaning of the state. The state is the product and the manifestation of the irreconcilability of class antagonisms. The state arises when, where, and to the extent that the class antagonisms cannot be objectively reconciled. And, conversely, the existence of the state proves that the class antagonisms are irreconcilable.

It is precisely on this most important and fundamental point that distortions of Marxism arise along two main lines.

On the one hand, the bourgeois, and particularly the petty-bourgeois, ideologists, compelled under the pressure of indisputable historical facts to admit that the state only exists where there are class antagonisms and the class struggle, "correct" Marx in such a way as to make it appear that the state is an organ for reconciling the classes. According to Marx, the state could neither arise nor maintain itself if a reconciliation of classes were possible. But with the petty-bourgeois and philistine professors and publicists, the state—and this frequently on the strength of benevolent references to Marx!—becomes a conciliator of the classes. According to

Marx, the state is an organ of class domination, an organ of oppression of one class by another; its aim is the creation of "order" which legalises and perpetuates this oppression by moderating the collisions between the classes. But in the opinion of the petty-bourgeois politicians, order means reconciliation of the classes, and not oppression of one class by another; to moderate collisions does not mean, they say, to deprive the oppressed classes of certain definite means and methods of struggle for overthrowing the oppressors, but to practice reconciliation.

For instance, when, in the Revolution of 1917, the question of the real meaning and role of the state arose in all its vastness as a practical question demanding immediate action on a wide mass scale, all the Socialist-Revolutionaries and Mensheviks suddenly and completely sank to the petty-bourgeois theory of "reconciliation" of the classes by the "state." Innumerable resolutions and articles by politicians of both these parties are saturated through and through with this purely petty-bourgeois and philistine theory of "reconciliation." That the state is an organ of domination of a definite class which cannot be reconciled with its antipode (the class opposed to it)—this petty-bourgeois democracy is never able to understand. Its attitude towards the state is one of the most telling proofs that our Socialist-Revolutionaries and Mensheviks are not Socialists at all (which we Bolsheviks have always maintained), but petty-bourgeois democrats with a near-Socialist phraseology.

On the other hand, the "Kautskyist" distortion of Marx is far more subtle. "Theoretically," there is no denying that the state is the organ of class domination, or that class antagonisms are irreconcilable. But what is forgotten or glossed over is this: if the state is the product of the irreconcilable character of class antagonisms, if it is a force standing above society and "increasingly separating itself from it," then it is clear that the liberation of the oppressed class is impossible not only without a violent revolution, but also without the destruction of the apparatus of state power, which was created by the ruling class and in which this "separation" is embodied. As we shall see later, Marx drew this theoretically self-evident conclusion from a concrete historical analysis of the problems of revolution. And it is exactly this conclusion which Kautsky—as we shall show fully in our subsequent remarks—has "forgotten" and distorted.

2. *Special Bodies of Armed Men, Prisons, Etc.*

Engels continues:

> In contrast with the ancient organisation of the gens, the first distinguishing characteristic of the state is the grouping of the subjects of the state on a territorial basis. . . .

Such a grouping seems "natural" to us, but it came after a prolonged and costly struggle against the old form of tribal or gentilic society.

> . . . The second is the establishment of a public force, which is no longer absolutely identical with the population organising itself as an armed power. This special public force is necessary, because a self-acting armed organisa-

> tion of the population has become impossible since the cleavage of society into classes. . . . This public force exists in every state; it consists not merely of armed men, but of material appendages, prisons and repressive institutions of all kinds, of which gentilic society knew nothing. . . .

Engels develops the conception of that "power" which is termed the state —a power arising from society, but placing itself above it and becoming more and more separated from it. What does this power mainly consist of? It consists of special bodies of armed men who have at their disposal prisons, etc.

We are justified in speaking of special bodies of armed men, because the public power peculiar to every state is not "absolutely identical" with the armed population, with its "self-acting armed organisation."

Like all the great revolutionary thinkers, Engels tries to draw the attention of the class-conscious workers to that very fact which to prevailing philistinism appears least of all worthy of attention, most common and sanctified by solid, indeed, one might say, petrified prejudices. A standing army and police are the chief instruments of state power. But can this be otherwise?

From the point of view of the vast majority of Europeans at the end of the nineteenth century whom Engels was addressing, and who had neither lived through nor closely observed a single great revolution, this cannot be otherwise. They cannot understand at all what this "self-acting armed organisation of the population" means. To the question, whence arose the need for special bodies of armed men, standing above society and becoming separated from it (police and standing army), the Western European and Russian philistines are inclined to answer with a few phrases borrowed from Spencer or Mikhailovsky, by reference to the complexity of social life, the differentiation of functions, and so forth.

Such a reference seems "scientific" and effectively dulls the senses of the average man, obscuring the most important and basic fact, namely, the break-up of society into irreconcilably antagonistic classes.

Without such a break-up, the "self-acting armed organisation of the population" might have differed from the primitive organisation of a herd of monkeys grasping sticks, or of primitive men, or men united in a tribal form of society, by its complexity, its high technique, and so forth, but would still have been possible.

It is impossible now, because society, in the period of civilisation, is broken up into antagonistic and, indeed, irreconcilably antagonistic classes, which, if armed in a "self-acting" manner, would come into armed struggle with each other. A state is formed, a special power is created in the form of special bodies of armed men, and every revolution, by shattering the state apparatus, demonstrates to us how the ruling class aims at the restoration of the special bodies of armed men at its service, and how the oppressed class tries to create a new organisation of this kind, capable of serving not the exploiters, but the exploited.

In the above observation, Engels raises theoretically the very same question which every great revolution raises practically, palpably, and on a mass scale of action, namely, the question of the relation between special bodies of armed men and the "self-acting armed organisation of the population." We shall see how this is concretely illustrated by the experience of the European and Russian revolutions.

But let us return to Engels' discourse.

He points out that sometimes, for instance, here and there in North America, this public power is weak (he has in mind an exception that is rare in capitalist society, and he speaks about parts of North America in its pre-imperialist days, where the free colonist predominated), but that in general it tends to become stronger:

> It [the public power] grows stronger, however, in proportion as the class antagonisms within the state grow sharper, and with the growth in size and population of the adjacent states. We have only to look at our present-day Europe, where class struggle and rivalry in conquest have screwed up the public power to such a pitch that it threatens to devour the whole of society and even the state itself.

This was written as early as the beginning of the nineties of last century, Engels' last preface being dated June 16, 1891. The turn towards imperialism, understood to mean complete domination of the trusts, full sway of the large banks, and a colonial policy on a grand scale, and so forth, was only just beginning in France, and was even weaker in North America and in Germany. Since then the "rivalry in conquest" has made gigantic progress—especially as, by the beginning of the second decade of the twentieth century, the whole world had been finally divided up between these "rivals in conquest," i.e., between the great predatory powers. Military and naval armaments since then have grown to monstrous proportions, and the predatory war of 1914–1917 for the domination of the world by England or Germany, for the division of the spoils, has brought the "swallowing up" of all the forces of society by the rapacious state power nearer to a complete catastrophe.

As early as 1891 Engels was able to point to "rivalry in conquest" as one of the most important features of the foreign policy of the great power, but in 1914–1917, when this rivalry, many times intensified, has given birth to an imperialist war, the rascally social-chauvinists cover up their defence of the predatory policy of "their" capitalist classes by phrases about the "defence of the fatherland," or the "defence of the republic and the revolution," etc.!

3. *The State as an Instrument for the Exploitation of the Oppressed Class*

For the maintenance of a special public force standing above society, taxes and state loans are needed.

> Having at their disposal the public force and the right to exact taxes, the officials now stand as organs of society above society. The free, voluntary respect which was accorded to the organs of the gentilic form of government does not satisfy them, even if they could have it. . . .

Special laws are enacted regarding the sanctity and the inviolability of the officials. "The shabbiest police servant . . . has more authority" than the representative of the clan, but even the head of the military power of a civilised state "may well envy the least among the chiefs of the clan the unconstrained and uncontested respect which is paid to him."

Here the question regarding the privileged position of the officials as organs of state power is clearly stated. The main point is indicated as follows: what is it that places them above society? We shall see how this theoretical problem was solved in practice by the Paris Commune in 1871 and how it was slurred over in a reactionary manner by Kautsky in 1912.

> As the state arose out of the need to hold class antagonisms in check; but as it, at the same time, arose in the midst of the conflict of these classes, it is, as a rule, the state of the most powerful, economically dominant class, which by virtue thereof becomes also the dominant class politically, and thus acquires new means of holding down and exploiting the oppressed classes. . . .

Not only the ancient and feudal states were organs of exploitation of the slaves and serfs, but the modern representative state is the instrument of the exploitation of wage labour capital. By way of exception, however, there are periods when the warring classes so nearly attain equilibrium that the state power, ostensibly appearing as a mediator, assumes for the moment a certain independence in relation to both. . . .

Such were, for instance, the absolute monarchies of the seventeenth and eighteenth centuries, the Bonapartism of the First and Second Empires in France, and the Bismarck regime in Germany.

Such, we may add, is now the Kerensky government in republican Russia after its shift to persecuting the revolutionary proletariat, at a moment when the Soviets, thanks to the leadership of the petty-bourgeois democrats, have already become impotent, while the bourgeoisie is not yet strong enough to disperse them outright.

In a democratic republic, Engels continues, "wealth wields its power indirectly, but all the more effectively," first, by means of "direct corruption of the government with the stock exchange" (France and America). . . .

We must also note that Engels quite definitely regards universal suffrage as a means of bourgeois domination. Universal suffrage, he says, obviously summing up the long experience of German Social-Democracy, is "an index of the maturity of the working class; it cannot, and never will, be anything else but that in the modern state."

The petty-bourgeois democrats, such as our Socialist-Revolutionaries and Mensheviks, and also their twin brothers, the social-chauvinists and opportunists of Western Europe, all expect "more" from universal suffrage. They themselves share, and instill into the minds of the people, the wrong idea that universal suffrage "in the modern state" is really capable of expressing the will of the majority of the toilers and of assuring its realisation.

We can here only note this wrong idea, only point out that this perfectly clear, exact and concrete statement by Engels is distorted at every step in the propaganda and agitation of the "official" (i.e., opportunist) Socialist parties. . . .

A general summary of his views is given by Engels in the most popular of his works in the following words:

> The state, therefore, has not existed from all eternity. There have been societies which managed without it, which had no conception of the state

> and state power. At a certain stage of economic development, which was necessarily bound up with the cleavage of society into classes, the state became a necessity owing to this cleavage. We are now rapidly approaching a stage in the development of production at which the existence of these classes has not only ceased to be a necessity, but is becoming a positive hindrance to production. They will disappear as inevitably as they arose at an earlier stage. Along with them, the state will inevitably disappear. The society that organises production anew on the basis of a free and equal association of the producers will put the whole state machine where it will then belong: in the museum of antiquities, side by side with the spinning wheel and the bronze axe.

It is not often that we find this passage quoted in the propaganda and agitation literature of contemporary Social-Democracy. But even when we do come across it, it is generally quoted in the same manner as one bows before an icon, i.e., it is done merely to show official respect for Engels, without any attempt to gauge the breadth and depth of revolutionary action presupposed by this relegating of "the whole state machine . . . to the museum of antiquities." In most cases we do not even find an understanding of what Engels calls the state machine.

4. *The "Withering Away" of the State and Violent Revolution*

Engels' words regarding the "withering away" of the state enjoy such popularity, they are so often quoted, and they show so clearly the essence of the usual adulteration by means of which Marxism is made to look like opportunism, that we must dwell on them in detail. Let us quote the whole passage from which they are taken.

> The proletariat seizes state power, and then transforms the means of production into state property. But in doing this, it puts an end to itself as the proletariat, it puts an end to all class differences and class antagonisms, it puts an end also to the state as the state. Former society, moving in class antagonisms, had need of the state, that is, an organisation of the exploiting class at each period for the maintenance of its external conditions of production; therefore, in particular, for the forcible holding down of the exploited class in the conditions of oppression (slavery, bondage or serfdom, wage-labour) determined by the existing mode of production. The state was the official representative of society as a whole, its embodiment in a visible corporate body; but it was this only insofar as it was the state of that class which itself, in its epoch, represented society as a whole: in ancient times, the state of the slave-owning citizens; in the Middle Ages, of the feudal nobility; in our epoch, of the bourgeoisie. When ultimately it becomes really representative of society as a whole, it makes itself superfluous. As soon as there is no longer any class of society to be held in subjection; as soon as, along with class domination and the struggle for individual existence based on the former anarchy of production, the collisions and excesses arising from these have also been abolished, there is nothing more to be repressed, and a special repressive force, a state, is no longer necessary. The first act in which the state really comes forward as the representative of society as

a whole—the seizure of the means of production in the name of society—is at the same time its last independent act as a state. The interference of a state power in social relations becomes superfluous in one sphere after another, and then becomes dormant of itself. Government over persons is replaced by the administration of things and the direction of the processes of production. The state is not "abolished," it withers away. It is from this standpoint that we must appraise the phrase "people's free state"—both its justification at times for agitational purposes, and its ultimate scientific inadequacy—and also the demand of the so-called Anarchists that the state should be abolished overnight.

Without fear of committing an error, it may be said that of this argument by Engels so singularly rich in ideas, only one point has become an integral part of Socialist thought among modern Socialist parties, namely, that, unlike the Anarchist doctrine of the "abolition" of the state, according to Marx the state "withers away." To emasculate Marxism in such a manner is to reduce it to opportunism, for such an "interpretation" only leaves the hazy conception of a slow, even, gradual change, free from leaps and storms, free from revolution. The current popular conception, if one may say so, of the "withering away" of the state undoubtedly means a slurring over, if not a negation, or revolution.

Yet, such an "interpretation" is the crudest distortion of Marxism, which is advantageous only to the bourgeoisie; in point of theory, it is based on a disregard for the most important circumstances and considerations pointed out in the very passage summarising Engels' ideas, which we have just quoted in full.

In the first place, Engels at the very outset of his argument says that, in assuming state power, the proletariat by that very act "puts an end to the state as the state." One is "not accustomed" to reflect on what this really means. Generally, it is either ignored altogether, or it is considered as a piece of "Hegelian weakness" on Engels' part. As a matter of fact, however, these words express succinctly the experience of one of the greatest proletarian revolutions—the Paris Commune of 1871, of which we shall speak in greater detail in its proper place. As a matter of fact, Engels speaks here of the destruction of the bourgeois state by the proletarian revolution, while the words about its withering away refer to the remains of proletarian statehood after the Socialist revolution. The bourgeois state does not "wither away," according to Engels, but is "put an end to" by the proletariat in the course of the revolution. What withers away after the revolution is the proletarian state or semistate.

Secondly, the state is a "special repressive force." This splendid and extremely profound definition of Engels' is given by him here with complete lucidity. It follows from this that the "special repressive force" of the bourgeoisie for the suppression of the proletariat, of the millions of workers by a handful of the rich, must be replaced by a "special repressive force" of the proletariat for the suppression of the bourgeoisie (the dictatorship of the proletariat). It is just this that constitutes the destruction of "the state as the state." It is just this that constitutes the "act" of "the seizure of the means of production in the name of society." And it is obvious that such a substitution of one (proletarian) "special repressive force" for another (bourgeois) "special repressive force" can in no way take place in the form of a "withering away."

Thirdly, as to the "withering away" or, more expressively and colourfully, as to the state "becoming dormant," Engels refers quite clearly and definitely to the period after "the seizure of the means of production (by the state) in the name of society," that is, after the Socialist revolution. We all know that the political form of the "state" at that time is complete democracy. But it never enters the head of any of the opportunists who shamelessly distort Marx that when Engels speaks here of the state "withering away," or "becoming dormant," he speaks of democracy. At first sight this seems very strange. But it is "unintelligible" only to one who has not reflected on the fact that democracy is also a state and that, consequently, democracy will also disappear when the state disappears. The bourgeois state can only be "put an end to" by a revolution. The state in general, i.e., most complete democracy, can only "wither away."

Fourthly, having formulated his famous proposition that "the state withers away," Engels at once explains concretely that this proposition is directed equally against the opportunists and the Anarchists. In doing this, however, Engels puts in the first place that conclusion from his proposition about the "withering away" of the state which is directed against the opportunists.

One can wager that out of every 10,000 persons who have read or heard about the "withering away" of the state, 9,990 do not know at all, or do not remember, that Engels did not direct his conclusions from this proposition against the Anarchists alone. And out of the remaining ten, probably nine do not know the meaning of a "people's free state" nor the reason why an attack on this watchword contains an attack on the opportunists. This is how history is written! This is how a great revolutionary doctrine is imperceptibly adulterated and adapted to current philistinism! The conclusion drawn against the Anarchists has been repeated thousands of times, vulgarised, harangued about in the crudest fashion possible until it has acquired the strength of a prejudice, whereas the conclusion drawn against the opportunists has been hushed up and "forgotten"!

. . . We are in favour of a democratic republic as the best form of the state for the proletariat under capitalism, but we have no right to forget that wage slavery is the lot of the people even in the most democratic bourgeois republic. Furthermore, every state is a "special repressive force" for the suppression of the oppressed class. Consequently, no state is either "free" or a "people's state." Marx and Engels explained this repeatedly to their party comrades in the seventies.

Fifthly, in the same work of Engels, from which everyone remembers his argument on the "withering away" of the state, there is also a disquisition on the significance of a violent revolution. The historical analysis of its role becomes, with Engels, a veritable panegyric on violent revolution. This, of course, "no one remembers"; to talk or even to think of the importance of this idea is not considered good form by contemporary Socialist parties, and in the daily propaganda and agitation among the masses it plays no part whatever. Yet it is indissolubly bound up with the "withering away" of the state in one harmonious whole.

Here is Engels' argument:

> . . . That force, however, plays another role (other than that of a diabolical power) in history, a revolutionary role; that, in the words of Marx, it is the midwife of every old society which is pregnant with the new; that it is the instrument with whose aid social movement forces its way through and shatters the dead, fossilised political forms—of this there is not a word in Herr Dühring. It is only with sighs and groans that he admits the possibility that force will perhaps be necessary for the overthrow of the economic system of exploitation—unfortunately! because all use of force, forsooth, demoralises the person who uses it. And this in spite of the immense moral and spiritual impetus which has resulted from every victorious revolution! And this in Germany, where a violent collision—which indeed may be forced on the people—would at least have the advantage of wiping out the servility which has permeated the national consciousness as a result of the humiliation of the Thirty Years' War. And this parson's mode of thought—lifeless, insipid and impotent—claims to impose itself on the most revolutionary party which history has known?

How can this panegyric on violent revolution, which Engels insistently brought to the attention of the German Social-Democrats between 1878 and 1894, i.e., right to the time of his death, be combined with the theory of the "withering away" of the state to form one doctrine?

Usually the two views are combined by means of eclecticism, by an unprincipled, sophistic, arbitrary selection (to oblige the powers that be) of either one or the other argument, and in ninety-nine cases out of a hundred (if not more often), it is the idea of the "withering away" that is specially emphasised. Eclecticism is substituted for dialectics—this is the most usual, the most widespread phenomenon to be met in the official Social-Democratic literature of our day in relation to Marxism. Such a substitution is, of course, nothing new; it may be observed even in the history of classic Greek philosophy. When Marxism is adulterated to become opportunism, the substitution of eclecticism for dialectics is the best method of deceiving the masses; it gives an illusory satisfaction; it seems to take into account all sides of the process, all the tendencies of development, all the contradictory factors and so forth, whereas in reality it offers no consistent and revolutionary view of the process of social development at all.

We have already said above and shall show more fully later that the teaching of Marx and Engels regarding the inevitability of a violent revolution refers to the bourgeois state. It cannot be replaced by the proletarian state (the dictatorship of the proletariat) through "withering away," but, as a general rule, only through a violent revolution. . . .

The replacement of the bourgeois by the proletarian state is impossible without a violent revolution. The abolition of the proletarian state, i.e., of all states, is only possible through "withering away."

American and Soviet Economies

This excerpt is part of a series of papers submitted by noted economists appearing before the Subcommittee on Economic Statistics of the Joint Economic Committee of the United States Congress. The Subcommittee was chaired by Congressman Richard Bolling of Missouri; the full Committee by Senator Paul H. Douglas of Illinois.

Commenting on the publications of the Subcommittee, Harry Schwartz, a major writer on the Soviet Union, described them as "the richest, systematic treasure trove of information on this subject which has become recently available in the public domain." Schwartz concluded by saying, "Some months ago a speaker at the National War College began his lecture by reminding his audience that the barbarian tribes which conquered Rome had a far smaller gross national product than did the rich, effete civilization they overcame. We need not labor the analogy, and of course our Soviet competitors are not barbarians, though there have been barbaric periods in not too distant Soviet history. I shall end by noting that the remark is a useful reminder that what is important for survival is not only the size of total production, but also the composition of that production and what it is used for."

W. W. Rostow, writer of the material below, became a special aide to President John F. Kennedy in 1961. The report is included in order to illustrate in part one of the major instruments of competition between the Soviets and the United States. Commentators have declared that the *real* struggle between the U.S.S.R. and the United States is ideological, or military, or economic, or spiritual, or any of a hundred other manifestations; actually, the struggle is total and includes every species of military and nonmilitary instrument.

[*Comparisons of the United States and Soviet Economies. Papers Submitted by Panelists Appearing before the Subcommittee on Economic Statistics, Part III,* Joint Economic Committee, Congress of the United States, Washington, D.C.: U.S. Government Printing Office, 1959, pp. 589–608.]

The fate of the United States does not depend on immutable laws of economic growth nor on the curving path of index numbers; it depends upon the actions we Americans take or fail to take; and ultimately it comes to rest on our faith in the democratic process. . . .

This paper begins with a brief summary of what the panelists have established; I shall then attempt to place their major findings in a general historical perspective; and finally, I shall try to identify what appear to me to be the real challenges which lie behind the Soviet statistics and the real implications of this study for American thought, policy, and action.

A SUMMARY OF FINDINGS

Doing some violence to the meticulously stated conclusions of the panelists, the relative position and prospects of the Soviet and American economies may be summarized as follows:

1. *Population and Working Force*

Soviet war losses and recent fertility rates set against the rise in the American birth rate have yielded over the past generation a dramatic narrowing in the relative size of the Russian and American populations. Between 1939 and 1959 the Russian margin in population size over the United States decreased from 46 to 18 percent. Although significant shifts in the structure of both populations will occur over the next decade, the gap is not likely to open significantly during this period either for the population as a whole or in those categories most relevant to economic and military activity. With respect to birth rates, there appears to be some stability in the surprisingly high American rate which emerged in the postwar decade, while there are scattered suggestions, at least, that accelerated urbanization and higher living standards may tend to depress somewhat the Soviet rate. In any case, it is important for Americans to realize that the old historic image of Russia—as a nation where the population mass was vastly greater than our own—is no longer correct. We are, roughly speaking, two nations of about the same population size. With respect to the two industrial working forces, there is a similar crude equivalence brought about despite the higher participation of females in Soviet economic activity because of the much higher proportion of the American population in nonagricultural pursuits. In attitudes toward productivity, the Soviet Union has moved away from an earlier concentration on manipulating masses of unskilled labor, in a situation of relative manpower abundance, toward a concern with productivity per man more nearly like that which has historically characterized the United States. This shift is dramatized by the reduction in the role of forced labor in the Soviet economy in recent years, and by the emphasis now placed on mechanization and automation in industry.

2. *Agriculture*

After a long period of notably sluggish productivity in agriculture, Soviet policy has moved with some success to improve incentives and organization and to increase output of higher grade foods. In addition, a radical increase in the use of commercial fertilizers is apparently now under consideration. Although Soviet productivity per man is likely to remain below the American figures over the next decade (and the Soviet proportion of manpower in agriculture to remain high by American standards) substantial improvements in the productivity of Soviet agriculture and in the food supply are in prospect.

3. *Capital*

The rate of Soviet gross investment (about 25 percent of GNP) is likely to persist and to remain slightly above the American rate (about 20 percent of

GNP including Government investment). Recent changes in investment criteria have probably improved somewhat the efficiency of Soviet investment; and the continued concentration of investment in industrial sectors—as opposed to services, transport, etc.—will probably continue to keep the Soviet rate of increase in GNP higher than the American rate.

4. *Transport and Power*

Transport and power, representing two sectors on which the whole economic structure depends, are useful indexes for comparison. With respect to transport, Russia remains and is likely to remain for the next decade, more heavily dependent than the United States on the intensive use of its railway net. In 1957 less than 40 percent of American intercity traffic moved by rail; the roughly equivalent Soviet figure was 90 percent. Some increase in Soviet road and pipeline transport is planned; but the major technical change appears to be a shift of rail lines to diesel and electric power. Total American freight traffic is about twice the Soviet figure. With respect to energy, both nations are well endowed with resources sufficiently economical to justify only a relatively slow introduction of atomic energy. . . .

5. *Management and Incentives*

Over the past 30 years the Soviet Union has devised a framework of education and administration, compulsion and incentives which yield men and institutions capable of operating a modern, rapidly growing economy. The working norms and methods of this system differ both from the initial standards of egalitarian communism and from those which have emerged in contemporary American society. Recent efforts have decentralized some areas of Soviet administration, without diminishing the ultimate ability of Moscow to allocate resources. Soviet education for management has typically a higher technological component than the typically more humanistic American general education. Although, to a limited extent, interesting similarities can be noted between Russian and American modes and problems of administration, the Soviet industrialist operates in a setting where his relations to the working force, to the consuming public, to the political process, and to the law are radically different from those of his American counterpart.

6. *Industrial Output, Productivity, National Income, and Growth Rate*

Despite enormous difficulties in useful comparative measurement, a high degree of consensus now exists among American experts on the Soviet Union with respect to the overall course and prospects of the Russian economy. In 1955, Soviet industrial output was not more than a third of American, perhaps substantially less; industrial productivity per man, certainly below one-third; and GNP, about 40 percent. Soviet industrial output is likely to continue to increase, despite some factors making for deceleration, at about 8 percent per annum, GNP at about 6 percent. Assuming optimistically a rise of 4.4 percent in the rate of increase of American GNP, the ratio of Soviet to American GNP would rise from its figure of 43 percent in 1958 to 48 percent in 1970, the equivalent per capita figures being 36 and 41 percent. A 3 percent U.S. growth rate would lift Soviet GNP slightly over 50 percent of the

American figure by 1970. Given the differences in growth rate this would mean that the Soviet Union would dispose for the first time of a larger annual increment in GNP than the United States, at the end of the coming decade.

7. *Standard of Living*

International comparisons of living standards are the most difficult of all relative measurements. But something like the following appears to be true: Soviet housing standards per family are about a fourth of the American average; food consumption per head somewhat better than one-half; clothing, a bit less than half; medical services, public parks, etc., similar to American standards. In durable consumers' goods and travel, the Soviet standard of living is, as it were, just entering the competition. The prospects for a significant improvement in Soviet food, shelter, and clothing for the next decade are good; and certain types of durable consumers' goods are under rapid expansion. No serious effort is now planned to manufacture and diffuse the automobile on a mass basis; and new housing will remain principally large urban apartment buildings. Except in a few particular categories (e.g., fish, woolen fabrics, and butter) there is little likelihood that Soviet consumption per capita will exceed the American figures, down to 1965. Taken all-in-all, a rise in the Soviet standard of living from something like one-third to about 40 percent of the American level is to be anticipated over the next decade.

8. *Military Expenditures*

When corrected for all the relevant factors, Soviet military expenditures are at about the same level as American outlays; that is to say, the Soviet Government is allocating more than twice the proportion of GNP to military purposes than the American Government.

9. *Foreign Aid*

Although Communist bloc foreign-aid figures in no way measure the scale nor define the nature of the Communist threat in Asia, the Middle East, Africa, and Latin America, Soviet military and economic assistance to underdeveloped areas was about half the level of American assistance in the period 1954–59. In addition, Moscow may have granted important assistance to Communist China over these years, although it is not certain. In 1959, some 4,700 Soviet technicians were engaged on work in the free world, about 75 percent of the number of Americans.

THE STAGES OF AMERICAN AND RUSSIAN GROWTH

To make sense of this broad picture, and to pose the questions it raises for American policy, it is important to look far back in the history of the United States and Russia. For in comparing the two countries, we are looking at societies at quite different points in their own evolution. I shall here use, if I may, the concept of stages of growth which I developed last year in some lectures at Cambridge University. This analysis would define societies as falling into the following broad categories: the traditional society; the preconditions for takeoff; the drive to technological maturity; the age of high mass consumption. . . .

In terms of these stages of growth, Russia is now roughly at the level of the United States in the first decade of the 20th century; but it comes to maturity at a different, more advanced level of technology. And Russia, like the United States and nations which have achieved technological maturity, confronts the question, To what larger purposes should its mature establishment be put—to enlarge Russian power on the world scene, to soften the harshness of the drive to maturity, or to enlarge consumption?

. . . on the eve of the 1960's we must assume that the Russian rate of growth will be higher than the American. This difference stems primarily from the way that Soviet Government has decided since Stalin's death to balance its choice among the three postmaturity alternatives.

Since 1953, the Soviet Union has, to a degree, reduced the harshness of police state rule and cut down on forced labor. To a degree it has increased the level of consumption of the Russian peoples. But its basic decision has been to use the annual increments in production to maintain a very large military establishment and to continue pressing for enlarged power on the world scene. Quite consciously, Soviet policy is postponing the age of the mass automobile and the single family house—the revolution which seized the United States in the 1920's, Western Europe in the 1950's—in order to make a bid for primacy in world power. Technically, this has meant that a much higher proportion of Russian investment than American has continued to go into manufacturing sectors rather than into construction and services. It is this relative concentration of Soviet investment in manufactures—and especially in industry related to military potential, which largely explains the higher Soviet than American rate of growth—now and for the next decade.

In historical terms, the challenge posed for the United States is whether a nation which has gone beyond the age of the automobile and suburbia and is concerning itself with larger families, travel, the refinement and differentiation of consumption, and the various uses of leisure can cope with a nation now arrived at technological maturity, pressing out on the world scene with high ambition, to see how far it can go, even at the expense of postponing the satisfactions (and problems) of the mass automobile and the single family house.

In policy terms, the challenge posed for the United States is symbolized —not defined, but symbolized—by the fact that a nation with less than half our GNP, living at about a third of our standard of welfare, is spending as much on military affairs as we are; putting 75 percent as many technicians and 50 per cent as much capital as we are into the non-Communist world, quite aside from its allocations of men and credit within the Communist bloc.

THE MULTIPLE DIMENSIONS OF THE SOVIET CHALLENGE

To understand the real nature of the Soviet challenge—and what the Soviet Government evidently means by "competitive coexistence"—it is necessary now to go beyond economic analysis and consider what Moscow is trying to accomplish.

Although Soviet policy objectives are primarily military, political, and psychological, they are based on an economic fact: the arrival of Russia at technological maturity. This means that the Soviet Union has the resources and technological capacity to mount a wider variety of military and economic programs than in the past. In the immediate postwar years, for example, the Soviet military threat was confined to the power of the Red Army. At the present time, it controls a full spectrum of military power ranging from ICBM's to conventional infantry and, one might add, "volunteers." A decade or so ago, Soviet trade and credit operations as well as technical assistance programs on the present scale would have been unthinkable. At the present time the Soviet Union has the evident capacity to conduct such operations on a regular expanding basis if it chooses to do so.

Here one specific aspect of the Soviet growth rate should be noted. A 6 percent rate of increase in Soviet GNP means that the Government disposes each year of something like the equivalent of $12 billion for whatever purposes it chooses. Although the level of American gross national product is more than twice that of the Soviet Union, an average growth rate of 3 percent means that the American economy as a whole—not the Government—disposes of an increment of, say, only some $15 billion. . . .

1. *The Threat of Major War*

The main weight of Soviet policy is being articulated to the Russian peoples and to the world in terms of a nonmilitary struggle, which is, indeed, being energetically and frankly pursued. But there is no evidence whatsoever that the Soviet military effort is being reduced; and there are no grounds for building American policy on the assumption that if the Soviet Government believed that it enjoyed a sufficient advantage in nuclear weapons to take out American retaliatory power at a blow, it would not do so. Inhibitions may well exist in the Soviet political system against such a course of action; but there is no objective basis for believing that the United States would be safe should the gap in military capabilities be permitted to open to such an extent. Put another way, we Americans have no right before man or God to tempt Moscow's planners with this possibility. At the present time and for some years—until we create a highly dispersed deterrent system—our ability to make this course of action irrational appears to hinge on an ability to get sufficient advance warning of a Soviet missile attack to put our bombers in the air; and on the pace at which we "harden" our bases. These slender threads on which American safety now rests illustrate the dangers of analyzing the Soviet threat in conventional economic terms. . . .

2. *The Threat of Limited War*

. . . there is no evidence in Soviet military allocations nor in Soviet military doctrine that the use of arms short of an all-out atomic war has been ruled out. On the contrary, the evidence remains that the Soviet Union has continued to modernize its ground force in ways which would make possible combat with either conventional or tactical atomic weapons. Moreover, just as the Geneva Conference of 1955 was accompanied by the disruptive Czech arms deal with Egypt, the present exploration of the possibilities of arms reduction and control is accompanied by Chinese Communist incursions across their southern border. This lively threat is, again, not illuminated by comparative economic analysis of the Russian and American economies. . . .

. . . the nature of the Soviet challenge—including the Soviet challenge to put forward concrete proposals for step-by-step movement toward the control of nuclear armaments—requires that we take the problem of deterring limited aggression much more seriously than we have done in the past 15 years.

3. *Diplomatic Blackmail*

Since the early months of 1956 down through the Berlin crisis, the Soviet Union has on a number of occasions used the threat of its missile capabilities to strengthen the hand of its diplomacy. Again, this is a form of threat which cannot be defined with reference to economic analysis. It comes, in the end, to a simple test of nerve and will.

4. *The Political Penetration of the Underdeveloped Areas*

Soviet policy in Asia, the Middle East, Africa, and Latin America is increasingly discussed under the heading of "The Economic Offensive." This leads to complicated efforts to compare the scale of Soviet and American aid on a quantitative basis. And, indeed, it is quite clear that Soviet technical and economic assistance to underdeveloped areas in the free world as well as Soviet trade policy have been significant forms for creating areas of political influence and sympathy in various parts of the world. But analysis confined to these familiar dimensions misses the main point and the fundamental nature of the Soviet threat. It is quite evident from Communist thought, writing, and policy that their goal in Asia, the Middle East, Africa, and parts of Latin America is a repetition in some form of the story of China from, say, 1927 to 1949; that is, Soviet analysts look to a progressive failure of the non-Communist regimes in these areas to solve the problems of modernization and economic growth, leading to frustration, internal turmoil, and to acceptance of the Communist alternative as a way of organizing these transitional societies. Thus, the central challenge confronting the United States and the Western World in the underdeveloped areas is not, somehow, to outstrip Russian loans and technical assistance. The challenge is to mount our own positive long-term policies designed to maximize the chance that these transitional societies will emerge into modernization without losing their independence and without foreclosing the possibility of progressively more democratic political development. Additional American and free world resources are required in this effort; and Soviet aid and trade policies play some role in the mounting of this challenge—which is, I believe, the route to world power that Moscow now regards as most likely. But to understand and deal with that challenge we must abandon a numbers racket approach and look directly and with insight at the problems of transitional societies and what we can do to help them.

5. *The Fragmentation of the Atlantic Alliance*

It is clear that Soviet policy is immensely alert to the possibility of exploiting schisms as among the Western European nations and as between Western Europe and the United States. Offers of East-West trade play some part in this Soviet policy; but its primary tools are military, political, and psychological—combined with the fact that Moscow controls Eastern Germany and, therefore, the possibility of German unity. This major Soviet effort is only obliquely related to Soviet and American growth rates; and the American response lies in the area of new ideas and institutional arrangements within the Western Alliance—which is now very rich—rather than in new American expenditures.

6. *The Psychological Image*

In support of these various efforts to achieve or to prepare for a breakthrough to world primacy, the Soviet Union is mounting a remarkable and sustained effort to project to the external world and to the Russian peoples a quite particular image. That image is of an ardent, energetic, and technically competent competitor closing fast on—and preparing to supersede—a front runner who has lost the capacity to deal with his problems and prefers to go down in the style to which he has become accustomed rather than to maintain his position. Leaving aside the various American contributions to the persuasiveness of this image in the outside world, this campaign has its foundations in three dimensions of Soviet policy: a somewhat dubious numerical approach to "catching up" with the American economy which, nevertheless, is rooted in the high momentum and technological maturity of the Soviet economy; an exceedingly solid set of Soviet achievements in missiles technology (military and nonmilitary) and a sporadically successful projection of the Soviet Union as the leader in the quest for peace. At home, the building of Soviet policy around the objective of catching up with the United States and with the American standards of living has proved an exceedingly successful device for unifying Soviet society, appealing as it does to three strong motivations evident in the Russian peoples: a deep nationalist pride, a desire for higher standards of living, and a passion for peace. In these dimensions of the Soviet challenge, the high momentum of the Soviet economy has played some part, but it is by no means the sole basis of the challenge.

THE AMERICAN AGENDA

We turn now to the following question: In the light of the purposes of our society, at home and on the world scene, what lines of action are suggested by these multiple Soviet challenges; and what role, if any, does the growth rate and economic policy play in shaping an effective American response?

The elements in an effective American military and foreign policy are, I suspect, quite clear to us all and likely to command something of a consensus. They come to this. By our military dispositions, we must continue to make either major or limited war an irrational undertaking for Communists. On this basis we must use our economic resources and our political and human insight to the full in doing what we can to insure that the nations of Asia, the Middle East, Africa, and Latin America remain independent and move through their difficult transitions to modernization in ways which keep open the possibility of a democratic evolution for their societies. In order to execute these military and creative missions, we must form up a new set of relationships with the resurgent nations of Western Europe and Japan. And from this solid free world base, we must maintain an endless diplomatic initiative and an endless sympathetic dialog with the Soviet leadership seeking to exploit every serious possibility for movement toward the effective international control of armaments. . . .

The potentials for American growth in the next decade would, I believe, permit us both chronic full employment and one of those surges of growth which transcend the long period average of 3 percent per annum increase in GNP. I am a little skeptical that we can attain 5 percent rate of increase; but a 4 percent rate of increase could be within our grasp if our growth potentials are fully and well used. I hold this view because there are three powerful expansionary forces now operating within the American economy: the rise in population, the acceleration of research and development, and the society's massive requirements for social overhead capital. A 4 percent growth in GNP would yield our society an annual increment for all purposes of well over $20 billion over the next decade. The first proposition is, therefore, that I can envisage no increase in American public outlays required to deal with the Soviet threats which could not easily be met by a society with over a $500 billion GNP and a more than $20 billion annual increment in GNP.

THE ALLOCATION PROBLEM

The root cause of our difficulty lies not in our income or our growth potential but in certain American habits of mind, carried over from earlier phases of our history, and in the workings of the political process, as they affect the allocation of resources. This interplay of intellectual conception and conventional politics conspires to make it difficult for Americans to increase the sale of public outlays except at moments of acute crisis. Here lies a danger to the national interest as well as a threat to the quality of American society.

Specifically, the working concepts of modern economics encourage the view that public outlays should be accommodated to the natural ebb and flow of the private sector, perhaps to be expanded at times of recession but certainly to be restrained when the private sectors exhibit high momentum. This perspective, carried over inappropriately from an era of depression and peace to a time of chronic cold war and secular expansion, constitutes a powerful deterrent to outlays in the public sector, especially at a time of chronic prosperity; for it renders difficult a rational choice between marginal outlays in the public and private sectors, without extraordinary exertions of political leadership which have not been forthcoming. Without such efforts, the calculation takes the form of a crude clash between the total claims of the state as against the individual family budget, in which the latter enjoys an evident prima facie advantage. The existing level of taxation acquires a degree of acceptability as citizens accommodate themselves to its burdens. Familiarity breeds not contempt but stoicism. Lacking a concerted effort of political leadership to dramatize the meaning of marginal shifts from the private to the public sector, it is difficult to generate the political base for tax increases or other forms of restraint on private outlays; e.g., checks on installment spending. This leads politicians, except under acute crisis circumstances, to work out the pattern of public outlays within ceilings determined by what the existing tax schedules—the arbitrary product of the last acute crisis—will yield at existing levels of income, if indeed it does not lead to inappropriate tax reductions.

It is essentially these two features of the American scene which have made our response to the changing directions of challenge in the cold war so sluggish on the one hand and convulsive on the other. Neither our concepts of political economy nor our notions of politics have made it possible to deal with threats to the national interest in a forehanded flexible way. We have shifted erratically from the moods and political economy of peace, to those of war. In the interval between, say, mid-1948 and the attack in Korea, for example, men in responsibility came to believe that a military budget beyond $15 billion was a threat to the American way of life. After the convulsive reaction to the Korean war had lifted military outlays more than threefold, this new range became again accepted as a line to be defended with a quite irrational ideological fervor.

The heart of the Soviet challenge lies, then, in presenting us with a situation where our interests may be eroded away, without palpable crisis, to a point where a traditional convulsive American response will no longer suffice. Our conceptions and methods of allocation to the public sector are inappropriate to a world caught up in a technological arms race and a slow grinding struggle for power and ideological conception in the underdeveloped areas. It is not the Soviet growth rate we need fear but a mode of American allocation which tends to imprison us at a level of public outlays determined by our arbitrary response to the last major crisis. . . .

THE RELEVANCE OF THE GROWTH RATE

Having tried to break through the Soviet economic data to identify the concrete dimensions of the Soviet challenge and to break through the American statistics to identify the real nature of our problem, let me say a word about the American growth rate. As Report IV of the Rockefeller Bros. Fund special studies project dramatized, a high rate of growth in gross national product makes it possible to enlarge both private income per head and public outlays, at existing tax rates. Put another way, the higher the growth rate, the less the potential clash between the claims of the two sectors. But, a high rate of growth, in itself, does not guarantee that the public sector will be adequately supplied with resources: for the American allocation system does not automatically maintain constant fixed percentage allocations to various purposes (assuming for a moment that such a system would yield increases adequate to the national interest at high rates of growth in GNP). Without purposeful efforts the natural tendency of the American system is for public outlays to decline as a percentage of total resources, except at intervals of acknowledged crisis.

In fact, as a rough approximation, it is quite accurate to identify the Soviet advantage over the United States as consisting in a more stable percentage allocation to military and foreign policy sectors, starting from a high initial percentage base, at a time of rapid increase in Soviet GNP. Soviet allocations follow a regular path of expansion accommodated to the high rate of growth of GNP. American allocations follow a convulsive path, moving from plateau to (downward sloping) plateau, as crises dictate.

There is every reason for us to seek a higher American rate of growth, and notably an accelerated increase in productivity. Such an achievement could ease the problem of allocation and ease the problem of inflation. But it would not automatically remove from us the hard choices of allocation, nor would it remove the challenge to the democratic process represented by the need to control inflation without stagnation or damping the rate of growth.

THE PROBLEM OF INCREASING AMERICAN PRODUCTIVITY

. . . in my view it would be wholesome . . . to place the issue of productivity high on the national agenda. It might be useful, for example, for task forces of private and public authorities jointly and systematically to examine the productivity potentials in various major sectors of the American economy with three objectives in mind. First, to identify the specific technical and institutional bottlenecks which need to be overcome in order to achieve more rapid expansion in productivity. Second, to see whether it might not be in the common interest to allocate increased research and development talent of the first order to those older and less glamorous fields where deceleration or decline has long since set in, but where very substantial proportions of the Nation's resources are still consumed; for example, cotton textiles, railroads, housing construction. The objective would be to correct a little the natural tendency, familiar to economic historians, for the new, rapidly expanding fields to absorb a disproportionate percentage of first-class talent. Third, we might systematically examine the extent to which entrepreneurship in the various sectors is or is not effectively bringing to bear the potentials which already exist for increased productivity, and we might then consider what incentives might be created to bring average levels of productivity closer to best-proved standards.

Among the particular sectors that deserve close examination is what might broadly be called staff work both within government and in the private economy. Some of us hold the view that we Americans have carried over into staff work criteria of specialization derived historically from notions of scientific management which originated in the problems of running a railroad system, an army in peacetime, and a machine shop. This leads to overmanned, overfragmented staffs, with tremendous inertia built into them, consuming their energies in maintaining the status quo, radically damping the pace of innovation. The increasing role of government in all our lives as well as the increasing role of staff work in the private sector, absorbing as staff work does so high a proportion of first rate human capital, may justify a serious examination of this prejudice.

It may seem odd to commend productivity teams to a nation which still leads the world in productivity and which, for so long, has been able to count on high productivity as an almost automatic byproduct of its evolution. But we must bear in mind that high productivity is not enough; it is the pace of increase that will help determine how easy or difficult it will be to meet our domestic and international challenges. And we should also bear in mind that the stage of growth which the United States has attained has altered the old tight connection between areas of high income elasticity of demand and high technological momentum. History appears to have decreed that, in order to remain a front runner, we shall have to continue to pioneer—in this case to pioneer in engineering productivity increases along a broad front. And in facing this challenge we should not complain, for a front runner's status is never automatically sustained. It must be constantly renewed.

CAN THE DEMOCRATIC PROCESS SOLVE THESE PROBLEMS?

The burden of this argument is, then, that the challenges the Nation confronts, finally, have major economic dimensions: The challenges of adequate and forehanded allocation to the public sector; of dealing with inflation without damping the rate of growth; of creating an environment and a public policy which would accelerate the rise of productivity on a broad front. Each of these is a direct challenge to the vitality of the democratic political process in the United States. As members of the Joint Economic Committee are well aware, there are many Americans (including, I would surmise, certain of your panelists) who would take the view that efforts by the American political process to come to grips with them would inevitably result either in more economic loss than the gain sought; or, in political damage to our society which would outweigh the possible economic gain.

One can reply that other democratic societies have, at various times, dealt more or less successfully with each of these problems, without losing their fundamental values; for example, the American Marshall Plan effort of 1947–48, conducted without the stimulus of military operations, but with strong political leadership which succeeded in getting support for a quite sharp increase in the public budget; for example, the efforts of the Netherlands to accommodate real wages to the average level of productivity increase in the economy; for example, the performance of western Europeans, at our strong urging, in stimulating substantial productivity increases after the Second World War.

But it would be wrong to rest the American case for accepting this tough agenda merely on the basis of analogy. Times are different, nations differ, and problems are never quite the same.

The real case must be negative on the one hand, positive on the other.

Negatively we know that four of our worst mistakes in modern history arose from a fear that our democracy could not deal with the problems it faced, without losing its essence. I refer, of course, to the belief of the Republican administration after 1929 that it could not deal with the great depression without risking unacceptable damage to capitalism; to the belief of isolationists in both parties that we could not deal with Hitler and the Axis without permanently damaging basic qualities in our society; to the belief of the Democratic administration before June 1950 that our society could not afford a military budget of more than $15 billion; and, I would add, the similar belief of the present administration that its overriding mission has been to reduce the public budget it inherited, despite the accelerated challenge it has faced since 1953 in many dimensions.

The lesson of our recent history is that every time the men in authority decided that some problem was too tough for democracy to lick, and that they had to evade the problem in order to save democracy, we have gotten into a quite deep hole; and in all but the fourth case, where the bill is still to be reckoned, democracy was, in the end, much more searchingly and dangerously threatened than if the challenge had been accepted in the first place, at an early stage of the difficulty.

But there is a positive case as well. The positive case is not only that the democratic technique, energetically applied, has proved capable of handling such awkward problems as severe unemployment, major war, and limited war; it is also the simple faith that if any problem is soluble by human beings it is best solved, in the long run, by responsible freemen, subject to the mixture of freedom and self-discipline which is the essence of the democratic process when it works. Without that faith the struggle in which we are engaged lacks meaning.

Our experience of the past century and three quarters should convince us that the democratic process in the United States is tough, resilient, and capable of handling whatever problems the flow of history may place on our agenda.

A CONCLUSION

Now, a final word. Khrushchev's Russia is not the first nation to arrive at technological maturity, feel its oats, look over the field, and decide the old front runner was ripe for the taking. In our own time we have faced such moods and policies from Germany and Japan.

In the past these fast-closing nations have been persuaded to accept the fact that the world was not their oyster and to settle down as part of the international community only by defeat in major war. Major war was then necessary because the older powers did not so conduct themselves as to make major war a totally irrational undertaking.

In Russia we do not face a nation irrevocably committed to pursue power by major war unless we tempt it beyond endurance by our weakness during the period of the missile gap. The main hope for Soviet world leadership lies in various other dimensions, notably in their hope that the Western World and the democratic principle will fail in Asia, the Middle East, Africa, and Latin America. Moreover, I believe that there may well be men in Russia who already perceive that the rise of new nations, in the southern half of the globe, and in China, in a world of atomic weapons, may require a much higher degree of collaboration with the United States than even Khrushchev's challenge to compete peacefully would imply; they may begin to count not on burying us, but on making common cause with us over a widening range of problems. The discussions about ending H-bomb tests, with all they imply about Moscow's worries concerning the spread of atomic weapons, are a small beginning in this direction. . . .

Between now and 1970 a decisive test will take place. The real lesson of your panelists' papers is that there is nothing in the structure or growth rates of the two economies that will automatically determine the outcome of this test. The answer lies in whether our political leadership mobilizes the evidently ample resources that lie to hand—resources of will, of skill, of talent, of commitment to the American heritage, as well as goods and services—to do the job.

Mao Tse-tung: Chinese Communism Is Democratic Dictatorship

It is a measure of the nature of the modern world that a book on major aspects of American government should find it fruitful to include material on China.

The American struggling to understand Chinese behavior and thinking confronts monumental difficulties. Nor is the difficulty peculiar to Americans. As recently as 1945, according to an entry by Harry Hopkins in his diary, Stalin remarked, "We do not regard the Chinese Communist Party as a serious factor. We recognize Chiang Kai-shek." (To be sure, Stalin did not always say what he meant or mean what he said.)

Doubletalk and perhaps doublethink are apparently reasonable designations for the Mao assertion that Chinese communism is democratic dictatorship; democracy for the decent people, dictatorship for the others: "These two aspects, namely democracy for the people and dictatorship over the reactionaries, represent the dictatorship of the people's democracy." But surely neither doubletalk nor doublethink is peculiarly Chinese. Witness the American politician who shouts simultaneously for more government services and reduced taxes, or the industrial mogul who wants no government interference in business, except that his business should receive substantial aids from government. In any event, the American is likely to respond with understanding to the Chinese as a person; any American adult who has on a thousand occasions sworn off smoking will appreciate the story of Mao who, seeking to stop smoking, broke his cigarettes in half as a way at least of curbing the habit.

One would guess that the warped character of the current Chinese view of the United States is equalled only by the uninformed nature of most Americans' concepts of the Red Chinese; one would add that the possibilities of correcting misconceptions are greater in the free, rather than the totalitarian nation.

The article from which the following excerpt was taken was written by Mao Tse-tung, chairman of the Central Committee of the Communist Party, in celebration of its 28th anniversary in 1949. In a preliminary note the publisher of Mao's article says that it "throws a brilliant light on the character and present stage of development of People's Democracy in China."

The Red Chinese view of Mao Tse-tung is illustrated by the declararation of Hsia Yen, Deputy Minister of Culture, that Mao has solved problems which Marx, Engels, Lenin, and Stalin had not solved. In point also is the declaration of the Vice President of the China People's University that "Mao Tse-tung's ideology glows a hundred thousand feet high."

Liu Shao-chi, leading Chinese Communist thinker, has stated that "Mao Tse-tung's great accomplishment has been to change Marxism from a European to an Asian form . . . he has created a Chinese or Asian form of Marxism."

An American view credits Mao with the leading role in activities which "won China and have succeeded in transforming a prostrate, disorganised mass into one of the most powerful, organised, and dynamic countries in the world."

[Mao Tse-tung, *On People's Democratic Rule,* published as a pamphlet by New Century Publishers, July, 1950, pp. 7–14.]

We are told: "You are establishing a dictatorship." Yes, dear gentlemen, you are right. We are indeed establishing a dictatorship. The experience acquired by the Chinese people over many decades shows us the need to establish a dictatorship of the people's democracy. This means that the reactionaries must be deprived of the right to express their opinion and that only the people shall have the right to vote and to express their opinion. Who are "the people"? At the present stage in China the people are the working class, the class of the peasantry, the petty bourgeoisie and national bourgeoisie. Under the leadership of the working class and the Communist Party these classes united to form their own state and to elect their own government in order to establish a dictatorship over the lackeys of imperialism—the class of landlords and bureaucratic capital—in order to crush them, allowing them to operate only within certain limits and preventing them from going outside these limits either in words or deeds. If they try either in words or deeds to go beyond this limit, they will be forbidden to do so and immediately punished. The democratic system must be realized among the people, granting them freedom of speech, assembly and organization. The right to vote is granted only to the people and not to the reactionaries. These two aspects, namely, democracy for the people and dictatorship over the reactionaries, represent the dictatorship of the people's democracy. . . .

We are told: "Don't you want to destroy state power?" Yes, that is so, but not just now. We cannot destroy state power at present. Why? Because imperialism still exists, because Chinese reactionaries still exist and because classes still exist in the country. Our task today is to strengthen the apparatus of the people's state, which means in the main, the people's army, the people's police and the people's courts, national defense and defense of the interests of the people. This is an essential condition if China is to steadily develop under the leadership of the working class and the Communist Party, if she is to develop from an agrarian country into an industrial country and to pass from a New Democracy to a Socialist and Communist society, in order to abolish classes and bring about world Communism. The army, police and courts of the state are instruments of classes to oppress classes. To hostile classes the State apparatus is the instrument of oppression. It is a weapon of violence and not of "benevolence."

We are told: "You are not benevolent." That is true. We are decidedly against benevolence in relation to the activities of reactionaries and reactionary classes. We apply benevolent administration only toward the people and not toward the activities of the reactionaries and reactionary classes who are outside the people. The people's state defends the people. Only under a people's state can the people apply democratic methods on a national scale and fully educate and re-educate themselves in order to cast off the influence of the reactionaries in their country and abroad (this influence is still very strong, will continue to exist for a long time to come and cannot be destroyed quickly), in order to discard the bad habits and ideologies acquired in the old society, in order not to advance along the incorrect path indicated by the reactionaries but to continue to advance and develop in the direction of establishing a Socialist and Communist society.

The methods used by us in this sphere are democratic: that is to say we are applying methods not of coercion but of persuasion. If people violate the law they will be punished, imprisoned and may even be sentenced to death. But these will be individual cases differing in principle from the dictatorship carried out against the reactionary class as a class. After the political regime of the reactionaries has been overthrown, the reactionary class and reactionary clique will also be given land, work and means of subsistence so that by working they will be able to re-educate themselves anew on condition that they do not attempt revolts, destruction or sabotage. If they refuse work, the people's state will compel them to work. Furthermore, political propaganda and educational work will be carried out among them as we did with those officers we took prisoner. This also can be regarded as benevolent administration. But this will be done through compulsion in relation to the former hostile classes and this work cannot be placed on a par with our educational work among the revolutionary people. Such re-education of the reactionary classes can be effected only in a state of the dictatorship of the people's democracy. . . .

Revolutionary dictatorship and counter-revolutionary dictatorship are diametrically opposed to each other. The former learned from the latter. This study is of great importance, for if the revolutionary people do not master the methods of dominating the counter-revolutionary classes, they will not be able to preserve their regime which will be overthrown by the clique of Chinese and foreign reactionaries. These reactionaries would then restore their domination in China and bring misfortune to the revolutionary people. . . .

In the twenty-eight years of its existence our Party has done one thing—we have achieved the main victory in revolutionary struggle. This is worth noting, for it is a people's victory and a victory in a great country such as China.

But much work still lies ahead. What has been accomplished in the past is only the first step along the 10,000-mile route. We still have to destroy the remnants of the enemy and we are faced with the serious task of economic construction. The work we have grown accustomed to will soon be laid aside and we will have to tackle a new job. This is where the difficulty lies. The imperialists think that we are incapable of handling the economic task confronting us. They are watching and waiting for us to fail. We have difficulties to overcome and have to master something new to us. In the sphere of economy we must learn to work from everybody, no matter whom. We must recognize them as our teachers and learn from them. We must not pretend that we know everything if we do not know something. We must not become bureaucrats. The job must be tackled and we shall ultimately master it in several months, in one or two years, or three to five years.

At the beginning also many Communists in the Soviet Union did not know how to work in the economic field and then, too, the imperialists expected them to fail. But the Communist Party in the Soviet Union emerged victorious. It carried out not only revolutionary but also reconstruction work under the leadership of Lenin and Stalin. It has already built a great and glorious Socialist state. The Communist Party of the Soviet Union is our best teacher from whom we must learn. The international and internal situation is in our favor. We can fully rely on the weapon of the dictatorship of the people's democracy in order to unite the whole people throughout the country, except the reactionaries, and steadfastly advance toward our goal.

Chou En-lai: "Stop Aggressive War and Safeguard World Peace"

The section below is from a speech by Premier Chou En-lai at a banquet given in 1960 in honor of trade union delegates of various countries attending the meeting in Peking of the World Federation of Trade Unions' General Council. The text of the speech has been taken from the *Peking Review,* "a weekly magazine of Chinese news and views" published in Peking, China.

Following is a biographical sketch of Chou En-lai: Politburo member; premier and former foreign minister; born 1898; classical education; studied at universities in China and Japan; went on work-and-study scholarship to France in 1919 and before returning to China studied for a year in Germany and visited England; he helped found a branch of the Communist Party in Paris; during the period of Nationalist-Communist cooperation was a leading political commissar; participated in the Long March (when the Red Chinese retreated from Chiang Kai-shek's troops over a period of a year, covering six thousand miles of rugged terrain, and involving the loss of seventy thousand men out of ninety thousand who started the March); became premier with the establishment of Communist government in 1949.

Chou En-lai is the only member of the Standing Committee of the Politburo who has traveled beyond the Communist bloc in the post-1949 period, and, says one scholar, "Among China specialists there seems to be a tacit assumption that Chou represents the eyes and ears of Mao as regards the outside world. No doubt there is much truth in this. Yet even Chou's extensive travels require a word of qualification. For practical purposes Chou has not been in an 'advanced' Western industrial city since his student days almost forty years back."

[Chou En-lai, "Speech at Banquet in Honor of World Federation of Trade Unions' Delegates," *Peking Review,* June 14, 1960, pp. 9–10.]

On the occasion of the holding in our capital of the 11th session of the General Council of the World Federation of Trade Unions, I would like, on behalf of the Chinese Government and people, to express warm welcome to you, the representatives of hundreds of millions of our working-class brothers throughout the world. . . .

Our epoch is one in which the forces of peace prevail over the forces of war, the forces of the people prevail over the forces of reaction, and the forces of socialism prevail over the forces of imperialism. The fundamental task facing the working class of the world and progressive mankind is to make full use of the present excellent situation to concentrate all energies to defeat the forces of war and aggression headed by U.S. imperialism, to continue to carry forward the cause of the peoples of various countries for world peace, national independence, democratic freedoms and socialism and attain the noble aims of lasting peace and human progress.

To stop aggressive war and safeguard world peace is the eager and universal desire of the working class and the broad masses of the people in all countries. Countless experiences have told us that in order to realize this desire of the people, reliance must be placed on the people themselves rising to fight imperialism. Peace can never be obtained by begging the imperialists for it. The aggressive, war-like nature of imperialism will never change, but imperialist activities for war and aggression can be smashed so long as the people of the world wage persistent and unremitting struggles against them. Since the Second World War, the imperialist colonialist forces have been compelled to withdraw from many areas of Asia, Africa and Latin America. The U.S. imperialist "positions of strength" and "brink of war" policies have been continuously frustrated; the "peace" fraud of U.S. imperialism has also been exposed again and again. . . .

The unity of the socialist camp headed by the Soviet Union and the unity of the working class of all countries constitute the surest guarantee for the cause of world peace, the cause of the emancipation of the working class and the cause of the liberation of all oppressed nations. Relying on this great unity, we will be able to unite all the forces which can be united with to form the broadest united front and isolate the imperialists and their lackeys to the greatest extent so as to finally triumph over imperialism. Precisely because of this, imperialism fears such unity most of all and tries to wreck it by every means. The most vicious, sinister tactics used by imperialism to undermine the unity of the working class of the world are to employ the modern revisionists to engage specifically in activities designed to split the working class. The modern revisionists try their utmost to spread illusions about peace within the ranks of the working class and obscure the dividing line between the enemy and ourselves, in an attempt to do away with the revolutionary struggle of the working class and perpetuate the reactionary rule of the imperialists. In this respect, the modern revisionists have played a role which the imperialists and their other lackeys are unable to play. Therefore, the working class of the world faces a serious militant task, that is, to continue to thoroughly expose the renegade face of the modern revisionists, thoroughly wash away the poisonous ideas spread by them and completely smash all their disruptive activities designed to split the working class. Only thus can the international unity of the working class be upheld and strengthened, and the revolutionary spirit of the working class brought into full play. Only thus can we deal mortal blows at the imperialists and their lackeys.

Liu Chang-sheng: Just and Unjust Wars

The article below is a summary of a speech delivered by Liu Chang-sheng at the General Council meeting in 1960 of the World Federation of Trade Unions (WFTU). Liu is vice chairman of the All-China

Federation of Trade Unions and is a member of the top formally governing body in China, the Central Committee.

The WFTU is a Communist-front organization; the General Council is the equivalent in its role to a Communist Party Central Committee. Claiming a total membership of about 95 million workers, about 75 per cent of whom are drawn from the Sino-Soviet orbit, the WFTU has been a faithful adherent of the Communist line; for example, Louis Saillant, secretary-general of the WFTU, said on one occasion: "We should state that one of the essential duties of the defenders of peace is the refusal to work on and produce war material in all capitalist countries."

Liu Chang-sheng's speech may be read in part as one of the manifestations of Sino-Soviet relationships illustrating the differing verbal positions of China and the Soviet Union on peace and war.

Richard Lowenthal, who has written widely on Soviet and international Communist matters and is now professor of international relations at the Free University in West Berlin, has analyzed the Liu Chang-sheng speech in a book, *The Sino-Soviet Dispute* (edited by G. F. Hudson). He notes that the speech represents a public ideological attack on the Soviet Union and adds "there is reason to suppose that even more comprehensive and outspoken criticisms of Soviet policy were communicated non-publicly at the same time, at least to selected leaders of the Communist world movement."

Two more points and the student can read for himself Liu's speech. One is that whether or not the speech is aimed partially at the Soviet Union leadership, it is hardly one whose content offers immediate comfort to the American. Second is a comment on Sino-Soviet disputation by Zbigniew Brzezinski, a noted analyst of Soviet affairs: ". . . these processes take place within an ideologically-oriented system that is highly hostile to the outside world. A situation of diverse unity can endure for a long time, with many ebbs and flows. . . ."

[Liu Chang-sheng, "On the Question of War and Peace," summarized in the *Peking Review,* June 14, 1960, pp. 13–14.]

Liu Chang-sheng said that the question of war and peace is one with which everyone is concerned and he wished to express some views on this question. With regard to the question of war and peace, he said, we have always stood for safeguarding world peace, for peaceful coexistence between countries with different social systems, for the relaxation of international tension and for disarmament. But on this question there still exist some problems involving basic principles that must be clarified, otherwise people would go astray in regard to the question of safeguarding peace.

As to what attitude we should adopt towards war, Liu Chang-sheng said, we must first of all make a distinction as to its nature. A war between imperialist countries in a scramble for colonies is an unjust war. An imperialist war to suppress the colonial people and the people at home and to commit aggression against other countries is also an unjust war. On the other hand, a revolutionary war waged by the colonial peoples and by the oppressed peoples of the imperialist countries for their own liberation is a just war. Since the imperialists use armed force to suppress the oppressed peoples and nations, the oppressed peoples and nations cannot but take up arms themselves. We must stand for and uphold just revolutionary wars, and oppose and stop unjust wars. It is wrong to talk indiscriminately about whether or not war should be supported or whether or not it should be opposed, without making a specific analysis of its nature.

Liu Chang-sheng continued: The question of whether or not war can be averted, in our opinion, refers mainly to a world war. As to whether a world war can be averted, it should be pointed out that, on the one hand, under the conditions of the steady growth of the forces of the socialist countries, the forces of the liberation movements in the colonies and semi-colonies and the forces of the revolutionary movements and peace movements of the peoples of the countries the world over, and the united struggle of these forces, there exists the possibility of stopping the imperialists from unleashing a new world war. But, on the other hand, so long as there is imperialism, the root cause of war remains, the breeding ground of war remains, and the war maniacs remain, and that is why there still exists the danger of imperialism launching a new world war. If we only talk about the possibility of stopping the imperialists from launching a world war, but not about the danger of imperialism launching a world war, and are not on the alert against the military adventures of the war maniacs, we will only lull ourselves and the people. This will only help imperialism in its arms expansion and war preparations and, once it launches a war, the peoples of various countries, taken off guard, may be thrown into a state of alarm and confusion and even suffer unduly heavy losses. It is entirely wrong to believe that war can be eliminated for ever while imperialism still exists. The spreading of such illusions about imperialism among the peoples of all lands will lead to evil consequences of a serious nature and, in fact, we can already see such consequences at present.

Liu Chang-sheng said that as to imperialist wars of suppression against colonies and semi-colonies, national liberation wars of the colonial and semi-colonial peoples against imperialism, wars of suppression against the people by the exploiting classes and people's revolutionary wars in the capitalist countries, wars of such nature have always existed in history, and have never stopped in the capitalist world since the Second World War. The wars in Indo-China, in Algeria, over the issue of the Suez Canal and in Cuba are all such wars. In the future, as long as imperialism and the exploiting system are still in existence, such wars of different nature will still be unavoidable. The belief that wars of the above-mentioned types can be avoided is entirely wrong and contrary to fact. Such views will deprive the oppressed peoples of their fighting spirit and in the face of armed suppression by the enemy, prevent them from arming themselves to actively fight the enemy, who is armed to the teeth, and to liberate themselves. This will, in effect, keep the oppressed peoples for ever in the state of enslavement.

Liu Chang-sheng went on: We stand for peaceful coexistence between socialist and capitalist countries. Since World War II, we socialist countries have spared no effort in striving for peaceful coexistence and have unswervingly pursued various policies of peace, but the imperialist countries headed by the United States have all along clung to their cold war policy, persisted in arms expansion and war preparations and created tension. We should make it clear to the people that they should not be intimidated by the cold war waged by imperialism, that they should resolutely oppose its cold war policy, expose its ugly face and wage a head-on struggle against it. Only thus can the cold war be prevented from developing into a hot one.

Liu Chang-sheng further stated: We must take into full account the fact that because internal crises are worsening day by day in the imperialist countries and because they want to intensify their oppression and rule over the people at home and in the colonial countries, the imperialists will, for a long time to come, keep up their cold war policy, impose cold war on the people of the world and continue to maintain their massive military forces and the entire state machine. To safeguard world peace and oppose imperialism will, therefore, be a long-drawn-out struggle for the peoples of various countries.

Liu Chang-sheng said: We support the disarmament proposals put forward by the Soviet Union. It is of course inconceivable that imperialism will accept proposals for general and complete disarmament. The purpose of putting forward such proposals is to arouse the people throughout the world to unite and oppose the imperialist scheme for arms drive and war preparations, to unmask the aggressive and bellicose nature of imperialism before the peoples of the world in order to isolate the imperialist bloc headed by the United States to the greatest extent, so that they will not dare unleash a war lightly. But there are people who believe that such proposals can be realized when imperialism still exists and that the "danger of war can be eliminated" by relying on such proposals. This is an unrealistic illusion. As to the view that after disarmament, imperialism would use the funds earmarked for war purposes for "the welfare of the labouring masses" and for "assisting underdeveloped countries" and that this would "bring general progress to people as a whole without exception"—this is downright whitewashing and embellishing imperialism, and indeed this is helping imperialism headed by the United States to dupe the people throughout the world.

Liu Chang-sheng pointed out that only when socialist revolution is victorious throughout the world, can there be a world free from war, a world without arms. Such a world is inconceivable while imperialism still exists. This is not a question of whether we want it or not; the question is that the imperialists will never lay down their arms of their own accord. They will not lay down their arms because they want to suppress the people of their own countries; they will not lay down their arms because they want to suppress the colonies; they will not lay down their arms because they want to carry on expansion and aggression against other countries. History has confirmed and will continue to confirm this.

Soviet and American Perceptions

The individual's value system is a central consideration in organizing his field of awareness—what he sees and what he remembers and how he interprets. That people tend to see what lies behind their eyes is no new insight; yet it must also be borne in mind that people tend no less frequently to perceive what lies in front of their eyes.

In any event, modern research documents the thought that "we strive to maintain internal consistency among our attitudes and beliefs, often at the price of doctoring reality." At the same time, of course, the fact is that people, whether deliberately or not, do manage to accept things as they are; one must be careful to avoid the notion that everybody always avoids reality.

An interesting experiment done inside the Soviet Union illustrates one aspect of "cognitive dynamics in the conduct of human affairs." The experiment consisted of showing one film shot spliced to different scenes. A simple, passive close-up of the well-known Russian actor, Mosjukhin, was joined to three different strips of film. In one strip, the close-up was followed by a shot of a bowl of soup on the table; in another it was followed by shots showing a dead woman on the table; in the third it was followed by shots of a little girl playing with a funny toy bear. The effects on an unsuspecting audience were described as prodigious: "The public raved about the acting of the artist. They pointed out the heavy pensiveness of his mood over the forgotten soup, were touched and moved by the deep sorrow with which he looked at the dead woman, and admired the light happy smile with which he surveyed the girl at play. But we knew that in all three cases the face was exactly the same."

Raymond A. Bauer, the author of the following article, has been a research associate at the Center for International Studies at the Massachusetts Institute of Technology, a lecturer in social psychology at Harvard University, co-director of research of the Harvard Project on the Soviet Social System, and a foremost writer on the Soviet Union. The article was presented as a paper to the International Psychological Congress, Bonn, August, 1960.

[Raymond A. Bauer, "Problems of Perception and the Relations between the United States and the Soviet Union," *The Journal of Conflict Resolution,* vol. 5, pp. 223–229, 1961.]

When a psychologist talks about "understanding another people" he usually talks about national character, and he is concerned with direct psychological observations to be made on some sample of people. However, my focus of attention is broader. I am concerned with the problem of understanding an ongoing social and political system—not only the people but also their institutions. I want to concentrate on some unconventional considerations that I personally found to be of practical importance. These considerations struck me most sharply specifically because preceding academic discussion had not alerted me sufficiently to them. Therefore, I am assuming they will fall outside the mainstream of what the reader, too, expects.

Let me state briefly the background which I bring to this task. For a period of about ten years I was engaged at least part-time in an effort to understand the Soviet Union. The magnitude of interest in this subject in the United States was stimulated largely by the practical considerations of the state of tension which existed between the Soviet Union and my own country. But, like many other American scholars, I was personally motivated to a very great degree by the intellectual challenge of understanding another social system. Our sources of information, regrettably, were poorer than we would have hoped them to be: official publications, occasional diaries of travelers, and, as in the case of some of my own work—the testimony of refugees. We did the best we could with the information available to us, but always with a feeling of dissatisfaction. When an opportunity came to visit the Soviet Union freely in the years after 1955, most of us leaped at this chance.

Having spent a number of years studying the Soviet Union with data with which I was not happy, I then undertook two studies of American institutions: one was an empirical study of the formation of American foreign trade policy; the other was a review of the role of mass communications in American society. In each instance I was going over ground that had been covered by many scholars before me. And in each instance, I was struck by the extent to which the data with which I was confronted led me into conflict with many opinions firmly held by scholars of great reputation. Furthermore, I met many Europeans who held opinions about the United States which they regarded as self-evident, but which I personally viewed as highly doubtful or plainly wrong. Finding out how difficult it was to establish with any degree of comfort what was happening in my own country, I was naturally intrigued by this opportunity to reconsider some of the problems of an American trying to understand the Soviet Union.

One's Intention toward the Object Shapes His Perception and Reporting

To the best of my knowledge, no American student of the Soviet Union has written or spoken anything other than what he believed to be the truth. Yet there is so much to observe and so much to say and write! What should be said or written at a given time? Over a period of several years I became intrigued with the extent to which the initiative did not lie with the writer.

To understand what I am saying here, you must appreciate the extent to which American students of the Soviet Union (correctly or incorrectly) take themselves very seriously as a source of influence on national policy. Here I speak from personal experience and assert that the problems many of us selected and the emphasis which we gave in our reporting were, to a very large extent, determined by our intention to counteract what we believe to be erroneous notions held in high quarters. There are others whose writing was shaped largely by the belief that the American public did not understand the "threat which Communism poses to the American way of life." The basic point I want to make is that the initiative did not lie with the writer but rather he was responding to an audience whose erroneous views he was attempting to correct. This means not only that the prospective audience influenced the questions which were asked, but probably that the scholars also overstated their own position somewhat in their attempts to counteract the opposing position.

A most clear-cut example occurred a few years after the close of World War II. Largely under the stimulus of articulate spokesmen of Soviet refugee groups, the belief developed in American government circles that there was a strong possibility of a popular revolution in the Soviet Union. This prompted many of us, particularly those of us who had contact with Soviet refugees, to turn our attention to the question of the stability of the Soviet order. Virtually unanimously we came to the conclusion that it was very stable indeed. I recall that we had a strong sense of mission to offset what we considered dangerous wishful thinking on the part of American political leaders. If other views had prevailed in Washington, the chances are that we would have concentrated on other problems and have paid less attention to the stabilizing features of the Soviet system.

When Stalin died, American students of the Soviet Union again felt compelled to affirm the stability of the Soviet system in order to forestall any official policy based on an overestimation of instability. After Stalin's death, there have of course been many marked changes in Soviet life. But the "Soviet specialists" have, as a group, continued to play their self-assigned role of guarding against overestimation of change in the Soviet Union.

At this point I will venture a rather rash speculation. As a result of their efforts to offset what they perceived to be official errors in the view of the Soviet system, American scholars have concentrated on the stabilizing elements in Soviet society, particularly the system of political and social control. As a result they may be less well equipped to anticipate and assess change. The original intention toward the object, to see it as a politically significant entity of which persons in a position of power held erroneous views, has shaped the conceptual apparatus with which it is presently viewed.

The Other Party's Position Is Overrationalized

This is the point at which to recall Metternich's reputed reaction to the death of a Russian ambassador: "I wonder what he meant by that." Game theory is based upon the assumption that one's opponent has complete information and has calculated his strategy with complete rationality. These may be optimal assumptions for setting strategy in a competitive situation, but they are scarcely a reasonable description of conditions that exist in the real world. Yet, years of reading American analysis of Soviet behavior and Soviet analysis of American behavior have convinced me that each party attributes to the other a degree of omniscience and omnipotence that he knows is manifestly impossible in his own situation.

To me this becomes particularly amusing when some blundering bit of

American policy is attributed to the subtle machinations of "Wall Street." I sympathize with the Soviet student of American politics. He can scarcely bring himself to believe that it is the complex shambles that it often is. Nor has he witnessed, as I have, the spectacle of Wall Street bankers fearing to speak up on a controversial political issue for fear of losing customers. A Soviet diplomat once interpreted American policy in the Middle East to me as being based solely on the desire to protect the interests of the large oil companies. I am sure that he was sincere. But he had no way of knowing that the American petroleum industry was split wide on the issue of foreign oil and that perhaps the politically more powerful segment of the industry—those who produce oil in the United States—would have been happier if Middle Eastern oil had never existed.

I am sure that Americans make similar overinterpretations of Soviet behavior—in fact that I myself have been guilty of such overrationalizations. The difficulty is knowing when this happens. Virtually every public action and utterance of a Soviet official is analyzed as a piece in a complex long-range strategy. Furthermore, it is assumed that if "the intentions of the Soviet leaders" can be deciphered, these "intentions" can almost automatically be assumed to be implemented. Since the Soviet Union seems to be a more thoroughly coordinated society than is the United States, one is probably warranted in attributing to Soviet leaders a greater freedom in setting policy deliberately, and a greater ability to implement that policy insofar as this implementation is contingent on control over Soviet society. But these leaders are also human beings subject to pressures and fallibility; and Soviet society is not the complete monolith that it is sometimes said to be.

Why then are we not content at times to shrug our shoulders, say "I don't know," or regard certain events as isolated "accidents" unrelated in any important systematic way to the main affairs of Soviet society, or as blundering rather than plotting? I think there are two major reasons.

The first is that the notion of "accident" is alien to the enterprise of understanding. We feel impelled to give cognitive structure to all the data available to us. This becomes a particular problem when the data are sparse. Where I have detailed knowledge of events in the United States I am often content to regard certain occurrences as unrelated in a significant fashion to "the American system." This is because I have concrete knowledge of what evoked these events. My need for cognitive clarity is satisfied. If I were a Soviet observer, however, I would probably be tempted to fit these events into some more determinate over-all scheme.

Secondly, we cannot ignore the fact that in the past decade or so, the United States and the Soviet Union have been in a competitive power struggle. This I believe produces a situation in which each party looks to each bit of evidence as a clue to what the other might do. In effect, this is the sort of conservative strategy advocated by the game theorist—i.e., the safest course is to assume complete rationality of thinking and behavior on the part of the opponent.

For the two reasons I have cited, I believe that both Soviet and American observers have overrationalized notions as to what transpires in the other society. This paper was in process of revision at the time of the aborted

Paris Summit Conference, and I would contend that both the principals and observers of that unfortunate event exhibited the tendency of over-interpretation to which I have referred.

For example, Soviet authorities probably interpreted President Eisenhower's assumption of responsibility for the U2 flight as a deliberately aggressive act. On the other hand, a popular interpretation of this act in the United States was that the President's press secretary had decreed that the President could no longer admit that he did not know what was going on in the country.

Theory Both Helps and Hinders

In our efforts to understand another country, or for that matter to understand our own, theoretical models play a crucial but complex role. One can scarcely begin thinking about a phenomenon as complex as a national state without employing some organizing principle. Thus, the typical American scholar approaches the study of the Soviet Union with a generalized model of "totalitarian communism," and the Soviet scholar sees the United States as an example of "monopolistic capitalism." Without such generalized models we could not begin to talk about so complex a phenomenon as a large-scale national state. Such models tell us which data are important and which trivial. They enable us to set up criteria for change since, in an ever-changing world, one cannot tell what is an "essential" and what is an "incidental" change unless he has some generalized model. Such models present some difficulties, however.

Perhaps the central problem of such theoretical models of national states is that like all models, they must always lag somewhat behind reality. Thus, the American student of the Soviet Union uses a model largely based on Stalin's reign, particularly during the periods of purges. The Soviet view of America, it seems to me, is based in part on the state of American society during the great depression of the 1930's. Now, one of the functions of such models—whether it is initially intended or not—is to help us interpret ambiguous data. A familiar example is the problem of interpreting the social significance of abstract painting. Thus, abstract painting is seen as creative experimentation in a free society by a person with one view of Western civilization, and as decadence by a person with another view. The statement of a Soviet leader that there will be an increase in consumer goods in the Soviet economy is accepted skeptically by the American scholar who sees the Soviet Union as committed to the Stalinist model of economic development. On the other hand, the Soviet scholar who reads about resistance to raising of personal property taxes for educational purposes in the United States sees this as opposition of the "landlord class," not realizing that in the present-day America, the opposition stems largely from individual owners of their own homes.

That a person will use a generalized model for the interpretation of ambiguous data is natural and probably proper. But what strikes me as extremely important is that a very high proportion of the data on the basis of which we assess trends even in our own society is ambiguous even to those who are best acquainted with them. A few years ago my wife and I reviewed a considerable amount of literature on American society. One of the salient impressions we derived from this literature is that for most of the criteria on the basis of which trends in American society were inferred, there simply were no unequivocal data. Thus, it is alleged that American society is marked by an increase in isolation of the individual, an increase in mental disorders, and an increase in juvenile behavior disorders. I assume that most of you have heard these statements so often that you take it for granted they are true. But the fact of the matter is that there are no unambiguous data on the basis of which to make such judgments. However, there are many illustrative bits of data which can be introduced as evidence, providing one's theoretical position leads him to the a priori conclusion that the statements are true.

The situation becomes exaggerated when the members of one country look at another country. When an American scholar studies the Soviet Union and a Soviet scholar studies America, the proportion of ambiguous data is higher than when one is looking at his own country. Hence, in this latter situation one's theoretical model becomes simultaneously more necessary and potentially more dangerous. There is an increased tendency to interpret the very data which would lead one to change one's model in such a way as to preserve that model. Without the model one could not say if change had taken place, but with the model one is less likely to see the evidence for change.

It is no accident, in the light of the above argument, that in my opinion American journalists and casual observers are more likely to see change in the Soviet Union since Stalin's death than are the so-called "Soviet experts." The experts would contend that laymen are misled by "nonessential" changes. To some extent I assume that the experts are right, but to what extent I do not know. But we must entertain seriously the alternative possibility that the "expert" tends to defend his own theoretical position by virtue of the selective interpretation of ambiguous data. This tendency is re-enforced by readily available methods of neutralizing data that do not clearly fit the model. This happens in slightly different forms for the two sides. If the Soviet leaders embark on a policy that does not fit the model of the American expert, this policy is labeled "a tactical retreat" which represents no "fundamental departure from the basic line." On the other hand, when American students of their own society report developments that do not fit the Soviet model of that society, these Americans are dismissed as "apologists."

My foregoing comments could be applied to the use of theory in any situation where the criterial data are ambiguous. The mystique of the "crucial experiment" on the basis of which a theory is accepted or rejected is scarcely relevant to such highly generalized notions as are applied to the analysis of national states. Theories, as desirable and inescapable as they may be, tend to be self-re-enforcing. While helping the scholar, they also place on him a tremendous burden of assessing the evidence on the basis of which he may change his theory.

When, however, we are dealing with two countries in a competitive situation *vis à vis* each other, the theoretical models of the two societies take on an additional role of differentiating the two societies from each other. My impression is that if a scholar from another century or another planet were to study the Soviet Union and the United States without the benefit of our existing statements of the differences between the two systems, he might be struck more by the similarities than by the differences. But, if he were to publish this conclusion it would be resisted by a majority of people in either camp. For example, some of us have stressed in our published works the extent to which the Soviet Union is an industrial society which shares features of all industrial societies. This position has been attacked in the Soviet press as an attempt on our part to deny the distinctive nature of the socialist state. It has been similarly attacked by some Americans as a failure to understand the "essential difference" between the Soviet Union and the United States. Actually, of course, we made no claims that there were not essential differences between the two societies, and we gave central consideration to many of these differences. But the ideologies in both camps are so concerned with the differentiation of one system from the other that a discussion of points of similarity is resisted. As a result, a considerable amount of social energy is devoted to exaggerating the distinctions.

Thus, American ideologists extol the virtues of a "free enterprise system" in contrast to a socialist system. Any person who gives a second thought to the matter knows full well that the American economy is not by any stretch of the imagination a "free enterprise economy" in the classical sense. The very same men who talk of it in such terms will on other occasions deplore a "drift to socialism" which must be stopped! However, a considerable portion of their energy is devoted to drawing up a nostalgic picture of American society that maximally differentiates American society from Soviet society.

Similarly, the realities of Soviet society have converged toward the realities of capitalist society in a number of ways. For example, the system of wage incentives which has evolved in Soviet industry is a drastic change from earlier socialist ideals and quite similar to the system of wage incentives used in capitalist countries. But Soviet ideologists go to great pains to point out that such a system of incentives is "essentially different" if carried out in socialist society. My frank opinion is that they feel no more free to admit they have learned from us than we feel free to admit that we have learned from them. (This is true so far as social and political institutions are concerned and does not pertain equally to science and technology.)

The practical result of this circumstance for the scholar studying either country is that there is a pervasive pressure on him to maintain models of the two systems that stress the differences between the systems. I cite this as another circumstance which discourages the revision of one's models.

However, I am pleased to report, although somewhat tentatively, the feeling that the scholar who reports convergence of the two systems is more likely to meet with approval in America today than he would have a few years ago.

Behind the attitudes toward similarities and dissimilarities of the two systems is a widespread fallacious assumption that conflict between two states is mainly a function of the dissimilarity of their political and economic systems.

Similarity to Traditional Problems of Psychology

The first familiar problem is that of the intention of the observer toward the object observed. We have recognized this as a crucial problem in personality diagnosis and made strenuous efforts to standardize and objectify our procedures and to reduce the element of individual judgment to a minimum. Few responsible psychologists, however, would claim that we have succeeded in avoiding the problem completely. In the field of social analysis the problem is, and will continue to be for some time, much more difficult because of the enormous task of developing an adequate model to be used for comparative social system analysis, and then of setting up standardized categories and procedures for gathering data. Limited models are available, but there are none to my knowledge that would not demand considerable ad hoc adjustment and elaboration if we were to turn it to the task of explaining and predicting developments in Soviet or American society.

The second familiar problem is that of deciding when "a system" has "changed." I doubt whether there is any psychologist who uses the concept of personality who would not contend that there can be "changes in behavior" which do not constitute "a change of personality." Similarly I know of no student of American or Soviet society who would not contend that there can be changes in the way of life of the people of those countries which do not constitute "changes in the system." It is my position that the notion of "change in a system" is inherently a matter of judgment of the observer—just as is the notion of "change of personality." True, if changes are sufficiently gross there will be a consensus of observers. But, by the time events reach this stage, what should have been a problem of diagnosis often becomes merely a post mortem. An early diagnosis is always desirable, and a prediction of incipient change is still more preferable. But, to predict or note "change in the system," the observer must be clear in his own mind what he considers to be essential to the system. This is fundamental for both the study of society and of personality so that the observer does not give equal weight to all data and fall into the trap of overly deterministic analysis to which I referred above.

A third problem is very similar to that to which the phenomenological psychologists address themselves. Formal institutional analysis is very much like the use of set categories in psychological observation. Both are essential for systematic work. Yet it is also vital that from time to time we return to raw observation on as naive a basis as we can manage. In social system analysis, it is extremely important to look repeatedly at the actual behavior of people within the institutional setting. This is crucial for assessing and predicting institutional change. It is a common occurrence for institutions to maintain most of their formal characteristics while important changes of function have taken place within their framework.

The distinctive contribution of the psychologist to social system analysis is, of course, his skill at systematic observation, whether it be on the level of description of overt behavior, or his measurement of variables which fall broadly in the area of personality. It is true that much data have been collected, but psychologists in my country at least have been slow at relating such data to the sort of formal institutional analysis which I have been arguing is inadequate without these data. This will probably take a long time and some institutional changes in American social science.

In the meantime, I think that my country and the Soviet Union face important problems of understanding each other. I look forward to the day when American and Soviet psychologists may work freely within each other's country making the observations which will give more sophistication to what I believe are overschematized models we have of each other's systems.

CHAPTER 11

PUBLIC ADMINISTRATION: AMERICAN GOVERNMENT AT WORK

ADDRESSING the National Association of Manufacturers on December 7, 1961, the President of the United States noted that he had not always thought of the NAM membership as among his strongest supporters and that he had been somewhat nervous about accepting the invitation to speak until he had studied the history of the organization. The President continued: "I learned that this organization had once denounced—on one occasion, our 'swollen bureaucracy' as among the triumphs of Karl Marx, and decried on another occasion new governmental 'paternalism and socialism.' I was comforted when reading this very familiar language to note that I was in very good company. For the first attack I quoted was on Calvin Coolidge and the second on Herbert Hoover."

At this point the *New York Times* transcript of the speech inserted the bracket [Laughter].

After the listener or reader has laughed, he ought to go on to see what data constitute the basis for the judgment "swollen bureaucracy," what is the behavior that is called "paternalism," what economic arrangements are labeled "socialism," and to examine the promise and the threat, the deprivation and the indulgence, the need and the waste embodied in the expanding public administration in the United States. If the citizen is to think competently about the bureaucracy and to be enabled to dissect intelligently the continuing commentary about public parasites and public officials, he should explore questions of administrative responsibility and bureaucratic effectiveness. Not inconceivably, he may even decide to go into government service himself.

The following four concepts identify salient ideas about governmental administration; they serve as an introduction to the excerpts from public hearings and other materials below illustrating various aspects of bureaucratic action and thought.

1. Value- and emotion-encrusted labels like "bureaucracy" or neutral terms like "public administration" are summary, simplistic designations for an enormous range of organizational and administrative species and forms that vary greatly in all important respects. Included in that range are the Federal Department of Defense and the local Departments of Health; agencies with hundreds of thousands of employees as against others with half a dozen; some whose utility is as obvious as the local fire and police departments and others whose contributions are more

recondite, like an Art Commission; some as prestigious as the Federal Bureau of Investigation, while others are objects of frequent verbal assault, like a local bureau of public welfare that provides home relief for needy people.

Within a specific agency, the bureaucrat may do any of a thousand things, such as supervising a unit concerned with personnel training, or making studies to improve agency organization and procedures, or serving as aide to a top executive, or directing a program of public housing. It is useful for the observer to translate "bureaucrat" into "senior accountant" or "city planner" or other specific terms as an early step in the effort to form opinions about public service.

2. Governmental activities have grown in response to the articulated wants expressed by institutions acting for the community. A welfare program, a road-building activity, an increased expenditure for missiles or satellites, or the production of information films, a library, an agency for making loans to businessmen or farmers, or for inspecting dance halls, or for doing anything else that the Federal, state, county, city, or other governmental unit does—any public administrative organ comes into being only after there has been a long line of prior events.

Representatives have been elected, laws have been passed, accountants and auditors have recorded and checked into past expenditures, administrators have requested budget appropriations. What is more, fiscal officers and administrative analysts have reviewed the requests and made recommendations to executives who have made requests to a legislative body which has approved the appropriation of money. Then an administrator has recruited or assigned staff to the function with the approval of a central civil service selection agency and has used material and equipment purchased by a central agency. There are many variants of this process, but generally the administrator has been required to make reports to justify and explain what he has been doing and plans to do.

All the while there have been continuing comment and investigation and other attentions focused on the government service by newspapers and other mass media, pressure groups, and diverse and knowledgeable people and organizations.

To be sure, not every public activity is a reflex response to a community need. Testifying before a Senate committee, George F. Kennan, famous as a practitioner and writer and teacher in international relations, said, "The appalling growth in numbers of personnel and the seemingly endless proliferation of competing agencies and committees has appeared to me to be only in minor part a response to real needs and in major part the result of some unhealthy internal compulsions." In the same vein is the witty reference to public officials who seek to build bigger and greater empires of power and authority as persons with "an edifice complex." The point has been made in what has been called Parkinson's Law: Work Expands to Fill the Time Available.

That governmental waste and ineptitude exist is unquestionable; no less unquestionable is the fact that waste and ineptitude are found outside governmental operations. In either case, public or not, it may be that an administrator sets out to acquire power and subordinates because of a psychological mechanism set in motion by neurotic anxieties about the Soviet Union or China or a frustrated childhood, rather than because the executive truly needs more assistants to get the agency's work done. No research illuminates a secure conclusion.

What we do know is that in and out of government there are a myriad of controls over the governmental bureaucrat, that the sum of these controls is equivalent to the organization of all the forces and institutions of the community, that the effectiveness of these controls in keeping unnecessary or wasteful work to a minimum is intimately correlated with the quality of the community itself.

Public agencies do not spring into being because a few left- or right-wingers dream them up, nor are public administrators people who work in the dark to inflate their egos by doing foolish things. In the final analysis, the scope and quality of government service in the United States are a response to the quality of the interests and the character of the American people and the technology and caliber of our democratic society itself. The task of the public administrator is to provide whatever creative services the community wants and just as responsibly as the community chooses.

3. The government bureaucrat has a central role in determining whether the United States will survive and the manner in which the nation will live. He helps decide whether America's defenses will be adequate, aids in regulating large sectors of the economy, assists in working out policies and processes concerned with America's nuclear efforts, helps to create a productive environment within which labor, management, agriculture, and other principal groupings can carry the nation forward, and contributes vitally in a thousand ways to make sure that we die neither of food poisoning nor thermonuclear fall-out, that we live in as happy a setting as can be managed by public education, social security, and other bureaucratic devices and activities. Parenthetically, we may say that two components interlock to influence the excellence of the public service performed by the bureaucrat. One is the administrative, political, and community context in which the bureaucrat works; the other is his personality make-up, his skills, attitudes, and interests. The men and women of talent, energy, and ambition who go into public service contribute to making America a superior civilization.

It is not only government which furthers the common good in the United States; so do the steel industry, oil producers, milk producers, manufacturers of electrical energy, aircraft companies; so do the scientists, the clergymen, the teachers, and a vast array of other people and organizations. Not only the public administrator serves the public interest. Equally, however, it is pivotally the public administrator who weaves together and coordinates facilities to serve the whole public.

4. The United States has always been somewhat "socialist," somewhat "capitalist." The American economic system has undergone continuing change; exact usage would talk of various economic arrangements that have existed in the United States.

To charge that governmental expansion is socialistic is apparently to equate socialism with enlarged scope of public activity. Three significant reasons would appear to blunt the point of the equation. First, governmental participation in the economy in the United States has been extensive in the past; it is hardly new. The principal textbook on government and the American economy remarks: "Despite myths of a Golden Age of laissez faire, politics and economics were early intermingled in the United States. Recent research has shown that state governments played a major role in promoting economic development from the Revolution to the Civil War. The economic concerns of the national government were slower to emerge, but, particularly in the last half century, they have expanded enormously."

Secondly, the whole country has grown. The accretion of governmental activities becomes in part one of the aspects of the extraordinary growth both qualitatively and quantitatively of the United States. An expression of a big and complicated country, big government becomes in part a counterweight to big business, big agriculture, and big private-interest groups.

Thirdly, the basic question in the matter of government "interference" is what combination of public and private enterprise will produce the optimum safeguards and services to the American people. For example, to object to any public administration of atomic energy on abstract grounds of "socialism" is to court disaster in our relations with other nations. The goal is to use our atomic resources and facilities most productively and most responsibly. To that end the task is to figure out the appropriate administrative organization and process, making use of the public bureaucracy and private organization as each may be valuable in complementing the other.

The sum of these three arguments is that the dispute about "socialism" as such is a semantic distraction rather than a carefully documented diagnosis of a major public administrative ailment.

Creative thinking about the modern bureaucracy would focus on the integral character of American society. So closely interdependent and intimately interwoven are the important activities of modern America that the boundaries of public administration blend into the private sectors of the economy. Similarly, the limits of local, state, metropolitan, and of national and international administration fuse the one with the other. Thus, when the United States budget is formulated, the management of virtually every significant enterprise is deeply affected within the United States and the world over.

Public Administration in Differing Perspectives

Senator Styles Bridges, Republican of New Hampshire, at whose request the following item was reproduced in the *Congressional Record,* had voted against the Area Redevelopment Act, the legislation to aid chronically depressed areas that forms the subject matter of the *Wall Street Journal* editorial. When he signed the bill on May 1, 1961,

President John F. Kennedy remarked that "This bill will help make it possible for thousands of Americans who want to work, to work. It will be of special help to those areas which have been subjected to chronic unemployment for many months, and in some cases for many years. In this free society we want to make it possible for everyone to find a job who wants to work and support their families, and this bill is an important step in that direction."

As the student reads the several alleged examples of "fiscal irresponsibility," cited below, he should be aware that Congress passed the law creating the area redevelopment program, that the Administrator is appointed by the President with the consent of the Senate, that the Administrator works with an Advisory Policy Board of Federal officials and a Public Advisory Committee of state and local officials and public members; that to be designated as one of the "redevelopment areas" an industrial area must have a rate of unemployment at least 6 per cent of the working force plus a past average unemployment rate of 6 per cent. The area must meet the unemployment rate criteria established by the Bureau of Employment Security of the Department of Labor to classify as an area of "substantial and persistent" labor surplus: (*a*) at least 50 per cent above the national average for three of the previous four years; or (*b*) at least 75 per cent above the national average for two of the previous three years; or (*c*) at least 100 per cent above the national average for one of the previous two years. Rural areas, including Indian reservations, may be designated as redevelopment areas where the Administrator finds that they "are among the highest in numbers and percentages of low-income families, and in which there exists a condition of substantial and persistent unemployment or underemployment."

Among the points of vantage from which the student may view the Senator's concern are: avoidable and inescapable waste in administrative activities, partisan politicking, executive-legislative conflict, mass-media attitudes toward public administrative programs, and newspapers' selection and organization of material for their readers and the availability to the citizen of alternative sources of data and interpretation.

["How to Make a Pork Barrel," editorial from *Wall Street Journal,* reproduced in *Congressional Record,* July 7, 1961, p. 11173.]

MR. BRIDGES. Mr. President, an editorial entitled "How to Make a Pork Barrel," which appeared in a recent edition of the *Wall Street Journal*, provides a shocking revelation of the extent to which the urban renewal program is used and abused.

The facts brought out in this revealing column make previous advocates of pork-barrel legislation look like skinflints. When, in the name of urban renewal, a town can receive as much as $478 in Federal funds for every one of its inhabitants, we have certainly hit a new high—or perhaps the word should be low—in fiscal irresponsibility.

I believe this commentary should be read by every Member of this body, and I particularly commend it to those Senators who champion the cause of a multi-billion-dollar urban renewal program. I ask unanimous consent that the editorial entitled "How to Make a Pork Barrel" be printed at this point in the *Record*.

There being no objection, the editorial was ordered to be printed in the *Record*, as follows:

HOW TO MAKE A PORK BARREL

If the phrase "urban renewal" conjures up any clear image it is that of a street scene in one of our great cities, with its rows of tenements swarming with people lacking not merely room to move but air to breathe, a congestion that chokes not merely the view but the community that surrounds it.

Such, anyway, was the image that supposedly moved Congress to pass the multi-billion-dollar urban renewal program. There was little inquiry as to why the slums and congestion existed or why the cities were unwilling to renew themselves. It was sufficient that the condition was, therefore, to apply the familiar remedy of billions from Washington.

Well, the actuality has turned out to be something different, as a detailed report in this newspaper the other day revealed. Whatever else this program may be, it isn't urban renewal.

A more accurate name today might be "the village landscaping program" or, if people were willing to be bluntly honest, the Federal pork barrel project. That old favorite of Congress, the rivers and harbors bill, just can't compare with this handy, bulging cask for dipping into.

Take just a few samples from the many reported in our recent story: The metropolis of East Granby, Conn., $246,000 of Federal funds for its 2,434 people. Lithonia, Ga., $102,800 for its 1,667 people. Atchison, Kans., $1,916,800 for its 12,500 people.

Or look a little more closely at the situation in Mercedes, Tex., a town of some 10,000 people. Here was a town which, by all the evidence, really did need a new sewer system, the cost of that program being about $234,000. In the words of the mayor, "We would never have been able to finance that by ourselves."

So what happened? In the name of "urban renewal" this small town got a Federal grant of $1.1 million not only to fix up its sewer system but also to pave streets and build a residential housing project. And now, again in the words of the mayor, "We're able to issue $350,000 in bonds for a new civic center without even raising the tax rate." They can now build a civic center when they were too poor to take care of their own sewage.

Or look at Wink, Tex. Here the Federal Government has allotted $478 for every man, woman, and child of its 1,800 population. This to completely remodel the town's business district, all three blocks of it.

To labor the evidence would be needless. As one of the officials of the Urban Renewal Administration quite frankly states, "There are no limits whatever on the size a city has to be to get urban renewal grants." And apparently none, either, on the kind of project for which towns and villages can tap the Federal till. The list of things which these happy folk are building with Federal funds includes parks, playgrounds, tennis courts, and swimming pools. All good things indeed for any town. And more blessed yet when they are paid by other people's taxes.

As a pork barrel this has the wonderful advantage that there's no need for any pretense about building a dam to preserve natural resources or dredging a creek for navigation purposes; the handouts can go to lovely, little towns like Princeton, N.J., or crossroad villages, like Wink, Tex., lost in the wide-open mesquite plains. All you need is a diligent representative in Washington.

It's hardly necessary to labor the editorial comment either. As the publisher of the *Wink Bulletin* remarked, "You can hardly spend money like this in a little town without doing some good." Or as the Mercedes mayor put it, "This is the greatest thing that's happened to us in years."

So it is. And also the greatest thing that's happened in years to the business of building pork barrels.

The New Pluralism and the Relative Decline of the States

There are intimate connections between Federalism and politics and administration in the United States, between the issue of centralization and decentralization in public administration, and continuing areas of concern like the maintenance of a free society and the administration of high-grade public services competently conceived and operated.

The article below was written by William G. Carleton, professor of political science and head professor of the social sciences at the University of Florida; it is reproduced here because it embodies a first-rate opportunity for the student to explore the relations between centralized administrative trends and other aspects of American government and politics.

[William G. Carleton, "Centralization and the Open Society," *Political Science Quarterly*, vol. 75, pp. 244–259, 1960.]

I

In 1952, the theme of Dwight Eisenhower's presidential campaign, at least in domestic politics, was the reawakening of the states, the restoration of their traditional place in the federal system, a return to the values and practices of decentralized federalism. Even scholars took another look at the federal system, and some became moderately optimistic about the prospects of revitalizing the states.

Among those who shared this optimism was the late Leonard D. White, one of our most distinguished scholars in the field of public administration. In a series of lectures at Louisiana State University, published in book form in early 1953 under the title *The States and the Nation*, Professor White set forth the grounds for believing that the federal government would relinquish some of its tax sources to the states, among others the gasoline tax, and that the states themselves would also explore new sources of tax revenue.

Professor White believed that the states would probably revitalize themselves in other ways. First, they would relinquish some federal grants-in-aid and assume independently some of the services they now render jointly with the federal government. Secondly, the states would experiment more widely with the interstate compact. Thirdly, they would make a much fuller use of their own powers in two general ways—they would enlarge their traditional services and keep these abreast of the great advances being made in criminology, penology, mental health and education; and they would resume their old role as laboratories of experimentation by taking on new functions such as adult education and training, government aid to superior students, health insurance, possibly even disability insurance.

This emphasis in 1952–1953 on the bright future of the states was, of course, a reaction from the enormous growth of federal power during the 1930's and 1940's. As late as the turn of the century, the federal government had affected the national economy only through its simple excise taxes, its protective tariff, its uniform currency, its marketing of federal bonds, the limited functions of the national banking system, and an inconclusive regulation of interstate carriers. By 1950, however, the activities of the federal government had come to touch vitally every aspect of American life. The old and original powers of the federal government had been prodigiously expanded by new demands in foreign affairs and national defense. And the New Deal and the Fair Deal, building on the earlier New Nationalism and New Freedom, had charged the federal government with vast new functions so as to assure a smooth functioning of the American economy. By 1950, American constitutional theory and practice had come to accept this and American opinion overwhelmingly to expect it.

In 1960, it looks as if the anticipation of a revived federalism in its old forms were unfounded. Aside from tidelands oil, there has been no significant return of functions or tax sources to the states. Since 1953, it is true, there have been demands for an enlargement of old state functions and for the initiation of new state functions, but most of the states fail to respond to the demands. At the same time, the federal government has been taking on and expanding functions hitherto regarded as largely state or private matters—road building, welfare, housing, slum clearance, urban renewal, individual and public health, hospitals, education, and so forth. The federal government has been concerning itself more and more with these activities, either directly, or indirectly through grants-in-aid. Older grants-in-aid are expanding, new grants-in-aid are being adopted, and federal money appropriations for grants-in-aid are increasing enormously. In 1901, they amounted to less than $3,000,000. In 1931, they amounted to about $220,000,000. In 1941, they rose to $615,000,000. By 1951, they had expanded to $2,280,000,000. Today, they are running close to $7,000,000,000, counting the so-called highway trust fund.

In effect, the centralization-decentralization issue has now shifted from the American economy to the American society. A new rationale to justify a new expansion of federal power is developing. More and more it is being said that our society is national, that as a society we are becoming more interrelated and interdependent, that we are a more mobile people than ever before, that health and education in one state affect health and education in all the states and in the nation.

At the turn of the century it would have taken a bold man to declare that since our economy was national, the government most concerned with that economy must be the national government and not the state. Today this is a commonplace. Now it is being said that because our society is national, the government most concerned with that society must be the national government and not the state. Today this is an advanced attitude, but tomorrow it may be a commonplace.

From many sides are coming demands for enlarged and new government services. Here are a few straws in the wind. In a recent series of articles on urban renewal, *The Christian Science Monitor* estimated that one out of every four city dwellers in the United States lives in a slum. A short time ago the New York State Department of Labor, commenting on the rising costs of health services, reported that today two out of every three dollars spent for medical and hospital services in the United States are still borne by the individual, that only one dollar in every three is covered by some kind of insurance. The National Education Association is insisting that our public schools need an additional eight billion dollars each year if American education is to be what it should be quantitatively and qualitatively, and it strongly implies that all estimates of federal aid up to this time have been trifling in comparison with existing need. From all sides come reports of skyrocketing costs for college and professional training. There is the much-publicized article of Benjamin Fine, who estimates that about two hundred thousand of our most gifted high school graduates each year cannot go on for college or technical or professional training for lack of financial help. And the nation is reacting to all this differently from what it would formerly. Yesterday people would have said: "But advanced education is for the individual to provide for himself." Today people increasingly say: "What a waste of national brain power!"

These new demands are coming out of new conditions. What are these conditions? Rapidly increasing population. Continuing and accelerating shifts of population to the urban areas. Disproportionately rising costs in medical services, hospital services and education. The expansion of the private sector of our economy, and the realization that as the private sector expands so also must the public sector—for otherwise we face grave imbalances. (For instance, when the private sector builds more automobiles, the public sector must build more roads.) The growing recognition that goods and services produced by the public sector are not just luxuries or consumer goods; that they are productive wealth, used to make more and better goods and services. (Better schools and better health facilities produce more effective workers, managers, scientists, technicians, technologists.) The deepening realization that we must keep ahead of the Soviet Union in industrial and military technology. The growing consciousness that desegregation is a vital ideological weapon in our world struggle to win the uncommitted peoples of Asia, the Middle East, Africa and Latin America, and that we can no longer regard this question as a domestic and local one. In short, crisis is the health of centralization, and we are in a continuing crisis.

II

Will the states do their part in meeting the nation's growing expectations? Have the optimistic predictions about the future of the states been borne out by subsequent developments? The evidence seems to be that they have not, that the states will not sufficiently revitalize themselves, that the trend to federal centralization will continue.

True, all states are making some progress; and a few states have taken constructive, even heroic, measures to tap water supplies, find new tax sources, provide regional planning, and reapportion their legislative seats. But what was the record of most of the legislatures meeting during 1959? It was largely a record of economy, retrenchment, and the slashing of budgets submitted by the executives. The truth is that most of the states are barely able to keep the old services abreast of increasing costs, increasing population, and the shifts of population to the cities.

Few of the things envisaged by Professor White have taken place. Have the states relinquished any federal grants-in-aid? Not at all. Not a single grant-in-aid has been relinquished. Here is the typical story. First, a grant-in-aid is made so as to get a necessary or desirable government service started and to soften opposition to it in the states. Then it becomes a going concern, vested interests are created, the controversial becomes customary, and the opposition vanishes. Therefore, grants-in-aid do not diminish; instead, they multiply.

What of the interstate compact? It still remains largely a potentiality rather than an actuality, although there is an encouraging tendency by the states to experiment with it more widely. The truth seems to be that the interstate compact works most successfully in the noncontroversial, that is, the relatively unimportant, areas of activity such as the regional educational councils, the return of parolees, and so forth. In the controversial areas—such as electric power, tapping water supplies, preventing water pollution, conserving soil and other natural resources—it has been less successful, although longer and wider experience may bring greater achievement. At the present time what is most impressive, considering the many possibilities for the use of interstate compacts, is this: how few are attempted; of the few attempted, how many founder in the process of negotiation and ratification; of the very few that materialize, how prolonged and difficult the process of negotiation and ratification. Proposed interstate compacts must be watched closely, for they sometimes contain built-in devices for local vetoes, disguises for obstruction. It is instructive that one of the reasons for calling the Constitutional Convention of 1787, to form a stronger general government, was the failure of the Potomac River states to conclude an interstate compact. In the light of the total situation and the many opportunities for employing this device, the use of the interstate compact is still negligible.

Are the states making an adequately fuller use of their own powers? They are not, emphatically not. This is so, chiefly because of the realities of group politics in the states. It is true that the groups that press for the expansion of government services to meet new conditions can be found in all states, but it is only in the industrial states that they can exert much influence. Generally speaking, they are more numerous and better organized on the national than on the state level. On the state level they frequently run into structural barriers erected by nineteenth-century horse-and-buggy constitutions. Some of these are so long and involved as to be in effect codes of law rather than constitutions. They place prohibitions on the taxing power, the borrowing power, the spending power and rigid limitations on the powers of the cities. Above all they provide for flagrant malapportionment of the legislatures.

Malapportionment of state legislatures is by now an old and a familiar story: how the rural areas are overrepresented and the urban areas underrepresented; how as little as 30 or 25 or 20 per cent or even less of a state's population frequently makes a majority in the legislature; how one vote in a rural area often equals one hundred or two hundred or even three hundred votes in an urban area.

What is not so well known is the extent of this malapportionment, how general it is, how flagrant, how today some of our states are as undemocratic as Great Britain was before the Reform Bill of 1832.

The consequences of all this are even less well known. Overrepresentation of the rural areas means not so much the rule of the rural folk as it does the rule of the rural politicians, who largely reflect the interests and values of the county rings, the large landowners, the small-scale and local-minded businessmen of the county-seat towns, and certain corporate businesses (themselves located in the cities) which would rather deal with a legislative oligarchy than a broadly representative and democratic legislature.

It is the legislatures dominated by rural politicians that favor the unrealistic proposals to amend the United States Constitution so as to limit the federal income tax, particularly in the higher income brackets. It is these legislatures which spawn the so-called "right-to-work" laws and other legislation designed to hamper the legitimate aspirations of organized labor. It is these legislatures which have a peculiarly tender regard for the small loan companies. (Recently, a bill sponsored by no one except the small loan companies was passed by the legislature of Florida; the "aye" votes in the house represented constituencies totaling 600,000 persons, while the "no" votes, which failed to stop the bill, represented constituencies totaling over two million people.)

Domination of the legislatures by rotten-borough rural politicians is especially dangerous in the one-party states, where these politicians become still more inbred and form a ruling clique unchecked by even a rival party clique. Nor does this situation prevail only in the South. About one half of all the states can be called one-party states, at least so far as state matters, especially the legislatures, are concerned.

These conditions are all roadblocks on the way to making the changes that would have to be made before the states could embark on that fuller use of their powers that was predicted by Professor White. Let us list some of these necessary changes: constitutional revision; genuine reapportionment; the exploration of new sources of taxation; the establishment of adequate civil service and merit systems in the states so that they could compete with private enterprise and the federal government for administrative personnel; emancipation of the cities from neglect and exploitation.

Thus the formidable task in most of the states is a twofold one. First, the structural barriers must be removed. Then the constructive battle must be fought to expand old services and introduce new ones.

The chances are that it will be another case of "too little and too late" since in the meantime the federal government will be moving in with new or expanded services which are given either directly, or indirectly through additional grants-in-aid. In fact, we may be nearer than many of us suspect to another great spurt in federal expansion. If the present Congress were not checked by presidential veto, we would be in the midst of it right now. After January 1961, a Mr. Veto may no longer be in the White House.

III

Yet we must beware of exaggeration. The federal system is moving in the direction of greater federal power, but it is not becoming extinct. Institutions are tenacious things, and they are transformed slowly. Local governments for experimentation, adaptation, apprenticeship in political leadership, and training for democratic citizenship will continue to function.

The states will continue to create and maintain counties and cities for local government. The states will continue to use the counties as agencies for the administration of state matters, though not as much as formerly, for the state today tends to administer more of its own functions directly and not indirectly. The states will continue to give their own grants-in-aid to the counties—so that the state will increasingly spend federal money it does not collect and collect state money it does not spend. The states will continue to exercise many powers independently of the federal government. Even where the federal government starts exercising a power formerly exercised exclusively by the state, the federal government does not always preempt the field, and thus cooperative federalism comes to operate in a wider way. (This whole subject of cooperative federalism is a large and intricate one in itself.) Finally, the state will continue to administer the joint federal-state projects under the federal government's expanding grants-in-aid programs.

Actually, in this century the state has been increasing its powers. State government does more than it did at the turn of the century. Some of these added powers have been taken from the counties, and some of them are new powers never before exercised by any government in the United States. However, the federal government, as we have seen, has taken on more powers, too. Some of these added federal powers have been taken from the states, but some of them are new powers never before exercised by any of our American units of government. The federal government has been increasing its powers at a more rapid rate than has the state, and its expanding powers are more significant and pervasive, more ramifying in their effects. Thus while the state has increased in power absolutely, it has declined relatively.

By now, we ought to face bluntly the implications of federal centralization for our open society. About this, there is profound and widespread confusion, even among our "liberals" and "progressives." The "conventional wisdom" places a high premium on the values of decentralized federalism, regarding it as the source of experimentation, adaptation to local variations, apprenticeship for political leadership, training in democratic citizenship, the very existence of democracy, the very preservation of liberty. Does this square with the facts?

J. K. Galbraith in *The Affluent Society* has shown how the conventional wisdom in economics—the discrepancy between our old stereotyped concepts of the traditional free market and the realities of today—clouds our thinking and actions in economic matters. Is it not high time to analyze the conventional wisdom in politics and to inquire whether there is not a similar discrepancy between the stereotyped concepts of the old decentralized federalism and the political realities of today? Is not the conventional wisdom in economics linked with that in politics? Do not our anachronistic, ritualistic and mythological notions about political decentralization help perpetuate our anachronistic notions about the "reality" of the free market today? Are not our horse-and-buggy state governments among the most formidable barriers to our meeting present-day economic and social needs? Do not people who recognize today's limitations on the free market but at the same time cling to the primacy of the local governments in effect nullify their insights into economics with a superstitious political faith?

It seems to me that an examination of the realities of contemporary politics would go far to show that federal centralization means wider economic and social fulfillment for the individual and the nation, and at the same time means not less democracy but more democracy, not less liberty but more liberty.

IV

Even if the federal system were becoming extinct—which it is not—there would still be local governments. It is a rather naive and parochial notion that we must have a federal system in order to have local governments with administrative and even discretionary powers. Even governments that are not federal at all—that are national in character—decentralize and allow for considerable creativity in local government. Most of the governments of western Europe are national, not federal, but they allow for local governments. These local governments provide apprenticeships for political leadership. Adenauer was mayor of Cologne. The Chamberlains saw service in the municipality of Birmingham. Attlee learned his politics in the London County Council. Many of the members of the French Chamber of Deputies served their towns and cities as mayors. If our American cities succeed in freeing themselves from some of the unreasonable restraints of the states, this might mean a further weakening of the traditional federal system, but it would surely result in a great energizing of local government!

In many ways experimentation in state and local governments is on the increase, particularly in technical and administrative matters. Home rule for the cities, where it exists, allows a wider scope for experimentation. The federal government, in gathering, organizing and disseminating data about state and local governments and in insisting that the states, under the grants-in-aid programs, keep better records and organize data, is actually stimulating experimentation and adaptation to local needs.

We must guard against an unwieldy federal bureaucracy, but we must also remember that federal administration and federal administrators are not the evil things they are often said to be. Federal administrators are in general better trained, better protected by civil service, and better audited financially than are state administrators. We should keep in mind that because a power is federalized it does not follow that its administration will be centralized in Washington. Federal administration may be regionalized, and indeed some of it is already regionalized. Even so, federal administrators do administer over a wider geographical area, and therefore minister to a larger number of groups, interests and values, and must be responsive to them. The people can influence federal administrators through their local congressmen and senators. Practical politicians frequently observe that people today have a greater feeling of intimacy with the federal government than they have with their own state and local governments, that people know their local congressman better than they do their local state legislator, that they bring him not only federal requests but many state and local requests.

Now, it is just as important to resist improper pressures as it is to respond to legitimate and democratic ones. Federal officials and administrators, since they minister to a wider area and to more groups, interests and values, are in a better position to resist improper pressures. If they offend some groups, they may compensate by increasing their popularity with other groups. Federal administrators are farther removed from particular local prejudices; they get a wider perspective; it is harder to convince them that a handful of people represent the whole universe. Usually, what we mean by an official's "growth" is the result of his transferring from a position of narrower horizons to one of wider horizons.

True, there recently have been disclosures of improprieties in some of the federal commissions in Washington—but that is just the point: in the federal government, because of the clash of more diverse and articulate interests, the federal commissions get the white heat of publicity, whereas the work of the state commissions all too often passes unnoticed. As a result of the recent disclosures, a great hue and cry has arisen to put the federal commissions beyond all pressures, to put them above and beyond the battle. In a democracy, this is dangerous nonsense. In a democracy, what we must avoid is secret and undue influence by some groups and interests; what we must guarantee is open access by all groups and interests.

There is a tendency to look back to the nineteenth century, when the state played a larger part in our federal system than it does today, and to say: "That was the day of real democracy, but now with all this growth of federal power, democracy is dying out." Now, it is romantic to think that we can return to an agrarian past. It is also romantic to think of that agrarian past as democratic. We look back and idealize the past. We visualize people in their rural neighborhoods and villages, in their town halls and county courthouses, all interested in politics, all participating in politics. Actually, politics in those days was largely a matter for professional politicians, for tight little caucuses and conventions, for county rings, for machines and bosses, for local bigwigs and notabilities. Politics was largely a matter for native, white, Protestant males, especially planters, big farmers, and the prosperous business and professional classes. Actually, nineteenth-century democracy was a limited and restricted democracy, a mere preface to our wider democracy of today.

Today, our democracy is mass democracy, metropolitan democracy, melting-pot democracy, group democracy. Politics centers less on caucus, convention, courthouse, town hall, and state capitol. People learn, discuss and operate in politics more through their functional groups—their economic, social, occupational, professional, business, labor, farm, ethnic and religious organizations. Today, there are more groups; they are better organized; they are organized nationally. The newer, popular, and numerically larger groups have learned how to use their national organizations on the federal level to by-pass the local traditional power structures, the local planter-lawyer-doctor-banker-realtor-insurance-business elites, to achieve a wider influence in public affairs and a larger respect for popular interests. This has not resulted in neglect of the interests of the traditional local elites—they still have an enormous influence—but it has resulted in a better and more democratic balancing of interests.

For people are still interested in local politics, and through their organizations they discuss and participate in local politics. Today, it is at the PTA meeting, the teachers' meeting, the League of Women Voters meeting, the woman's club meeting, the Junior Chamber of Commerce meeting, the civic club meeting, the union meeting, and the farm organization meeting that people learn about and discuss local politics. Thus today, more people, more different kinds of people, participate in local politics than ever attended the old courthouse rallies, which were largely composed of the politicians, the officeholders, their families, their friends, and those who wanted political jobs. Today, even in semirural states, widely representative community organizations, like the local and state PTA and the local and state League of Women Voters, are playing a relatively larger part in politics, and the old county rings are playing a relatively smaller part.

In general, the most undemocratic areas in America are the small rural counties, the very ones vastly overrepresented in the legislatures, for these counties usually have the smallest number of diversified and organized groups, and the professional politicians, with the voters atomized and less aware, can be less responsive to needs and more free to operate on their own, to serve their own interests or to serve interests at variance with those of their rural constituents. Today, it is the heavily rural counties, where the traditional local elites still predominate, which continue to operate most like the way the "democracy" of the nineteenth century operated.

People who look back to the past emphasize "the freedom of the states." People who would come to grips with present-day realities emphasize freedom of association, the importance of group organization, and fair representation on all levels of government.

Last, and most important, what of liberty? The "conventional wisdom" in America has it that liberty is nurtured by local government and dries up when government becomes far away and remote. This does not square with the realities. Most tyrannies in history, and some of the most onerous, have been local. Indeed, a central trend of western civilization has been the breakdown of the rule of local feudal lords and local magnates and the development of the national democratic state, which has done much to free individuals from local shackles.

The most frequent violations of constitutional processes and civil liberties in the United States have been in the states and localities. Let us mention a few examples: the shoddy treatment of Negroes, aliens and migratory laborers in many states; the Lusk gag laws of 1919 in New York State and the expulsion of the Socialist assemblymen from the New York State legislature in the same year; the control of Indiana by the Ku Klux Klan in the mid-1920's; the Huey Long dictatorship in Louisiana; the existence of prohibition in many states long before and long after prohibition on the national scene. Traditional decentralizers are in the habit of saying that prohibition in Kansas is all right because it is an adjustment to a local variation, but that prohibition on the national scene is a mistake. Are not a person's liberties as much impaired by prohibition from Topeka as by prohibition from Washington?

Think back, too, over our judicial history. Have not most of the judicial miscarriages been in the state courts, and not in the federal courts? There would be more of these were it not for the due-process-of-law clause and the equal-protection clause of the Fourteenth Amendment, and for judicial review in the federal courts by federal judges removed from local prejudices, sustained by a broad national opinion, and taking the large and long view.

In historical perspective, periods of extremism and hysteria on the national scene have been infrequent, short-lived, and relatively mild. Three of these stand out. One was the "black cockade" reaction of the John Adams administration, which gave us the Alien and Sedition Laws. Another was the Palmer Red Hunts of 1919. The third was McCarthyism and the spate of congressional investigations into subversion, without due regard for civil liberties, in the early and middle 1950's during and following the Korean War. All of these proved to be abortive. Witch-hunting on the national scene created a furor and collapsed several years ago, but it continues on the state level, where little McCarthys in some of our state legislatures have set up committees which are currently investigating subversion, un-Americanism, socialism, communism, the NAACP, immorality, and sundry other things. It goes without saying that many of these investigations are being conducted with no nice respect for personal civil liberties. On the national scene these would produce furious indignation and vigorous countermeasures, but in the states there is apathy.

Even during the national trauma of the Civil War, the conduct of President Lincoln was moderate compared to the highhanded methods of a Governor Oliver P. Morton in Indiana.

There are several reasons why liberty is better safeguarded in the nation than in the state. The chances are greater of having independent citizens and newspapers to speak out against passion and injustice. It is harder for a single group or faction to get control of the government. It is more difficult to form a majority, and even more difficult to form an opinionated majority. Within the wide scope of the nation there are many more classes, groups, interests and values which check, restrain and counterbalance one another. All of this is stated in *The Federalist,* and it is as true now as when it was first written.

Is it not a curious paradox that today, when we are much more national than we were in 1789, these truths in *The Federalist* have almost ceased to be expressed, that they are all but drowned out in the steady drumfire of expressions of fear of federal centralization? Why do those who favor federal centralization today put their case almost exclusively in terms of concrete measures and refuse to put it in a wide and philosophic setting as the centralizers of 1789 did so admirably and successfully?

There are more groups today than there were in the early days of the Republic; they are better organized; they are more nationally organized. These groups help check big business; they help check big government; they help check one another. The group process is coming to be recognized as another of our guarantees of liberty along with the written Constitution, judicial review, separation of powers, and federalism. The states have declined somewhat and the federal system has become somewhat weaker, but the group checks have become stronger. Liberty is better safeguarded in those areas where there are many and well-organized groups than in the areas where they are fewer in number and less organized.

In the earlier days of the Republic, the states thundered at the government in Washington, and legislators often instructed United States Senators out of their seats. Those days are gone. Today, it is the groups that restrain government and our political parties, and thus play a vital role in the processes of both democracy and liberty. Fortunately our two major parties in America are center parties; neither runs to extremes. But when the Republicans are in power in Washington and incline too far to the right, they are checked not so much by the states as by the activities of the nationally organized liberal groups. And when the Democrats are in power in Washington and incline too far to the left, they are checked not so much by the states as by the activities of the nationally organized conservative groups.

What happens when a national organization gets too ambitious and overreaching? Then other groups tend to ally themselves against it. And it is important to note that if government is necessary to regulate such a group, it is the federal government which must do it, for our leading national organizations are now too large for effective state regulation. Also, any hidden collusion of groups would ultimately bring resistance of other groups and intervention by the federal government.

Are the rank-and-file members of America's mass-group organizations exploited by their own leaders, their own elites? This and other aspects of our increasingly corporate and group society (particularly the spiritual and personality aspects) are beyond the scope of this discussion. However, it should be said in passing that it is a safe guide to assume that farmers, wageworkers and Negroes are better judges of their own interests and leaderships than are outside elites, and it seems indisputable that the individual members of mass groups now have better economic conditions, enjoy wider civil liberties, and exercise more political influence than they did in the days when they were unorganized and atomized.

All parts of America are becoming more alike, but more alike in their diversity. Formerly, the diversity of America was geographical; diversity expressed itself in differences from locality to locality and from section to section. Today, as industrialization and urbanization spread, every community is becoming more diversified, coming to contain within itself a larger number of different groups and values. This new pluralism, found on all levels but particularly on the national level, will do much to offset the relative decline of the states, prevent the dangers of federal centralization, and preserve and extend both democracy and liberty.

Toward a Responsible Bureaucracy

One of the popular sports in America is to point to the enormous rise in public expenditures, the great expansion in the numbers of public employees, the vast proliferation of public services and activities, the monumental alteration in the nature, organization, and locus of the public bureaucracy. Thus, an investment advisory service included with its suggestions to its clientele for reaping profits in the stock market a page reproducing a map of the United States. A little above the approximate center of the map was a heavy dot. Take a good look at the speck on the map, said the investment service. The speck is Armstrong County which lies in South Dakota; 53 people live there and they have seven farms. "It is also the only county left in the entire United States which does not have a Federal civilian employee at work within its borders."

Concern about the possibility of an irresponsible bureaucracy is natural indeed, and in fact, vital in a democratic society. The article below, by one of the nation's great professors of political science, furnishes persuasive evidence that public administration in the United States is a network of responsible people at work.

[Peter H. Odegard, "Toward a Responsible Bureaucracy," *Annals of the American Academy of Political and Social Science,* vol. 292, pp. 18–29, 1954.]

A government without bureaucrats is like a centipede without legs, unable to move—even to save itself—and powerless to accomplish any of the goals for which governments are instituted among men. For it is upon the bureaucrats that we depend to see that these goals—or policies—are realized in practice. Without administrative officers—that is, without a bureaucracy to carry them into effect—the most fine-spun schemes for promoting the common defense, insuring domestic tranquillity, promoting the general welfare, and preserving the blessings of liberty to ourselves and our posterity would be stillborn.

Yet there is a widely current notion that bureaucracy and democracy are somehow incompatible—that the bureaucrat and the democrat must forever be at odds. This popular antithesis between bureaucracy and democracy is, as Professor Friedrich says, "an oratorical slogan which endangers the future of democracy. For a constitutional system which cannot function effectively, which cannot act with dispatch and strength, cannot live."

Nevertheless, the fears expressed by the demagogues pose problems which cannot be denied for those who want government to be both effective and democratic. Not the least of these is the problem of enforcing responsibility upon the bureaucracy. For among the so-called immutable principles of democratic theory is the assumption that power and responsibility must go hand in hand. Power without responsibility is the very definition of tyranny, and the transition from arbitrary to responsible government involves more than popular control of the legislature, the so-called policy-making branch of the government. It involves also popular control of the executive establishment and the bureaucracy through which public policies are translated from law into life.

As the functions of the state expand and the size and complexity of the bureaucracy increase, the search for ways and means to make these minions of Leviathan more responsible becomes both more important and more intense. But if bureaucratic accountability is to be real and equitable, the bureaucrat must know for what and to whom he is responsible. . . .

Implications of Responsibility

But "responsibility" implies more than mere accountability for what is or is not done, and more too than a strict adherence to policy mandates as they come from the legislature and/or one's administrative superiors and associates. It implies also a high level of technical competence for the job one is called upon to do, a personal character that is loyal, honest, and reliable, a dedication to duty, and faith in the basic values of the society one serves. These values in turn will in final analysis determine the quality of the public service and the character and conduct of its servants.

A truly responsible bureaucrat is, then, a man of not one but many responsibilities. He owes a political responsibility to those who have final say as to policy and ultimately to the people who make and unmake them. He owes both a "political" and an administrative responsibility to his superior officers. He owes a legal responsibility to the courts (both administrative and judicial), lest he transgress the rights of citizens by abusing or exceeding his powers. He owes a professional responsibility to his fellow bureaucrats to maintain high standards of integrity and competence, lest he bring dishonor or disgrace to the "guild" of which all are members. He owes a moral responsibility to the highest ethical and moral principles of the state and society in which he lives and to which he professes allegiance. And finally he owes a responsibility to his own soul—to the honor and integrity of his own person—for without self-respect he can scarcely be expected to have respect for others or to deserve their respect in turn.

To explore fully these multiple loyalties and responsibilities is beyond the scope of this brief essay. It may, nevertheless, be useful to suggest some of the problems and perplexities that occur in thinking about a responsible bureaucracy in the modern state.

Responsibility for Subordinates

As far as the mass of bureaucrats have any political responsibility, it must be vicarious and not direct. A President, a Prime Minister, and the chief executive officers appointed to serve with them must, above all things, be politicians (and partisans, at that) and, as such, politically responsible not alone for their own acts but for those of their subordinates, however numerous and widespread.

As the leader of the government, and under the principle of collective responsibility as it operates in Great Britain, the Prime Minister is the center and focus of political responsibility. If the deeds of wayward and incompetent civil servants in the Home Office are attributable to the Home Secretary, so in like succession are they—through the Home Secretary—attributable to Her Majesty's Prime Minister. And all together the ministers of the Crown must assume collective political responsibility not only for major lines of policy but also for administrative acts of thousands of civil servants of whose very existence they may be but dimly aware. It is in this combination of individual and collective responsibility to Parliament that the great strength of British democracy is to be found.

Political responsibility for the mass of bureaucrats in the American government is much less clearly defined. The President, to be sure, in final analysis must "take the rap" for what is or is not done. The heads of the major departments are political officers appointed by and accountable to him; and as they must answer for the acts of their subordinates, so the President in turn must answer for them. But the locus of responsibility is by no means as clear as in Great Britain. James Burns says:

> The Founding Fathers did not clearly distinguish between the President's executive authority and the supervisory powers of Congress over administration. On the contrary, they deliberately divided administrative power between the two branches as part of the system of checks and balances.

The Issue Confused

The President's power to control the bureaucrats derives mainly from his powers to appoint (and presumably by inference to dismiss) "officers of the United States whose appointments are not otherwise provided for" and to "require the opinion, in writing, of the principal officer in each of the executive departments." But these powers are by no means unlimited or exclusive, and at a hundred points Congress has, from the beginning, pared them down and impaired their effectiveness. The organic act establishing the Treasury Department, to cite one example, requires the Secretary "to make report and give information to either branch of the legislature, in person or in writing, respecting all matters referred to him by the Senate or House of Representatives or which may appertain to his office." And, although the Secretary was described in a subsequent law of September 11, 1789, as an "Executive Officer," he and the Treasurer of the United States were nevertheless required to make annual reports to Congress.

Legislation setting up other major departments or executive agencies has not followed this pattern, but Congress has nevertheless found ways and means for interposing itself between the President and his executive subordinates and thus confusing the clear line of bureaucratic responsibility. The creation within major departments of numerous bureaus over which particular committees of Congress and even particular Congressmen exercise more control than the department chief is but one of several such devices.

Nor is this confusion confined to the central corps of executive departments and agencies. It has been confounded by the creation of "independent" boards, commissions, corporations, and authorities, responsible (if they may be so described) not to the President, but to Congress. This so-called "headless fourth branch of government" has posed problems of administrative organization, management, and responsibility for which no one seems to have found satisfactory solutions. . . .

Constitutional Division of Powers

The problem of the "independent agency" is obviously too complex and too important to be resolved by mere structural or procedural reform. It involves a restudy of at least one basic principle of American constitutional law—the principle of separation of powers. Although not expressly spelled out in the United States Constitution, the principle has always been implied from the language of Articles I, II, and III, vesting the legislative, executive, and judicial powers in three distinct branches of the government. But there is scarcely an agency or official of the government that does not in one way or another exercise two or more of these "distinct" powers.

Wherever an official has discretion to decide controversies among persons or between private persons and the government, he may be said to exercise judicial power; wherever he has power to issue rules or regulations to which penalties for violation are attached, he exercises legislative power; and wherever he has power to direct, or control, conduct in terms of these decisions or rules, he may be said to have executive power. Mean is the official, and humble indeed is his station, who does not in some measure combine these powers in the performance of his duties. To call them quasi-judicial and quasi-legislative may help the judicial conscience to rationalize departure from fundamental doctrine, but to justify the "independence" and hence the practical "irresponsibility" of an agency of government because it exercises quasi-judicial or quasi-legislative power may be to establish a principle which, if extended to all officials or agencies whose powers may be similarly described, can undermine the democratic principle that public officials—including bureaucrats called commissioners—must be politically responsible to the people through their elected representatives.

Representatives of the People

It is too often forgotten that the President—no less than the Congress—represents the people, and that it is through him, perhaps more effectively than through Congress, that bureaucrats can be held responsible. Although the political responsibility of bureaucrats is a vicarious responsibility in either case, in the Presidency it comes to fairly clear focus at one time and in a single office, whereas in Congress it appears in fragments and at uneven intervals. And whereas through Congress the bureaucrat's responsibility to his state or local "clients" is emphasized, it is through the President that the bureaucracy can be most effectively held to account for promoting the "general welfare" of all the people. Fortunately it is not necessary to choose between Congress and the President in our search for a responsible bureaucracy. Both are essential, provided we understand what it is we are striving to accomplish.

Not the least of the heavy burdens the President must bear is political responsibility for the conduct and misconduct of the executive establishment. Insolence, inefficiency, incompetence, and corruption in any executive official or agency are properly chargeable to him. He ought not to escape this responsibility, as Grant and Harding, and others too, have sought to escape, by talk of "betrayal" by "faithless men in high places." These men are his agents and for better or worse their deeds are his.

Party Responsibility

And the President's responsibility is the responsibility of his party. Yet how often have we seen not only the President, but the party whose leader he is, seek (often successfully) to escape responsibility for the "evil deeds of evil men"—forgetting that these same "evil men" were his agents and those of his party! In final analysis political responsibility in a big democracy can be effectively enforced only through well-organized political parties. Hence it is that the search for a more responsible bureaucracy must be sought not merely in administrative reorganization or the redefinition and reallocation of powers and responsibilities, but also through a more responsible party system.

And if this is true of the President, it is equally true of the Congress. Congressmen no less than the President owe their election to the party in whose principles presumably they believe. Without responsible parties to organize and discipline Congressmen in terms of policies upon which as partisans they agree—the Congress itself becomes an undisciplined, irresponsible body of "freewheelers," each seeking his own exaltation and each owing allegiance to state and local pressure groups upon which—rather than the party—his political future comes to depend.

We need to inquire, then, whether party responsibility is more direct and meaningful when applied to Congress or to the President. There is reason to believe that our major political parties—as far at least as concerns the general welfare of the nation—are less responsible at the congressional than at the Presidential level. Although it is true that our major parties may be described as loose federations of state and local parties, it is also true that they function more effectively in Presidential years than at any other time in presenting to the voter meaningful alternatives as to candidates and policies. The higher ratio of actual to eligible voters at Presidential elections is one evidence of this. Another is the identification of the President by the voters as the responsible leader of his party in the nation. It is also true that—for a variety of reasons—party labels mean less at state and local levels than at the national level; and party organization is less efficient and less disciplined at off-year than at Presidential elections.

The relative weakness of the parties at the state and local levels is reflected, as both cause and effect, in the greater power and influence of special interest groups. Many Congressmen, and some Senators, owe more to powerful pressure groups within their states or districts than they owe to the party under whose label they aspire to office. In any case the issues over which congressional campaigns are fought in off years are more likely to reflect state and local interests than the issues over which Presidential campaigns are fought.

What is said here of the relative effectiveness of political parties in enforcing political responsibility in national affairs as between the President and Congress applies, with even greater force, to state and local governments and as between the governor and the legislature. The situation is of course complicated in the states by hydra-headed elective executives and in local governments by the widespread tradition of nonpartisanship.

General Welfare versus Special Interest

If this analysis has any validity, it follows that a bureaucracy responsible to the legislature will be more responsive and more responsible to local and special interests than a bureaucracy responsible to an elective chief executive.

It is to be expected that a Congressman quite properly answerable and responsive to the cattle growers of his district should seek to "liberalize" grazing regulations in federal forest reserves or on other federally owned lands within his state. If the bureaucrats responsible for the making and enforcement of these regulations are answerable to the Congressmen, they will find it difficult to resist such demands for "liberalization" even though they conflict with general policies of the nation concerning the conservation and use of our natural resources. And what is true of grazing regulations is likewise true of countless other policies.

This is not to argue that Congressmen (taken together) are less concerned about the "general welfare" of the nation than is the President. Nor is it to lose sight of the intense pressures from special interests that are felt in the White House. It is, however, to say that the President, because his constituency is the nation, because he has at his beck and call mass communications facilities beyond the reach of any other person, because he is the dominant figure in his party, because of the power and prestige of his office, is less vulnerable to such special or regional pressures than is the average Congressman. Moreover, it is his responsibility to see that the general welfare is not sacrificed to special or parochial interests, and where he finds faithless bureaucrats who betray this trust, he has or should have power to discipline, expose, and if necessary remove them.

The Legislature as a Safeguard

But, as I have said, the choice between a bureaucracy responsible to the executive (President, governor, mayor) and one responsible to the legislature (Congress, state legislature, city council) is not to be made in *either-or* terms—nor under our system is such a choice open to us.

For, although the weight of constitutional authority, the dictates of practicality, and considerations of democratic theory point to the elected executive as the channel through which the bureaucracy is made responsible to the people, the legislature will continue to challenge this solution and to claim its share of control. And within proper limits it is a legitimate claim.

For surely one of the basic functions of a representative legislative body is to maintain eternal vigilance over the bureaucracy to the end that the spirit as well as the letter of the law be observed in its execution and that the liberty of the citizen and the due processes of law be not sacrificed to the insolence of office masquerading under "reasons of state."

Legislative bodies discharge this function through the enactment of laws which define the goals and standards of administrative action and the limits of administrative discretion; through the appropriation or denial of funds to administrative agencies, and the examination and evaluation of administrative policies and procedures when budget requests are under review; through more or less continuous inquiries of appropriate legislative committees, and special investigations launched in response to demands for more searching examination of particular agencies; and through the virtually continuous and informal contacts that individual legislators maintain—usually in response to requests from their constituents—with administrative agencies.

All these are legitimate and, under our system of government, inevitable devices available to legislative bodies for enforcing political responsibility upon bureaucrats.

Nevertheless, under present circumstances, it is not easy for the legislature to maintain effective surveillance and control over the vast and far-flung bureaucracy of the modern state. Even in the determination of the basic structure and powers of administrative agencies, the legislature is severely handicapped. To an ever increasing extent it has lost the initiative in the formulation of policy. Moreover, the scope and complexity of the problems with which legislation must now deal require that legislative standards be more general—not to say vague—leaving to the executive great discretion in the development of supplementary legislation (rules and regulations) to meet particular situations.

Nor can the modern legislative body hope to have access to information necessary to effective control of the bureaucracy, except through the bureaucracy itself. Even the power of special investigation may be limited by considerations of national security. The ever expanding scope of governmental activities shrouded in secrecy—if not mystery—makes effective control by a numerous legislative body difficult if not impossible. Congress, for example, is in these days called upon to authorize expenditures of fantastic dimensions for the development of atomic energy, for national defense, for foreign policy, often without the benefit of more than the most sketchy and elementary information. Such information as there is, is in the hands of the executive and subject to his control.

Under these circumstances, a responsible bureaucracy is possible only through a partnership of the legislature and the executive, based on mutual respect, trust, and confidence.

Congressional-Executive Relations

Certainly no one observing the American scene in these latter days would argue that such a partnership has characterized executive-legislative relations at the national level. Hearings before committees of Congress take on the appearance of adversary proceedings, with Congressmen as prosecutors and executive officers as defendants. Loose, exaggerated, and often unsupported charges of corruption, incompetence, moral depravity, and disloyalty have been hurled at administrative officers and at entire agencies by presumably responsible chairmen of committees. Observers watching the cold war between the White House and the Hill, even when both are controlled by the same party, might well conclude that the American government had indeed fallen on evil days. The very term bureaucracy has become a "snarl" word, symbol not of loyal and devoted public servants, but of functionless hangers-on—of doubtful honesty, morality, and loyalty. Obviously this is the way to ensure not a responsible, but a bitterly resentful, bureaucracy, crippled by fear, internal disunity, and dissension. Vigilance is indeed the price of liberty under law, but the line between the vigilant and the lawless vigilante must be maintained lest we betray the very freedom we seek to defend.

So much has been written about the dangers of executive usurpation and abuse of power that we have become less alert to threats of legislative usurpation. "The legislature," warned James Madison, "is everywhere extending the sphere of its activity and drawing all power into its impetuous vortex," and ". . . it is against the enterprising ambition of this department that the people ought to indulge all their jealousy and exhaust all their precautions."

Madison's warning has a peculiar timeliness today, when some congressional committees have presumed to exercise not only powers of investigation and legislation normally associated with the legislative branch, but also executive and even judicial powers. Legislative intervention in the appointing power of the President has recently gone far beyond the so-called custom of senatorial courtesy. Attacks on prospective appointees as "security risks," loudly expressed doubts as to the loyalty of incumbents, and riders on appropriation bills forbidding the payment of public funds to named individuals are among the more recent devices of legislative usurpation, although the Supreme Court has branded this latter maneuver as being in effect a bill of attainder and hence invalid.

Illustrations of legislative intervention in administrative management are numerous and occur in virtually every major department of the government. And Senator McCarthy's "negotiations" with Greek shipowners concerning trade with Communist China mark a new level of legislative impertinence and usurpation. Only the so-called Bricker amendment, which would cripple Presidential control of foreign policy, compares with McCarthy's conduct as an example of congressional arrogance.

No better formula for producing a confused, timid, ineffective, and irresponsible bureaucracy could be imagined than this tug of war between the executive and the legislature for control. James Burns says:

> Responsibility for policy and administration becomes shrouded in a fantastically complicated network of ever shifting relationships among President, administrators, staff agencies, Senate, House of Representatives, committees, sub-committees, chairmen, individual legislators and among infinite combinations and permutations thereof.

There is no easy escape from this situation. No reforms of structure or procedure, and no admonitions concerning good behavior will suffice without strong leadership on both ends of Pennsylvania Avenue.

If the major burden of enforcing bureaucratic responsibility should fall to the elected executive, it is imperative that the executive establishment be adequate, in terms of both the scope and structure of power, to make its control effective. The diffusion and confusion of power in a plural executive (as in the states), the intervention of the legislature in strictly executive functions, and the denial to the executive of power commensurate with his responsibility, all militate against a responsible bureaucracy. . . .

The President is not only harassed by congressional interference and usurpation. He is denied many of the powers essential to effective executive control of the administrative machine. He lacks, for example, real authority to determine the organization and structure of the executive branch, and a large number of important executive functions in the so-called "headless fourth branch of the government"—the "independent" agencies—are outside his control. He lacks effective control over the federal budget, is "handcuffed and hog-tied" with line-by-line appropriations, and is denied the item veto. And he has only a limited control over personnel policy and administration, even within the regular executive departments and agencies.

Political Responsibility versus Partisan Loyalty

How far up or down the hierarchy of administrative authority the principle of political responsibility should extend has been a subject of prolonged and intense debate. The issue has been confused by failure to distinguish between political responsibility and partisan loyalty. The former is a salutary and indispensable characteristic of democratic government and should extend from the outermost reaches of the bureaucracy to the White House. The latter, unless carefully confined to top administrative posts which share with the President in the determination of high policy, can become a mask for the place seeker and the spoilsman. . . .

To say that civil servants should not be held to any partisan loyalty or responsibility is not to say that they should also be exempt from political responsibility. Political responsibility in this sense implies that the civil servant carry out faithfully and to the best of his ability the policies of the administration, or government, of whatever party, in which the people have placed their trust. As former Prime Minister Attlee once observed, "We always demand from our civil servants a loyalty to the State, and that they should serve the government of the day, whatever its political colour." Anyone who cannot give this elementary loyalty to the state he serves cannot justly claim the security and immunity from partisan responsibility that characterizes membership in the permanent civil service.

Legal Responsibility

A responsible bureaucracy implies not only political but legal responsibility as well. The legal definition of bureaucratic powers and responsibilities is the heart of administrative law and an important part of the criminal code. Laws against bribery and corruption, fraud and deceit, misfeasance and malfeasance, are, of course, part of the machinery for enforcing this legal responsibility. . .

Moral Responsibility

But a truly responsible bureaucracy will depend as much—perhaps more—upon its own code of professional and civic ethics as upon external controls. Excessive regulation may hinder rather than help in the development of such a code, by cultivating "timidity" and government by rule book at the sacrifice of imagination and initiative. "Infinitely more important than compelling administrative officials to live up to minutely defined requirements of control is their acceptance of an ethical obligation to account to themselves and to the public for the public character of their actions."

The growth of professional pride and esprit among civil servants, without which no professional code of ethics can have much meaning or effect, has had to wait upon victory over the spoilsman. Although the final battles in that war have yet to be won, it is not too early to make some conscious and concerted effort to create among public servants a greater sense of professional loyalty, discipline, and responsibility. Indeed, signs are not lacking that, in some sectors at least, this new professional spirit has already begun to emerge. Numerous organizations of public servants already exist through which higher standards of competence, integrity, and responsibility can develop.

The experience of other professions—medicine, law, and teaching, for example—can offer stimulus but also a warning to bureaucrats. For too often such associations become primarily concerned not with their responsibility for higher standards and better public service, but with the promotion of narrower and more selfish ends. Associations of civil servants have a special obligation to avoid these pitfalls and to cultivate at all times an intense and pervasive sense of public service and responsibility.

Loyalty to high standards of honesty, "scientific management," and technical competence are, of course, of transcendent importance. But equally important is the bureaucrat's responsibility to know and respect the wishes, values, and goals of the community he serves, not in supine response to the pressures of special interest groups, but through a dogged devotion to the basic policies of the state—even though this means resistance to these same special or parochial groups.

Although we have far to go in this country in achieving a truly responsible bureaucracy, we can take comfort in the progress that has been made. No longer has the patronage peddler or the spoilsman the hold he once had on the federal service. No longer can it be fairly said that American city government is a failure, conspicuous or otherwise. No longer can it accurately be said, as George S. Taylor once said of Britain in the eighteenth century, that politics is "the trade of managing the state in the interests of the men in possession and their friends." Standards of character and competence, of integrity and industry, in the public service will stand comparison with those in other walks of life. But it is not enough that they be "just as good"—they should be better. Just as government should be a model employer, so the public service and the public servant should be models for the community, as I believe they are even now.

It is fitting and proper for the community to expect higher standards among its public servants than in private life. But in the end administrative morality will reflect the morality of the community it serves. A society in which "caveat emptor" is still a basic principle of business, in which the clever man who can make a "fast buck" is eulogized, and in which private peculation is often concealed in acts of so-called public policy, ought not to be surprised if an occasional bureaucrat strays from the straight and narrow path. The ancient English jingle has relevance even to our own times when it says:

> The law locks up both man and woman
> Who steals the goose from off the common
> But lets the greater felon loose
> Who steals the common from the goose.

The old aphorism that "every people gets the kind of government it deserves" is at best a half-truth, for the American people probably gets better government than it deserves. In a country where the "politician" is a symbol of corruption and dishonesty, if not dishonor, where a large majority of parents, as reported by the Gallup poll, prefer not to have their children enter the public service, where the bureaucracy is regarded as a legitimate object of ridicule and even revulsion and the term "bureaucrat" is a nasty name, how can one expect high standards of public service and responsibility? The wonder is not that we have not achieved a competent, devoted, and responsible bureaucracy, but that we have come so close to doing so.

Irresponsible attacks upon public servants are a luxury we can no longer afford—when our prosperity, our freedom, and even our survival may depend upon them. A responsible bureaucracy requires a responsible democracy—and a responsible citizenry. To create the one we must also create the other. To do so will require the best efforts of all who value our democratic institutions, whether they be in education, business, labor, or the professions.

AUTHORS OF SOURCE MATERIALS

INDEX